Praise for *Marie-Thérèse*

"This highly detailed, exhaustively researched, often riveting account will appeal especially to all those readers who've immersed themselves in the many recent books about Marie Antoinette."

—*Booklist,* **starred review**

"A powerful story told with wonderful verve: a triumph."

—**Amanda Foreman, author of** *Georgiana: Duchess of Devonshire*

"Unlike her mother, the subject of so much historical attention, Marie-Thérèse, the sole survivor of her nuclear family, has been neglected by posterity. If she's remembered at all, it's as a figure typical of the restored Bourbons, who had famously forgotten nothing and learned nothing. In this biography, the account of what she endured is harrowing . . . Contrary to received wisdom, the woman in these pages emerges, after much evidence cited, as a veritable prototype of saintly Catholic forgiveness."

—*Atlantic*

"If there is a more fascinating or unbelievable life than the one led by Marie-Thérèse-Charlotte, Marie Antoinette's sole surviving child, I certainly am not familiar with it . . . Royal orphan and republican bête noire, the subject of fervent monarchist adoration and the object obsessive conspiracy theories, this princess emerges in Nagel's telling as one of the nineteenth century's most captivating heroines. A must-read for lovers of French history and royal biography alike."

—**Caroline Weber, author of** *Queen of Fashion: What Marie Antoinette Wore to the Revolution*

"Relates the dramatic highs and lows experienced by the woman known as 'Madame Royale' . . . Highly detailed and sympathetic."

—*Publishers Weekly*

"Few historical tales can match the family drama of Louis XVI and Marie Antoinette . . . Author Susan Nagel puts to rest most of the doubts about the Bourbons via a thorough analysis of DNA samples and handwriting in family letters. But the best part of the tale isn't the clarification of the historical record—it's the engaging portrait Nagel paints of a young woman who gave up everything for the love of France and her family."

—*Virtuoso Life*

"Enlivened by intriguing asides about the young Marie-Thérèse, such as the special sign language she developed to communicate with her parents in prison and the impact on her own development of her mother's bravery in the face of the French Revolution."

—*Kirkus Reviews*

"Taking one of those fascinating lives that have remained too long untold, Susan Nagel's *Marie-Thérèse* is a well-researched, entertaining and often poignant biography that recreates royalty, terror, tragedy, revolution, and restoration with verve and vividness."

—Simon Sebag Montefiore, author of *Young Stalin* and *Stalin: The Court of the Red Tsar*

BY THE SAME AUTHOR

The Influence of the Novels of Jean Giraudoux on the Hispanic Vanguard Novels of the 1920s–1930s

Mistress of the Elgin Marbles

MARIE-THÉRÈSE

THE FATE OF
MARIE ANTOINETTE'S DAUGHTER

SUSAN NAGEL

BLOOMSBURY

NEW YORK BERLIN LONDON

Published by Bloomsbury USA, New York

All papers used by Bloomsbury USA are natural, recyclable products made from wood grown in well-managed forests. The manufacturing processes conform to the environmental regulations of the country of origin.

LIBRARY OF CONGRESS CATALOGING-IN-PUBLICATION DATA

Nagel, Susan, 1954–
Marie-Thérèse, child of terror : the fate of Marie Antoinette's daughter / Susan Nagel.
p. cm.
Includes bibliographical references and index.
ISBN-13: 978-1-59691-057-7 (hardcover)
ISBN-10: 1-59691-057-7 (hardcover)
1. Angoulême, Marie-Thérèse Charlotte, duchesse d', 1778–1851. 2. France—Kings and rulers—Children—Biography. 3. Marie Antoinette, Queen, consort of Louis XVI, King of France, 1755–1793—Family. 4. France—History—Louis XVI, 1774–1793. 5. France—History—1789–1815. I. Title.

DC137.2.N34 2008
944'.035092—dc22
[B]
2007044472

First published by Bloomsbury USA in 2008
This paperback edition published in 2009

Paperback ISBN-10: 1-59691-058-5
ISBN-13: 978-1-59691-058-4

1 3 5 7 9 10 8 6 4 2

Typeset by Hewer Text UK Ltd, Edinburgh
Printed in the United States of America by Quebecor World Fairfield

For Hadley,
my passionate historian

CONTENTS

ACKNOWLEDGEMENTS

This book could not have been written without: the love, support and great tolerance of Hadley and Jon Nagel; the help and encouragement of His Serene Highness, Prince Charles-Henri de Lobkowicz; and the singular Tina Bennett, my personal and professional OnStar.

Thank you to my wise and talented editor, Colin Dickerman; the beautiful and very thorough Lindsay Sagnette; and the rest of the US Bloomsbury team – Laura Keefe, Natalie Slocum, Sabrina Farber, Michael O'Connor, and Gary J. Antonetti and his staff at Ortelius Design. As they all know, this book would certainly not have taken its full shape without the tenacity and brilliance of Michael Fishwick at Bloomsbury UK and Kate Johnson. Thank you also to Trâm-Anh Doan, Emily Sweet and the rest of the fastidious, hard-working bunch at Bloomsbury UK.

I am eternally grateful to Leila and the late, wonderful Hank Luce for their extraordinary kindness, and to a young Sorbonne student, Maialen Berasategui (who has a superb website, http://madameroyale.free.fr). Others who have also been exceedingly generous with their help have been the fantastic Delphine Renaut; the brilliant and scholarly Christophe Levantal; the extraordinarily knowledgeable historian Philip Mansel; the indefatigable and dedicated David Smith of the New York Public Library; and the very knowledgeable, kind and patient Tammy Wofsey of the Marymount Manhattan College Shanahan Library.

A million thanks to: Svetlana Katz; Thomas Meyhöfer (and his fascinating website www.madame-royale.de); Marc de Gontaut Biron; Stefan Ottrubay of the Esterházy family; Clementina di Levetzow Lantieri; Dr Serenella Ferrari Benedetti of the Fondazione Coronini Cronberg; Dr Leopold Auer and Dr Ernst Petretsch at the Österreichisches Staatsarchiv; Peter Prokop at the Österreichische Nationalbibliothek; Dr Jean-Jacques Cassiman; Wayne Furman for the use of the Allen Room at the New York Public Library; Paul LeClerc, President of the New York

Public Library, and his assistant, Elaine Cunningham; Jason Baumann and Elizabeth Novelo, also of the NYPL; Claudia Solacini, the New York Society Library and Sara Elliott Holliday; New York City District Attorney Robert Morgenthau and Martha Bashford in the DA's office; David Linton and Cecilia Feilla of the Humanities Department at Marymount Manhattan College; Paul Smart with the Church of the Latter Day Saints in Salt Lake City, Utah; and Christine Kohl-Langer of the Archiv und Museum in Landau, Germany.

Also to: Mary Brown, Teresa Yip and Henry Blanke of the Marymount Manhattan College Shanahan Library; Carolyn Holmes at Ash Lawn-Highland in Charlottesville; Arik Bartelmus; Paul Anditsch of Frohsdorf Immobilien; Peter Berg of the Michigan State University Library Special Collections; Steven J. Herman at the Library of Congress, Washington D.C.; Katie McMahon at the Newberry Library in Chicago; and Antoine Treuille and the Bic Corporation.

And last but not least, a heartfelt thank you to my comrades in books: Tina Brown, Lenny Golay, Jeanette Watson Sanger and Vicky Ward, for understanding the long and winding road to publication and indulging me with their infinite empathy.

LIST OF ILLUSTRATIONS

The Comte d'Artois, later Charles X, Marie-Thérèse's uncle and father-in-law. (*Courtesy of Collection of His Serene Highness, Prince Charles-Henri de Lobkowicz*)

The dashing duc de Berry, Marie-Thérèse's brother-in-law. (*Courtesy of Collection of His Serene Highness, Prince Charles-Henri de Lobkowicz*)

A cartoon depicting 'The New Antigone', as King Louis XVIII referred to his niece.

Abbé Edgeworth, the priest who had accompanied Louis XVI to the scaffold, on his deathbed, with Marie-Thérèse. (*La duchesse d'Angoulême au lit de mort de l'abbé Edgeworth by A. Menjaud courtesy of Musée des Beaux-Arts, Bordeaux*)

Madame Campan, first lady-in-waiting to Marie-Thérèse's mother, to whom Marie-Thérèse refused to speak following the Bourbons' return to France. (*Madam Campan by Gérard courtesy of Ash Lawn-Highland*)

The sculpture marking the graves of King Louis XVI and Queen Marie Antoinette in the royal crypt at Saint-Denis.

Marie-Thérèse and her husband, the Duc d'Angoulême, arriving to cheering crowds in Bordeaux at the beginning of March 1815. (*Entrée de LL RR Mgr Duc et Duchesse d'Angoulême dans la ville de Bordeaux le 5 mars 1815 by Boccia courtesy of Musée des Beaux-Arts, Bordeaux*)

Marie-Thérèse bidding farewell to adoring crowds at Pauillac after her failed attempt to orchestrate the defeat of Napoleon's troops at Bordeaux. (*Embarkation of the Duchess of Angoulême in Pauillac by Antoine-Jean Gros courtesy of Musée des Beaux-Arts, Bordeaux*)

A portrait of Marie-Thérèse in Toulouse in the summer of 1815. (*Portrait of Marie-Thérèse by Guillaume-Joseph Roques Collection de l'Etablissement Thermal de Vichy*)

A portrait of Marie-Thérèse which is reminiscent of the pregnant Gabrielle d'Estrées. (*Duchesse d'Angoulême by J.B.J. Augustin 1818 courtesy of the Philip Mansel Collection*)

Marie-Thérèse depicted in a royal diadem, her mother's pearls and white Bourbon plumes. (*Marie-Thérèse, duchesse d'Angoulême by Antoine-Jean Gros courtesy of The Bowes Museum, County Durham, England*)

Marie-Thérèse's niece and nephew, Louise and Henri. (*Courtesy of Collection of His Serene Highness, Prince Charles-Henri de Lobkowicz*)

Villeneuve l'Etang, which became the country retreat for Marie-Thérèse and the children. (*Courtesy of Collection Musée de l'Île de France, Sceaux. Photograph by Pascal Lemaître*)

Hartwell in Buckinghamshire, the English country estate where the Bourbons resided until Napoleon's defeat. (*Photograph courtesy of Historic House Hotels website, www.historichousehotels.com*)

Frohsdorf Castle, outside Vienna, where Marie-Thérèse spent her last years.

The young Comte de Chambord, later Henri V. (*Courtesy of the collection of His Serene Highness, Prince Charles-Henri de Lobkowicz*)

The heart of little Louis Charles in the royal crypt at Saint-Denis.

CHRONOLOGY

1754 Louis-Auguste, the future Louis XVI of France born at Versailles on August 23

1755 Marie Antoinette, daughter of Empress Maria Theresa of Austria, born in Vienna on November 2; the Comte de Provence born on November 17

1757 Comte d'Artois born on October 9

1764 Madame Elisabeth born on May 3

1768 Marriage agreed between Marie Antoinette and the French Dauphin, Louis

1770 Marie Antoinette leaves for France on April 21; arrives and is married at Versailles on May 16

1774 King Louis XV dies on May 10

1775 Coronation of Louis XVI at Reims on June 11; Louis-Antoine, Duc d'Angoulême born on August 6

1778 Death of Voltaire and Rousseau; third child, Charles Ferdinand, Duc de Berry, born to the Comte and Comtesse d'Artois on January 24; Ernestine (Marie-Philippe) de Lambriquet born on July 31; **Marie-Thérèse-Charlotte, Child of France, 'Madame Royale', born on December 19 at 11.30 a.m.**

1781 Louis Joseph, Dauphin of France born on October 22

1785 Louis Charles, Duc de Normandie born on March 27

1786 Sophie Hélène Béatrice, Child of France born on July 9; dies 10 days later

1788 Philippine de Lambriquet dies on April 30; Queen Marie Antoinette adopts Marie-Philippine re-naming her 'Ernestine';

King Louis XVI establishes pension of 12,000 *livres* for Ernestine on November 9

1789   Opening of the États Généraux on May 5; Louis Joseph, Dauphin of France dies at 1 a.m. on June 4, Louis Charles becomes Dauphin; Third Estate constitutes itself on June 17 as National Assembly; Oath at the Jeu de Paume on June 20; Necker dismissed on July 11; Bastille stormed July 14; Declaration of the Rights of Man on August 26; Versailles attacked on October 5; on October 6, royal family forced to flee to Paris

1790   Marie-Thérèse and Ernestine receive First Communion on Easter Sunday, April 4; Joseph II dies on February 20; Fête de la Fédération on July 14

1791   Royal family captured at Varennes on June 21, return to Paris on June 25

1792   France declares war on Hungary and Bohemia on April 20; mob attacks Tuileries Palace on June 20; Prussia declares war on France, Duke of Brunswick issues manifesto on July 25; mob slaughters Swiss Guard members on August 10, royal family incarcerated at the Temple Prison on August 13; Princesse de Lamballe murdered on September 3; monarchy abolished on September 21; trial of Louis XVI begins on December 11

1793   Execution of Louis XVI on January 21; France declares war on England and Holland on February 1; separation of the Dauphin and the Queen on July 3; Marie Antoinette guillotined on October 16; Philippe Égalité (d'Orléans) executed on November 6

1794   Madame Elisabeth guillotined on May 10; Robespierre executed on July 28

1795   Louis XVII dies on June 8; Renée de Chanterenne becomes companion to Madame Royale in the Temple Prison on June 20; royalist insurrection crushed by Barras and Napoleon on October 5 ending the Revolution; Marie-Thérèse leaves Temple Prison at midnight on December 19, and arrives in Basel on December 26

1796   Marie-Thérèse arrives at the Hofburg in Vienna on January 9

1797   Treaty of Campo Formio signed on October 17

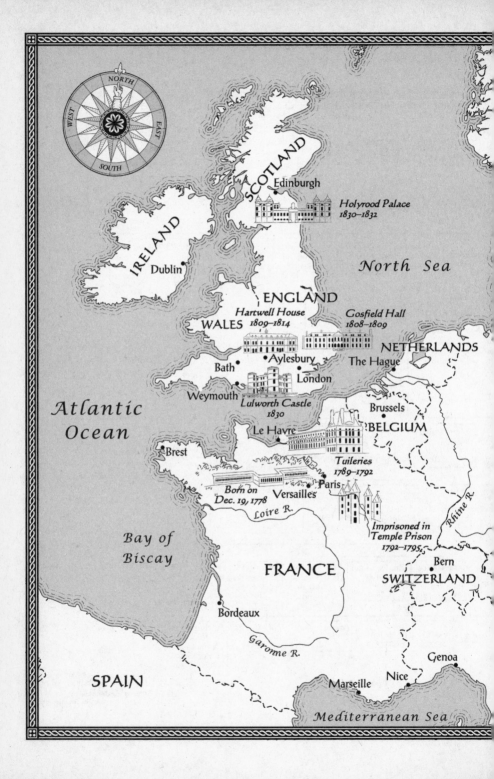

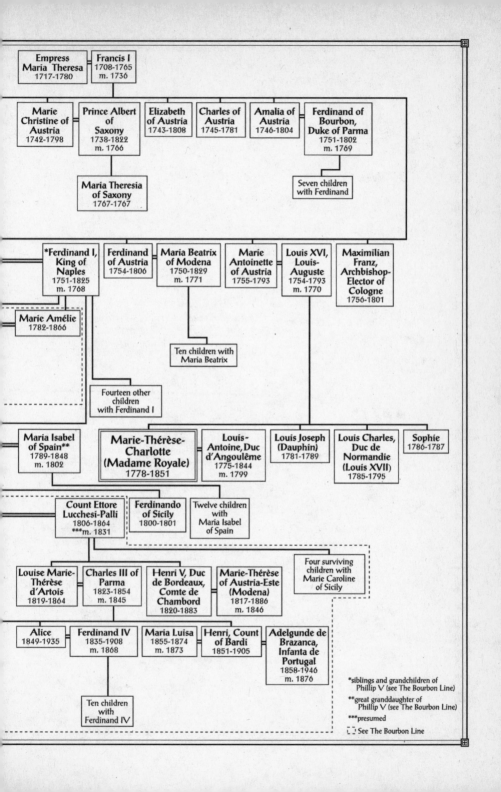

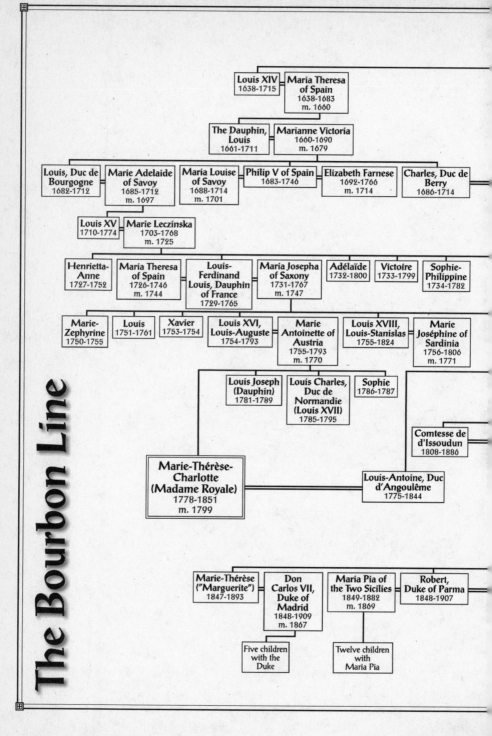

The Bourbon Line

Louis XIV
1638-1715

Maria Theresa of Spain
1638-1683
m. 1660

The Dauphin, Louis
1661-1711

Marianne Victoria
1660-1690
m. 1679

Louis, Duc de Bourgogne
1682-1712

Marie Adelaide of Savoy
1685-1712
m. 1697

Maria Louise of Savoy
1688-1714
m. 1701

Philip V of Spain
1683-1746

Elizabeth Farnese
1692-1766
m. 1714

Charles, Duc de Berry
1686-1714

Louis XV
1710-1774

Marie Leczinska
1703-1768
m. 1725

Henrietta-Anne
1727-1752

Maria Theresa of Spain
1726-1746
m. 1744

Louis-Ferdinand Louis, Dauphin of France
1729-1765

Maria Josepha of Saxony
1731-1767
m. 1747

Adélaïde
1732-1800

Victoire
1733-1799

Sophie-Philippine
1734-1782

Marie-Zephyrine
1750-1755

Louis
1751-1761

Xavier
1753-1754

Louis XVI, Louis-Auguste
1754-1793

Marie Antoinette of Austria
1755-1793
m. 1770

Louis XVIII, Louis-Stanislas
1755-1824

Marie Joséphine of Sardinia
1756-1806
m. 1771

Louis Joseph (Dauphin)
1781-1789

Louis Charles, Duc de Normandie (Louis XVII)
1785-1795

Sophie
1786-1787

Comtesse de d'Issoudun
1808-1886

Marie-Thérèse-Charlotte (Madame Royale)
1778-1851
m. 1799

Louis-Antoine, Duc d'Angoulême
1775-1844

Marie-Thérèse ("Marguerite")
1847-1893

Don Carlos VII, Duke of Madrid
1848-1909
m. 1867

Maria Pia of the Two Sicilies
1849-1882
m. 1869

Robert, Duke of Parma
1848-1907

Five children with the Duke

Twelve children with Maria Pia

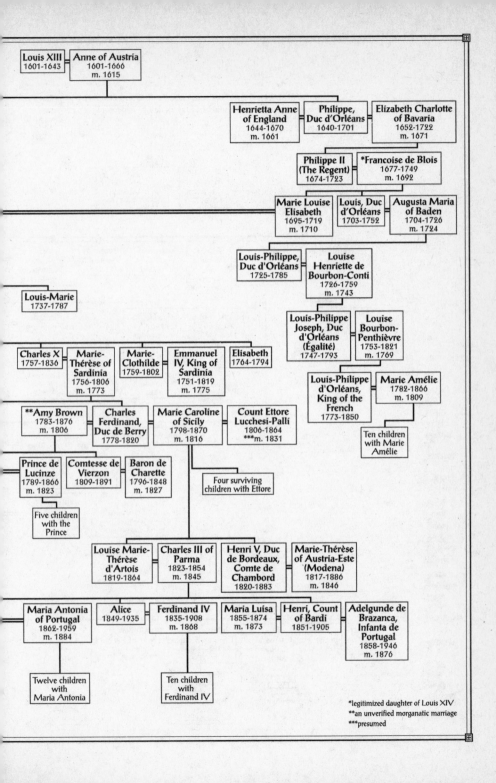

Louis XIII
1601-1643

Anne of Austria
1601-1666
m. 1615

Henrietta Anne
of England
1644-1670
m. 1661

Philippe,
Duc d'Orléans
1640-1701

Elizabeth Charlotte
of Bavaria
1652-1722
m. 1671

Philippe II
(The Regent)
1674-1723

*Francoise de Blois
1677-1749
m. 1692

Marie Louise
Elisabeth
1695-1719
m. 1710

Louis, Duc
d'Orléans
1703-1752

Augusta Maria
of Baden
1704-1726
m. 1724

Louis-Philippe,
Duc d'Orléans
1725-1785

Louise
Henriette de
Bourbon-Conti
1726-1759
m. 1743

Louis-Marie
1737-1787

Louis-Philippe
Joseph, Duc
d'Orléans
(Égalité)
1747-1793

Louise
Bourbon-
Penthièvre
1753-1821
m. 1769

Charles X
1757-1836

Marie-
Thérèse of
Sardinia
1756-1806
m. 1773

Marie-
Clothilde
1759-1802

Emmanuel
IV, King of
Sardinia
1751-1819
m. 1775

Elisabeth
1764-1794

Louis-Philippe
d'Orléans,
King of the
French
1773-1850

Marie Amélie
1782-1866
m. 1809

Ten children
with Marie
Amélie

**Amy Brown
1783-1876
m. 1806

Charles
Ferdinand,
Duc de Berry
1778-1820

Marie Caroline
of Sicily
1798-1870
m. 1816

Count Ettore
Lucchesi-Palli
1806-1864
***m. 1831

Prince de
Lucinze
1789-1866
m. 1823

Comtesse de
Vierzon
1809-1891

Baron de
Charette
1796-1848
m. 1827

Four surviving
children with Ettore

Five children
with the
Prince

Louise Marie-
Thérèse
d'Artois
1819-1864

Charles III of
Parma
1823-1854
m. 1845

Henri V, Duc
de Bordeaux,
Comte de
Chambord
1820-1883

Marie-Thérèse
of Austria-Este
(Modena)
1817-1886
m. 1846

Maria Antonia
of Portugal
1802-1959
m. 1884

Alice
1849-1935

Ferdinand IV
1835-1908
m. 1868

Maria Luisa
1855-1874
m. 1873

Henri, Count
of Bardi
1851-1905

Adelgunde de
Brazanca,
Infanta de
Portugal
1858-1946
m. 1876

Twelve children
with Maria Antonia

Ten children
with Ferdinand IV

*legitimized daughter of Louis XIV
**an unverified morganatic marriage
***presumed

The Habsburg Line

| Elizabeth of Austria 1737-1740 | Maria Anna of Austria, Abbess of Klagenfurt 1738-1789 | Caroline of Austria 1740-1741 | Isabella of Parma 1741-1763 m. 1760 | Joseph II of Austria 1741-1790 | Josepha of Bavaria 1739-1767 m. 1765 |

| Theresa of Austria 1762-1770 | Christina of Austria 1763-1763 |

| Leopold II of Austria 1747-1792 | *Maria Louisa of Spain 1745-1792 m. 1765 | Maria Caroline of Austria 1748-1748 | Joanna of Austria 1750-1762 | Josepha of Austria 1751-1767 | Maria Carolina of Austria 1752-1814 |

| Fourteen other children with Maria Louisa | | Franz II of Austria 1768-1835 | Maria-Theresa of the Two Sicilies 1772-1807 m. 1790 | Louis-Philippe d'Orléans, King of the French 1773-1850 m. 1809 |

| Three other wives, but none with surviving children | Twelve children with Franz II of Austria | Ten children with Marie Amélie |

| Maria Clementine 1777-1801 m. 1797 | Ferdinand of the Two Sicilies 1777-1830 |

| Charles Ferdinand, Duc de Berry 1778-1820 | Marie Caroline of Sicily 1798-1870 m. 1816 |

| Marie-Thérèse ("Marguerite") 1847-1893 | Don Carlos VII, Duke of Madrid 1848-1909 m. 1867 | Maria Pia of the Two Sicilies 1849-1882 m. 1869 | Robert, Duke of Parma 1848-1907 | Maria Antonia of Portugal 1862-1959 m. 1884 |

| Five children with the Duke | Twelve children with Maria Pia | Twelve children with Maria Antonia |

1830 Charles X abdicates on August 2; Duc d'Angoulême becomes King Louis XIX for twenty minutes and, until her husband's abdication, Marie-Thérèse becomes the last Queen of France of the senior Bourbon line

1832 Duchesse de Berry attempts to regain the throne for her son

1836 Charles X dies on November 6

1837 The Dark Countess, 'Sophie Botta', dies on November 25

1844 The Duc d'Angoulême dies on June 3

1845 'Vavel de Versay', real name Cornelius Van der Valck, dies on April 8; Louise d'Artois marries Charles de Bourbon, the future Duc de Parme on November 10

1846 Henri V marries Archduchess Marie-Thérèse d'Este of Modena on November 16

1851 Marie-Thérèse dies on October 19

1799 Madame Royale marries the Duc d'Angoulême in Mitau on
      June 10

1801 King Louis XVIII forced to leave Russia on January 22; Marie-
      Thérèse and Louis arrive in Warsaw on March 6

1803 A mysterious couple referred to as 'the Dark Count and
      Countess' arrive in Ingelfingen, Germany

1804 Napoleon declares himself 'Hereditary Emperor of France' on
      May 18

1805 Marie-Thérèse returns to Mitau in April; Napoleon victorious
      at Austerlitz on December 2

1806 Holy Roman Emperor Franz II abdicates on August 6

1807 Arrival of the Dark Count and Countess in Hildburghausen on
      February 7; Louis XVIII arrives in England on November 2

1808 Marie-Thérèse arrives at Gosfield Hall in England on August
      24

1809 The French royal family in exile moves to Hartwell House in
      April

1810 Comte Fersen murdered on June 20; Queen Louise of Prussia
      dies on July 17; the Dark Count and Countess flee to Eishausen
      Castle in September

1814 Abdication of Napoleon on April 6; King Louis XVIII enters
      Paris on May 3

1815 Napoleon's rule of 'Hundred Days', from March 20; Louis
      XVIII returns to Paris on July 8; Napoleon boards British man-
      of-war *Bellerophon* on July 15, reaches St Helena on October
      15; Marie-Thérèse returns to Paris on July 27

1816 The Duc de Berry marries Princess Marie Caroline of Naples on
      June 17

1819 Princess Louise born on September 21

1820 Assassination of the Duc de Berry on February 13; birth of
      Henri, Duc de Bordeaux (later Comte de Chambord) on
      September 29

1824 King Louis XVIII dies on September 16; Comte d'Artois
      ascends the throne as Charles X

1825 Coronation of King Charles X at Reims on May 29; *Il Viaggio
      a Reims* by Rossini debuts on June 19

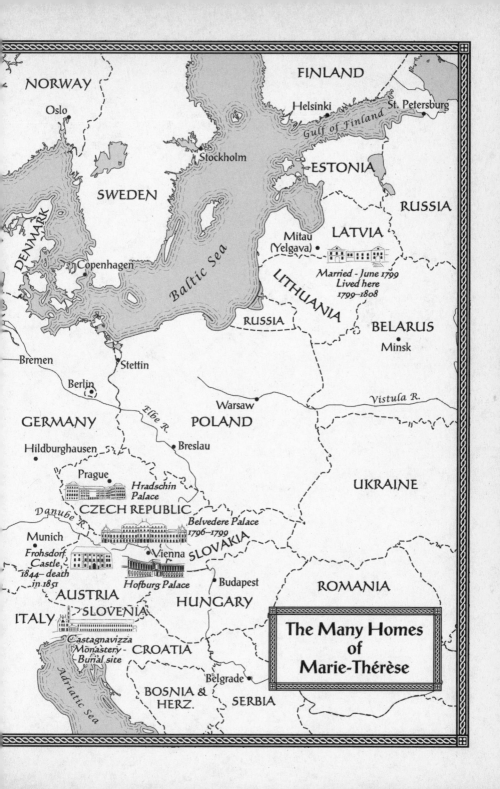

NORWAY

Oslo

FINLAND

Helsinki

St. Petersburg

SWEDEN

Stockholm

ESTONIA

RUSSIA

DENMARK

Copenhagen

Baltic Sea

Mitau
(Yelgava)

LATVIA

Married - June 1799
Lived here
1799–1808

LITHUANIA

RUSSIA

BELARUS

Minsk

Bremen

Stettin

Berlin

Elbe R.

Vistula R.

Warsaw

POLAND

GERMANY

Hildburghausen

Breslau

Prague

UKRAINE

Hradschin
Palace

Danube R.

CZECH REPUBLIC

Belvedere Palace
1796–1799

Munich

SLOVAKIA

Frohsdorf
Castle,
1844– death
in 1851

Vienna

Hofburg Palace

Budapest

ROMANIA

AUSTRIA

HUNGARY

ITALY

SLOVENIA

Castagnavizza
Monastery -
Burial site

CROATIA

Adriatic Sea

Belgrade

BOSNIA &
HERZ.

SERBIA

The Many Homes
of
Marie-Thérèse

PREFACE

After the brutal beheadings of King Louis XVI and Queen Marie Antoinette in 1793, dozens of young men and women around the globe came forth with astonishing tales of escape and adventure, claiming to be the long-lost children of the slaughtered Bourbon King and his Austrian-born wife. The royal couple had four children: their eldest, Marie-Thérèse-Charlotte, named for her maternal grandmother, the Empress of Austria; Louis Joseph, known as the Dauphin; Louis Charles; and the youngest, Sophie. Louis Joseph and Sophie both died in early childhood of natural causes. Marie-Thérèse and Louis Charles, who became the Dauphin after his brother's death, accompanied their parents to the notorious Temple Prison in Paris where they lived a life of physical and mental deprivation from 1792–95.

Sadly, we now know for certain what became of Louis Charles, the adored son whom Marie Antoinette called her *chou d'amour*. In 2000, two scientists, Jean-Jacques Cassiman of the University of Leuven in Belgium and Bernard Brinkmann of the University of Munster in Germany, using a lock of hair from the head of Marie Antoinette, proved through exhaustive DNA testing that the heart of a little boy who had died in the Temple Prison was, in fact, the heart of Louis Charles, Dauphin of France, known after his father's death as Louis XVII. The tiny heart had apparently been cut from his body by the doctor performing the autopsy and smuggled out of the prison in a handkerchief. The doctor brought the heart to his home, placed it in a jar, and kept it. After the doctor's death, during a time of continuing political upheaval in France, the heart was removed from the house, making a fantastic clandestine journey from palaces to churches and libraries over a period of two hundred years. In June 2004, the jar containing the boy's heart was ceremoniously laid to rest in the royal crypt in St Denis, outside Paris, where it will remain in perpetuity.

The DNA results put to rest the scores of claims fabricated by desperate, delusional or merely greedy pretenders and finally offered conclusive evidence that there was only one surviving child of the royal couple: Marie-Thérèse-Charlotte, known as 'Madame Royale', and as the daughter of the King, 'Child of France'. For years after the French Revolution, Marie-Thérèse, who escaped the Temple Prison at midnight on her seventeenth birthday, lived under the threat of abduction or assassination. Two of her cousins were murdered long after the French Revolution had ended, and it was widely known that the daughter of the King of France remained a key target. She was also the subject of intriguing rumors and conspiracy theories.

Through letters scattered among the aristocracy, a story circulated that Marie-Thérèse had been raped in prison and was pregnant when she fled her captors. Further commentary claimed that she was not only pregnant, but so mentally frail that she was in no way fit to be a royal bride to her intended husband, the Austrian Archduke Karl, brother of the Holy Roman Emperor. These allegations fueled suspicion that the daughter of Marie Antoinette and King Louis XVI had changed places with another girl.

The nineteenth-century world was obsessed with the idea that the royal children in the Temple Prison had in fact changed places with doppelgängers. C. S. Forester alludes to the idea of there having been a 'switch' in his novel *Lord Hornblower*, in which he creates an encounter between the swashbuckling British naval hero Horatio Hornblower and Marie-Thérèse, then the Duchesse d'Angoulême. Hornblower is charmed by the 'high-spirited' and 'lovely' Duchess, and adds that he finds her warmth and familiarity 'very un-Bourbon-like'. He ponders why she is 'acting with a condescension a trifle excessive in a king's daughter, a future queen of France', but decides that it must be because she is 'the only living child of Marie Antoinette, whose charm and vivacity and indiscretion had been proverbial. That might explain it.' Rumors of a 'switch' and suspicions as to the fate of the Dauphin even spread to the American frontier, where satirist Mark Twain alluded to the phenomenon in four of his most popular novels: in *Huckleberry Finn*, for instance, Huck declares himself to be the missing 'little boy *dolphin*'.

In 1814, upon the return of the Bourbons to France, the Duchesse d'Abrantès wryly remarked that it had been over twenty years since anyone had seen a Bourbon, and 'no one quite knew who was who anymore'. In the days before the invention of photography and mass media, people relied on portraiture, which was wildly unreliable, to know the faces of their ruling families. In the case of the French Revolution, where so many of the courtiers were executed, there were very few people living afterwards who could serve as eyewitnesses, or say with any certainty, 'That is Madame Royale.' After all, Marie-Thérèse had entered the Temple Prison a girl and vacated its walls, after more than three years of isolation, a young woman. Various portraits of her, one supposedly executed days after her escape from the Temple Prison, do, in fact, show facial changes including a nose that is inexplicably different from the pictures of her as a young teenager.

Only months after Marie-Thérèse made her dramatic journey from the Temple Prison to Vienna, the American Gouverneur Morris, who had known Marie-Thérèse as a little girl, saw her at the Prater. Morris remarked that she was 'much improved' since he had seen her in France and that she looked so much like the late King, that he could with certainty dispel one rumor – that she was the daughter of Marie Antoinette's alleged lover, the Swedish Count, Axel Fersen.

Another rumor, which also originated at the court of Louis XVI, concerned the birth of a young girl named Ernestine de Lambriquet. Gossips whispered that Ernestine was not the daughter of a chambermaid and a manservant of King Louis XVI's brother as was claimed, but the illegitimate daughter of that same chambermaid and King Louis XVI himself, making her Marie-Thérèse's half-sister. That certainly would have explained not only why Ernestine looked so much like the King but also why she and Marie-Thérèse were often called 'twins' and why she was raised alongside the young Princess as her 'playmate'. Ernestine was just a few months older than Madame Royale, and it was not uncommon for illegitimate children of a monarch to be brought up under royal protection alongside legitimate heirs to the throne.

Two hundred years after the demise of the Holy Roman Empire and the thousand-year-old Capetian dynasty, of which the Bourbon branch was its last, there remained one final nagging controversy. It is claimed that a woman known as the 'Dark Countess', who lived as a recluse at Eishausen Castle near Hildburghausen, Germany, was, in fact, the real Marie-Thérèse and that Ernestine de Lambriquet posed as Marie-Thérèse, went on to become the Duchesse d'Angoulême, Dauphine of France, and, to legitimists, the Queen of France in exile. The 'Dark Countess' was said to appear in public only infrequently, and when she did, she wore a dark veil to cover her fair hair, high coloring and blue eyes. Her companion was a man who referred to her as 'Your Grace', and the pair spoke with each other in French. Eishausen had a subterranean cave and tunnel, an escape route into a forest, and local inhabitants noted that the couple would often receive mysterious visits from courtiers and servants of Europe's royal houses.

The Dark Countess died on November 25, 1837, and was buried before dawn. Her death did nothing to dispel the rumors, however. The public records stated that the dead woman's name was 'Sophie' – the name that Marie-Thérèse used when traveling incognito. The documents also state that 'Sophie' was 'fifty-eight' at the time of her death – making her the same age as the daughter of Marie Antoinette. Among the contents of Sophie's estate was furniture and clothing emblazoned with the Bourbon family crest, the fleur-de-lys, and an ornately chiseled turquoise and gold *collier* also engraved with the fleur-de-lys, which has since been authenticated as having belonged to the murdered Queen of France. Also among the Countess's personal effects was a *livre d'heures* – a liturgical prayer book – written in French, which had been published in 1756 by the Austrian Imperial imprinter, Thomas Trattner, in Vienna, and which contained white and blue bookmarks decorated with Bourbon escutcheon and symbols. On one page within was a hand-drawn portrait of a woman with her nose erased. It was widely known that Marie Antoinette had had her *livre d'heures* with her on the day of her execution, and it was believed that the book had traveled through many hands, including those of the French revolutionary leaders Robespierre and Marat, before turning up at auction in England. Shortly after the auction, and long before the story of the Dark Countess became known, it was told in England that Marie Antoinette's prayer book had been sent to a small town in Germany called Hildburghausen. Today, the book resides in a museum in France. In 1954, a member of the German noble family of Saxe-Altenburg, Frédéric de Saxe-Altenburg, wrote the book *L'Énigme de Madame Royale*, in which he contested that various members of his family had inherited possessions that had belonged to the Dark Countess along with a pledge to never reveal the secret story that there had, indeed, been a 'switch'.

On October 16, 1851 – some fourteen years after the death of the Dark Countess – the Duchesse d'Angoulême, suffering from pneumonia, rose to observe, as she did every year, the anniversary of the death of Queen Marie Antoinette of France. She died at Frohsdorf Castle near Vienna three days later on October 19, holding the wedding band that had belonged to King Louis XVI. On October 28, her nephew, the Comte de Chambord, eulogized her, stating that she lived according to 'not only the double majesty of virtue and sadness but also to the grand principles in which rest our future'. Her body was laid to rest at the peaceful convent of Castagnavizza in Slovenia, the crypt selected by Charles X for his exiled Bourbon family.

The story of Marie-Thérèse is one laden with paradoxes. The French considered themselves to be the most refined of Europe, the guardians of the most civilized society and their court the most rarefied; yet they became embroiled in the most barbaric and bloodthirsty revolution that, for the royal Children of France, was a Moloch. As a young girl, the public perceived Marie-Thérèse as a sinner – a spoilt and arrogant little girl; but she was, of course, just a child trained to perform. By the time of the Terror, hatred for her bloodline had grown to such a level that she was vilified by the masses, declared 'evil', and locked away in prison. However, when the nation needed to expiate itself for its crimes, it proclaimed her a saint. While Ernestine, the King's putative child, was neither damned nor noticed, Marie-Thérèse, as the legitimate daughter of the King and Queen of France, was scrutinized from the day she was born. Both women may have shared a father, a history, and a legacy that connected them back to the Merovingian Kings of France, but only one of them was the daughter of Marie Antoinette, and only one of them was raised to fulfill her duty as the standard bearer of a thousand-year-old dynasty.

Part One

Sinner

CHAPTER I
SEX AND POLITICS

W HEN HOLY ROMAN EMPEROR Joseph I died without a male heir in 1711, the crown passed to his brother, Charles VI. At that time, twenty-six-year-old Charles had no children. If Charles were to have a son, that boy would have been next in line to inherit the throne; but, if Charles were to have daughters, his late brothers' daughters would have precedence over his own female issue. In order to ensure continuation of his own dynasty and to preempt any claims to the throne by his nieces or other branches of the mighty Habsburg family, Charles, still childless in 1713, drafted a document called the Pragmatic Sanction. The Sanction laid down a code of succession in which Charles's eldest child, male or female, would inherit all the disparate Habsburg lands – including Austria, Hungary, Bohemia, and parts of Italy. However, before the Sanction could become law Charles had to negotiate fiercely with his nieces, cousins and various regional princes to persuade them to accept the measure.

Charles had one son who died in infancy and two daughters who would survive him. The eldest, Maria Theresa, became heiress to the throne and because Charles assumed that whichever husband she chose would, in reality, rule the Empire, she was allowed to marry for love. In 1736, nineteen-year-old Maria Theresa married Francis of Lorraine and by the marriage settlement the region of Lorraine was ceded to France, and Francis was given the title Grand Duke of Tuscany and with it vast territories and riches.

In 1740, Charles died and Maria Theresa ascended the throne, becoming Queen of Hungary and Bohemia, Archduchess of Austria, and Duchess of Parma, Piacenza and Guastalla. Despite the fact that during his lifetime Charles had devoted his diplomatic energies to having the Pragmatic Solution accepted by the major rulers of Europe, after his death Bavaria, France, Prussia and Spain immediately contested the document, advancing claims to great portions of the Empire. A war fought on many fronts, the War of Austrian Succession lasted for eight years during which time Charles of Bavaria was elected Holy Roman Emperor. The Austrians were able to defeat the French and Bavarians in Bohemia, sign a short-lived armistice with Frederick of Prussia, and, at last, when Charles of Bavaria died, secure the title Holy Roman Emperor for Maria Theresa's husband, Francis. Through her husband's election as 'Holy Roman Emperor, Francis I', Maria Theresa received the title 'Empress'.

Maria Theresa was acutely aware that as a female ruler her position would remain tenuous as without a male heir the legitimacy of the Sanction would be continually challenged. She and Francis would have sixteen children together – ten of whom would reach adulthood – but for the first three years of her marriage Maria Theresa gave birth only to daughters. Finally, in 1741, she gave birth to a son, Joseph, and was able to consolidate her position.

Despite Francis's widely acknowledged philandering, the royal couple successfully created a public image of family, piety, sobriety and good works. Although the royal tribe presented a somewhat casual family lifestyle – moving between the Hofburg Palace in Vienna and the nearby summer home, Schönbrunn Palace – there was nothing haphazard about their plans for their children. Each child was groomed for a specific role or marriage. Joseph was destined for and trained to be Holy Roman Emperor; Leopold II inherited his father's title, Grand Duke of Tuscany, when Francis I died in 1765; and Max Franz became Elector of Cologne. To the other young Archdukes and Archduchesses Maria Theresa applied the Habsburg family motto: 'Let other nations wage war; you, happy Austria, achieve your ends through marriage,' and she busily sought out and arranged marriages for them that would benefit the Empire. Eighth-born Maria Amelia fell in love with Prince Charles of Zweibrücken. The Empress and her minister Kaunitz disapproved of what they thought was an inferior match and forced the twenty-three-year-old Princess to marry the Duke of Parma, five years her junior and mentally impaired, in 1769. Maria Carolina, thirteenth-born, became Queen of Naples and Sicily. And in 1768, in what would prove the most tragic and ill-fated union, thirteen-year-old Maria Antonia was informed that she would be sent to France as the bride of Louis-Auguste, the Dauphin and future King of France.

In the 1750s, after centuries of hostility, Austria and France united against the British, but their alliance proved a disaster when, at the end of the Seven Years War in 1763, a British victory left France without much of her American territories and with heavy debts from a series of defeats. Maria Theresa and King Louis XV of France hoped that the marriage of their children would engender a more lasting truce between the two defeated Empires. Although many in France decried the proposal as a crime of miscegenation, Maria Antonia and Louis-Auguste were, in fact, both descended from Anne of Austria, the mother of France's King Louis XIV (although as the daughter of the Spanish King Philip III, she had never actually set foot in Austria and came to the French court directly from Spain).

Until the time of her engagement, Maria Antonia had been largely ignored by her mother. She had been raised by a series of tutors, maids and courtiers. Like most aristocrats, Maria Antonia was fluent in French, though she had never ventured further than the outskirts of Vienna. She loved music and was a talented ballet dancer – her graceful carriage always regarded as one of her finest attributes. The rest of her education was poor, however, and it was later discovered that the pretty and beguiling young Archduchess had been able to persuade her tutors to allow her to skip key subjects such as history and culture. These instructors, afraid of losing their posts, often completed Maria Antonia's homework for her, telling the Empress that it was the work of the child.

Before Maria Antonia could be presented to the French court as their future Queen, the young Archduchess had to undergo certain preparations including painful teeth straightening and an intensive course in French court customs. On April 19, 1770, Maria Antonia was married by proxy to Louis-Auguste of France. She was fourteen years old; the future Louis XVI, fifteen. The couple had never met, and both had reservations about the marriage. Maria Antonia was anxious about leaving her home forever. Louis-Auguste, convinced by courtiers and tutors that the Austrians were to be mistrusted, was far from happy about the exogamous union. Despite the bride's misgivings, she wrote to her new King informing him that the wedding by proxy had taken place, 'yesterday according to every ecclesiastical ceremony required'. She assured him that she would but 'occupy all my life to your care and to what pleases you to merit your confidence and goodness . . . to submit to your wishes', and, revealing a certain persuasive charm that she would become famous for, addressing His Majesty as 'my very dear grandfather', the new Dauphine added, 'I know that my age and my inexperience might require your indulgence.'

On the eve of her departure, Maria Antonia received a present from her mother: a gold, enamel and amber watch and chain that had belonged to the Empress herself. The following day, Saturday, April 21, Maria Antonia, sobbing uncontrollably, embraced her mother for the last time, said her goodbyes to the Austrian courtiers and left the Hofburg Palace, the place she would always recall as idyllic. She carried with her a list of instructions from her mother that included guidelines on French diet, religion, and acceptable reading material. The Empress bid her daughter farewell, announcing to all within earshot that she was sending France 'an angel'.

The fifty-seven-carriage cortège that departed Vienna splendidly befitted the occasion. The teenage bride's entourage rode in carriages upholstered in vivid-colored velvets, embroidered with crests and symbols. Maria Antonia's own carriage, sent especially by the King of France, had been designed to show off her beauty to the world. The berlin's panels were made of brilliant glass that shimmered like diamonds encasing the Dauphine as the new crown jewel of France, each panel set by finely wrought white, yellow and rose-colored gold that wrapped vine-like around the windows. The roof of the coach, a solid-gold encasement with bouquets of flowers, again in tri-colored gold, was so delicately crafted that the flowers actually swayed in the breeze as the procession headed west.

In an attempt to elicit favorable public relations around the Empire, the Austrian court had set out a travel itinerary for the new bride, which took her around Western Europe, allowing its subjects to behold the young beauty, lavish tribute upon her, and feel optimistic about their reigning family. From Melk to Ulm to Freiberg, Maria Antonia traveled for up to ten hours a day as enthusiastic throngs of people waved her on. Finally, after meandering through a week of pomp and celebration, she reached the Rhine near the town of Kehl, the final stop before she left the borders of her homeland.

Maria Antonia was to meet her new family on an island in the middle of the Rhine, signifying neutral ground – the same island where Maria Josepha of Saxony had been handed over to the French to become Dauphine some twenty-three years earlier. A group of citizens from nearby Strasbourg had erected a wooden pavilion decorated with tapestries in which to receive their new Dauphine. Oddly, one of the tapestries hurriedly nailed to a wall depicted a scene from the story of Jason and Medea, recalling the monstrous mother who kills her own children. The writer Goethe, a young man studying law in Strasbourg at the time, had visited the site a few days prior to the Dauphine's arrival, and, in his memoir, commented on the horrific inappropriateness of the imagery.

Maria Antonia arrived on the island in the afternoon of May 7, beneath gathering storm clouds. She was deposited inside the pavilion by her Austrian courtiers, who were then asked to leave. The French, insisting on a clean break from the past for this daughter of the Holy Roman Empire, demanded that the Dauphine proceed to France accompanied only by Prince Starhemberg, former ambassador to France and special assistant to Chancellor Kaunitz. Even her pet was banished: the fourteen-year-old was forced to leave her pug dog, Mops, with the Austrian delegation.

Although her magnificent trousseau had been crafted in France, it too was deemed to be 'Austrian'. She was stripped and her clothes thrown to waiting female attendants, who squabbled over them. Maria Antonia was then symbolically transformed into the future Queen of France. Completely re-attired in a second set of French-made, French-styled clothing, she was led to the next room in the pavilion, where she was received by various members of the French nobility. No longer Maria Antonia, Archduchess of the Holy Roman Empire, she was now Marie Antoinette, Dauphine of France.

According to the French courtiers who were present at the official *remise*, Maria Antonia committed a serious faux pas the moment she was presented to her French entourage. Tradition demanded that the person of the King and, by extension, his family, were absolutely sacred and therefore the body of the Dauphine was not to be touched by anyone. Overcome with emotion and desiring to make a fine first impression, Maria Antonia reached out and hugged the particularly severe Comtesse de Noailles, who had been appointed the Dauphine's Lady of Honor. The Countess, stunned at the young girl's impulsiveness and informality, cringed and remained rigid. Maria Antonia was immediately judged ill-prepared to serve as Queen.

The ceremony completed, the French procession made its way westward through the provinces. The bride, greeted with cheers and showers of flower petals, remained deeply anxious about meeting her new husband and seeing her new home, the incomparable Palace of Versailles.

The entourage arrived at the palace, west of Paris, on May 16. Six thousand people, dressed in their finest couture, assembled for a wedding celebration of heart-stopping splendor in the Opera House at Versailles, which had been built for the occasion. The young bride was lovely, declared the throngs of people. The aging Louis XV, who liked his women young and whose own mistress, Madame du Barry, was only two years older than his new granddaughter-in-law, was confident that the Dauphin would be extremely attracted to this 'delectable' Princess and that the dynasty would be preserved. To everyone's surprise, however, when the bridal bed was examined the next morning, it became clear that the couple had not consummated their marriage.

It seems that neither the fifteen-year-old Dauphin nor his fourteen-year-old bride had been taught anything about sex and neither of them had the slightest idea of what to do when they climbed into the marriage bed. It did not help that the two were temperamental opposites. Marie Antoinette was charming, graceful and outgoing, though deficient in formal education; the young Dauphin was plodding, reserved, of a solitary nature, and bookish. In 1763, having already read David Hume's *History of England*, the nine-year-old future Louis XVI was the only member of the royal family who was genuinely thrilled to meet the philosopher when he visited the French court (the rest of the royal family snubbed Hume). The Dauphin also enjoyed solving complicated geographical puzzles and creating intricate locks that took great ingenuity to pry open. He maintained a private smithy at Versailles where he would retreat to construct these devices. However, he expended most of his physical energy on hunting – going out almost every day, from early morning through a good deal of the afternoon. Gossip immediately spread among the thousands of courtiers at Versailles: the Dauphin preferred his smithy and the hunt to the company of his beautiful young wife.

In contrast with his grandson, Louis XV was a gregarious presence at court. He had little interest in serious thought and believed that a man's steady stream of mistresses was the true testament to his masculinity. He thought there was something very wrong with his grandson. Others said the same, and embarrassing pornographic cartoons began to appear, ridiculing the Dauphin's masculinity. In one, he appeared as a locksmith unable to work the key, an obvious insult to his lack of prowess. One picture showed the future king riding a giant phallic ostrich (*autruche* – a pun on the word for Austria: *autriche*) while Marie Antoinette stroked it. The Dauphin was a tall man; but as the number of caricatures increased, his height in them diminished leaving for posterity an image of him as a small, portly, inept little fellow.

The bride, so malleable, young, and desperate to fulfill her destiny, quickly became the ensnared pawn of rival factions at court, and of her own mother, the Empress. Week after week, month after month, Marie Antoinette received scolding letters from her mother who reminded her that her primary duty was to produce an heir to the throne.[1] Maria

Theresa also relentlessly nagged the Dauphine, stressing that she should serve the Austrian Empire, gain favor with the French King, find out as much information as she could and send that information back to Vienna. The great and powerful Empress of Austria, who fought dazzling political duels with the formidable Frederick II of Prussia, proved equally skillful at manipulating her own daughter; her letters to her frequently included comments such as 'If you loved me, you would . . .' and 'You don't listen to a word I say'. And when it came to exerting even further pressure on her daughter with regard to producing an heir the Empress wrote, 'seeing you in this state [pregnant] . . . would be the only thing that would give me a reason to prolong my sad days.' Later, Marie Antoinette would be accused of spying for Austria. These accusations – which could never be proved – were to a degree well founded because, owing to her complete naivety, Marie Antoinette unwittingly imparted information to her mother and brother who then used guile and trickery to obtain further intelligence from other sources.

Mother and daughter would communicate through letters carried by a private courier who left Vienna at the beginning of each month. This trusted messenger would journey from Vienna to Austrian Belgium and arrive in Paris about ten days later. He would remain in Paris until the middle of the month and would return via the same route in reverse, arriving in Vienna around the 25th of each month, though in the case of a family crisis, the Empress would dispatch extra couriers.

Such a system was essential to maintain a type of privacy. It was widely known that elaborate spy cabinets operated in every European court to digest and profit from potentially important and secret information. Among the most successful of the eighteenth-century nefarious Black Chambers – the teams of espionage who worked at deciphering and encrypting messages sent among the embassies – was the Austrian Geheime Kabinets-Kanzlei. Before any letter arrived at its intended location in Vienna, it would be sent to the Black Chamber at 7 a.m. for examination. Seals were melted, letters copied, and messages decoded. Language specialists, stenographers and cryptologists assisted in this treachery. The letters would then be resealed to perfection and delivered to the addressee by four in the afternoon, seemingly intact.

Despite the fact that Marie Antoinette signed her letters 'Your submissive daughter', the Empress was not at all convinced that she would receive completely honest news, and she was equally confident that her somewhat frivolous daughter, inattentive to world events, could not possibly offer any substantive political information. Therefore the

Empress placed two spies at the French court. One, the Abbé de Vermond, instructed Marie Antoinette on religious matters and listened to her most personal confessions; the other, Comte Mercy-Argenteau, served as the Austrian ambassador to France. On February 13, 1772, the Empress wrote to her daughter, 'If you love me, you will listen to all of his [Mercy's] advice without exception . . . follow, without hesitation and with confidence, everything he will tell you or demand of you', even if it placed her in conflict with her own husband.

These two spies, whose letters were included in the packets transported by the private courier, reported on every misstep, misdeed, and failure of the young Dauphine. The Empress would let her daughter know she had heard rumors, but would never reveal the true source of her information. Instead, she led her daughter to believe that the King of Prussia was behind the stories. The Empress's implications had the desired effect: Marie Antoinette assumed that the Prussian had spies at the French court and often complained to her husband that the Prussians were slandering them. In the meantime, the Empress received the most personal and invasive information, including reports on where the Dauphine slept, how late she stayed up in the evening, the fact that she was horseback riding despite her mother's directive not to do so (for fear that such activities might interfere with pregnancy), and even accounts of her monthly periods (which were termed 'General Krottendorf' after a private family joke about the General's dour wife).

The most pressing issue for Maria Theresa, however, remained her daughter's inability to become pregnant. In a similar observation to that of Louis XV, the Empress noted that there must have been something wrong with the Dauphin because he did not seem to be aroused by her daughter. While royal houses all over Europe were increasing their numbers, Marie Antoinette remained childless. Finally, in 1773, after three years of marriage, the couple had what they thought was sex. Still, there were no pregnancies. Doctors puzzled over their 'infertility'. The Empress continued to receive updates from Comte Mercy, and she continued to harangue her already very anxious daughter, instructing Marie Antoinette to use all of her energy and charm to seduce her husband.

In a letter to Comte Mercy dated November 6, 1773, Maria Theresa wrote: '*Voilà!* Three grandchildren this year and I expect a fourth in December . . . as for the Dauphine . . . nothing . . . I burn with desire at this moment to see her pregnant.' Mercy wrote to the Empress on November 12, that the pregnancy would not be as soon as she would like. In response Maria Theresa wrote that she would keep hoping. Shortly after the New Year, on January 3, 1774, the Empress reiterated her frustration with the Dauphin saying that his seeming indifference to her daughter was a mystery to her and that he should get on and do his duty.

On May 10, 1774, King Louis XV died of smallpox. The following year, on June 11, Louis-Auguste was crowned Louis XVI at the cathedral of Reims, as French monarchs had been for hundreds of years. The nineteen-year-old King was advised by his ministers that the Seven Years War had left the French treasury in a precarious position and that in order to save the money of the realm they would need to forego an official coronation for the new Queen. This was largely an excuse, however. In truth, Louis XVI's ministers were beginning to discuss the notion of persuading the King to divorce his childless wife and send her back to Austria. Many people were already deeply concerned by the monarch's failure to produce an heir, though the King's brothers, the Comte de Provence and the Comte d'Artois, second and third in line for the throne respectively, were content to see their brother remain without issue. Their cousins, the Orléans clan, descended from the younger brother of King Louis XIV, maintained that they had a superior claim to the throne, questioned their cousins' legitimacy and were quietly amused by the royal couple's failure to procreate.

After the Orléans cousins failed to attend Louis XV's funeral, King Louis XVI banished his young cousin Philippe, the Duc de Chartres, from court. Chartres – who would soon inherit his father's title of Duc d'Orléans, placing him one step closer to the throne in the line of succession – thus began a long and personal campaign against the young King that would have dire consequences for the entire country. Young Orléans took special pleasure in a rift he had engineered between the King's youngest brother, the teenage Comte d'Artois, and the King. Orléans, it was said, had deliberately introduced d'Artois to the world of gambling and brothels at the Palais-Royal in Paris. Louis, a sober and pious young man, strongly disapproved of the evenings of debauchery, and suspected his cousin had even more nefarious motives. Venereal diseases were rampant in the brothels of Paris and a number of the Bourbons' relations and friends had fallen ill and had perished without issue. There would be no better way to step even closer to the throne than to render the King's youngest brother sterile or to indirectly cause his death.

D'Artois and the King's other brother, the Comte de Provence, had recently married the daughters of the King of Sardinia, who were regarded as being ugly and as having very poor personal hygiene. The brothers, thoroughly repulsed, initially refused to sleep with their wives. The Comte de Provence remained steadfast in his refusal but d'Artois, feeling the pressure of the dynasty upon his shoulders, soldiered through his performances with disgust but regularity for the good of France. On December 17, 1774, Marie Antoinette wrote to her mother that she was upset because the Comtesse d'Artois had become pregnant. Mercy wrote the Empress that although Marie Antoinette was behaving very kindly toward her sister-in-law, it was apparent to him that the Queen was jealous. The next day Mercy wrote again saying that Marie Antoinette had now confided her extreme pain to both the Abbé de Vermond and himself.

The King may not have spent much time with his bride, but the Queen was never alone. Owing to a surveillance system designed to protect the virtue of every French queen since the time of the fourteenth-century monarch Philippe IV, Marie Antoinette's every move was made in front of courtiers or in public. Even her outlandish hairdos, which took hours to construct, were concocted for public entertainment. As if at the theater, onlookers would sit for hours in the Queen's chambers, looking on while the Queen's hairdresser, Léonard, sculpted lavish headdresses for her to wear to any one of a number of balls she would host, night after night. On Monday night, for instance, it was masked quadrilles. Aside from the constant galas and card parties offered to amuse the courtiers, any visiting dignitary or foreign head of state was feted in a style intended to impress. The Queen's rising, eating, daily worship and bedtime were ceremoniously acted out for public consumption. If she wanted to stroll in the gardens, she was accompanied. If she wanted a glass of water, there was a chain of people who would perform small tasks until a gloved person of honor would hand her a glass.

Marie Antoinette became increasingly unhappy. While her siblings were sending portraits of their growing families to their mother, she had nothing more than sketches of her hairdos to dispatch. To escape the constant glare of the spotlight, the constant criticism of her mother, and the pain of her inability to bear a child, she removed herself to the 'Petit Trianon'. This bauble of a country home, built on the grounds of Versailles but separate from the *grand palais,* was where Marie Antoinette withdrew to host only her closest friends. It was here that the Queen, exhausted from the etiquette of the French court, banished curtsying and insisted that she be called by her first name.

The Empress once again criticized her daughter – this time for isolating herself at the Petit Trianon. Maria Theresa warned Marie Antoinette that by doing this she was not only insulting the French court, but avoiding her husband's bed. When the Empress further learned that her daughter spent many late evenings playing cards at the gambling tables long after her husband had retired for the evening, Maria Theresa admonished her daughter for her frivolity and self-indulgence, warning her that the French people would never accept their Austrian-born Queen unless she gave birth to a French child. The Empress feared that any opprobrium directed toward the Queen would worsen relations between the two countries; in this Maria Theresa was proved correct. Marie Antoinette's critics began to call her 'l'Autri*chienne*' – 'the Austrian' – placing an emphasis on *chienne*, or 'bitch'. Critical pamphlets appeared, some rumored to have been penned by the King's own brothers. The public further expressed its distaste for things Austrian when Marie Antoinette's favorite composer, the German Gluck, whose music she had grown up with in Vienna, arrived in France and his compositions were reviled.

Marie Antoinette encouraged Gluck to persist, and when he presented such works as *Orfeo et Euridice* as *Orphée et Eurydice* and *Iphigénie en Tauride* with French libretti, the audiences were won over, offering tribute to their Queen as the arbiter of good taste. Enjoying her success as his patron, she spent many evenings at the opera while her husband was at home in bed. Her mother, again, complained that she was neglecting her wifely duties in the bedroom. Marie Antoinette gave excuses explaining that it was also her duty to promote the arts in France and that joining in the gaming parties was expected of her. On October 17, 1775, Mercy informed the Empress that, while the Comtesse d'Artois was pregnant again, Marie Antoinette and her husband maintained very different schedules – a sure impediment to procreation. The following year, Marie Antoinette received further news that her favorite sister, the Queen of Naples, and the wives of her brothers Leopold and Ferdinand were all pregnant.

In despair, Marie Antoinette unburdened herself in a letter to her brother, the future Emperor Joseph II of Austria, and, on November 30, 1776, she received a letter from her mother informing her that Joseph would come to France to see her. Joseph made it clear that he wanted no part of the French formalities at Versailles and insisted on a quiet, private visit. Although he toured hospitals and factories, his real mission was to investigate the cause of his sister's unhappiness, though what he dis- covered made him roar with both laughter and disbelief. On June 9, 1777, he wrote their brother, Archduke Leopold, of his findings.

The great King of France does not ejaculate inside his wife, Joseph explained:

> [he] has good strong erections, he introduces his member, stays there without moving for perhaps two minutes and never ejaculates, still erect, he withdraws, and bids good-night . . . he sometimes has nightly emissions, but once in place and going at it, never, and he is content claiming that he is only doing it out of a sense of duty but not because he has any pleasure . . . if only once I could have been there, I would have . . . whipped him so that he would have ejaculated out of sheer rage like a donkey.

It was true that Louis and Marie Antoinette had married as young teenagers without any instruction in the subject of sex, but Joseph thought that after seven years of marriage the French King might have worked out what to do. Marie Antoinette was the object of admiration, and lust, on the part of many men. Her friendship with the handsome Swedish Count, Axel Fersen, for example, had ignited much gossip. Sadly, the King remained neither excited nor inflamed by jealousy. After he learned of the King's complete ineptness in the bedroom, Joseph went for a long walk with Louis during which he explained in great detail what the King needed to do in order to complete the act of intercourse. Satisfied that he had accomplished what he had set out to do, Joseph returned home.[2]

Comte Mercy, who had been sending the Empress his own detailed reports of Joseph's visit to France, wrote Maria Theresa on June 15 that the King of France had expressed his sadness about not having children to his brother-in-law, and that Joseph had given the King some advice. In that same letter Mercy reassured the Empress that Joseph would tell her in person what had transpired. On June 16, 1777, Marie Antoinette wrote to her mother that the Comtesse d'Artois was pregnant once again and, although after seven years of marriage the 'outlook was unpleasant' for herself, she was 'not without hope; my brother will tell my dear Mama all about it. The King talked to him on this point in a friendly and trusting way.'

On August 18, between 10 and 11.15 in the morning, after the Queen's bath, the King and Queen completed 'the sexual act' at last. On August 30, Marie Antoinette wrote:

> My dear Mother . . . It has already been more than eight days since my marriage was perfectly consummated; the proof has been repeated and

yesterday even more completely than the first time. At first I thought of sending my dear Mama a courier. I feared that it would be such an event as to cause talk.

On September 12, Mercy confirmed Marie Antoinette's claim in a letter to Maria Theresa stating that the Queen had also told him that her husband 'had succeeded'. In October 1777, Joseph wrote his brother Leopold, 'the King of France has at last succeeded in the *grande oeuvre* and perhaps the Queen will become pregnant . . . they both have written to thank me attributing it to my counsel'.

One of the unforeseen results of the King's new interest in sex was that various factions, knowing that by placing a mistress in the King's bed they could gain influence over the monarch, began to scheme. Mercy commented on this danger and wrote the Empress on November 19, 1777, that Marie Antoinette had dismissed the possibility, claiming her husband was too shy and had not enough energy to chase other women. Marie Antoinette went so far as to joke among friends that if Louis had dallied she would not be the least bit angry. Mercy admonished the Queen, saying that speaking about her husband with such indifference was not amusing, and that if the King learned of her banter he would be stunned. The Empress agreed and wrote to her daughter, once again warning her to behave herself. Both Mercy and the Empress were acutely aware that if the Queen were unable to bear children, she could be returned to Vienna and a papal annulment granted.

Louis knew this, but, as a man of very strict morals, he had neither desire for mistresses nor favorites. He did, however, want to know for certain who would be at fault if his wife did not conceive. There was a young chambermaid at court named Philippine de Lambriquet, whose husband, Jacques, served on the staff of the Comte de Provence. The King proceeded with his agenda and, it seems, after her liaison with the King, she became pregnant – though as she also had a husband, Louis was still not quite certain of his own fertility.

On January 5, 1778, Maria Theresa greeted her daughter with the New Year wish 'that a courier may bring me news of a pregnancy . . . at sixty, one cannot wait long'. Marie Antoinette replied on January 15: 'I am ashamed and upset to have to tell my dear Mama that I had my period yesterday morning.' On February 1, Maria Theresa wrote that Marie Antoinette's sister, Maria Carolina, Queen of Naples and Sicily, was pregnant again, commenting 'they come one after the other'. At the same time, she urged Marie Antoinette to convince her husband that he ought to be a good son-in-law and side with the Empress against Frederick II of Prussia. Louis responded negatively, at first, stating: 'It is your relatives' ambition which is causing all the trouble; they started with Poland, now they are doing it again in Bavaria; I am sorry for this because of you.'

On February 13, Marie Antoinette once again conceded failure to conceive when she wrote to her mother that 'on February 8 my period came. That is six days early.' In March, Marie Antoinette promised her mother that she was sincerely trying. 'The King sleeps with me three or four nights a week and behaves in such a way as to give me great hopes.'

A week later Marie Antoinette wrote,

My first impulse a week ago, which I regret not following, was to write to my dear Mama about my hopes. I was prevented by my fear of causing too great a sorrow if my hopes were to vanish; they are still not completely assured, and I will only count on it at the beginning of next month, the time for the second period. In the meantime I think I have good reason to feel confident; I have never been late, on the contrary always a little early; in March I had my period on the third; today is the nineteenth and nothing has happened.

In addition, she was thrilled to add, 'Yesterday, coming back from Evensong, I vomited a little.' She took advantage of her mother's excitement about her potential pregnancy, and turned the tables on her, using a potential pregnancy quite deftly to evoke guilt. She asked her mother to stop pressuring her about the political situation, going so far as to warn that if she were with child and suffered a miscarriage it would be a result of the strain cause by the Empress. 'I would be too happy if the [Bavarian] business could be settled and free me from worry and the greatest misfortunes that could happen to me.'

On April 20, Comte Mercy wrote the Empress that everyone at court was whispering about the fact that Marie Antoinette had not had her period at the beginning of the month. Dr Lassone was called to examine her. The doctor stated that the Queen was premature in her calculation, explaining that when two cycles had passed, they could then confirm that she was pregnant. In the meantime, while Marie Antoinette rested between fear and hope, the King was delirious. A couple of weeks later the Empress warned her daughter that if she were pregnant she had better get plenty of rest and refrain from playing billiards, sleeping in chaise longues, wearing court dress, and taking recommendations from anyone at Versailles other than Dr Lassone as to whom she should choose as her obstetrician-midwife. 'Even your nausea pleases me and I hope it will all go on . . . The Queen of Naples's joy will be extreme; I bet that she will be moved to tears,' she wrote.

On May 5, Mercy wrote Maria Theresa that Marie Antoinette had virtually succeeded on two fronts: she had still not had a period and had apparently softened her husband's stance toward Austria. After pleasing her mother over 'the Bavarian business', Marie Antoinette was briefly tempted to meddle further in politics, but quickly found herself otherwise occupied.

After eight long years, Marie Antoinette was pregnant at last. Blissfully preparing for the birth of her first child, she chose the brother of her priest, Vermond, as obstetrician. He would be paid 40,000 *livres*[3] if he delivered a boy and 10,000 for a girl. As head of the child's household, the Princesse de Guémené would oversee a staff of nearly one hundred people to surround, serve, and educate the child. On June 11, Maria Theresa wrote to her daughter that everyone in Vienna was thrilled for her and that no one was talking of anything but Marie Antoinette.

Louis XVI's brothers and cousins, however, were less than thrilled by the news which threatened their positions of succession. The Comte de Provence actually admitted in a letter to King Gustav III of Sweden, whose own wife was pregnant, that he put on a happy face in public but that he was finding the change in his fortunes hard to cope with.

For the first time in years, Marie Antoinette was utterly content, growing fat – by June, she had gained four and a half inches on her tiny waist – and, for the first time in years, she was able to write to her mother without anxiety or hesitation. On Friday, July 31, Marie Antoinette felt the baby's first movement. Teasing her husband, she told him that one of his subjects had the audacity to kick her in the stomach. Madame Campan, Marie Antoinette's amiable and witty First Lady-in-Waiting, reported that the King, with tears in his eyes, had given a triumphant shout. That same day, Philippine de Lambriquet gave birth to a daughter, Marie-Philippine, who closely resembled the King.

The summer of 1778 was unbearably hot, with no rain to alleviate the burning sun. In a letter to the Duchesse d'Enville, the King's recently dismissed Finance Minister, Turgot, wrote that a rumor had spread among the populace that the American scientist and inventor Benjamin Franklin, who was living near Paris at the time while serving as his country's ambassador, had electrified the weather in order to prevent any storms until Marie Antoinette's first child was born. At Versailles, to combat the stifling heat, the Queen wore flowing, lightweight muslin maternity gowns designed by her couturier, Rose Bertin, and her *parfumeur*, Jean-Louis Fargeon, created soothing scents with iris, benzoin, wild roses, and sandalwood. Still, Marie Antoinette remained uncomfortable and stayed inside during the daytime. In the very late evenings, long after the King had gone to bed, the air cooled sufficiently for the Queen to walk about. Her brothers- and sisters-in-law would join her on quiet promenades along the terraces, leaving all of the candles burning in their rooms for illumination. These nightly outings became a regular event for the group and, knowing of the Queen's fondness for music, someone suggested that a small group of musicians who performed in the chapel provide soft music for added ambience. These simple, refreshing evenings seemed almost dream-like as Versailles glowed dimly from within and music flowed in the nocturnal air.

Such private moments of pleasure did not last for long, however. Word traveled among the courtiers and townspeople of Versailles, who had open access to the gardens, that the Queen was out and about in the evenings. The tiny procession swelled to an enormous group of people; the tiny cluster of musicians expanded into an orchestra; candelabra were placed in the gardens to accommodate the assemblage, and it became necessary to station sentinels to stand guard. These grand festivities even attracted the now-banished Madame du Barry, the late King's mistress, whom Marie Antoinette had detested. More lethal to the Queen at this moment were her enemies who chose to feed the imagination of the people of France against her. These detractors, including the Orléans clan and the King's own brothers, published pamphlets portraying these evenings of innocence as scandalous revelries.

One usual source of criticism, however, abated for the moment. As the summer turned to autumn, the Empress changed tack and lectured her daughter on a different front, this time offering unsolicited advice on childrearing. She should not swaddle the child too tightly; she should not keep the baby too warm; and she should find a very good wet nurse. Maria Theresa did not have to point out to her daughter that she was the mother of sixteen children, most of whom had attained adulthood – in those days a rarity. Marie Antoinette responded with the plans she had made: the child would not be swaddled at all, a tiny *grille* was being installed for the baby to hold onto to facilitate walking on parquet floors, and, in fact, because of the family lore that Bourbons were often born with teeth, four wet nurses had been engaged. The Empress wanted everything prepared to perfection. At the beginning of December, Marie Antoinette took to her bed to wait for the baby's birth; her hairdresser,

Léonard, climbing into bed and lying down beside her each day to style her hair. The two joked that with all of the stories about her infidelities, she was, actually, finally in bed with a man not her husband.

The King of Spain, Charles III, agreed to be the baby's godfather. Marie Antoinette asked her mother to be the baby's godmother and to create a list of potential names for the child. The Empress was again delighted and asked Mercy to inform her of what she would need to do to comply with French custom. What gifts would she need to buy? Who would stand in her place? She had looked forward to this day for years, and with increased anticipation, she awaited the moment that would give her peace: the delivery of the letter that would bring her news of the birth of the heir to the throne of France, her hope for the perfect alliance between the two great monarchies. She counted on Mercy, her son-in-law, and her children – with their vast network of contacts and friends – to keep her fully informed. There were, however, some details about the impending birth of the child that no one, not even Mercy, dared tell the Empress.

CHAPTER II
CHILD OF FRANCE

I N 1777, as American colonists fought a bloody war with the British for independence, life in England seemed a time of frothy enjoyment. Richard Sheridan's *The School for Scandal* amused British theatergoers and the Royal Crescent in Bath attracted vacationers to the popular spa. On the European continent as well, with Mozart delighting audiences, war against tyranny seemed a world away. In 1778, eight-year-old Beethoven was introduced as a prodigy by his father; the world-famous La Scala opera house opened in Milan; and both Rousseau and Voltaire, the *bêtes noires* of King Louis XVI, died. As an antidote to the maddening *philosophes* and their liberal, anti-monarchial, pro-republican rhetoric, the Société des amis de la Religion et des Lettres was founded, awarding prizes for literary achievement that praised religion and the status quo in government and condemning the voices of the Enlightenment as provocateurs of anarchy.

For Louis XVI, reigning monarch of the oldest continuous kingdom in Europe and awaiting the birth of his first legitimate child, all was right with the world. He was not at all disturbed when his mother-in-law, Empress Maria Theresa, with a typical lack of confidence in her own daughter, made a bet with him that Marie Antoinette would not succeed in giving him a (male) heir. Louis had openly stated that since a son had been born to King Gustav III of Sweden that same year, because he believed no two kings would be born in the same year, he, too, felt that his wife would deliver him a daughter. Having fathered one child, he was confident that there would be more children, and among them an heir. In a magnanimous mood, Louis accepted the wager from the Empress and was happy to take a loss.

Such was Louis's confidence in the perpetuation of his dynasty that he also signed two treaties with the 'upstart Americans', offering the Colonies official recognition as a nation as well as money on an 'as needed' basis. Impressed by the skillful, tenacious yet patient negotiations of Benjamin Franklin and keen to participate in any defeat over the British, Louis XVI viewed the American independence movement as an experiment, like Franklin's scientific probing.

Although the agreements between France and America increased hostility between England and France, there was little personal animosity between the French King and George III of England. The two exchanged friendly notes, with King George offering Louis his sincere delight that he was about to become a father. The entire family of European royalty – all, in fact, related, as brothers, sisters and cousins – considered the impending birth of the child created by the union of Marie Antoinette and Louis XVI a joyous event that would impact on future alliances.

It was customary for witnesses to be present at royal births in most European countries. In England, for example, when the future George IV was born, half a dozen courtiers were on hand to attest to the fact that the baby born was indeed the child of the Queen. In France, however, it was another matter altogether: the birth of a royal child was a public event with an audience on a first-come, first-served basis. When the young Duc d'Angoulême was born on August 6, 1775, the Queen, along with the family and members of the court, remained in her sister-in-law's chambers for an entire day until the birth of her nephew; but the birth of a child of the King brought people to Versailles from all parts of the realm. Marie Antoinette may have thought she was prepared for the birth of her child but she did not anticipate the frenzy that would accompany the baby's arrival.

When the Queen began to feel contractions just after midnight on Saturday, December 19, the tocsin sounded at Versailles. This initial alarm set off a chain of bell-ringing throughout France. By two o'clock in the morning, the Queen was in labor and crowds began to arrive. In an attempt to provide a measure of privacy for the Queen, the King constructed a tent by tying together the tapestry screens that surrounded the antechamber, which contained her bed; the tent, however, proved useless as a crush of onlookers poured in. First Lady-in-Waiting Madame Campan recalled seeing two Savoyards standing on the furniture. Windows that had been nailed shut for the winter were smashed in order to provide air for the Queen as well as the hundreds present. The circus-like atmosphere reached a fever when nearly ten hours later, at around 11.30

a.m., in full view of hundreds of people, the Queen delivered a healthy, fair-haired, blue-eyed daughter. Marie-Thérèse-Charlotte would be called a Child of France, as any child of the King would be known, but her formal title would be 'Madame Royale'.

Immediately upon her arrival, the most anticipated baby in Europe upstaged her mother. The King exuberantly grabbed his daughter and carried her in the air, proceeding into a larger antechamber for the baby's baptism. While crowds of people followed the King, the Queen, who by this time was completely ignored by all, convulsed then slipped into unconsciousness. She knew neither whether her baby had survived, nor what sex it was. Although Marie Antoinette had established a signal with her good friend, the Princesse de Lamballe, to inform her immediately of the baby's gender, the Princess, swept along in the crowd, had no time to deliver the news before the Queen lost consciousness. Lamballe was supposed to say, in Italian, '*Il figlio è nato*', if it was a boy, or '*Una figlia è nata*', for a girl. From the midst of the crowd, Lamballe, overwhelmed with emotion, mistakenly declared, '*La regina è andato!*' ('The Queen came!') and promptly fainted. The Marquise du Deffand wrote to her friend Horace Walpole that the Queen had actually bled from her mouth before anyone noticed her dire condition, and, after a few minutes, during which Marie Antoinette almost perished, the chief surgeon grabbed a knife and sliced into her foot, causing it to bleed and the Queen to revive.

The extensive household staff of nearly a hundred, carefully selected before the baby's arrival,[1] included a head governess, four *sous* governesses, a royal hairdresser, dentist, cradle rocker, the mandatory wet nurses, and servants to serve the servants. The expenses for the baby's household totaled 299,000 *livres* before her first birthday and by the age of two, the cost of serving the Princess a bowl of soup was estimated to be 5,000 *livres*. Furniture-makers and carpenters would also benefit. An entire suite of rooms had been designated to serve as the nursery. The apartment would face Versailles' resplendent gardens, where the child, when she was ready, would stroll accompanied by a retinue of retainers.

The birth of the Princess also brought wealth for industries across the realm, as merchants all over France worked feverishly to prepare offerings and lavish gifts of thanks for her little royal highness. Representatives from the provinces and from a cross section of guilds arrived in Versailles to present their finest silks, porcelains, silver, crystal and cabinetry to the newborn, hoping to please and potentially gain favor – and commissions. The Church, too, organized services of thanks, and towns celebrated the momentous event with festivals and fireworks. Coins of the realm were minted featuring mother and child. The Opéra in Paris offered free performances and refreshments to the populace. Rousing shouts of 'Santé!' echoed in the hall as the masses drank to the health of the newborn Princess, descendant of the great Eudes who ascended the throne of France in 888. The little girl was the latest member of the Capet family, France's ruling dynasty since the tenth century. From the time of the great Charlemagne, the French kings had been considered God's lieutenants, a symbol of divinity on earth, and French subjects regarded the daughter of King Louis XVI as almost a goddess.

Despite the baby's lineage, Marie-Thérèse's baptism was accompanied by some quite un-regal behavior. France's *grand aumônier*, or chief chaplain, Cardinal de Rohan of Strasbourg,[2] baptized the tiny Princess on the day of her birth in the presence of her father, his brothers and sisters-in-law, courtiers, and the mob of citizens who remained for the sacrament. The Comtesse de Provence stood in for Maria Theresa of Austria, and her husband, the Comte de Provence, for King Charles III of Spain. Both were overjoyed that the baby was a girl because she would not disturb the line of succession to the throne. Despite his relief, Provence simply could not resist passing comment. When testifying to the parentage of the girl during the service, he made a remark implying that his brother was not the baby's father, causing the King – and everyone who heard the insult – to bristle.

After the service, Marie-Thérèse was handed to her governess, the Princesse de Guémené, who carried the newborn back into the bedchamber to be reunited with her mother. When Marie Antoinette saw that the baby was a girl she realized that she had disappointed her husband, as there was still no heir. Privately, however, she delighted in her baby girl. The Duc de Croÿ, who had been Louis XV's First Gentleman of the Bedchamber, and Madame Campan both reported that as the new mother held her baby in her arms, she whispered, 'Poor little girl, you are not what was desired, but you are no less dear to me on that account. A son would have been the property of the State. You shall be mine; you shall have my undivided care; you will share all my happiness and you will alleviate my sufferings.' Someone in the crowd reminded the King that he had lost his bet with his mother-in-law. He nonetheless appeared besotted with his new daughter and lovingly repeated some verses in Italian by Metastasio. He may have lost the bet, said the King, but the whole world had won.

The day after the birth of Madame Royale, the Queen met with Comte Mercy to compose what she knew would be a disappointing letter to her mother. Mercy protested that the Queen was in too weak a state to correspond with her mother and explained that he had already taken care of informing the Empress judiciously, though omitting details of her daughter's near death. That same day, in its 'news from Versailles' section, the *Mercure de France* – a publication that enjoyed the King's patronage – reported that:

> Yesterday at 11.30 in the morning, the Queen had happily given birth to a wonderful, marvelous daughter, and Her Majesty was doing as well as could be expected. The day of this happy event was the same day that Philippe, Duc d'Anjou had been born in 1683.

The baby was healthy, the Queen was recovering, and all thought it best to spare the baby's grandmother most of the details. The January 5, 1779, edition of the *Mercure de France* reported under the headline 'NEWS FROM VERSAILLES ON DECEMBER 31, 1778', that the Queen was recovering as well as could be expected. The article also contained an aside that the baby had been baptized privately immediately after its birth, which, according to the newspaper, was quite unusual for the French, whose ancient custom was to wait a few years before baptizing children. For a newspaper that enjoyed the royal blessing, this comment, a reminder to the public that their own Queen had strange, foreign ways, was considered audacious and disrespectful.

Despite the court's careful attempt to conceal the Queen's arduous labor, greatly embroidered tales spread throughout the realm. One rumor said that the Queen had been gravely wounded during the birth of her daughter. Such stories reached the ears of Empress Maria Theresa who became convinced that there was a conspiracy afoot to hurt her daughter. She even stated that she was certain that there were people who wanted to make sure that the Queen of France would bear no more children and no heir to the throne. And indeed there were those who were so inclined. One such instance surfaced a few weeks after the birth of the baby, when the curé of the Madeleine de la Cité approached Madame Campan and asked for an audience with the Queen. Campan wrote that the priest delivered into the hands of the Queen a tiny box containing her wedding ring with a note which read, 'I have received under the seal of confession the ring which I send to your Majesty, with an avowal that it was stolen from you in 1771, in order to be used in sorceries, to prevent your having any children.'

The King and Queen, doting on their new baby, stated that they wanted to create a cocoon of beauty and love around their daughter.

Each of them had grown up acutely aware that they were not their parents' favorite child. Louis-Auguste, like his wife, had been neglected as a child; he had not got along with his father at all, and the two had spent very little time together. By the time Louis-Auguste was twelve, both of his parents had died. Marie Antoinette, though adored by her father, was nonetheless very young when he died and when the Empress had time to consider her children, she focused on the future Emperor and her older daughters.

Louis XVI was determined that his daughter would never feel unloved or rejected and he cancelled many of his outings and engagements in order to spend as much time as possible with his wife and baby daughter. Attentive courtiers joined the King passing many hours and days by the Queen's bedside and in the nursery. In order to provide her well-wishers with comfort, Marie Antoinette had ordered specially designed chairs. By January 3, the Queen invited about fifty guests at a time to her rooms. Little entertainments were devised to amuse the Queen as she recuperated. Guests were encouraged to visit Marie-Thérèse in her nursery, but were not allowed to touch her. On January 19, Madame Royale's one-month birthday, Marie Antoinette moved to a chaise in order to greet the Spanish ambassador who arrived bearing a spectacular gift for the baby from her godfather – a pair of diamond earrings and a diamond Saint-Esprit pendant suspended on a silk cord.

In many ways, the birth of Madame Royale heralded a sea change in the royal couple's relationship. Louis XVI, so enthralled with his wife and new baby, regaled 120,000 *livres* on the Queen as a present for her to spend as she saw fit. Marie Antoinette was moved by her husband's tenderness and viewed him in a more loving light. She decided that she would try to get pregnant again as soon as possible. She was also doubtless aware of the fact that she could escape many of the rigors of protocol when pregnant. Motherhood consumed her days. If the newborn baby had been a boy, as the heir to the throne he would have been immediately whisked away to wet nurses; but as the Queen had predicted, by giving birth to a daughter she was able to enjoy far more latitude in raising and caring for the baby herself. For eighteen days, the Queen breastfed her own child – an act that horrified her mother. The Empress immediately sent instructions to her daughter to cease such 'barbarism' and warned her that breast-feeding would prevent her from getting pregnant again, believing it in effect a contraceptive. Marie Antoinette stopped breastfeeding her daughter.

Before the birth of Madame Royale, the Queen had spent hours each day sitting before her hairdresser as he created the hairstyles that had been the talk of Europe. Pregnancy, however, had caused the loss of a great deal of her hair causing Léonard and the Queen's *parfumeur* Jean-Louis Fargeon to work together in creating a pomade to strengthen the roots of her hair. Marie Antoinette wanted to spend more time with her baby and fewer hours in front of the looking-glass, and so although her hair had been repaired, she displayed a new penchant for a simpler coiffure and manner of dress, preferring loosely tumbling tresses tied by a large silk ribbon in the style of a little girl, as Vigée-Lebrun would often paint her.

The royal couple also made public statements reflecting their happiness. The Queen commissioned her dressmaker to create a splendid gown for the statue of the Virgin of Monflières as an offering of thanks, and she paid off the debts of women imprisoned for not having had enough money to pay their own baby's nurses. The Queen also offered alms to the poor in the name of the newborn princess. The King, as the nation's father, passed an edict three weeks after the birth of Madame Royale on behalf of all orphans in France whose fathers could not or would not 'protect them against the dangers at so tender an age'. Until that time in France, orphaned children were often transported great distances in open vehicles to the foundling hospital in Paris, even in inclement weather, regardless of their health. The edict ended this practice and by it local charitable institutions were compelled to assume responsibility for the forsaken children. In addition, Louis opened his treasury to provide the extra revenue needed in the provinces to support the welfare of these orphans.

Despite the great joy at court, the Queen's first public appearance, called the *cérémonie de relevailles,* or the 'ceremony of getting up', on February 8, 1779, was not an unqualified success. First, the King and Queen broke with tradition, celebrating in grand style as if a male heir to the throne had been born. If a boy had been born, the French people would have expected the Queen to attend a service at Notre Dame in Paris as well as the Church of Sainte-Geneviève, the patron saint of Paris, but not in the case of the birth of a daughter. Marie Antoinette and King Louis XVI proceeded as they saw fit and defied precedent. The crowds mumbled that the Queen's audacity proved her domination and manipulation of the King, and that all of the fanfare must be just one more offensive foreign custom; for why would the King and Queen hail the birth of a girl?

As part of this grand celebration, one hundred wedding ceremonies were performed simultaneously in all of the parishes of Paris, the brides dressed at the Queen's expense. Marie Antoinette announced that she was going to give each young couple an additional dowry of 500 *livres* and that she would pay for the care of children born of these marriages – 15 *livres* a month if the mothers nursed their own babies but only 10 *livres* if they sought outside help. Despite her mother's disapproval, Marie Antoinette informed the Empress that she wanted to encourage French mothers to breastfeed their own children. Despite her husband's loathing for the late writer, Marie Antoinette believed that her obvious nod to Rousseau and his prescription that mothers ought to breastfeed and care for their own babies would make her more popular with the citizens of France who had embraced the concepts of the recently deceased *philosophe*. The Queen, however, had miscalculated. It had been a particularly barren year for the French farmers, the cost of food had soared, and French citizens, more acutely concerned with their stomachs than with theoretical notions, had been angered by reports that Marie Antoinette's exorbitant spending had caused their misery. The Queen's detractors denounced her largesse to the newlyweds as gratuitous. As she rode through the streets of Paris, ordinary citizens scowled at her not only for what they considered her disrespect for French tradition, but also because they perceived her to be insensitive to their hardships.

At the court of Versailles, as well as the other courts of Europe, there was immediate speculation about marriage prospects for the newborn Princess. Although the ancient Salic law in France precluded girls from inheriting the throne, Marie-Thérèse was heiress to vast properties and wealth. Among possible future husbands for the daughter of the King of France were the future King of Sweden, the brother of the future King of Spain, an Austrian archduke, and the son of Marie Antoinette's favorite sister, Queen Maria Carolina of Naples and Sicily. In France, the most junior branch of the Bourbon family, the Orléans faction, whose members had been asserting claims to the throne since the days of Louis XIV, proposed a union with Louis-Philippe, son of the then Duc d'Orléans. Marie Antoinette was also a cousin to the Orléans branch through her father. Remembering her own suffering when she left Vienna, Marie Antoinette liked the idea of her daughter remaining at home. She determined that if she were to have no sons, Marie-Thérèse should marry the young Duc d'Angoulême, the eldest son of the Comte d'Artois, third in line for the throne of France after his childless uncle and his own father. Madame de la Tour du Pin recalled in her memoirs that although the Duc d'Orléans 'wanted his son, [Louis-Philippe] the Duc de Chartres, to marry Madame Royale . . . the Duc d'Angoulême . . . was the marriage favored by the Queen. The Duc d'Orléans' request was therefore refused, and he took it as a mortal affront.'

Louis-Philippe, who had always coveted the throne, now had an even more spiteful reason to wage a vengeful campaign to wrest the throne from his own cousin, Louis XVI. The Duke would become infamous. Madame de la Tour du Pin called him 'the Regicide'. In her memoirs of the French Revolution, de la Tour du Pin wrote that she was convinced that Orléans was behind the riots in the lead-up to the Revolution. Thomas Carlyle, in his dramatic account, *The French Revolution*, agreed, and, referring to Orléans's betrayal of the King, named Orléans 'Iscariot'. The contemporary French historian Montjoye called Orléans the 'atrocious Philippe', and those who stormed Versailles 'the prostitutes of Orléans'.

By April, the Empress was again putting pressure on her daughter to get pregnant. On April 1, 1779, she wrote, 'What you write about your dear daughter pleases me greatly, and especially the King's love. But I must admit to being insatiable; she needs a companion, and he must not delay too long.'

That month, the Queen contracted measles and sequestered herself so that she would not infect the King or her infant daughter. She once again caused a stir when she allowed the Ducs de Coigny and de Guines, the Comte Esterhazy and the Baron de Besenval, and no female companions, to keep her amused. The month-long illness delayed any hope of pregnancy and kept her from watching over her daughter's progress. However, by early May, she reported to her mother that the baby girl could recognize people around her with whom she was familiar. The Empress received reports from two Russian friends who said the baby looked like her mother, but based on two portraits, the Empress wrote that she disagreed.

Marie Antoinette was aware that certain individuals remained determined to find a mistress for her husband. In order to show where he stood on the subject, the King made a public declaration of his undying affection for his wife and daughter in front of the entire court. Meanwhile, the Empress wrote Mercy that he should instruct her daughter on how to hold on to her husband's love, and if this failed, how to handle herself in the event of a rival. Foremost, she cautioned, Marie Antoinette needed to provide the King with an heir.

That summer, Marie Antoinette became pregnant again but suffered a miscarriage in the early stages of the pregnancy. She and the King wept together, but Louis then sought solace in the company of another woman, though not just any woman: Gabrielle Yolande de Polignac was Marie Antoinette's closest friend at court. Louis started visiting Madame de Polignac without his wife, a development that disturbed Mercy and the Empress. She had a husband – Comte Jules de Polignac – and a lover – the handsome and entertaining Comte de Vaudreuil, one of Marie Antoinette's favorite companions, whom the King would appoint Grand Falconer. When Madame de Polignac became pregnant in the second half of 1779 after not having had a child for a good many years, Marie Antoinette feared her worst suspicions confirmed, but she said nothing to the King hoping that his 'infatuation' would subside.

The Empress, though concerned for her daughter's health after the miscarriage, remained preoccupied about the future of the dynasty. When yet another portrait of Marie-Thérèse arrived in Vienna with a note reporting that the baby was 'beginning to walk in her basket' and, to the delight of the King, had said 'Papa', the Empress replied:

> Your letter of August 16 gave me great joy . . . the hopes you give me of a companion for the dear child whose portrait you sent me; she is charming, strong, healthy and has caused me the greatest joy. I have her portrait opposite me on a chair and cannot let it go; but I think also that she looks like the King.

Most people disagreed, complimenting the child for her likeness to her mother. She was said to be graceful and to have the Queen's features and coloring. In September, Marie Antoinette reported that the baby was in very good health, in October, 'a marvel!' – Madame Royale was beginning to teethe and had taken a few baby steps. In December, the Empress wrote that, thrilled as she was with the details on her namesake's progress, the letter did not 'make us happy concerning another pregnancy which I am awaiting with eagerness. Your daughter will soon be one year old; you must give her a little companion, we all hope.'

On behalf of her daughter, Marie Antoinette began another battle with hundreds of years of French tradition, which again caused resentment at court. The Queen reduced the number of *sous* governesses and determined to remove the Princesse de Guémené as her daughter's educator. The King and Queen agreed that the little Princess ought to receive as rigorous an education – secular as well as religious – as would any son, and the Queen felt that de Guémené was not the best person to do this. To separate the title from the duties entailed a long legal process and caused no small embarrassment to the King. Mercy reported to the Empress that the baby's household staff performed with great order and exactitude and that, by January 1780, the baby was very strong, healthy and pleasing to the eye. Mercy wrote that the King and Queen remained besotted with their daughter and spent much of their time attending to the Princess and all her concerns.

Marie Antoinette proudly wrote to her mother that by March the child was so robust that one would take her for a two-year-old. Marie-Thérèse sat, got up and walked by herself, and had never been sick a day. The little girl still did not speak very much but charmed a crowd of people, including the visiting Princesses Charlotte and Louise of Hesse, Marie Antoinette's best friends since childhood. Surrounded by staff and visitors since the moment of her birth, Madame Royale demonstrated that she could differentiate between those who served and entertained her and the woman who loved her. Marie Antoinette wrote to her mother with maternal pride that when someone asked the Princess, 'Where is your mother?' Marie-Thérèse ran to the Queen with outstretched arms. Marie Antoinette gushed, 'I felt the greatest joy.'

When Diane de Polignac, Gabrielle Yolande's conniving sister-in-law, suggested that the Queen give a ball despite the fact that she was feeling unwell, Marie Antoinette magnanimously hosted an all-night fête that lasted until eleven the following morning. Privately, however, the Queen was in poor spirits. She was desperate to wean her husband from her best friend and to be pregnant again.

In April, the Queen wrote to her mother that she was longing to give her daughter a sibling. She also admitted that although she was painfully aware that the King was enamored of her best friend, she would not ask him to give up his special friendship, even though it was widely discussed that the King visited Madame de Polignac at her townhouse and that hers was the only private house in Paris he visited since he had become King. Mercy reported to the Empress that Madame de Polignac was gaining more and more prestige and favor and was to be given a great deal of money and the title Duchess after the birth of her baby. The practical reason for the King bestowing this title on the Queen's friend was so that de Polignac could remain in the inner circle at Versailles, as protocol demanded that she retain a certain rank. Mercy assured the Empress that her daughter was bearing the situation with a dignity that Maria Theresa would be proud of.

In early May, Gabrielle Yolande de Polignac gave birth to a son, Jules Auguste. The Comte de Provence, later King Louis XVIII, wrote in his memoir that the birth of this boy was celebrated as if he were a 'prince of our blood'. Although Jules Auguste was Madame de Polignac's youngest by many years, the boy would be ennobled a prince by both the Pope in 1822 and the King of Bavaria in 1838, honors none of her older children received. The birth of Jules Auguste sent the Empress into a rage, and even though she received glowing reports from her messenger that her own granddaughter was thriving, was in perfect health and was a beautiful little girl, she responded to her daughter that it was absolutely imperative for her to give birth to a boy, a dauphin.

The following month Marie Antoinette suffered another miscarriage. This time the Empress convinced herself that the loss was no accident and she accused the Polignacs of somehow being behind the nefarious deed.

Marie Antoinette, by contrast, maintained her composure. Although she felt estranged from the friend whom she believed had betrayed her, that summer she recommenced the musical evenings at Versailles and invited Gabrielle Yolande to join her, in part so she could keep an eye on her. During the day, Marie Antoinette took harp lessons and encouraged the King to keep busy by resuming his hunting parties, thereby keeping him out of Madame de Polignac's arms.

In Vienna, Empress Maria Theresa launched a two-pronged attack on what she saw as 'the French situation'. She continued to demand that her daughter produce an heir ('You must give us a dauphin . . .'), but also instructed her ambassador to circumvent Marie Antoinette and go straight to the King's favorite to obtain influence. On August 31, 1780, for example, the Empress ordered Mercy to persuade Madame de Polignac to influence the King's decision in a matter of politics that would suit Her Imperial Majesty. Other developments merely added to the pressure on the Queen. The young Duc d'Angoulême, now five years of age, was removed from female care that autumn – two years earlier than was customary for the Royal Children of France – and taken to a house in the country belonging to the Marquis de Seran, who was placed in charge of the boy's education – a decision that was understood to be a move to prepare him as heir to the throne.

Marie Antoinette nervously tried to maintain her focus on a new pregnancy and the progress of her daughter. She believed that Marie-Thérèse needed to spend as much time as possible out of doors and away from the stuffy apartments of the older castles like Compiègne and Fontainebleau, where the court moved from time to time. On September 17, as a result of teething, the toddler suffered febrile convulsions. Marie-Thérèse experienced three weeks of fever and pain during which, her mother reported, she was completely sweet and good-tempered. While the court moved on to the Château Marly, where Louis XIV had gone to escape Versailles and his own stringent protocol, Madame Royale convalesced at Versailles with her mother by her side. Other than her bout of teething, the child exhibited excellent health overall and the Queen pointed to her remaining at Versailles as the reason for this. The arrangement, of course, made it all the more convenient for Marie Antoinette to spend more time at her beloved Petit Trianon. The Empress saw right through Marie Antoinette's ruse and reminded her daughter that Rousseau and his notion of living in simplicity with nature might be fine for the masses, but the Queen of France and her daughter had inherited responsibilities, and these they could not escape.

Marie Antoinette had often remarked on how young and pretty her mother looked, even after she was widowed. Indeed the Empress had always taken great care and interest in her own health and that of her family. (She was an early proponent of inoculation, and after a smallpox epidemic in Austria in the late 1760s, the Empress received an injection of the vaccine, which prompted many of her countrymen to follow suit.) However, during the autumn of 1780 the Empress's health suddenly deteriorated. She had joined a hunting party and been caught in a downpour. Over the next few days she grew weaker, coughing and wheezing. Realizing she would not recover, she wrote letters to her children and made additional bequests in her will for the country's soldiers, schools and poor.

On November 29, Maria Theresa died at the age of sixty-three of 'hardening of the lungs'. Almost immediately after her death, Marie Antoinette became pregnant with the son both she and her mother had longed for.

CHAPTER III
PLAYMATES

D URING THE 1780s, dignitaries from across the globe made pilgrimages to Versailles to observe court custom and to see for themselves the Queen's personal style, which was copied around the world. French-style gardens, furniture, fashion, porcelain and etiquette echoed in the most unlikely places; even the Ottoman court at the Topkapi Palace installed a garden and French interiors *à la française* when a young French woman, kidnapped and offered to the Sultan as a present, became his favorite. Marie Antoinette's most cherished friends and family members, such as her childhood companions, the Princes and Princesses of Hesse, also made their way to Versailles to greet little Madame Royale and to expose themselves to French etiquette.

The Hessians, however, were among the least important sovereigns to cross the threshold of Versailles during Marie-Thérèse's childhood. Her parents would play host to some of the world's most powerful emperors and monarchs, including her uncle Joseph – now Holy Roman Emperor Joseph II – Gustav III of Sweden, the future Czar Paul I of Russia, and various rulers of the Habsburg dynasty. Marie-Thérèse would be presented to all of them, endear herself to many, and retain close ties with some who would help her after her parents' death.

In the summer of 1781, Marie-Thérèse's uncle Joseph, once again traveling incognito under the name Comte Falkenstein, returned to Versailles to visit his pregnant sister. He saw for himself the young girl who was his late mother's namesake and agreed that she was indeed very much like the portraits that had so pleased the late Empress in Vienna. She was everything her mother had said she was – robust, active and clever. The Queen herself, entering the third trimester of her latest pregnancy, was in excellent health and spirits. Brother and sister – Emperor and Queen – strolled in the gardens at the Petit Trianon, watching illuminations in the sky. It was a bittersweet time for the pair as they each faced the prospect of fulfilling the destinies planned for them by their mother.

Mindful of her condition and taking advantage of her brother's presence, the Queen sought to scale down the numbers of those attending the entertainments laid on for her brother's visit that summer. She objected especially to the hordes of *noblesse présentée* who usually turned up for such occasions often expecting handouts or entitlements. In order to be presented at court in France, a person had to prove that he or she was descended from a noble family that went back to the year 1400. By the time of the reign of Louis XVI the numbers of *noblesse présentée* had risen to thousands. The Queen regarded most of these as dull 'hangers on' who just added to the excruciating rigidity and formality of the court. She preferred company that was more interesting and fun – such as writers, artists and, very often, foreign ministers and their wives. The King, excited by the possibility of an heir to the throne, relaxed court rules and allowed presentations to be made at court on the basis of achievement rather than lineage (during the 1780s, 30 per cent of those presented at court would come from this bracket). Louis ignored the complaints of the many excluded from the festivities and hoped his subjects would put the Queen's health before their own pettiness. However, in this he miscalculated. By the time of the Queen's confinement, much of the nobility harbored even more bitterness and resentment toward the 'Autri*chienne*', insisting that this change in protocol was due to her foreign influence. Some of those disgruntled members of the out-of-favor *haut monde* issued pamphlets, once again, accusing the Queen of infidelity.

Still, anyone could wander the grounds of Versailles, as long as he or she arrived suitably dressed, and any subject could present a petition to the King on his way to Mass or to the hunt. Such openness to the public had created the zoo-like conditions under which the Queen had given birth to Madame Royale three years earlier. For the birth of his second child, the King decided to take far greater control. He announced that only members of the royal family, a few ladies of the Queen's household and the Lord Chancellor would be permitted to witness the birth of the baby. Again courtiers whined that they were being deprived of a historic moment. The King issued a directive to all, including the Queen's closest friends, that no one was to tell of or signal in any way the sex of the baby until he himself felt that the Queen was recovered enough from the birth to learn of it.

The King also personally orchestrated a search for a wet nurse, which became a nationwide competition. The successful candidate given the honor of suckling the next Child of France was a buxom woman, whom Marie Antoinette nicknamed 'Madame Poitrine', or 'Madame Breasts'. 'Madame Poitrine' was the wife of a gardener who, according to courtiers, added humor to her post when she sang the song 'Marlbrouck s'en va-t-en guerre' to the little boy while she nursed him. The song, which she brought with her from her small, country village, was about the first Duke of Marlborough's defeat in France and was sung to the tune of 'For He's a Jolly Good Fellow'. Apparently, she sang it so often that others at court, including the Queen, frequently joined in.

The King too was in an effervescent mood and proved justified in his optimism. On October 22, 1781, at 1.15 p.m., Louis Joseph, the Dauphin, was born. The King, in tears, lifted the male infant in front of the window to the crowds below. The Queen nervously awaited the news, and, when the King gave him to his mother he said in a raised but solemn voice, 'I present the Dauphin to his mother, the Queen.'

The newborn boy was baptized, as Marie-Thérèse had been, by France's *grand aumônier*, Cardinal de Rohan. The Comte de Provence once again stood in for a godfather – this time, the Holy Roman Emperor, Joseph II of Austria – and the King's sister, Madame Elisabeth, for the King's younger sister, Clothilde, Princess of Piedmont. The Dauphin was immediately invested with the blue ribbon of the Saint-Esprit and the cross of Saint-Louis. Madame Campan recalled that upon seeing his newborn cousin, the Duc d'Angoulême, who had just lost a place in line for the throne, remarked to his father, the Comte d'Artois, 'Look how tiny he is!', to which the Comte replied: 'The day will come when you will think him great enough.'

The nation, however, was jubilant. Fireworks lit up the skies of Paris. Fountains flowed with wine. Prayers were said in every chapel. The festivities around the country lasted for two weeks. Once again, the Opéra opened for a free performance: a few hundred people were expected but nearly six thousand showed up cheering '*Vive le Roi!*', '*Vive la Reine!*' and '*Vive Monsieur le Dauphin!*' As if to express the fact that the baby's smallest functions were deified, a new color, a drab olive green, was given the name '*caca-dauphin*' ('the heir's excrement') and became sought after by the fashionable, adding to the silliness of the delirium. And when the Queen, having once again lost a considerable amount of hair in pregnancy, asked Léonard to fashion something attractive, he created a short, feathery cut, which he named *coiffure à l'enfant* in the little boy's honor; this, again, caught on among the fashionable.

Long processions of tradesmen jammed the roads leading to Versailles, offering gifts befitting a future king of France. Butchers and pastry chefs offered foods. Clothiers fashioned suits and shoes of the finest materials for the little boy. A group of chimney sweeps brought a beautiful chimney from which a young boy emerged and delivered a congratulatory message to the King. Locksmiths brought a lock from which when opened a model of a dauphin popped out. The only eerily inappropriate statement in all of this seemingly universal adoration was made by a group of gravediggers who came to Versailles bearing gifts of their trade. The King's aunt, Madame Sophie, intercepted them and turned them away.

Representing the brand new and very grateful nation, the United States of America, which had just defeated Britain in the decisive battle at Yorktown, Benjamin Franklin made the pilgrimage to Versailles and reported to Madame Brillon, 'Before he was yet a day old, I was there, not in the capacity of an Eastern King, but rather the contrary, and from the West.' Franklin, who referred to the King of France as the 'father of America', professed that he was 'joyous' to see 'his friends happy'. In Austria the populace perceived the delivery of a Bourbon-Habsburg heir to the French throne as a triumph for all of Austria, and they too celebrated with abandon. In Vienna, the Queen's brother, Emperor Joseph (who had grown even fonder of his sister after his recent visit, writing that she was 'charming' and 'bewitching'), was elated. The Queen received congratulations from the Hessian Princesses and King Gustav III. In a note to Princess Charlotte of Hesse-Darmstadt on November 26, Marie Antoinette thanked her friend for her compliments and added, 'My son progresses marvelously. I wish you could judge for yourself this winter.'

When the Queen had made her first entrance into Paris for her *cérémonie des relevailles* after the birth of Madame Royale there had been a definite froideur from the crowds. Now, in January 1782, when the Queen appeared for a service of thanks at the churches of Notre Dame and Sainte-Geneviève, the crowds cheered. A splendid dinner for hundreds was prepared at the Hôtel de Ville. Afterwards, the Queen requested her coachmen take a detour to the Hôtel de Noailles, where the hero of the American revolutionary war, Lafayette, was staying. As the royal couple greeted him, the crowds roared with thunderous approval.

Unfortunately, the Queen and King mistook the crowds' screams as being in honor of their son rather than a tribute to the man who personified the notion of liberty for the masses. The following day the royal couple dined with the Comte d'Artois at his home, the Temple Palace, a sinister place with a medieval dungeon that would, just over a decade later, serve as their prison.

When Madame Royale was born, the King had given his wife a generous cash gift of 120,000 *livres*. After the birth of the Dauphin, the Queen received the enormous sum of 300,000 *livres*. Even though Louis Joseph inevitably eclipsed his elder sister in terms of public adoration, his birth in no way removed Marie-Thérèse from her father's affection. From the time when, at eight months, she uttered her first word – 'papa' – Madame Royale was the apple of her father's eye. The Marquis de Bombelles recounted in his journal that the little girl once told him that she loved her father better than her mother because the Queen, famous for her regal carriage and imposing walk, always walked 'straight ahead of me and doesn't even look to see whether I am following her . . . whereas Papa takes me by the hand and looks after me'.

In the spring of 1782, Grand Duke Paul, the future Czar Paul I of Russia, visited Versailles traveling with his wife under the names the Comte and Comtesse du Nord. The future monarch was treated to a masked ball and illuminations, and although there were far fewer servants at Versailles than at the time of King Louis XIV, the palace still inspired awe. The Grand Duke, overwhelmed by his hosts' hospitality, gallantly addressed the royal family by stating to three-and-a-half-year-old Madame Royale that it would be his honor to host her in his dominions some day when she became a woman. The two young Children of France were considered the most privileged and blessed on earth, and neither the future Czar nor the Princess could possibly have foreseen the tragic circumstances under which that invitation would later be accepted.

By autumn, about the time of the Dauphin's first year birthday in October, the Princesse de Guémené had resigned her post as Governess to the Children of France owing to a scandal involving her husband's debts. The Queen decided to use the opportunity to mend fences with Madame de Polignac. As the Polignacs were always in need of money, Marie Antoinette offered the Duchess the position. The Queen, who had grown comfortable in her role as mother of the heir to the throne, seemed again willing to forgive as she handed her children to Polignac with the comment that their first governess had been entrusted to provide the children with correctness while their new governess would be trusted with their future because of friendship. While it seemed the two women had reconciled their differences, some courtiers whispered about the wisdom of this choice. The post of Governess to the Children of France was traditionally a prestigious one offered only to women of noble birth. Madame de Polignac, born Gabrielle Yolande de Polastron, was certainly not that and few believed that the newly minted Duchesse de Polignac was qualified for the job.

The Queen dismissed this last concern because she intended to supervise her children's education herself. Her brother, Joseph, chided her for this: he wanted his sister to become more involved in European politics and spend less time on motherhood, and accused her of squandering her position as Queen of France. Nonetheless, Marie Antoinette oversaw her children's academic tutors with rigor and personally instructed her daughter in needlework. Madame Elisabeth, the King's pious sister, was placed in charge of Madame Royale's religious and moral education. The King, who had a passion for geography, commissioned the construction of a gigantic globe for his children, attended their geography lessons whenever he could and made up games as a method for his children to retain information.

Marie Antoinette demonstrated sensitivity and intelligence as a mother. Madame Campan recounted one time when the King requested that four-year-old Marie-Thérèse be brought to meet his aunt, Madame Louise. Madame Louise, who was lame and a dwarf, had become a Carmelite nun. To prepare Marie-Thérèse for her visit, the Queen had Madame Campan dress in the Carmelite habit and, in addition, had a doll made up wearing the same clothes so that Marie-Thérèse would neither be afraid nor express any shock when she arrived at the convent. The exercise was a success. The nuns found the little girl so well behaved that one of the women commented that she would be fit to take the veil. Fearing that she might have offended the Queen with that remark, the nun apologized. The Queen said, on the contrary, it was a great compliment to her daughter. Before departing the convent, the Queen asked her daughter if she had anything she would like to ask the ladies. Madame Royale made a lasting impression when, at only four years of age, she requested that they all pray for her at their Mass. She appeared to be a little angel.

Shortly before the Dauphin's second birthday Marie Antoinette suffered another miscarriage – her third. By the following summer, to her great relief and that of the King, she was pregnant again. Ostensibly to celebrate his increasing brood, the King purchased the castle at Saint-

Cloud, with its fabulous cascading waters and bird's-eye view of Paris. However, the real reason behind the purchase was the Dauphin's health. By 1784, it was becoming clear that Louis Joseph had severe health problems. In May, the two-year-old became violently ill and stopped urinating. He seemed to make a quick recovery, which made the Queen a little more optimistic, but his health remained a constant worry to the royal couple. As he grew, his body formed with one shoulder higher than the other, and he was quite frail and unable to join his sister in games. Many members of Europe's royal families had suffered deformities and fragile health and it seemed that the Dauphin would not escape this fate.

With another pregnancy under way, Marie Antoinette began to consider marriage matches for Madame Royale once more. As the daughter of the King of France, little Marie-Thérèse was known as the 'King's Choice' and considered to be the most eligible lady in Christendom. One contender for her hand was Gustavus Adolphus, the future King of Sweden. His father, Gustav III, visited Versailles in the summer of 1784, traveling incognito under the name 'the Count of Haga'. The Swedish King had professed to consider the late King, Louis XV, a second father and had not only received financial aid from the French, but was also a staunch ally in political affairs and a personal friend to the Bourbons. Gustav was invited to both formal events at Versailles and the less formal 'en famille' garden parties and celebratory illuminations at the Petit Trianon. A hot air balloon emblazoned with the monograms of both kings and the name 'Marie Antoinette' floated above as a special treat for the visiting Swedish monarch. Marie Antoinette made a specific point of introducing the young Madame Royale to the man who might become the girl's father-in-law, and he was charmed. After Gustav returned home to Sweden in the autumn, he had his son send a letter with his own portrait to the Queen, so beginning the process of royal matchmaking. Under her mother's guidance, Marie-Thérèse wrote thanking her 'brother' and 'cousin' – a customary address – and sending him great compliments. Marie Antoinette affirmed to the King of Sweden that it was clear that his son was 'superior' and 'advanced'. Marie Antoinette further flattered Gustav III, telling him that the ruler had made a lasting impression on her young daughter.

Another marriage prospect for Marie-Thérèse was the son of her mother's favorite sister, Maria Carolina, Queen of Naples and Sicily, who sent an emissary, the Chevalier de Bressac, in the summer of 1787 to negotiate on behalf of the hereditary Prince. Often, in the case of a future queen when a marriage arrangement was agreed upon, the young girl would be taken from her own country and brought to the palace of her fiancé so that she could be groomed according to the customs of her adopted country. Although Marie Antoinette adored her sister, the Queen was not yet ready to send her little girl abroad and she therefore ignored the proposal.

On March 27, 1785, Easter Sunday, the Queen gave birth to a second son, Louis Charles. This delivery was the easiest of all of her children and from the moment of his birth, the new 'Duc de Normandie' was the sunniest as well. Louis was ecstatic, ignoring the gossip that he was not the boy's father. Critics of the Queen and jealous family members, now even further from the throne, had been spreading rumors that the infant's real father was the Queen's alleged lover, Comte Fersen, aide-de-camp to King Gustav III. Fersen had indeed been at Versailles with the Swedish King the previous summer when the Queen had conceived. The timing was unfortunate but the King, who knew the times of his own conjugal visits, seemed completely satisfied that he was the Duc de Normandie's father and was thrilled with his new robust son.

A year after the birth of Louis Charles, the Queen gave birth to her fourth child, whom they named Sophie. When the King informed the Spanish ambassador that his wife had given birth to a girl, the ambassador gallantly responded, 'As Your Majesty keeps his Princes at his side he now has a means of bestowing presents [his daughters] on the rest of Europe.' Madame Vigée-Lebrun was commissioned to paint a joyful family portrait of the Queen surrounded by her children with the baby Sophie in her cradle.

Unfortunately, Sophie was born with an abnormally large head and other deformities not unknown to the Bourbon and Habsburg families. Although the King and Queen tried to ignore the baby's shortcomings and hoped for the best, Sophie died eleven months later. The bereft Queen's favorite artist then painted the baby out of the family portrait leaving a happy and glowing Queen Marie Antoinette, her three children and an empty cradle, a lamentable reminder of the family tragedy.

The entire court was in mourning during the summer of 1787. Eight-year-old Marie-Thérèse was taking the death of her baby sister especially hard. In a touching gesture, one of Marie Antoinette's least favorite sisters, Marie Christine, traveled to Versailles under the name 'Comtesse de Bellyé' to offer comfort. The sisters spent time together at Versailles and included Marie-Thérèse in their walks around the gardens at the Petit Trianon. After Marie Christine's departure, the Queen wrote to her sister that she was 'sitting on a bench where we sat together' and that her visit had been a tonic for the entire family. She also wrote that, while she was writing the letter, Marie-Thérèse was watering Marie Christine's favorite garden of chrysanthemums, tending them in her honor, poignantly observing that the little girl was zealously focused on making the flowers live. The Queen expressed in her note to her sister her great relief that Marie-Thérèse, who had been so silent at the beginning of the summer when she first met her aunt, shortly after baby Sophie's death, was talking once again. She assured Marie Christine that the King himself had not stopped talking about his sister-in-law. That winter, as Marie-Thérèse turned nine, the King's aunt, Madame Louise, the Carmelite nun, died and the court was in mourning once again.

Little Louis Charles, although at an impressionable age, was simply too young to understand the sadness around him, and he provided the levity so hungered for by his family. The adorable '*chou d'amour*', as the Queen referred to her second son, quickly became his mother's favorite. She wrote that he was 'a peasant child . . . big . . . fresh-faced and fat', and remarked that, while Louis Joseph was being prepared for his serious role, and was in fact quite proficient in history at a very young age, little Louis Charles was simply the family pet. Significantly, no one in the family had been bestowed with the title 'Duc de Normandie' for centuries – not since the fourth son of Charles VII. It had been the King's idea to give his second son the title after an excursion to the Norman town of Cherbourg in 1786, during which the infant was hailed with gusto by the local population. Louis XVI would regularly embrace Louis Charles thereafter and say with great effusiveness and tenderness, 'Come here, my little Norman, your name will bring you happiness!'

François Hüe, a servant to the boy who later became a trusted member of the Restoration regime, recounted many anecdotes in his memoir about Louis Charles. One day, according to Hüe, the little boy began to 'hiss' and 'boo'. Both the Queen and Hüe told him to stop his antics. The boy responded: 'I did my lesson so badly that I'm booing myself.' Hüe also recalled that to get the very active boy to sleep, Marie Antoinette would sometimes play softly on her harp. One evening at Saint-Cloud, while the Queen was playing him a lullaby, Madame Elisabeth commented '*Voilà!* Charles is sleeping.' Louis Charles immediately popped up and said, 'Ah, my dear aunt, could anyone sleep when listening to my mother the Queen?'

Louis Charles adored his mother and she loved to read him the fables of La Fontaine. Hüe reported that Louis Charles had an especially sensitive understanding of his mother's temperament and knew that she loved flowers. Every morning at Versailles the boy would go outside accompanied by a chambermaid and his dog, Coco, to pick flowers for his mother's *table de toilette*. The King became aware of his son's routine and offered him a small garden and some tools of his own. Louis Charles worked enthusiastically and diligently on his garden, exerting effort even on the hottest days. One day, a courtier came to offer the boy help but Louis Charles refused. He thanked the man but said that the flowers would be less pleasing to his mother if someone else had tended them.

Louis Charles also liked to make his sister smile. Sometimes, during her lessons, when she could not recall a fact, he would whisper something sweet to rid her of her frustration. The two were inseparable, and Marie-Thérèse took on a very protective and maternal role toward her youngest brother, treating him like her own baby. She doted on him and indulged him, petted him and pampered him like a favored doll. To look at, Louis Charles was irresistible; he was the most beautiful of Marie Antoinette's children. His pale, ash blond, shoulder-length ringlets appear in painting after painting; and courtiers wrote of his cerulean blue eyes and long lashes. Everyone found him delightful and his cherubic appearance mirrored a truly loving and sweet-natured child.

A physiognomic assessment of his sister, however, who also possessed truly angelic features, would have completely missed the mark. Madame Royale was proving that she could be decidedly difficult.

CHAPTER IV
ONCE UPON A TIME

F ROM HER EARLIEST days Marie-Thérèse was a witness to and parti-
cipant in extraordinary times. In the second half of the eighteenth
century most of the world considered life at Versailles to be the zenith of
refinement and civility. Many courtiers in the orbit of King Louis XVI and
Queen Marie Antoinette as well as foreign visitors chronicled its dizzying
opulence. First-hand accounts by loyal courtiers such as Pauline de Béarn,
Madame de la Tour du Pin, Madame Campan and others have invited us
into the celebrated court at Versailles and portrayed with great sympathy
the much-maligned Queen of France. American writers including Benjamin Franklin, Thomas Paine, Gouverneur Morris, and Thomas Jefferson
also sent home their own impressions to colonists eager to glean details;
though they were democrats, they too seemed to have had great admiration for Marie Antoinette. Politicians, soldiers and historians have exhaustively documented the last days of the glory of the Bourbon regime,
its demise all the more shocking for the incredible savagery that destroyed
it. No one, however, but Marie-Thérèse, Child of France, knew what it
was like to take one's first steps along the red carpet surrounded by the
world's most dazzling diamonds and blinding candles, reflected in the
thousands of mirrors in the fabled Galerie des Glaces.

At the moment of her birth, guns had blasted, heralding her arrival. She
was the cynosure of thousands of people on a daily basis. Every person in
her presence, aside from her parents, was required to bow or curtsy at her
feet. From the moment she could walk, all within reach would kiss the
border of her gown. As a little girl she attended state events where, in a
powdered wig and formal dress, she was seated near her mother on a
raised platform in full view of foreign potentates and dignitaries, the

entire European aristocracy, the clergy and the people of France. The Comte de la Ferronnays recalled that Madame Royale as a young girl once asked his sister, Félicie, if she had ever seen the Princess in her *grand panier* – the extremely wide and heavily weighted hooped skirts worn at court. Félicie responded that she had not. According to de la Ferronnays, Marie-Thérèse sighed gravely and advised, 'Well, come tomorrow to the King's Mass and there you will see.' As the *grand panier* weighed as much as she did, Marie-Thérèse was not at all happy having to spend hours in the massive costume.

It was a singular existence with very stringent protocol. On ordinary days, rising, dining and bed times were all ceremonial events with designated procedures and parades of servants, foodstuffs and accoutrements. Many of these rituals dated from the Middle Ages and served to demonstrate deference to the deified Most Christian King of France and his family. At noon every day, the entire royal family attended Mass in the two-story marble Palace Chapel escorted by equerries, pages and officers of the guard. On Sundays, the ritual was repeated with even more splendor. All attending were expected to be attired in their finest clothes while the King's extended family proceeded to the chapel accompanied by the music of an orchestra.

Madame de la Tour du Pin reported that the program of activities – the changes of clothing and rigid routine – was excruciatingly exhausting. Holidays and days of feasting proved even more tiresome and Madame Royale was required to partake of the pageantry for what seemed to be endless hours. Soldiers and noblemen received their decorations,[1] each honor given great import; each foreign ambassador afforded his speech. These tributes and gatherings were enacted at the half-a-dozen palaces in which the royal family lived – Compiègne, Fontainebleau, Versailles, Saint-Cloud, Marly, Meudon. Each royal palace had its own history, architecture, furniture, tapestry, and style and color of livery – and its own set of inconveniences and rules – and wherever the King, Queen and their children went, the entire court and its trappings followed.

At Versailles, the children's quarters opened onto the Orangerie gardens whose spectacular fountains and gilded statues provided the morning panorama. One monthly account from the 1780s shows that among the orders commissioned for Madame Royale were eight dozen white gloves, three dozen pairs of dog-skin mittens, twelve bottles of lavender, twenty bottles of wine spirits, twenty-two pots of pomade, eighteen pots of powder and untold orders for ribbons and colored taffetas. Against this backdrop of unparalleled luxury the royal children received their academic and religious lessons and played their childhood games. While ushers, silver cleaners, hairdressers, valets, porters, laundresses and others who served the Children of France observed the children in their natural, private moments, this freedom and innocence was abruptly curtailed whenever they were asked to perform before the eyes of France.

The Queen noticed a duality in the personality of her firstborn child – brought about, she believed, by the demands of her divided life: Madame Royale was acutely attuned to duty, formality and protocol, but she flourished when allowed to be a child and act her age. Those simple moments were mostly private ones. Sometimes very early in the morning when a chambermaid would bring the Queen a basket of fresh linen for the day, Marie-Thérèse, acting the pixy, would sneak beside the servant into her mother's room in order to spend time alone with the Queen before the usual crowds of people came to absorb her attention. The King, who rose before eight in the morning and worked near the window of his study, had no time to escape the crowds of people once his official rising ceremony – the *lever* – was under way at 11.30 a.m. and his courtiers were admitted. In the 1780s, the royal household employed four times as many people as the central government. The Children of the King had to compete with musicians, librarians, pages, equerries, falconers, food staff, military personnel, clergy and foreign ministers for a moment of their busy parents' time.

Like her mother, Marie-Thérèse sometimes chafed at life at Versailles, and Marie Antoinette sympathetically and lovingly dubbed her daughter 'Mousseline Sérieuse' – 'serious muslin' – an oxymoronic appellation. On the one hand, Marie-Thérèse looked light, bright and breezy, like muslin – blonde, fair (almost transparent) skinned. She laughed and played gaily, even robustly, in the gardens at the Petit Trianon, and at her mother's Hameau, the whimsically constructed farmhouse with its very own menagerie and chicken run, where the Queen and her chosen company would play at being peasants – although their milk pans were designed by Sèvres. On the other hand, frequent pomp and pageantry took its toll on a young girl who, dressed in formal gowns and uncomfortable wigs, often appeared glum, grumpy and humorless in the presence of grown-ups. Seeing her daughter's demeanor, Marie Antoinette worried that her little 'Mousseline Sérieuse' was in fact missing out on the carefree childhood that she herself had enjoyed in Vienna. As a treat one afternoon, the Queen arranged for a swan-shaped sleigh to take Marie-Thérèse for a ride around a park, a gesture that delighted the Princess and one that softened her heart considerably toward her mother.

The author and statesman, François-René de Chateaubriand, described her as proud and beautiful in the nobility of her rank and in the innocence of a young child. Citing *Guirlande de Julie*, he wrote that she seemed, to him, 'like the orange blossom'.[2] No one dared utter but the highest praise and compliments in the presence of Madame Royale. She was flattered and fawned over by all, and she felt herself to be unique and remarkable. One day the Queen saw a lovely child at court around the same age as Marie-Thérèse. (The little girl, named Julie Bernard, would later become Madame Récamier, famous for her beauty and her liaison with François-René de Chateaubriand.) The Queen was so enchanted with the child that she sent her off to the nursery to play with Madame Royale. When the girl was introduced to Madame Royale, the Princess was decidedly frosty, annoyed that her mother found another little girl worthy of praise, and even more annoyed to be compared with a 'commoner'.

Many negative accounts portray Madame Royale as a spoilt and impossible brat, haughty and unkind; however, a deeper reading shows a strong-willed, intelligent and precocious child, whose patience was frequently tested as she was forced to live and perform in an adult world of unrelenting pomp and circumstance. The Baronne d'Oberkirch was a visitor at Versailles in the 1780s. In her memoirs she recounts that she had offered kind and obsequious words to the girl telling her how pretty she looked. Marie-Thérèse answered rudely that she thought the woman had displayed great audacity to speak to *her*. When *sous* governess Madame de Mackau gently corrected her, Madame Royale extended her tiny hand for the Baroness to kiss and then curtsyed to display good manners. The Baroness, who thought the little girl resembled the Queen, was charmed. In her memoirs, she reported that the girl was 'a miracle of beauty, spirit, precocious dignity', recalling that on one occasion, Madame Royale asked if the name Oberkirch was a German name and the lady replied 'no', she was from Alsace. 'Oh, that is better! I would not like to like foreigners,' replied the young Madame Royale. Madame Royale's *sous* governess recalled one day, after having instructed the nine-year-old Princess on Plutarch and the Stoics, she accidentally stepped hard on the girl's foot. Marie-Thérèse said nothing. That evening, the governess noticed that the Princess's foot was bruised with dried blood on it. She asked her charge why she had not complained, and Marie-Thérèse replied: 'At the moment when you hurt me and I was in pain, it would have pained you more to know that you hurt me.'

Another time, Madame Royale stunned the Abbé de Vermond and all within earshot when, informed of the very good news that the Queen had not died after a bad fall from her horse, Madame Royale remarked that if her mother had died, she would be free to do what she liked. Like any child resentful of grown-ups controlling her life, Marie-Thérèse responded with the childish frankness that lacked any guile.

Though the Queen understood that as the one implementing correction and discipline she was bound to be the less favorite of the parents, she was nonetheless determined to provide her daughter with some lessons in humility. Every Sunday, Marie Antoinette arranged for her daughter to host dances for any child, not just the children of the nobility, who arrived properly dressed. Madame Royale was also encouraged to write homilies on the evils of 'the airs of grandeur' and 'the virtues of affability', use her needlecraft skills to make socks for the poor and to offer some of her own allowance money to the poor. One New Year's Day, expecting her usual presents, Marie-Thérèse and her brothers arrived at the Queen's sitting room where all of the newest dolls and mechanical toys were spread out for what they thought was their choice. The Queen, however, informed her children that the toys were only theirs to look at. As it had been a very bad winter, and other children were starving, she wanted her own children to understand why they should not receive any toys that year. She explained that the money she would have spent on purchasing the toys was instead going to buying necessities for other children. The toys were all wrapped up and returned. The startling lesson, at a time when Marie-Thérèse was old enough to comprehend the example of sacrifice, guided her throughout her life and later, Marie-Thérèse would be known for her kindness to others.

Another of the Queen's ideas was to take Marie-Philippine de Lambriquet to the castle every day as a playmate for Madame Royale. Madame Royale was instructed to take turns waiting table on her new friend, whom the Queen re-named 'Ernestine' after the heroine of a popular novel by Madame Riccoboni. Ernestine went home to her parents every evening until her mother died on April 30, 1788, at which time the Queen adopted her and brought her to stay at Versailles. The two little girls, who looked very much alike, lived alongside one another as sisters. All legal documents refer to the girl as the daughter of Philippine de Lambriquet but do not include the mention of Jacques, who, by the end of 1788, had been promoted to serve on the staff of the King. Ernestine received the same education as Marie-Thérèse, and the Queen spared no expense. She happily paid for additional tutorial services by A. M. Gattescky, master of languages, to teach the ten-year-old Italian and geography.

On November 9, 1788, the King signed a formal document giving
Ernestine, 'in consideration of the services of her deceased mother', a
pension of 12,000 *livres*. The accounting records of Versailles showed
staggeringly high purchase orders for the child's comfort and pleasure.[3]
Fine furniture, a pianoforte, the most expensive candles, games, books,
satin dresses and the white Bourbon feathers for her hair, taffetas, gloves,
and powders created a gilded childhood for this daughter of a chambermaid. When the royal family traveled to their other palaces, Ernestine
went with them. The Duchesse de Polignac treated her as if she were
another royal child. Those on less intimate terms with the royal family
referred to Ernestine as 'the girl who is always with Madame Royale'. She
stood, slept and grew up side by side with her best friend, her putative
half-sister, Marie-Thérèse, and the two girls, inseparable, enjoyed their
similarities. They appeared, almost as a decorative ensemble, with the
Queen at the theater, at military spectacles, and at Mass. And when the
royal family eventually faced doom, the Queen seemed as frantic for the
safety of Ernestine as she was for her own children. 'What will become of
us is uncertain, but . . . never forget that Ernestine is my daughter,' Marie
Antoinette once told *sous* governess Madame de Soucy, and the Queen
added that she and Ernestine 'would love each other for eternity'.

Although Madame Royale could be impudent, and impatient, she was
also extremely caring and kind-hearted, showing great tenderness toward
Ernestine, Louis Charles, her maiden aunts, and, of course, the King. On
June 29, 1786, when the King arrived home from a trip, Marie-Thérèse ran
to the balcony shouting, 'Papa! Papa!' Carrying one brother and dragging
the other behind her, the trio waved and screamed as the King leapt out of
his carriage, bounded up the stairs and rushed to lift his daughter in the air.
On December 11, 1787, Marie Antoinette wrote to her friend, the
Hereditary Princess of Hesse-Darmstadt, that Marie-Thérèse had had a
mild case of the measles and that the Queen had spent three weeks with her
daughter while the child recovered. The Queen remarked with pleasure in
the letter that her daughter had become quite 'a person' and that, despite
her infirmity, she had been 'a very nice companion'.

Although she was expected to behave in a manner beyond her years,
Marie-Thérèse was, of course, still a child. She was not at all privy to her
parents' private thoughts and plans concerning her future, despite the fact
that her uncle, the Comte de Provence, would later assert otherwise.
During the 1780s, she was innocent of the fact that her place and position
as the heiress to the legacy was the cause of infighting among the different
branches of the Bourbon family. The deaths of her baby sister and aunt

and an awareness of growing tensions around her, however, affected her deeply. Madam Campan wrote of Madame Royale's fear of a man named Castelnaux from Bordeaux who was obsessed with the Queen. The pale and sinister-looking Castelnaux fantasized that he was the Queen's lover and stalked Marie Antoinette and her children. He would appear at the Petit Trianon when the children were in the gardens with their mother, and at Versailles when the Queen had card parties. He would travel to Fontainebleau to be the first to greet the Queen when she descended from her carriage, and he would arrive at the theater to stare at Her Majesty whenever she attended a performance. Although he made many courtiers nervous, the Queen, anxious for her children's safety, charmed him into docility and chose to treat him as a naughty schoolboy.

There were those who were certainly not as fanatically attached to the Queen and, in fact, her detractors became as frightening and insidious a presence to Madame Royale. Unlike other children, Marie-Thérèse was very often included in her parents' social outings, and she became acutely aware of the growing animosity toward her mother. By the late 1780s, more and more courtiers were openly expressing dissatisfaction with their Queen and what they perceived to be insulting behavior toward the majority of those who were not among her intimate circle. Instead, such courtiers began spending more time in Paris, enjoying the gaiety of the theater, the opera and dinner parties. When the Queen – who actually agreed with their notion that there was much more fun to be had in Paris – took Marie-Thérèse to Paris to attend the theater, not for publicity, but for the little girl's enjoyment, the public vociferously criticized Marie Antoinette for exposing the daughter of the King to 'the common people'.

At the end of July 1788, Marie-Thérèse, usually the picture of good health, suffered a severe fever. The Queen, frantic with worry, spent two nights awake by her daughter's side; the King joined them for one of the nights, he too staying awake and keeping vigil the entire time. Marie Antoinette wrote to her brother, the Holy Roman Emperor Joseph II, that their daughter's sweetness and stoicism in bearing up to her illness made her and the King 'weep'.

Marie-Thérèse recovered in time to meet the envoys of Tippoo Sahib, King of Mysore, India. Their exotic appearance with turbaned slaves in tow fascinated the entire court. In August, the foreign guests were treated to fountain spectacles, rides in barouches and a formal ceremony in the Salon d'Hercule during which Marie-Thérèse sat by her parents' side and watched in amazement as the Indians made presentations to her father wearing native headdress and suits made of Moroccan leather. The easterners had never seen women in décolletage, and the French court had never seen anything like them. The Queen was so dazzled that she commissioned Madame Tussaud to sculpt them in wax to immortalize their visit. This would prove to be the last state dinner hosted by King Louis XVI and his Queen.

Although Marie Antoinette appeared to radiate excitement and enthusiasm, in private she was in great anguish. The Dauphin's health was rapidly declining. He had become a pitiable little boy who had grown a hunchback and had trouble breathing. In early 1789, the decision had been made to move him to the royal palace at Meudon, the official residence of the Dauphin of France. Situated on an elevation, the air at Meudon was believed to have therapeutic properties. The castle was close enough for the King and Queen to visit, yet it was a world away from the hectic court life. To spare the King and Queen, the doctors told his parents that he was simply teething. It was, of course, untrue, and as she told her dearest friends and family, the Queen admitted to them and to herself that she knew her son was dying. The Dauphin himself understood that he was not getting better, and he would frequently state so, adding to his parents' already unimaginable heartache. For his seventh birthday, on October 22, 1788 – the 'age of reason' when his education was transferred from a governess to a male tutor – there had been a great celebration at Versailles. Among the many presents the Dauphin received from courtiers and family members were jeweled animals. His favorite present, however, was a movable gold and enamel swan given to him by his mother. When, barely a few months after the party, he was taken to Meudon, his servants packed a few of his toys but forgot to pack this particular toy, so precious to him. Louis Joseph insisted that they wait until it was found, and when it was not, he overheard someone remark that it was, indeed, a bad omen. From that day forth, the boy believed that he would languish. His sister, who had already mourned the death of one younger sibling, braced herself for his death by clinging to her other little playmate, Louis Charles. Although they were over six years apart, Marie-Thérèse determined to protect him at all costs, and she kept her baby brother constantly at her side.

While the family anguished over the Dauphin they also had to contend with the deteriorating health of the dynasty. The King had been experiencing renewed trouble with his cousin, Louis-Philippe, who had now inherited his father's title Duc d'Orléans. At a meeting of Parlement on November 19, 1788, Orléans challenged the King. The role of this ancient judicial body of noblemen was to enact the King's decrees, and it was not in its own best interest to change the status quo. Orléans, however, seized the opportunity to foster discord, committing what the King perceived as a crime of *lèse-majesté*. Marie Antoinette wrote to her brother that Louis, annoyed and embarrassed, banished Orléans 'to Villers-Cotterêts and forbids him to see anyone but his family and household'. The estate being in Picardie, some 80 kilometers from Paris, this was mostly a symbolic punishment, but the King hoped that his action would chasten his cousin.

It did not. Distanced from the court, Louis-Philippe was still able to cause damage. As for the Queen, it certainly may not have been wise to alert foreigners to the schism between the King and the Duc d'Orléans, but it soon became common knowledge anyway as Orléans came out into the open as a leader of a political movement with grievances against the King, and one of his minions made a public suggestion that a second throne be established with Orléans as constitutional monarch. A combination of spite and worry about the Dauphin's health prompted Marie Antoinette to refuse to consent to an engagement between the Duc d'Angoulême and Orléans's only daughter, Eugénie Adélaïde Louise. The Queen was perfectly in her right to withhold permission, but her actions only served to inflame Orléans's resentment. Marie Antoinette simply claimed that she was keeping all options open for her own daughter. The Comte d'Artois, father of the Duc d'Angoulême, was thrilled with the idea that his son, who would probably not inherit the throne, might nonetheless marry Madame Royale when she could have married any other crowned head of Europe. To Orléans, however, the Queen was keeping his own daughter away from the crown of France.

Madame Royale later recalled how she had overheard her 'papa' being angry with his cousin, but at the time she was unaware of the larger issues facing the King. The country was going bankrupt after decades of failure to implement fiscal reforms. Two expensive wars with the British and an inequitable system of taxation and famine had exacted a heavy toll. Although Louis's finance minister Turgot had suggested radical fiscal reforms in the 1770s, the King's other advisors warned him against Turgot's measures. Although they would have been good for the country, his ministers argued, they would have made many among the nobility and in the powerful guilds unhappy. Louis XVI had personally whittled down the costs of the court and although he maintained that court cost nowhere near the fiasco of the Seven Years War, and nor could it trump the total of monies loaned to the Colonies, the populace blamed the King, and even more his wife, 'l'Autri*chienne*'. Frenchmen who did not benefit from the feudal system of privilege, inspired by the American Revolution, clamored for change. Among their demands was a more equal distribution of the tax obligation. Ninety-eight per cent of the population who paid taxes had no say in their own government, and the greatest burden fell on the Tiers État – the Third Estate – the middle classes and peasants, rather than on the First (the clergy) or the Second (the nobility).

In July 13 1787, faced with opposition to reform from the First and Second Estates, an Assembly of Notables demanded that the King call the États-Généraux – the legislative body that included representatives from all sections of French society, bar the very poorest. A convention of the body had not taken place since 1614 and many of the new and rising classes of the bourgeoisie would see its calling as a rare opportunity to make their pitch for power.

By December, the King agreed to convene the États, although he was deliberately vague about when it would occur. The following summer, faced with the arrival of a new finance minister – Jacques Necker, notoriously sympathetic to the rights of the Third Estate – the King agreed to convene the États in May of the following year.

CHAPTER V
STORM CLOUDS OVER THE PALACE

THE KING'S PREVARICATION over convening the États-Généraux, prompting the body to instead summon their King, had handed Orléans and his supporters a delicious victory. The États would meet at Versailles in early May 1789. It was the first stumble in a rapid loss of footing for the monarchy. The backdrop against which this political drama was being played could hardly have been more unsettling. The 97 per cent of Frenchmen who were members of neither the clergy nor the noble classes, and who were responsible for paying all of the taxes to the crown, were clamoring for reform. They looked to the nascent republic in America, and to their neighbors, the British, whose House of Commons gave more of its citizenry a voice in government, and now the Tiers État representatives were heading to Versailles to demand change.

Worse still, the winter of 1788/89 was as harsh as any in France could remember: temperatures remained below zero degrees Fahrenheit for months and windmills were brought to a standstill, creating bread shortages. While the increase in prices had only minor impact on the nobility and the clergy, most of the people of France faced unemployment and starvation. As discontent and tension rose across the country, an uneasy mood blanketed Paris. The Seine had frozen, causing bridges to crumble and houses that had stood on the famous *ponts* for centuries to collapse. Ramshackle medieval tenements housing the poorest Parisians barely hung on in the inclement conditions. While the masses starved in the shadow of the Knights Templar fortress and Saint-Antoine, near the Bastille, the inhabitants of the opulent new stone mansions along the Place du Palais-Royal and the Faubourg Saint-Honoré, built during the reigns of Louis XV and XVI, seemed impervious to the harsh winter. The grand façades of these testaments to privilege welcomed a glittering assortment of noblemen – including the Duc d'Orléans whose expulsion from Paris had been short-lived – and an array of artists, philosophers and heiresses to Paris's now legendary salons.

The Palais-Royal, the Paris seat of the Ducs d'Orléans since earlier in the century, had been recently renovated by Louis-Philippe. With towering new arcades housing galleries, cafés, an indoor riding ring, and shops of every kind, it teemed with insouciant life. The Duke had spent a fortune constructing a kind of city unto itself. During the day, jewelry merchants displayed their wares; children came to watch marionette shows and curiosity seekers observed freak shows. At night, the Palais-Royal sizzled as libertines chased women and clandestine meetings took place in the subterranean Grotte Flamande, where pleasure seekers of all classes and inclinations congregated.

Madame de la Tour du Pin recalled that at Versailles the King and Queen quietly distributed significant quantities of aid to the poor, a gesture that gained them a measure of momentary popularity; but, it was the Duc d'Orléans with his great fortune and his high visibility in the heart of Paris who was able to make the most flamboyant and extravagant show of benevolence. Opening the Palais-Royal to the public gave the Duke a patina of liberalism and it also raised morale at a time when the ordinary Parisian was hungry for diversion from cares. Restyling himself a man of the people, Orléans changed his name to 'Philippe Égalité', though he continued to a live a life far more sybaritic than that of the King and Queen. He was known for his racehorses, his mistresses and an expensive taste in clothing, and for throwing money at crowds so that they would cheer him on the street. He was a great friend of the equally debauched Prince of Wales (the future King George IV).

Orléans continued his campaign against Marie Antoinette, denouncing her as a 'traitor' in pamphlets and at social and political gatherings. The Queen found the Duke's ruthless ambition and continuing hostility toward the crown troubling, and wrote of her contempt for 'Philippe Égalité' to her brother, Emperor Joseph II, the person who had saved her marriage. She was certainly not alone in her opinion that Orléans was intent on stealing the crown. Madame de la Tour du Pin, whose father-in-law would later that year become minister for war, was a witness in late April 1789 to the riots that had broken out at the Réveillon wallpaper factory after rumors of wage cuts. Madame de la Tour du Pin recalled that she was traveling home from the races at Vincennes, where she had witnessed the horses of the Duc d'Orléans run against those of the Comte d'Artois:

> It was after the last of these races, as we were driving home along the Rue Saint-Antoine with Mme de Valence, that we found ourselves in the midst of the first riot, the one which destroyed the worthy Réveillon's wallpaper factory . . . M. de Valence was at the time First Equerry to the Duc d'Orléans and as we passed through the crowd of four or five hundred people which filled the street, the sight of the Orléans livery roused their enthusiasm. For a few minutes they held up the carriage shouting 'Long Live our Father! Long Live King d'Orléans!' and a few months later, when I had certain knowledge of the scheming Duc d'Orléans, they returned to my mind. The popular movement which ruined Réveillon had been organized, I have not the slightest doubt.

La Tour du Pin returned to court later that day and wrote of her relief that the Duc d'Orléans was not at Versailles that day, 'and so I avoided being embraced by that monster'.

The deputies began arriving at Versailles for the convention of the États-Généraux toward the end of April. Many of them, wrote Madame de la Tour du Pin, carried with them a proclamation that the Duc d'Orléans had 'sent to all the bailiwicks where he owned property'. These representatives, many from provincial towns, had been told incredible stories about the Queen and they all wanted to see the Petit Trianon. Marie Antoinette was a perfect hostess, allowing the members of the États-Généraux to wander freely through the grounds of the palace as well as some of its interior. Some looked for the diamond-encrusted closets, others for the columns wreathed in rubies and sapphires – none of which existed except in fabulists' accounts. Some members of the group believed that they would see the King in an intoxicated state every day – information also gleaned from hostile pamphlets and rumor-mongers.

Although May 5 was the day designated for the formal opening of the États-Généraux, the convocation began a day before on the 4th with a religious preamble to the political wrangling. The two churches in the village of Versailles – Notre Dame on the rue de la Paroisse and Saint-Louis on rue Satory – were to be the start and end points of a massive cavalcade. Tapestries had been hung along the route and locals rented out their windows for handsome prices to onlookers who came to cheer on the deputies. Although some members of the États-Généraux arrived at the church of Notre Dame at 7 a.m., it would be another three hours before the King and Queen emerged from the palace, with Madame Royale in tow, to take to their carriage at the head of a procession of soldiers and deputies – the Tiers État dressed simply in black, the nobility attired in ceremonial splendor and the clergy, led by Cardinal de la Rochefoucauld, dressed in purple.

En route, the King and Queen indicated their acknowledgement of a most important spectator who was seated near a window in the Lesser Stables at the Place d'Armes. The Dauphin had been allowed to come to Versailles from Meudon for the day in order to watch the procession. The seven-year-old boy, whose weight had plummeted, lay propped up on pillows, covered in sores, hunchbacked and ravaged by rickets, his legs no longer able to support him. His frail appearance caused noticeable distress on the faces of his parents.

The cortege continued, passing crowds of people along the streets shouting '*Vivat Orléans! Vivat Orléans!*', but when the King, Queen and Madame Royale descended from their carriage at Notre Dame they were greeted with virtual silence. Stepping out into the sun, Louis XVI blinded in gold cloth strewn with diamonds – diamonds as buttons, diamonds as buckles on his shoes, diamonds on his garters, and on his ribbons and medals. He also wore the famous 140-carat cushion-shaped Regent diamond on his crown, which he had worn at his coronation, and a diamond sword. The Queen shimmered in violet and white embroidered with silver *pailletes* and displayed some of the world's most famous diamonds: in her hair the pale yellow 55-carat flawless 'Sancy', and, on her body, the De Guise and the Mirror of Portugal, whose suite included the fifth and sixth Mazarin diamonds.

For this momentous occasion, however, the Queen chose to leave her décolletage bare. Marie Antoinette, who understood theater and cere-mony better than anyone, was still stinging from the accusations sur-rounding the 1785 scandal that became known as the 'Diamond Necklace Affair' and she wanted to issue a public statement of her own discontent. The controversy had involved a con artist named Jeanne de Lamotte who had forged the Queen's signature, duping the Cardinal de Rohan into colluding with her so that she could obtain an outrageously expensive necklace from the Crown Jeweler without paying for it. Despite the fact that the courts of Paris determined that Marie Antoinette was absolutely blameless and had been ignorant of the swindle, there were many skeptics who still thought the Queen was guilty. When, in the 1770s, Louis XVI's ministers had denied Marie Antoinette a formal coronation, she had gleefully – and not without a little spite – substituted outlandish hairdos for a tiara.

After the assembly concluded its devotions at Notre Dame, it moved on to the church of Saint-Louis. Though the Duc d'Orléans had been elected as a deputy, he opted, in direct violation of the King's orders, not to march with the other Princes of the Blood but rather with the politicians – leaving his fifteen-year-old, the Duc de Chartres, to walk with the nobility in his place. Inside the church, the Bishop of Nancy preached a sermon on the profound disparity between the poor of France and the intemperate, self-indulgent aristocracy. Hatred for the Queen, whom many of the people called 'Madame Deficit', had escalated to a level of mania. Illustrated pamphlets flooded the streets depicting the Queen variously as a nymphomaniac, a lesbian, and, in another, using a dildo. The Bishop now played to the crowd, roundly condemning the Queen for her extravagance. He failed, however, to mention the millions of *livres* spent by the Duc d'Orléans on the Palais-Royal or the fact that he had turned his Parisian palace into a playground for all that was profane and profligate.

The King's response to the Bishop's attack on his wife was to appear to be asleep. Marie Antoinette had told Léonard, her hairdresser, that she was going to perform like an actress and she sat unmoved throughout. Gouverneur Morris, who observed the Queen for much of the gathering of the Assembly of Notables, remarked that to him the Queen often looked as if she were mentally plotting revenge. After a day of insults hurled at both King and Queen, their majesties returned to the palace in separate coaches. Although Marie Antoinette was exhausted from the day's events, she spent the evening listening to her husband rehearse the speech that he was going to deliver in front of the entire États-Généraux the next day.

The États-Généraux convened at 9 a.m. in the grounds of Versailles in the neo-classical building, the Salle des Menus-Plaisirs. The building, constructed to house spectacles for the amusement of the King of France, could accommodate up to five thousand people. Approaching noon, about twelve hundred members representing the clergy, the nobility and the rest of the citizenry were seated in the room, the Duc d'Orléans with his minions. At 1 p.m., ten-year-old Madame Royale accompanied her parents to the assembly hall where they were received in silence. (The Duc d'Orléans, on the other hand, had been applauded wildly.) At the very moment at which the King's subjects should have kneeled in solemn reverence before their sovereign ruler, the members of the Tiers État remained on their feet – a deliberate affront to the puissance and dominion of the King of France. His Majesty's throne in the Apollo Salon had always been curtsyed and bowed to – even when the throne was empty and the King elsewhere. His Most Christian Majesty, dressed in the Order of the Holy Ghost ablaze with diamonds, noticed his cousin seated among the commoners and beckoned to him to join his own family. Orléans, however, declined. Then, in a moment of grand gallantry, the King gestured to his wife to sit; she refused and curtsyed to her husband so deeply and with such elegance that some in the crowd, at last, responded with 'Vive la Reine!'

The damage, however, was done. Marie-Thérèse was present at the moment when a monarchy that had ruled by divine right for over thirteen hundred years had, in one defiant gesture, been diminished, and she watched in stunned and incomprehending silence as her beloved father was ridiculed and her mother disdained.

The King tried to rise above the insult and proceed on a conciliatory note. Beginning with the now famous statement, 'Gentlemen, the day my heart has waited for for so long has finally arrived,' Louis acknowledged the financial difficulties burdening the country and promised reform. Stating that he believed that 'a happy accord' could be reached, he insisted that his intentions stemmed from 'my love for my people'.

Louis had not been unaware of the need for drastic reform, but he had relied on a series of finance ministers with varying methodology and opinions. Turgot, Calonne, Brienne and Necker had all failed to rescue the drowning economy. Between 1786 and 1788 the King himself had cut the cost of the court from 37,650,000 to 31,650,000 livres. By 1789, that cost had dropped to just over 24 million livres, 1.3 million of which went on his children. The number of servants at Versailles totaled considerably less than during the days of Louis XV and the number of horses in the King's stables shrank from 2,215 to 1,195 in the three years up to 1787. A good part of the King's expenses was spent on maintaining the habits of his brothers and their households, which, according to records kept at Versailles for the year 1789, totaled 8,240,000 livres in addition to court expenditure of approximately 24 million. Other than those expenses, many of the costs of the court of France were expenditures of the state, it being the obligation of the King to pay for certain services for the people, and this included pensions. All of this took place at a time when the average annual income of a doctor or lawyer was between 1,000 and 6,000 livres and that of a nobleman 80,000 livres. While the people of France condemned the King and Queen for their self-indulgence and extravagance, Louis XVI ran his entire court of thousands of people on about 30 million *livres*. In contrast, his cousin, the Duc d'Orléans, enjoyed a personal annual income of almost 7 million *livres* – significantly higher than any other individual in France.

France's financial situation was indeed bleak, but the fault did not rest solely with the monarchy. Years of war had cost the nation nearly 3 billion *livres*. The first two Estates, the clergy and the nobility, comprising only about 600,000 people, controlled most of the wealth in the country. Mindful of the need for reform, Louis XVI had made concessions from the moment of his coronation. Throughout the years of his reign, Louis XVI had been a sober if not boring man to most courtiers. He preferred to go to bed early and was not considered charismatic, as had been Louis XIV and XV. Louis XVI envisioned himself as a father figure rather than a playmate. Louis was by nature benevolent and tolerant. In the late 1770s, Louis XVI and his minister, Turgot, abolished many unfair feudal laws including personal servitude – serfdom – in the royal domain and the *corvée*, wherein, owing to a lack of metal money, labor was supplied as a form of tax payment, and, in an attempt to improve trade with England, opened the port of Cherbourg.

As Louis had not impressed most courtiers with an amiable and winning way, he did not seduce this crowd of twelve hundred, and many of them, predisposed to dislike him, were waiting to hear what finance minister Necker had to say. The King, however, continued to address the assembly. He spoke of the inhumane treatment of inmates at the Conciergerie prison in Paris (which, ironically, would be the last residence of his own wife) and insisted on removing debtors from captivity with criminals. And again, ironically, it was he who had insisted on helping the colonists in America in their struggle for independence from King George III, an act that would bring the country to financial ruin. The King's absolute power was very different from the constitutional monarchy of his 'cousin' and 'brother', King George III of England. England had gone through its transition from rule by absolute monarchy to a constitutional one over one hundred years earlier. However, as Madame de la Tour du Pin wryly reported in 1789, in France there was a mania for all things English, from style of dress to silver design. It became a compliment to tell a woman she seemed 'English'. Britain's form of government was also greatly admired. Although Louis did not approve of the English kind of constitutional monarchy for France, he was prepared, he said, to accept the diminished role in order to preserve his own dynasty.

Madame Royale sat on the royal dais until 6 p.m., through long, drawn-out orations, including Necker's three-hour harangue in which he called for more loans but no drastic reform, and during which the minister grew so hoarse that someone else had to finish his speech. Madame Royale, on the other hand, took her cue from her mother and remained collected. Exhibiting great stamina and poise, the Queen impressed many with her dignity. Madame de la Tour du Pin noticed, however, that although Marie Antoinette appeared contained, she fluttered her fan almost convulsively, a sign that the Queen was agitated. Madame Royale appeared every inch a princess, precociously regal. She sat, listened and watched as commoners hurled accusation after accusation at her parents. From this time on, despite her religious education, she learned to hate, developing a lifelong grudge against the enemies of her parents – especially the Duc d'Orléans and his family.

For the rest of the month, the factions battled each other – the noblemen remaining intransigent for the most part while the Tiers État waged their campaign that 97 per cent of the population deserved to be heard. While the debate continued, the King and Queen became preoccupied with their own personal tragedy, making frequent visits to Meudon in order to spend time with the Dauphin. One evening toward the end of May at Versailles, Madame Campan placed four candles on the Queen's vanity table and attempted to light them. The first blew out. The lady-in-waiting re-lit it. Shortly afterwards the second and then the third extinguished. Marie Antoinette grabbed Madame Campan's hand, squeezed it in terror, saying that if the fourth taper went out like the rest, 'then she could look on it as nothing but a sinister omen'.

The King and Queen made frequent trips to Meudon to see their son, who was failing fast. One day at the end of May, as the Queen sat by her son's bedside, she could not stop herself from crying. Her son asked her to try to stop, adding, 'because soon you will need all of your courage' – an eerily prophetic prognosis. On the afternoon of June 4, when the King and Queen arrived at Meudon, M. Lefèvre, the Duc d'Harcourt's secretary, informed the royal parents that they could not see their son. The King immediately anticipated the worst and said, 'Ah! My son is dead.' 'No, Sire,' Lefèvre replied; 'He is not dead, he is worse.' Lefèvre reported that the ensuing scene was a memory that he would never forget: the King crumpled onto a sofa and the Queen sank to her knees beside him, both weeping over their beloved son.[1]

Later that night, at about 1 a.m., Louis Joseph died. The cause of death was given as a combination of rickets and pneumonia. When the King was told, he commanded M. de Villedeuil, Secretary of State in the Department of the King, to announce to the four-year-old Duc de Normandie, in the presence of his governess, that he was now proclaimed Dauphin of France. The King asked the Archbishop of Paris to hold one thousand Masses for the soul of his late son. When the Archbishop enquired who, at this time of economy, would fund these services, the inconsolable King replied: 'Sell the silverware.'

For a while the nation seemed to unite in its grief for the Dauphin. All around the King and Queen, their friends and courtiers donned black. The Tiers État prepared a statement expressing its profound sorrow, stating that the Assembly had been penetrated by sadness upon the death of the Dauphin, and authorized M. le Doyen to present this sentiment to the King and Queen. The following day, on June 5, M. le Duc du Châtelet, on behalf of the nobility, presented a motion to the Assembly that a statement of condolence should be delivered to their Majesties as well. One well-meaning member of the Tiers État arrived unannounced at the King's chambers with holy water and although the King did not wish to see anyone, he received the man out of courtesy to the Tiers État.

At Meudon, the Dauphin's body was embalmed and put on view in a white velvet-lined casket. Neither parent was permitted to see it or attend the Dauphin's funeral: French tradition stipulated that the Kings of France and their Queens could not associate themselves with the sick or dead. Nor were they permitted to attend funerals, as the King was regarded as the incarnation of the nation and therefore 'never died'.

On June 12, the Dauphin's body was placed in the royal crypt at St. Denis; his heart, also according to custom, at Val-de-Grâce. For the second time in her short life, Marie-Thérèse was in mourning for the death of a beloved sibling. The King and Queen were suffering from insomnia and two days later the royal family moved to Marly to grieve in private.

The knell of church bells and the shutting-down of amusement venues around the country was the least that could be expected when a Dauphin of France died. In the past, the death of a Dauphin would have caused the country to come to its knees for many months; but a year after her son's horrendously painful demise, the Queen would write to her brother Leopold, who by that time would succeed their brother, Joseph, and become Holy Roman Emperor Leopold II, that she felt the people of France had made no more than a perfunctory show of respect. While a deep sadness took hold of the royal family, and their royal counterparts in other courts of Europe expressed sympathy, the nation went on with its business. Versailles, which had always teemed with faces familiar to Marie-Thérèse, or at least with people she would get to know, now burgeoned with strangers as the Tiers État persisted on a path of insubordination. On June 17, 1789, while the King was still grieving at Marly, the Tiers État banded together to form a National Assembly, vowing that they would create a new, written constitution; they urged the clergy and the members of the nobility to prepare for change. The people wanted equality. On June 19, the clergy voted 149 to 137 to join the États-Généraux. The next day, when they all arrived in the pouring rain at the Salle des Menus-Plaisirs, they discovered that they had been locked out of the meeting hall. Dr Joseph Guillotin suggested that the group convene at the Jeu de Paume, a grubby gymnasium on the rue du Vieux-Versailles. In this most inelegant place, the Tiers État drew up its own Declaration of Independence, now known as 'The Tennis Court Oath'. The Comte d'Artois, in a show of protest, reserved the hall for the next day so that the assembly could not reconvene there.

The nobility itself was splitting into factions. One, led by the Comte d'Artois and supported by the Queen, wanted no change at all. Marie Antoinette's loyalty toward her brother-in-law and his coterie caused their enemies to publish a pamphlet illustrating the pair having sex, 'doggy style'. In addition it was widely believed that the Queen had stolen money and sent it to her brother, the Holy Roman Emperor. Another, more liberal, faction tried to convince the King to make further concessions and to follow the suggestions proposed by finance minister Necker, who was popular with the Tiers État. It was widely known that the Queen disliked Necker and his policies. The Queen, having learned the power of her own mother's manipulation and theatrical tactics, gathered Marie-Thérèse and Louis Charles together, thrust them into their father's arms, and dramatically pleaded with the King to stand firm for the sake of their children. The King, as usual, wanted to please everyone, and remained centrist.

On June 23, Louis XVI, in style and demeanor still very much the regal, divinely ordained monarch, presided imperiously over a *séance royale* during which he reminded the deputies that it was he who granted the people favor and not the reverse. The King declared the June 17 and June 20 proceedings, documents and oaths null and void. Never had a king done so much for his people, said Louis, but, as a minor concession, he accepted a watered-down version of Necker's proposals. Necker was conspicuously absent from this meeting called by His Majesty. It was an act of defiance noted by the crowd. Immediately after the King stated his position, the errant Marquis de Mirabeau, serving as a representative of the Tiers État, issued the chilling threat: 'We will not back down without the force of bayonets!' An angry crowd made its way through the palace of Versailles toward the Queen's private chambers. Leaders of the new National Assembly vowed to press on with their demands for equality and fiscal reform. The angry mob would not back down until at least thirty citizens were arrested. The deputies, who in the past had thought of their King as well-meaning but impotent and bumbling, now mistrusted and feared him. The impressionable Madame Royale was shocked by the appearance of these oddly dressed, ill-spoken, belligerent people at the palace. They seemed antipathetic to her family's sorrow. The death of her brother, however, would be the first of many traumatic and devastating losses for Marie-Thérèse that year.

Madame de la Tour du Pin noted that tensions were high in the salons of Paris that June. She was aware that food was intentionally being withheld from Parisians in order for some to pursue a more radical political course, and that the encroachment on the King's authority was so 'novel', that the royal family was simply unprepared for it.

A moment of respite occurred for the royal family in late June when the amiable, fun-loving Georgiana, Duchess of Devonshire – a great friend of Marie Antoinette's from more carefree days – traveled to France to offer comfort. Georgiana arrived in Paris like a welcome breeze on June 22. The Englishwoman had mixed in English political circles for years and understood that contention was part of the reform process; yet even she was shocked by the degree of agitation caused by the Duc d'Orléans, another old friend. On June 25, the Duke led another insurrection, becoming even more popular among the masses, when he ceremoniously joined the Tiers État, encouraging other aristocrats to follow. Thousands of people gathered at the Palais-Royal to complain about the government, and the cafés became places of ferment for political clubs. Georgiana entertained her old acquaintances in Paris, but kept the warring parties apart. Although the Princesse de Lamballe was the widow of the brother of the Duchesse d'Orléans, Georgiana understood that Lamballe was supremely loyal to Marie Antoinette and therefore did not invite the Queen's friend to her suite at the same time as the Duke. Georgiana attended the opera two nights in a row – one evening she sat with the Comte d'Artois, the next with his former friend and now hated rival, the Duc d'Orléans. The usually friendly rivalry between Artois and Orléans at the races had taken on a different tone. As the enmity between the two men had intensified, their horses served as a symbol for each man's desire to vanquish the other. Artois, enraged about Orléans's role in the recent political upheaval, spoke publicly for hours against him. Orléans, however, had gained so much momentum that the King was forced to order the dissolution of the first and second États on June 27. The National Assembly had defeated the crown, the common man enjoying a heady empowerment while an ancient monarchy tottered.

At Versailles, Georgiana was struck by the Queen's appearance. Marie Antoinette seemed withered and distracted and had lost her elegant gaiety. Georgiana reluctantly returned to Paris, and by the beginning of July the atmosphere was so turbulent in the city that her husband decided they ought to leave. Despite the crowds and foreign troops lining the road to Versailles, Georgiana insisted on seeing Marie Antoinette once again. On July 8, dressed in mourning attire, the Duchess of Devonshire tackled the road to the chateau where she and her friend, the Queen, spent some time together. Both women feared for the future of the royal family, and it was the last time they would see each other. The Devonshires fled to Brussels where they awaited word on the emigration of many of their friends during the explosive days of July 1789.

That July, the King removed Jacques Necker from his post. The populace rioted, gathered arms, and invaded the Bastille prison looking for gunpowder. A rumor had spread that the King himself had planted explosives to blow up the National Assembly and that the Comte d'Artois and the Polignacs were going to quash the new government with force. Immediately after the fall of the Bastille on July 14, people began to advise the King to leave the country, or at least to let his children slip away for their own safety, but the King and Queen refused to part from each other or to be separated from their children. On July 16, 1789, two days after the storming of the Bastille, a council was held in the King's bedroom. With crowds threatening to assassinate the Polignacs and the Comte d'Artois, the Queen begged the royal governess to escape, but Polignac refused. Marie Antoinette then asked the King to order their friend to depart. The duchess could not refuse an order issued by her king. A sad farewell took place in the evening as all of the people, except for her parents and brother, closest in the world to Marie-Thérèse, fled France in various disguises. The Queen, trying to keep her friend's imminent departure a secret, passed a note to Madame de Polignac that read, 'Adieu! The most tender of friends. The word is terrible to pronounce but it must be said. Here is the order for the horses. I have no more strength left except to embrace you.'

The King assured the Polignacs, as they hurriedly packed for Switzerland, that he would continue to support them, and the Queen gave Madame Campan money to give to the Duchess for their traveling expenses. The King arranged for troops to accompany his youngest brother, the Comte d'Artois, the Comtesse d'Artois, and their sons, the young Ducs d'Angoulême and de Berry, to safety. These two young boys, Marie-Thérèse's first cousins, were among her closest playmates. She was distraught at their departure but relieved to learn of their safe arrival in Italy. Artois's father-in-law, the King of Sardinia, welcomed his daughter and her family and the Condés as well as a growing number of French aristocrats settled in Turin out of reach of the revolutionaries. Marie Antoinette, certain that she, the King, and their children would be forced to flee, asked Madame Campan to help her burn papers and gather her jewelry in preparation for their own hasty escape, but that plan was dashed, according to Campan, when a 'small committee' instead agreed that the King would go to Paris to face the insurrection. Marie Antoinette, convinced that the King would be harmed or held hostage in Paris, planned to ask the Assembly for asylum for herself and her children if he did not return.

The next morning, July 17, the King went without his family to Paris to approve a new mayor and the appointment of Lafayette as military commander. The Queen, shaking, locked herself and what was left of her family inside private chambers. The children did not leave her for one instant. The Dauphin, constantly looking out the window, assured his mother, 'He will return. He will return. My father is so good that no one will hurt him!' The day seemed without end as they waited to hear word or the sound of the approach of the King's coach and horses. Finally, at 11 p.m., Louis arrived, rushed straight to the Queen, and heartily hugged his crying children. People filled the courtyard to get a glimpse of the King, who had put on the tricolor cockade of the revolution to demonstrate his support of the new government and the rights of the citizens of France.

The Queen and their children joined the King on the balcony twice to receive acclaim from the crowd. News had reached the masses that the King had agreed to call Necker back to his job, and, for the moment, Louis seemed to have appeased his enemies. The cabals continued to meet at the cafés in Paris – Marie Antoinette referring to them as the 'enraged' people of the Palais-Royal. In the meantime, she sought a replacement for the Duchesse de Polignac. She summoned the forty-year-old widow, the Marquise de Tourzel, whose husband had died in 1786 while on a hunt with the King. It was a dangerous time to serve the royal family at

Versailles and aristocrats were fleeing in droves, but Madame de Tourzel accepted the post.

On July 25, the Queen wrote confidential instructions to the Marquise in order to prepare de Tourzel for her new job. It was a touching and honest letter revealing each child's shortcomings and strengths. Marie Antoinette welcomed the new governess saying, 'Madame, I had entrusted my children to friendship; today, I entrust them to virtue.' She also asked the new governess to pay as much attention to Madame Royale as to the Dauphin. The Queen explained that it was the women who had been with Madame Royale since her birth, such as Mesdames Fréminville, Brunier and seven other ladies, who had made the greatest impression on Marie-Thérèse, and those women were very important to her daughter. They had attended Marie-Thérèse with diligence and care. The Queen confided, however, that 'the men with her since birth are absolutely insignificant'.

Delineating the failings of various servants, including complaints about both mother and daughter Mesdames de Mackau and de Soucy, the Queen also sketched intimate details of life in the royal nursery. The Queen revealed that although the Dauphin, now almost four years and four months old, was of robust health, and that he had been 'born happy', he was a sensitive boy and his nerves were delicate. Louis Charles could be indiscreet, the Queen warned, and he would innocently repeat things that he had overheard, embellishing imaginatively. She rightly understood this as the innocent babble of a small child; some people, however, would not be so forgiving.[2] The Queen also stressed that the four-year-old Dauphin found apologizing – for example, after a temper tantrum – quite a challenge. She added that he did, however, have many redeeming qualities. One of his finest was that he 'loves his sister deeply, and with a full heart. Every time that something gives him pleasure, whether to go somewhere or something that someone gives him, his first inclination is to always request that his sister have the same'.[3]

Madame de Tourzel, who would later be honored with the hereditary title of Duchess, arrived at Versailles at the beginning of August. She slept in the Dauphin's room, guarding him day and night. Displaying great loyalty, she brought along her own teenage daughter, Pauline, whom she could have sent out of the country to safety at any time. The children adored Pauline, and, although genuinely fond of the Marquise, they teasingly called her 'Madame Sévère'.

The royal couple kept up as regular a correspondence with the Duchesse de Polignac as was possible. In a letter to his former 'favorite', dated July 29, the King wrote that he was happy that she was safe, and closed with the tender words, 'Goodnight, my dear Madame; you know the unchanging sentiments of your very humble and obedient servant.' The Queen, knowing that Polignac would long to hear news of the royal children, put in place a chain of sympathizers who would send oral reports to the émigrée, now situated in Basel. The King and Queen smuggled letters to their refugee friends and family through the Queen's long-time advisor (and her mother's former spy), Comte Mercy. On August 12, the Queen wrote to Polignac that she had no doubt that word had arrived about the appointment of Madame de Tourzel and that although it pained her heart to replace her friend, it was necessary to find someone who had been far from all of the accusations and intrigue at court, someone who was above reproach. She also reported that the two girls were trying their best to be exemplary: 'My daughter and Ernestine had been perfect for you, and, consequently, for me. As for my son, he is still too young and too scattered to deeply sense a separation.' On August 31, the Queen's letter to Polignac included a handwritten note from Marie-Thérèse, which said, 'Madame, I was very angry to learn that you had left. Please know that I will never forget you.'

While many of the émigrés, which included hairdressers and couturiers who lived off their rich patrons, believed that what they were encountering was a temporary hiatus, and that they would return to France as soon as the situation stabilized, Marie-Thérèse clearly believed in her heart that things would not get better. The ten-year-old was aware of the growing impatience of the populace with the legislators whom they themselves had put in place. Tensions escalated and the personal rights and very freedom of the royal family were eroded. In August, members of the National Assembly were busily constructing a manifesto based on the American Declaration of Independence, called the 'Declaration of the Rights of Man'. Two weeks before the Declaration was passed on August 26, it was announced that no one in France would ever kneel before anyone else again. On August 25, the Fête of Saint-Louis, even the Mayor of Paris did not bow before the King and Queen on the King's own name day. In September, Necker announced that the King and his household would drastically cut its expenditure. Rumors at the Palais-Royal spread that the King was going to live with the Dauphin at the Louvre Palace while the Queen was going to enter a convent. On September 13, in Paris, a baker was hanged for supposedly favoring his more affluent customers and offering only poor quality bread to those of lesser means. As the violence became random and more prolific, the

King called upon the Flanders regiment, whom he believed loyal, to provide protection at Versailles.

Garrisoned at the frontier, 1,100 men arrived at the palace on September 23, most with enthusiasm, though this was somewhat diluted when they came into contact with and fraternized with the National Guard, organized by the National Assembly of France. To honor their newly arrived Flemish comrades, the *gardes du corps* – the King's own palace guards – planned a feast, inviting the Swiss and National Guards as well. The banquet was held on October 1 in the Opera House at Versailles, the very same place where the royal couple's spectacular wedding reception had taken place nearly twenty years before.

The King and Queen were advised to make an appearance. Marie Antoinette was afraid that she would be harmed, so she sent Madame Campan ahead to spy on the crowd. Campan surveyed the scene accompanied by one of her nieces and Ernestine. When the girls joined some soldiers in singing a chorus of 'O Richard, oh my king!' and shouted *'Vive le Roi!'*, a deputy chided them for screaming outrageously for the life of one man who, according to the Declaration of the Rights of Man, had no more importance than any other. Madame Campan's niece responded sharply and Campan herself told the man to shut up. Suddenly, without having waited for a signal to enter, the royal family arrived: the Queen, dressed in white and pale blue and wearing a turquoise necklace and a feather in her hair, carried the Dauphin – dressed in a lilac sailor suit – in one arm. Marie-Thérèse, in green and white, held her mother's other hand. Madame de Tourzel and Pauline walked behind. A soldier approached the Queen and asked if she would permit him to take the Dauphin to join the men downstairs, and although she complied graciously, she was terrified. The boy was lifted onto a table and as he walked along it fearlessly, the convivial crowd sang with gusto. Some of the soldiers saluted the boy with their swords and the Dauphin received a spontaneous ovation. A few members of the National Guard turned their cockades inside out displaying the white lining as a tribute to the Bourbons and then the entire militia escorted the royal family back to their quarters.

As the royal family prepared for bed, they felt more optimistic than they had for many months. Soldiers sang and danced under the King's windows, and one belonging to the Flanders regiment climbed up onto the King's balcony loudly shouting, *'Vive le Roi!'* The euphoria lulled the royal family into a false sense of calm. They quickly tried to recover their customary daily domestic routine and pursue normal activities. Meanwhile, rumors proliferated that the soldiers' revelry at Versailles had been no less than an orgy and a counter-revolutionary celebration that was held to restore all powers to the King. On the morning following the festivities, October 2, an inflammatory and excoriating article appeared in the newspaper *L'Ami du Peuple*, published by revolutionary leader Marat, portraying the previous night's revelries as a gross affront to the people, and a song about the King's surfeited guards, glass in hand, called 'L'Orgie des Gardes françaises', became an overnight anthem. Members of the National Assembly met to denounce the evening.

According to the stories, the Queen had gorged herself with the most delectable, succulent food and had become drunk on the 'gallons of fine wines' at the festivities. When, on October 4, the peasants of Paris were told there was no bread in the entire city, they rioted, turned violent, and hanged another unfortunate baker on the spot. Later, they would learn that the Duc d'Orléans had secretly amassed an immense hoard of grain with the intent of causing a shortage, in effect starving and killing many of the people who thought him a savior. Ignorant of the Duke's malevolence, a mob of six to seven thousand Parisians, angry and hungry and armed with guns, pikes and iron hooks, gathered at Place Louis XV and set out in the pouring rain on the twelve-mile walk to Versailles, to get their hands on bounty.

CHAPTER VI
THE END OF
THE FAIRY TALE

M ARIE-THÉRÈSE reported in her journal that Monday, October 5, 1789, began as a rather tranquil day at Versailles. She and her brother were playing in the gardens at the Petit Trianon and they joined their mother for lunch at 1.30 in the afternoon. The Comte de Provence and his wife were at Versailles, and her favorite aunt, Madame Elisabeth, was on a drive toward Montreuil. The King, hunting at Meudon, was feeling quite happy with his booty of forty-one birds when a gentleman on his staff interrupted. The servant informed the King that a mob was en route to Versailles from Paris. Madame Elisabeth was eating lunch at Montreuil when she, too, was alerted. According to Marie-Thérèse, her aunt immediately headed back to Versailles, where she went to her brother's apartment. The Comte de Provence said he had heard rumors of a march, but did not believe them. Madame Elisabeth assured her brother that the story was true and the two of them went directly to the Petit Trianon where they found the Queen dining with her children. Marie Antoinette realized there was something gravely wrong as soon as she saw her sister-in-law and left the room so that she could receive her news in private. That was the last time that Marie Antoinette would see her beloved Petit Trianon.

The Queen, the children, her brother and sisters-in-law returned to the palace and sequestered themselves for the remainder of the afternoon while courtiers paced silently. The children remained on the second floor with their mother and were forbidden from going outside. Soldiers slammed shut the palace's massive iron gates. The rain intensified and then subsided, then poured down again – a mirror of the ebb and flow of emotion and resolution that the royal family would experience during their last few hours at Versailles.

Félix d'Hézecques, a young page in the King's service, recalled that the King was so worried about the safety of his wife and children that he refused a carriage, mounted one of the strongest horses in the Meudon stables and galloped at full speed the five miles to Versailles. People on the roads who saw the King charging on horseback at breakneck speed were so stunned, they simply scurried out of his way to the side of the road. Traditionally, there would have been about a hundred of the elite Swiss guard inside the palace to protect the King's person or to be on call for ceremonial duties, with another nine hundred posted in the palace grounds. The King had agreed, as part of the cost-cutting measures for the royal household, to reduce the number of these soldiers. It was an admirable public relations attempt, stating in effect that the King had full confidence in the National Assembly, but as a security measure, it was a disaster. Many of the King's personal guard, now let go, had defected to the National Guard, led by the Marquis de Lafayette, an aristocrat who had gained fame and glory as a war hero in the American battle for independence from the British. Other soldiers remained but had little desire to risk their own lives for this King and the despised 'l'Autrichienne'.

Panic consumed the entire court during those last few hours at Versailles and versions of events vary with almost every testimony. Most accounts agree that the King raced back to Versailles believing that he and his family could escape the palace before the onslaught of rioters. Some eyewitnesses state that the King arrived at Versailles at three in the afternoon; others claim it was two hours later. Intent on moving his loved ones to Fontainebleau or Rambouillet, the King began making escape arrangements. It was not a simple process, however, as it necessitated the cooperation of his ministers and a few loyal courtiers. As always, notwithstanding the fact that the King had suffered an immeasurable loss of status, he could not simply abandon one palace without detection and without considering public opinion.

Some bystanders' accounts claim the rioters arrived at the palace gates at about four in the afternoon; Marie-Thérèse and Monsieur Hüe both, however, place that event at about six that evening. When the *poissardes* – the women from Paris's fish markets – arrived at the head of the mob, shouting obscenities through the bolted gates, they came face to face with the King's *gardes du corps,* poised for battle. These coarse and brawny women, who earned their living eviscerating fish, came in their blood-and-gut-stained white aprons armed with their tools of the trade. They appeared unafraid of the Flanders regiment stationed in the vast court-yard of the chateau. Some insist that General Lafayette accompanied the mob to the palace, arriving at the same hour; others place his arrival five hours later, in a deliberate attempt, despite the fact that he had known about the march on Versailles since early that morning, to stall his soldiers and appear just at the moment of crisis.

Conversation inside the palace walls took place in whispers as ministers including Necker, the Comte de Saint-Priest, the Marquis de La Tour du Pin, and Marshal Beauvau came and went to speak with the King to discuss whether he and his family should evacuate the palace. These discussions are recorded in accounts with great variation. Saint-Priest suggested that the Queen, the children and Madame Elisabeth depart for Rambouillet. The famous literary figure Madame de Staël, who was present, saw her father, finance minister Necker, as the voice of wisdom. Necker, ever the financier, advised against the departure of the royal family, explaining that moving would be expensive. He also suggested that if the King did not stand his ground, he would be playing right into the Duc d'Orléans's hands. Although the Queen had ordered her belong-ings to be packed, she refused to be separated from her husband and children. The King maintained his desire to stay and help his people, and when he ruefully rejected the idea out of hand with the comment 'A king in flight?', Marie Antoinette told her staff that the family would be staying put.

Jean-Joseph Mounier, the President of the National Assembly, also traveled to Versailles that day. Until then, the King had refused to sanction the reforms passed by the National Assembly in August and September, including the 'Declaration of the Rights of Man', and, in reaction, there had been discussion to pass a resolution declaring the Duc d'Orléans King. Mounier arrived to tell His Majesty that he needed to agree to the Assembly's decree, 'the Rights of Man', and nineteen articles of the new constitution. Mounier explained that the rioting had now spread beyond Paris to the provinces. There had been reports of the sacking and burning down of chateaux. Mounier reasoned that it was necessary for peace in the country to give the National Assembly his blessing, warning the King that there could be civil war. Mounier later recalled that when he stood to face the King he saw a frightened man. He reassured the monarch that General Lafayette was on his way and that the royal family would not be harmed. Marie-Thérèse later reflected that she thought Mounier meant well; Hüe, on the other hand, thought that Mounier's understanding of the situation was simplistic, and, thus, a recipe for disaster. For several hours, Mounier went back and forth to the Salle des Menus-Plaisirs, where Assembly leaders were gathered to debate and negotiate.

To Mounier's satisfaction, the King agreed to ratify the Assembly's decisions. Marie-Thérèse recalled that she saw Mounier come to the chateau several times that evening. First, he came on an errand on behalf of the new government; he then returned as a mediator, in what he perceived to be a conciliatory role. Mounier believed that the citizen army was rioting for a fair and proper cause, so he asked the King to allow a small group of the female peasants to be permitted through the gates. This designated group of women, representing the larger mob, would speak with the King, he said, in a civilized manner, and express the concerns of His Majesty's subjects.

Madame de Tourzel counted that twelve representatives of the citizen army were let inside the palace to see the King; others claimed there were five. In either case, the small delegation was ushered to the Salon de l'Oeil-de-Boeuf, so named by Louis XV who liked to joke that the oval window in its cornice looked like a bull's eye. Seventeen-year-old Louise Chabry was the designated spokesperson. Some have since regarded her as a 'Palais-Royal mole', claiming that she then theatrically feigned a state of near collapse in order to gain a measure of notoriety and sympathy, though, in truth, the march itself would have exhausted even the fittest. When the King exhibited concern for the young woman and asked her what it was she wanted, Chabry tearfully replied: 'bread'. Louis XVI immediately requested that a glass of wine be served to the shaking Mademoiselle Chabry, and he further ordered that bread from two of the palace's granaries be distributed among the women. The group seemed appeased, even stunned, by His Majesty's compassion. Mounier again assured the King that, since Lafayette was en route and the King had complied with the National Assembly, His Majesty should demonstrate even more good faith and disperse his soldiers.

At about seven o'clock, the delegation of women returned to their comrades outside the palace gates with a handwritten promise from the King, shouting, 'We will have bread!' A small group responded, '*Vive le Roi!*' One woman in the crowd told her friends to shut up because the demand for bread was merely a pretext. One of the *gardes du corps*, on horseback, claimed he heard a woman cry, 'Go back to the palace and tell them we will be there soon to cut off the Queen's head.' Another shouted, 'We will roast the Queen's heart tomorrow!' The onset of rain did not deter the crowd from their mission of finding a way to enter the palace.

While a struggle conveniently erupted among some soldiers in the Place d'Armes, a group of the brigands found a small, unprotected gate, slipped onto the grounds of the palace and made their way to the kitchen, where they broke in. When confronted by members of the King's staff, some broke down, claiming that they had been forced to march. The Marquis de La Maisonfort, later a royalist spy, and Madame Campan both referred to the female rebels as 'furies'; to others, the hordes of screaming women were 'harpies' or 'Orléans's prostitutes'. Hüe alleged that Orléans had engaged real Parisian prostitutes to seduce the soldiers away from their posts at Versailles, that some of the regiments, led by aristocratic officers, resisted temptation, remaining strong, but some succumbed, abandoned their King and donned the tri-colored hats of the revolutionaries, causing confusion in the ranks.

While chaos infiltrated the militia, inside the palace the plans were changing moment by moment. The children – the Dauphin, Madame Royale and her playmate Ernestine – would be with the King and Queen one moment; then they would be suddenly whisked to their own rooms to protect their ears from a barrage of hostile news; at last, at play, they would once again be brought back to the King and Queen for their own safety, and then, again, returned to their own chambers. At eight o'clock, the Queen went to the children's quarters and told the staff they were to get the children ready to leave in fifteen minutes. Half an hour later, she rescinded her command and took the children with her back up to the first floor where they spent the evening under the watchful eye of the King, the Queen and the King's ministers.

At nine o'clock in the evening, there was an extraordinary commotion right outside the children's quarters near the Orangerie as a carriage raced out of the stables and pulled up near the terrace, ostensibly to take away the royal family. Félix d'Hézecques recalled seeing a column of the King's *gardes du corps* move from the Place d'Armes closer to the chateau. According to one account, this regiment, whose job it was to guard the person of the King, saw the escape carriage and lost faith in their sovereign.

Another eyewitness described how, as the rabble began to multiply, with more and more men coming out from behind the women and getting closer to the King's inner sanctum, the King's personal men stood in place as the last line of protection between His Majesty and the citizen army. At nearly ten o'clock, the skirmish among soldiers had spread from the courtyard to the gardens. Marie Antoinette, who, Madame de Tourzel later wrote, expressed her concern for everyone but herself that evening, instructed the children's governess that if, after the children went to bed, there was the slightest noise inside the palace she must bring Marie-Thérèse and Louis Charles to the Queen's chambers.

The Queen changed her mind later in the evening and gave new orders: if the children grew afraid, Madame de Tourzel was to bring them to the King's rooms, which Marie Antoinette thought would be safer. Marie-Thérèse's own recollection was different. She remembered her mother having said, 'bring my son instantly to the King', with no specific mention of her daughter, or Ernestine. Courtiers begged the King to escape with his family. Even Mounier, genuinely surprised that the crowd had not retreated, and in fact, had grown even more ferocious, pleaded with the King for the royal family to leave, offering them the protection of the National Assembly. At that late hour, as the mob had now surrounded and had partially penetrated the palace, the plan to have a carriage carry them away proved impossible and had to be abandoned.

Only about fifty loyal soldiers remained inside the corridors of the palace immediately near the family's quarters. A storm raged all evening, the sound of wind snapping around the brickwork of the chimneys. While courtiers walked the length of the mirrored Galerie des Glaces, Madame de la Tour du Pin recalled that she was exceedingly agitated, and did not sit still for one minute. Towards midnight, General Lafayette finally appeared at the palace to see the King. Lafayette, unaware – or at least, pretending to be – of the dissension that Orléans had already perpetrated among the ranks of his own command, assured the King and his courtiers that there would be no further mischief. It is not known whether it was the King who instructed some of his most loyal *gardes du corps* to ride to Rambouillet to anticipate the arrival of the royal family in case of an escape, or if it had been Lafayette who took that decision. In either case, members of the guard were dispatched to the Chateau de Rambouillet, leaving Versailles and the royal family even more vulnerable.

Lafayette then instructed everyone to go to bed. Some of the exhausted women on the Queen's own staff reluctantly followed the General's directive, but they decided to remain fully dressed nonetheless. The Queen insisted on sleeping apart from her children and the King as she was convinced that if anyone came into the palace, she would be the intended target. She felt that it was the Duc d'Orléans who had master-minded the attack on Versailles and that if Lafayette could not subdue the mob it was she that they would come after. As it turned out she was quite correct. Among Lafayette's soldiers were mercenaries hired by the Duc d'Orléans for that very purpose. As the Russian ambassador to France,

Mr de Simolin, wrote Russian Chancellor Ivan Ostermann, 'the Duc d'Orléans was without doubt inculpated in weaving the plot of the 5th and 6th of October'.

Madame Royale, in awe of her mother's coolness and courage, obeyed her governess and went to bed. At about midnight, all seemed quiet. A little while later, once the King was alone, he summoned Hüe, requesting that the loyal servant deliver a message to the Queen: the King desired that the Queen 'rest tranquilly' and sleep, as he, the King, would also do. Madame de Tourzel recalled, however, that the Queen did not go to sleep until two in the morning, encouraging the governess to get some sleep as well. General Lafayette also decided to take a nap in the early hours of the morning, and while he was sleeping in town at the home of the de Noailles, the rebels struck. This mistake would earn him the sarcastic appellation 'General Morpheus', an ironic reference to the Greek god of dreams. Not only did the General sleep that night, but he was also under the illusion that he was in command and that everything was under control.

Marie-Thérèse recalled that all was quiet until about five in the morning of October 6 when the iron gates of the chateau were forced and a crowd, led by the Duc d'Orléans, made their way to the palace. Madame de La Tour du Pin wrote that she believed that it was about four in the morning when she looked out her window after having heard voices screaming in the courtyard: 'Kill them! Kill them!' She then saw the Duc d'Orléans ride through the gate to cheers of 'Long live our King d'Orléans!' The Duke, who had told his cousins that he was in Paris for the General Assembly, had in fact been hiding out in Versailles. Madame de la Tour du Pin's servant, Marguerite, who knew him, claimed that she was certain that she had seen him with his boots 'splashed in mud', riding whip in hand. Madame Campan wrote that others testified before the National Assembly when it made its inquiry into the events of the day, that they had seen the King's cousin 'in a greatcoat and slouched hat, at half-past four in the morning, at the top of the marble staircase, pointing out with his hand the guard-room, which led to the Queen's apartment'. A small group of attackers, led by someone who knew the layout of the palace well, then headed straight for the Queen's guardroom.

Outside in the garden, a big bearded man named Nicolas Jourdan – who would earn the name 'coupe-tête' or 'head chop' – decapitated a soldier of the gardes du corps with an axe, placed the head on a pike and paraded it outside the windows of the children's rooms. Inside the palace, a group of insurgents, led by the Duc d'Orléans, threatened the Swiss

Guard stationed at the foot of the marble staircase leading to the rooms of the royal family. The guards had their throats slit and some were completely decapitated. The remaining *gardes du corps* proved their loyalty as well when two of the guards, Miomandre de Sainte-Marie and Durepaire, though badly wounded, made their way to the Queen's door, pounded on it with the butts of their muskets and shouted, 'Madame, you must flee! . . . there are men here who have come to kill you!'

Baronne Cécile de Courtot, lady-in-waiting to the Princesse de Lamballe, recalled hearing axes hacking the Queen's door while she and the Princess helped the Queen grab a yellow striped underskirt. The two women opened a secret panel in the wall next to the bed where the Queen had given birth to her children, which led to a small chamber, and shoved her inside the panel. Once inside, the Queen climbed down a hidden passage leading beneath the Salon de l'Oeil-de-Boeuf to the King's chamber, the walls of the antechamber, painted with charming scenes of children at play, providing a surreal backdrop to such a terrifying moment. One report stated that a second after the Queen escaped, the rebels broke down the door to her room; finding no queen, they angrily sliced into her bed, chopping it to bits, and left to search the entire palace. Félix d'Hézecques wrote that the invaders did not penetrate the Queen's private bedroom and only got as far as the door to her room. He claimed that he examined her bed two days later and found that no trace of violence had been perpetrated within. Madame Campan also dismissed this story, but she let her readers know that she received her information concerning the events of October 5 and 6, just hours after they had happened, from her sister, Madame Auguié, also in the service of the Queen, who was on duty during that time.

The unfolding tragedy contained elements of farce. When Marie Antoinette arrived at her husband's private chamber she found it empty, the King having taken another secret passage to find her. When the King did not find the Queen in her chambers, he returned to his own room and found her waiting for him. Madame de Tourzel reported that it was she who, following the orders of the Queen, had brought the little Dauphin to the King's room, and when the Queen arrived, relieved that her husband and son were together, she frantically descended a secret staircase, not to Madame Royale's bedroom, but to Madame de Tourzel's apartments, where the terrified Marie-Thérèse had spent the night and was fast asleep near Pauline. According to the account of another member of the royal staff, the Queen spoke softly and tenderly to her daughter, lifted Marie-

Thérèse into her arms and fled, once again, to the King's room. Pauline, who was in the room, told yet another variation. According to her recollection, Pauline believed that it was the Queen who suddenly appeared in the governess's chambers, lifted Madame Royale in her arms and told Madame de Tourzel to carry the Dauphin from his bed to the King's room. Pauline remembered that, as discombobulated as she was, the Queen took the time to take her by the hand and tell her: 'Don't be afraid. Stay calm.' Pauline remained in her mother's apartments, trying her best to follow the Queen's advice, listening to the fracas of shouting and doors being opened and slammed shut.

The King's elderly aunts, Adélaïde and Victoire arrived, as had a handful of soldiers, bearing the grim news that many of the Swiss Guard and *gardes du corps* positioned in the Cour Royale had been executed. The bodies of Des Huttes, de Varicort and others known well to the royal family lay mutilated and strewn about the halls. Marie-Thérèse heard the order to find Madame Elisabeth and the Comte and Comtesse de Provence, who were still asleep. The children saw people at the windows with pikes threatening to attack. Marie-Thérèse was shocked at the tattered clothing of some and later wrote that some of the women were half-naked. One man, wearing a guard's uniform, shot into the crowd, enraging the mob further. The King appeared on a balcony to beg the marauders for mercy, to spare the life of his family and his guards.

Lafayette, now the subject of ridicule by many present (Hézecques called him an imbecile, and 'the incarnation of Cromwell') arrived from the de Noailles townhouse at about ten in the morning, having once again avoided most of the drama. The royal couple resigned themselves to the fact that it was time to leave Versailles, and Lafayette went out onto the balcony and informed the multitude that the King would accompany them all back to Paris. The crowd shouted for the King who once more came out and confirmed to the crowd, whose numbers had risen to an estimated 40,000, that the royal family would indeed be leaving for the capital. General Lafayette asked the crowd to remain calm while the royal family, still in their nightcaps, dressed for the journey.

Jean-Joseph Mounier, who would resign four days later and return home to the Dauphiné, would publish his own account only weeks after the invasion of Versailles. In his *Exposé de ma conduite à l'Assemblée nationale et les motifs de mon retour en Dauphiné*, Mounier recalled having crossed paths with the Comte de Provence that morning and that it was he who informed the Prince of the rioting, stating that the Assembly had voted that the King must go to Paris. Mounier revealed that Provence reacted philosophically, ' "What do you expect? We are in the middle of a revolution," said the King's brother, adding an old French proverb, "*On ne fait pas d'omelettes sans casser des oeufs.*" ' ('One cannot make omelets without breaking eggs.')

Although she had sometimes disobeyed the Queen and had treated her with less deference than she did her father, Marie-Thérèse saw something in her mother that day that affected her profoundly. She would recall and recount with the greatest admiration the enormous bravery her mother exhibited under extreme duress, and she would hold on to that example to guide her throughout her life.

The mob demanded that the Queen come to the balcony. Madame de Staël reported that all those who were present in the room advised Marie Antoinette not to go, but that the Queen, who had turned very pale, took the hands of her two terrified children and walked toward the windows. Hézecques and Pauline both recalled that the Queen went out on the balcony with both of her children, as does almost every other eyewitness and testimony. Marie-Thérèse, however, recalled that the Queen went out on the balcony with only the Dauphin in her arms. Marie-Thérèse said that she felt 'mortal anxiety' that morning and may have been so traumatized at this time that she simply blocked the event from her mind.

The crowd chanted for the Queen to face them alone. Marie Antoinette left the balcony for a moment, and, according to all present, placed both of her children in the King's custody. Again, Marie-Thérèse reported that the Queen placed only her brother in the King's arms. All she could recall of the event is that her mother then returned to the balcony to face the baying crowds on her own – this time, expecting to die. From her position near the window, Marie-Thérèse could see a man dressed in the National Guard uniform aiming a musket at her mother. The Queen made a deep curtsy, which caught the mob off guard. Her courageous gesture inspired a few in the crowd to shout '*Vive la Reine!*', but the majority continued to hurl obscenities at her.

The Queen returned from the balcony to a roomful of friends and family who stood silently in awe. According to accounts from those in the room, she took the Dauphin in her arms and, as she wept from emotional exhaustion, planted kisses all over his face, turned to the King and said, 'Promise me, Sire, I hold up to you, in the name of all you hold most dear, for the good of France, for your loved ones, for this dear child, Oh! Promise me that if a similar circumstance presents itself, and you have the means to go away, that you will not allow the opportunity to escape.'

A few members of the court staff watching the rioters from the windows and balconies eyed them with suspicion. For peasants, some seemed to have good teeth and clothes of good quality. It was clear to many that this was a bought-and-paid-for piece of theater – subsidized most probably by the Duc d'Orléans. Skeptical about the King's honesty and Lafayette's own ability to deliver, the citizen army waited in the palace grounds to see that the King kept his word.

The royal family scheduled their departure for noon, but they were not ready until one or two o'clock in the afternoon. Madame de la Tour du Pin claimed that a mournful King asked her father-in-law to watch over Versailles, which was being pillaged as the family packed. The Queen quickly handed out personal mementos to some loyal friends and servants. The King's elderly aunts were escorted to their estate at Bellevue. The children, hurrying to leave, saw blood, entrails and human body parts strewn about the marble floor outside the King's room; as they were leaving, they heard the sounds of hatchets ripping through *boiserie*, and the shrieks and moans of humans in combat to the death as fighting continued. The royal family then crossed the Cour des Cerfs and climbed into their carriage. Marie-Thérèse recalled that the King, Queen and Dauphin sat in the back of the coach, while she sat in front with her aunts, Madame Elisabeth and the Comtesse de Provence. Sandwiched in between her aunts were the Comte de Provence and Madame de Tourzel. Again, doubtless owing to the dazed state of the entire group, there are varying accounts of the journey. Madame de Tourzel claimed that Marie-Thérèse sat between her parents in the back while she sat in the front with the Dauphin on her lap, Madame Elisabeth at her side, the Comte and Comtesse de Provence at each window.

The Queen carried as many of her diamonds as she could put in a case. As the carriage was built for six, the ride was an uncomfortable one. General Lafayette rode his famous white horse at one door and the Comte d'Estaing, commander of the guards of Versailles, rode at the other. A second carriage bearing the Princesse de Chimay, the Duchesse de Duras, the Marquise de la Roche-Aymon and Pauline followed. More carriages containing servants and courtiers completed the royal cortège. Anticipating the pathetic procession, the Duc d'Orléans had rented a house in Passy, and he stood on a balcony with his family and his children's governess, Madame de Genlis, who was also his mistress, and, according to those loyal to the King, gloated and mocked as the carriage passed.

Just five months earlier, at the opening of the États-Généraux, the thrilling sound of trumpets had hailed the royal cortège as it left Versailles. On this afternoon, the air was filled with the sound of rage.

Furious crowds along the route, some with loaves of bread on spikes, shrilly called the King and Queen 'the baker and the baker's wife'. Peasants screamed for Marie Antoinette's heart to be cut out; others made obscene or threatening gestures. The Dauphin, who cried and complained of hunger, climbed onto his mother's lap. When the procession reached Sèvres, a local wigmaker was forced to powder the bloody hair of the severed heads of two of the murdered *gardes du corps*. These heads were then placed on spikes and brandished at the King's carriage again for the children to see; they were the heads of men whom the children had known and been fond of, people who had escorted them, humored them and who had faithfully protected them for many years. Madame de Tourzel claimed that someone tossed a small package inside the carriage, which landed on her knees. Without allowing her to look at it, the King tossed it outside. The coach was shot at three times and lanced with pikes. While Marie-Thérèse watched in horror, Pauline recalled how she herself kept her eyes down, heard the cannon shots, and refused to look up for most of the journey.

Although the capital was only twelve miles away, it took the royal cortège six hours to reach the gates of Paris where the Mayor, Bailly, greeted them with the words, 'What a beautiful day, Sire, for the people of Paris to have in their city Your Majesty and his family!' As Bailly presented the King with the keys to the city, the King replied: 'It is always with pleasure and confidence that I find myself among the people of my good city of Paris.' Bailly, repeating the King's response for the crowds, omitted the words, 'with confidence'. Marie Antoinette shouted out at him, 'Repeat: with confidence!' The King added, 'I sincerely hope that my sojourn will restore peace, harmony and submission to the law.' Although the royal party was weary and shaken – the children having witnessed unimaginable horrors – Mayor Bailly and General Lafayette showed little sensitivity. The two men insisted that the cortège proceed to the Hôtel de Ville so that the people of Paris could see their king. For three hours, the King's family rode slowly in circles around the city. The Marquis de La Maisonfort spied them en route, noticing that Lafayette looked as pale as his horse. La Maisonfort thought Lafayette looked stupefied – puzzled, as if he wondered what on earth was going to happen next. According to La Maisonfort, himself an experienced soldier, Lafayette and his fellow revolutionaries had begun a battle without having an endgame, a war without an exit plan. Ironically, their enemy, His Most Christian King, was also the Pacifist King, the ruler who consistently refused to fire on his own people.

For one thousand years, France had been governed by the axiom, 'As wills the King, so wills the law.' No longer was the King's *demande* his command. He and his family were now at the mercy of the people he had once called his subjects. As the royal family wound their way around the streets of the capital, longing for rest but dreading their new resting place, they all knew that their new guards would be neither faithful nor friendly, and although for those who had lived through the events of the day, it would be indelible, the trauma of the whole experience would remain personal and relative. Marie Antoinette said of the events of October 5–6, 1789, 'I saw everything, knew everything, and forgot everything.' Marie-Thérèse would pen her own version of those two days some ten years later.

CHAPTER VII
A NEW HOME

THE ROYAL PARTY arrived at the Tuileries Palace, bewildered and exhausted, at around 10.30 that night. Out of the darkness a stranger reached in and lifted the Dauphin from the carriage, causing the Queen to almost faint. The stranger made no effort to kidnap the little boy, but stood calmly with the Dauphin in his arms. The man, Jean-Baptiste Cléry, had long ago been promised a job in service of the first the Dauphin. However, when Madame de Polignac forgot to assign him a post, he wrote to the Queen who assured Cléry that she would not forget about him and that some day, if she had another son, she hoped that he could serve the royal family by looking after him. When Cléry learned of the march on Versailles, he set out on foot to come to the aid of the young prince. Realizing that he would not arrive in time, he went to the Tuileries and waited to assume his new responsibilities. Like Madame de Tourzel, who joined the royal family after the fall of the Bastille, both Cléry and the governess placed their own lives in danger in order to serve the royal children, and both would prove extraordinarily faithful. With the four-year-old boy in his arms, Cléry walked with the royal family into their new quarters.

The Tuileries Palace, on the right bank of the Seine, next to the Louvre, was commissioned by Catherine de Medici in 1564, following the death of her husband King Henri II. It had not been inhabited as a major royal residence since the mid-seventeenth century. Louis XIV lived there for a short time while Versailles was under construction, spending the winters there from 1667 to 1671; but for the most part the building had been abandoned for well over a century. The royal family occasionally used the Tuileries as their pied à terre when they were in town for changing between official events. According to Félix d'Hézecques, there had not even been a fire lit in this building since Louis XV and the castle was, for the most part, sparsely furnished and contained no mirrors. It was dark, dank and smelly, and the children immediately hated the place. When the Dauphin complained that the house was ugly, the Queen apparently replied: 'My son, Louis XIV lived here and liked it. We do not want to be more difficult than him.' The King apologized to his family on the first night because they were forced to sleep on chairs, rugs and tables.

The next morning the Queen penned a note to her longtime confidant, Comte Mercy, who had fled to Brussels. 'I am fine, be at ease,' she wrote the Austrian ambassador; 'I am sorry that we have been separated, but it is better that you stay where you are for a while. Adieu, you can depend on my everlasting feelings for you.' Mercy, her mother's eyes and ears at Versailles for ten years, had performed his duty to the Empress often to Marie Antoinette's detriment; however, as Marie Antoinette had matured and had become the matriarch of her own family, Mercy had grown to admire the woman he had observed as a frivolous, young Dauphine, and the two had developed a very strong bond after the Empress's death.

Marie Antoinette was most definitely not 'fine': as she addressed the staff on October 8 her voice quavered and her eyes filled with tears. The King silently stood by her side. Life at the Tuileries would be a time of continual strain for the royal party, comprising the King, Queen, Madame Royale, the Dauphin, Ernestine, Madame Elisabeth, and their loyal servants (the Comte and Comtesse de Provence were moved on the second day to the Palais du Luxembourg). The atmosphere was tense and unpleasant. To establish his own authority at the Tuileries, General Lafayette had installed Major Gouvion, an officer he could trust, who was to ensure that the troops served Lafayette and not the King. The hundreds of soldiers posted by Lafayette stood in the hallways and outside in the gardens, demonstrating the power of the people over the monarch and piercing the royal family with fear. Madame Campan revealed that the Queen, who kept a bowl of powdered sugar near her bedside to mix with water to make it palatable, asked her lady-in-waiting to change the bowl frequently in case it had been poisoned.

One hostile element had, however, been removed from Paris – albeit temporarily. General Lafayette had no intention of repeating the blunder that he had made on the evening of October 5, and once he learned of the Duc d'Orléans's perfidy in the insurrection, Lafayette brought his evidence to the King. Although the royal couple were convinced of their cousin's culpability and would have preferred to be completely rid of him, they chose not to discuss such matters in public and instead put on a united front. Lafayette and the royal couple determined that the Duc d'Orléans should be banished, and that the public would be told that the Duke was being sent on an important mission to England. It was hoped that such a gesture would send a conciliatory message to the people. Some, who had been surprised by Orléans's actions and now mistrusted him, asserted that he was probably an English agent anyway and had been on a mission to dethrone his cousin and cause destabilization in France on behalf of King George III.

Writing to Mercy, Marie Antoinette conceded that reports of the bloody carnival at Versailles were true and she asked him not to attempt to return to the French court. Mercy replied that he together with the Holy Roman Emperor hoped to hatch a plan to help the royal family escape; but on October 10, Marie Antoinette instructed her friend to resist writing to her brother Joseph for the moment. The Emperor himself, ever the loving brother, wrote his own sentiments in a letter dated October 12, 1789, which was smuggled into the Tuileries by the Baron d'Escars. (Although the royal family was under close surveillance, they were able to pass some correspondence through a chain of loyal sympathizers and spies.) In his letter, Joseph reassured his sister that he was indeed their loyal ally and that the 'most beautiful monarchy in the entire world' would never be destroyed. Both Louis XVI and his youngest brother, Artois, contacted Charles IV of Spain, who had succeeded his own father in 1788, requesting that the Spanish king stand by his cousins. Louis had no desire to encourage invasion by a foreign country, but the King of France was hoping that a public statement accompanied by diplomatic protest would remind the Assembly that their King had friends in high places with armies at their disposal.

Describing their new life at the Tuileries, Marie Antoinette wrote that she saw no society and that she and her children slept in two rooms – Marie-Thérèse right by her side. A few days later the rooms were rearranged so that the royal family would be more comfortable in the long term. The King slept on the first floor (where Napoleon would later sleep), with the Dauphin near his bedroom. The women – the Queen, Madame Royale, Ernestine, Madame de Tourzel and Pauline – were on the second floor with a private staircase joining their rooms to those of the King and the Dauphin. The only non-royal person to be given a key to the private stairwell was the children's governess, Madame de Tourzel.

The Queen had wanted the sleeping arrangements that way for the children's safety. Besides, the children remained traumatized. Madame Royale had become distinctly quiet and withdrawn. Though still only a child, Marie-Thérèse already felt nostalgic for her childhood at Versailles. The Dauphin had recurring nightmares. By day he was often confused and asked questions. Why did the King no longer have his *gardes du corps*? The Queen replied that the King of France did not need protection from his people. The Dauphin asked a guest why people use the saying 'happy as a queen', as 'my mother is never happy. She often cries.' Pauline de Tourzel wrote that every person who came to the Tuileries to see the royal family was nonetheless enchanted with the little Dauphin, exclaiming him to be a beautiful child. Madame Campan described a touching scene in which the four-year-old told his father that he had something serious to discuss with him, and asked his father why the people of France, who had loved him, were now so angry with him. The King sat his son on his knee and explained that although he tried to make the people happy, it was their leaders who were angry with him and it was these leaders from the provinces who had not been able to curb the excesses. They needed to work together to correct the financial problems. He begged his son not to blame the people of France, and the Queen instructed him to be kind and affable to everyone. When the Mayor of Paris arrived to see the family just days into their confinement, the little boy made a great effort to be charming, and then whispered in his mother's ear: 'Was that right?'

The fiction that poured out of the drama of the French Revolution chronicled the daring exploits of heroes like the Scarlet Pimpernel and Dickens's doomed Sydney Carton. In fact, contemporary accounts confirm that there was great gallantry in the face of peril together with acts of great kindness. Reports from the borders tell of how chivalric Swiss men took pity on young women fleeing France and underwent marriages of convenience, thereby allowing the women to enter Switzerland with their escorts. In some cases, the 'husbands' were found to have married eighteen or twenty times.

After the insurrection of October 6, it became nearly impossible to get a passport to leave France and the new National Guard stepped up its patrols of the borders. Yet, from Brussels to Parma, Coblenz and Russia, sympathizers and expatriates gathered, building nests of intrigue, hatching plots to rescue the King, or just the Queen and the children. All of these plans included the final destination of Vienna where most assumed that the Queen and her family would be welcomed with open arms.

On the morning after their arrival at the Tuileries, the Queen met with her secretary, Jacques Matthieu Augeard, who wrote that he had scarcely entered and closed the door when the Queen went to see if they were being overheard. 'We are not safe here,' whispered the Queen, 'let us go somewhere else.' The Queen took Augeard to another room where Madame Royale was sitting. The Queen asked her daughter to leave them as they had something secret to discuss. While they spoke, Augeard noticed the tiny ottoman upon which Madame Royale slept. The secretary had come armed with an escape plan for the Queen and the children. The Queen thanked him, but declined, stating she could not leave her husband.

As a king, Louis XVI was prone to indecisiveness, but as a husband and father he immediately understood the importance of creating some semblance of normality for his family, in spite of the highly restrictive circumstances. Marie-Thérèse's pianoforte was brought from Versailles along with some other pieces of furniture and a few portraits, lending familiarity and comfort to the Tuileries. To distract her daughter from their unpleasant new surroundings, the Queen asked Madame de Tourzel to hold tea parties for Marie-Thérèse and to invite other children. For a few hours, Madame Royale, Ernestine and Pauline laughed and played hide and seek with their guests. On Thursday evenings, the King held public dinners. He continued to rise early, pray and meet the Queen and their children for breakfast. For their displaced courtiers, the King and Queen re-established a measure of the routine they had known at Versailles. The royal family received diplomats on Sundays and Thursdays; the *grand couvert*, the King's formal public dinner, when his entire family was in attendance, was scheduled for Sundays. The King's *lever* and *coucher*, his ceremonial rising and goodnight, were resumed to honor those who wished to continue to serve His Majesty. Among their faithful servants, however, were those who came with other intentions. The King and Queen were convinced, and quite rightly, that some of the servants and soldiers around them, many of whom had been appointed by Lafayette or who had received their new posts as favors from the National Assembly, were spies. Others, they were convinced, were in the pay of the Duc d'Orléans.

At ten years old, Marie-Thérèse learned to conduct her conversations carefully, to censor every thought before she uttered a word; she also learned to communicate with her parents through a special sign language concocted by the Queen, a secret code used only by the royal family. She was old enough to understand that it was not a game and that her family's very existence depended on her discretion; it was a burdensome responsibility for such a young child. There were no moments of privacy, none like the special times she had shared with her family at the Petit Trianon. Like her mother, Marie-Thérèse longed for a return to Versailles. She missed the countryside, her very own menagerie at the Hameau, and the beautiful aromas of the gardens. The city stank and was dirty. The gardens at the Tuileries, a popular place for Parisians to stroll, were tiny by comparison, and now that the royal family was in residence the courtyard was constantly filled with curiosity-seekers hoping to catch a glimpse of the children playing outdoors or of the King and Queen on a promenade. Hordes of people would trample through the gardens, come right up to the palace windows and peer inside in order to watch the King, the Queen and their children or shout for them to come out so that they could get a closer look. Sometimes the Queen would suffer so much for the cooped-up children that she would insist on taking them to the great public park, the Bois de Boulogne, leaving the palace by a discreet staircase in the Pavilion de Flore. To attend Mass, they had to walk on a terrace through an arcade where throngs of people gathered to leer at them.

Marie-Thérèse also learned a cynical lesson about politics at this very young age. She knew that people had cried for bread, yet from the tiny windows of her room she saw wagon after wagon filled with flour sacks, said to have been spoiled for having been in storage too long, driven to the Seine where their contents were dumped into the river. Marie-Thérèse kept a close watch as her parents' attempts to reach out to the people were rebuffed. The Queen, although deprived of many of her own luxuries, continued to give openly to charities. Young Madame Royale accompanied her mother to visit the factories at the rue Saint-Antoine, the hotbed of hatred against the Queen, and the Queen took the Dauphin to visit orphanages to show him how fortunate he was. The people of Paris, however, grew more openly hostile, and the royal family retreated more and more behind the palace's walls. The Queen gave up her box at the theater to avoid public scrutiny. The outings to the Bois de Boulogne became fewer and further between: the abuse hurled at the family disturbed the children so much that the guards would often have to whisk them back to the Tuileries.

That October, the National Assembly moved from the Salle des Menus-Plaisirs to Paris. Because of the level of unrest a form of martial law was placed on the city, though this proved to be ineffective. Having whittled down the powers of the King, the constitutionalists now sought to dismantle those of the Church. On October 10, a proposal came to the floor of the Assembly that stated that the government would subsume all property owned by the Catholic Church in France. Ironically, it was the Bishop of Autun – Prince Charles-Maurice de Talleyrand – who initiated the bill that would be passed one month later. A further blow was struck to Church authority, again from within, when, in October 1789, a political club at first comprising mainly deputies to the National Assembly from Brittany convened at the Jacobins' friary on the rue Saint-Honoré, not far from the Tuileries. Dominican friars had set up their first monastery on the rue Saint-Jacques in Paris, thereafter acquiring the name 'the Jacobins'. The political club, initially calling itself 'The Society of Friends of the Constitution, meeting at the Jacobins in Paris', soon acquired the same sobriquet. As they gained political momentum as the party of the people (calling all other political factions 'elitist'), they enacted policies that resulted in widespread violence against French priests and the complete intolerance of religion in general.

While plans were under way to cut every thread that had woven together the fabric of life in France for the past thousand years, the royal couple, like ordinary bourgeois French parents, spent their days supervising their children's studies and writing letters to their friends and family. The Queen oversaw her daughter's embroidery lessons as Marie-Thérèse worked on large pieces of tapestry. The King heard his daughter recite geography and history. The Dauphin, who had promised his mother that he would learn to read by the New Year, also practiced his skills out loud. Less aware than his sister of the forced effort to maintain the appearance of tranquility, he commented to a courtier that he was very excited to be able to spend so much time with his parents.

The Queen continued to correspond with Comte Mercy, whom she regarded as a lifeline, and with Madame de Polignac, who had joined the Comte d'Artois in Italy. The King, using the pseudonym 'M. d'Hanaud', also wrote long and touching letters to his former favorite, assuring her that she could always count on him despite the distance. In December, Marie Antoinette assured the Duchess that the children were fine, and wrote that she knew that her exiled friend would be pained to hear anecdotes of her former charges, adding 'my poor little girl has been a marvel to me'. Marie-Thérèse wrote her own letter to her former governess. The royal couple also received letters of concern from the Kings of Spain, Sweden and England, the formidable Empress Catherine of Russia – who advised the King to steer his own course undisturbed by the people – and, of course, Emperor Joseph, who remained steadfast and reassuring. To her childhood friends, the Princesses of Hesse, Marie

Antoinette wrote adoring accounts of the children, who, she said, were constantly with her and who provided her with her only source of happiness.

Such idle moments were few, however, and often shattered by the arrival of crowds in the palace courtyards and politicians arriving with the latest news from the National Assembly, apprizing the King of some new article of law that took away this or that privilege. The Jacobins, whose members now included Robespierre as leader, the Marquis de Mirabeau, who was widely known for his prodigious spending habits, and the orator and politician Antoine Barnave, created the beginnings of a political machine. The Jacobins' goal was to carve up France like a geometric grid into a new, uniform, socio-economically level playing field. There would be one code of taxation for all, one system of weights and measures and departments instead of unruly provinces. Although the plan appeared consummately rational – a product of the Enlightenment – their agenda provoked a spontaneous outbreak of raw passion, anathema to the Age of Reason. Turmoil, disequilibrium and widespread brutality would result in a destabilized France rather than the equitable utopia the political club had originally dreamt of.

One of the Jacobins' first proposals, meant as a grand, symbolic gesture, came across more as an attempt to mock the royal family. The Marquis de Mirabeau advised the National Assembly to insist that the King, Queen and their children wear revolutionary colors, even indoors. Madame Campan wrote that the Queen had told her that Mirabeau had previously been turned down for the post of ambassador to Constantinople. She believed the ambitious Mirabeau, thwarted in one arena, was 'a dangerous man' and that he was out for revenge as he sought to mold and influence the new government.

As the year came to a close it was apparent that tensions between the more moderate legislators and their angry counterparts were escalating. On New Year's Day, 1790, the sixth new President of the National Assembly since Mounier's resignation on October 10 came to the Tuileries Palace to offer his good wishes. His name was Jean-Nicolas Démeunier. Démeunier was an author, a Freemason and a great supporter of America, whose cause he had written about eloquently. Madame de Tourzel recalled that Démeunier was evidently touched by the sight of the Queen flanked by her two children: one, full of life and joy and too young to comprehend the misfortune that menaced him; the other, who should have known only those same innocent emotions, appearing sorrowful, yet all the more brave for her understanding. Sympathizers such as Démeunier were very much a minority, however. Three days after his visit to the Tuileries, he, too, resigned his position. The Queen wrote to Madame de Polignac that it was becoming increasingly difficult for her to correspond as they were 'under surveillance like criminals'. In the New Year, Comte Mercy, having returned to Paris despite the Queen's warnings, turned up at a Tuileries diplomatic evening and surreptitiously exchanged packets of letters with Marie Antoinette.

On February 4, 1790, the King addressed the National Assembly asking that the new order proceed in a calm fashion and without a repeat of the violence of the previous July and October in which thousands had died. Louis had arranged for the purchase of foreign grain, and he called on the National Assembly to forge a path to financial solvency without further bloodshed. The King offered the legislators his support, declaring that he was raising his son, their future king, to understand the new France and that the National Assembly would have his full support if they could make the French people happy. He implored the Assembly to establish peace and stability so that those French men and women who had fled the country could return without fear or anxiety.

Sixteen days after the King's conciliatory speech, the Queen's brother, Emperor Joseph II, died aged forty-eight. Joseph had been sick for two years after having accompanied his army into battle against the Ottomans. The war had not only turned out to be a fiasco, but it had also ruined his health. Joseph had been Marie Antoinette's champion, her father figure, and the man, with his vast armies and allies, who loomed over Europe as his sister's protector. On February 27, the day that Marie Antoinette learned of Joseph's death, her brother Leopold was crowned his successor. Leopold, less close to his sister than Joseph, nonetheless wrote an affectionate letter to the Queen of France offering her and her family support, including refuge at the Hofburg Palace. Marie Antoinette replied expressing her gratitude but remained adamant that she would not be separated from her husband, who was not prepared to leave France.

On Sunday, April 4, 1790, Easter Sunday, Marie-Thérèse was due to have her first communion, but even a day meant for celebration turned into a subdued affair. Like any other French girl, she dressed in white and waited with excitement to receive the sacrament. Customarily, the daughter of His Most Christian King would have been feted on this day with cheering crowds hailing her on her way to the church and a grand reception afterwards. The fear of an ugly spectacle, however, forced plans to be scaled down. As any event attended by the King would, at this point, have required the presence of a battery of soldiers, and permission from the National Assembly to sanction the expenditure, Marie-Thérèse was to be deprived of both her father's presence at her communion and that of her brother. The day before, the Dauphin surprised his governess, revealing that he was more aware of his own unfortunate situation than he had let on. He explained to Madame de Tourzel that he longed for his garden for if he still had it he would have gathered beautiful flowers to make a bouquet for his sister for her special day.

Before leaving the Tuileries, Marie-Thérèse appeared before her adoring father for his approval. In the presence of a small group of courtiers, which included Madame de Tourzel, Pauline and Hüe, who each recorded an account of the event, the Queen instructed Marie-Thérèse to kneel before the King and receive his benediction. The King addressed his eleven-year-old daughter solemnly:

It is from the bottom of my heart, my daughter, that I bless you and ask Heaven to give you the grace to understand the great action you are about to take. Your heart is innocent and pure in the eyes of God; may your vows be agreeable to Him. Offer them to Him for your mother and for me. Ask Him to impart me with His grace necessary for me to provide happiness to those in the empire which He has given me, to those people whom I consider my children. Ask Him to deign to conserve the purity of religion in this realm, and remember well, my daughter, that this holy religion is the source of happiness and the sustenance against the adversities of life. Do not believe that you are without shelter. You are so young, yet you have seen your father afflicted more than once. You do not know, my daughter, what Providence has destined for you: whether you will stay in this kingdom or if you will live in another. Wherever the hand of God places you, remember that you will teach by your example, do good every time you find the occasion. But, above all, my child, alleviate the unfortunate with all of your power. God had us born on the rung where we are to work for their happiness and console their pains. Go to the Altar where you are awaited, and beseech God for mercy to never allow you to forget the advice of your loving father.[1]

The King then held his daughter in his arms and added, 'Pray, my child, for France, and for us. The prayers of the innocent might soften divine anger.'[2]

In addition to a grand reception, it was also customary for the daughter of the King of France to receive a suite of diamonds on this special day;

however, that tradition was also dispensed with for Marie-Thérèse, as the King explained to his daughter:

> I know that you are too reasonable, my daughter, to believe that at the moment when you should be entirely occupied with the care of adorning your heart and making of it a dignified sanctuary of the divinity, to attach a great price to these artificial ornaments. Moreover, my child, the public's misery is extreme, the poor abound, and undoubtedly you would like it better to go without gems than to know that others are going without bread.[3]

Marie-Thérèse, Ernestine, who was also receiving her first communion, Madame de Tourzel and Pauline, Madame de Mackau and the Duchesse de Charost made their way from the Tuileries to the local parish church, Saint Germain-l'Auxerrois. This was a small medieval chapel used by the kings of France when they had lived at the Louvre. The Queen, determined not to let her daughter feel that she had been abandoned, made her way to the church on her own, disguised in simple clothes. Although Marie Antoinette sat quietly apart from the royal party, Marie-Thérèse knew that her mother was in the audience. The only public statement or acknowledgment that their majesties had chosen to make on the occasion of Madame Royale's communion was an offering of alms to various churches in Paris. Privately, however, the King expressed his delight in a letter to Madame de Polignac. He wrote that her 'little friend had had her first communion at Easter. We have all been content with the way she comported herself. I also see with pleasure that she remembers you, as she should. The other is fine and is reading well enough at present.'

The 'other' – the Dauphin – who had expressed such sadness at not having been able to grow flowers to give to his sister on her special day, was shortly afterwards given a small garden by his father near the Seine. This same little plot of earth would later be given to the King of Rome by his father, Napoleon I; to the Duc de Bordeaux, by his grandfather, Charles X; and to the Comte de Paris by his grandfather, King Louis-Philippe. Every time Louis Charles went to tend his plot armed soldiers of the National Guard would escort him. The Dauphin was so excited about having 'his very own soldiers' that he asked to have his own National Guard uniform made for him, which he would wear whenever he went to the garden. The tiny royal soldier chatted away with his guards about 'paparoi' – 'daddyking' – and his mother 'mamareine' – 'mummyqueen', which was said to have melted the most hardened hearts among them.

Word of the gatherings spread among the Parisians and the Abbot Antheaume approached the King for permission to form a corps called the 'Regiment of the Dauphin' made up of young boys who wanted to emulate the little Dauphin. With Louis Charles as their patron, the boys became cadets, and got to dress and parade like soldiers. Twice a week, they held military drills under Antheaume's supervision and they would march on the streets in the prelate's neighborhood and every now and then present themselves at the Tuileries for inspection.

Five days after Marie-Thérèse's first communion, the National Assembly passed a vote declaring that the Catholic Church would no longer be the official state religion. In the south of France, Catholics and Protestants resumed old battles. The National Assembly also issued an order that commanded all priests to swear oaths of loyalty to the State instead of the Church. Some monarchs like Marie Antoinette's late brother Joseph whose public role was to uphold the power of the Church were privately admirers of the Enlightenment, and were not especially religious. Louis, however, was deeply pious and considered such moves to erode the Church's powers as blasphemous.

On May 23, Louis XVI and Marie Antoinette led the Holy Sacrament procession to Saint Germain-l'Auxerrois and attended the Fête de la Pentecôte accompanied by some of the members of the Assembly who believed that the attacks on the Church in France were overly harsh and vindictive. Marie-Thérèse was not feeling well that day, so she and her brother stayed behind and watched their parents through a window at the Louvre Palace. Over the course of the year, while the National Assembly turned their powers against the Church, Marie-Thérèse observed very closely the awful conflict of conscience that caused her father so much suffering. For Louis, daily prayers and strong Christian faith were inseparable from the notion of the King's divine right, and the apostasy of the French revolutionaries was appalling and incomprehensible.

As the first anniversary of the storming of the Bastille grew closer, General Lafayette, the National Assembly, and the royal family all feared another potentially violent insurrection. A great celebration called the Fête de la Fédération was planned for July 14, which, it was hoped, would appease the masses. In the meantime Lafayette urged the powers of the Assembly to permit the King and his family to leave for Saint-Cloud. The castle, on the outskirts of Paris, would keep the King and Queen somewhat out of harm's way, but it was close enough to the capital for the King to maintain a presence. Soldiers were posted around the estate to keep the royal party safe and at the same time reassure those who worried that the King and Queen might try to flee. It was announced that the entire family would return to Paris for the festivities that would take place on the fourteenth.

The royal family left for Saint-Cloud on June 4, the first anniversary of the death of the first Dauphin. They had been under house arrest at the Tuileries for eight months. Saint-Cloud would give them an opportunity to hunt, garden, and receive visitors, which would include the Comte de Provence who had leased a house just inside the city gates in order to visit his brother every day.

Madame Royale, having received her first communion, now ate every meal with her father, according to the ancient rules of court etiquette. No one except the Princes of the Blood and those invited by the King who had been presented at court could dine at the same table as the King, but Louis broke with such etiquette and invited Pauline de Tourzel to join them for meals. Pauline was not a member of the Bourbon royal family and, because of her age, she had not even been presented at court. The King's aunts pointed out that the rules of the court must never be broken, but Louis declared that extraordinary times required a change of attitude, and Pauline acquired a regular place at the King's table, sitting between her mother the governess and Madame Royale. Once in a while, the King would seat Pauline near him as a sign of honor; Pauline also recalled her delight at being asked by the Comtesse de Provence to sit next to her. His Majesty tried to entertain the teenagers, and, one evening, in a jovial mood, Louis taught an awestruck Pauline to play billiards. Pauline recalled later that it was that particular summer, the summer at Saint-Cloud in 1790, which cemented the beginning of a lifelong friendship with Marie-Thérèse – a friendship from which Pauline would be the beneficiary of many kindnesses. Pauline would always dismiss criticism that Marie-Thérèse was 'haughty', insisting that these tales had circulated among people who had no real acquaintance with Madame Royale and that the Princess possessed 'an excellent heart'.

Marie-Thérèse observed her parents and their constant agony – their profound grief for the first Dauphin, the absence of their friends and family, and the violent scenes of July 14 and October 6, which intruded into everyone's thoughts. The King admitted in a letter sent to Madame de Polignac from Saint-Cloud that despite the summer break from the strife in Paris, he had not been able to divert his mind from the difficulties that had befallen his family and those dear to him in exile. 'I arrived in the countryside. The air will do us well, but this sojourn we appear changed.

The luncheon salon – how sad – none of you is there. I do not lose hope that we find each other.'

Political infighting had resulted in the creation of splinter factions from the Jacobins. The Queen had been correct when she privately remarked that Mirabeau possessed unbounded ambition. The Marquis, while professing his devotion to the new government, was hoping that there would be a return to absolutism with himself as the King's right hand. He also needed money. In early July, Mirabeau came to Saint-Cloud to visit the royal couple. Marie Antoinette did not trust him but she understood that he was now in a position to benefit her family. The two struck a deal: Mirabeau would work for the good of the royal family and Marie Antoinette would pay him the handsome sum of 5,000 *livres* a month. They were an unlikely pair of conspirators. Mirabeau's enemies, already suspicious, noticed that he was spending a great deal of money and that he had bought an impressive house in Paris. The high-living aristocrat was denounced as a traitor to the revolution. He retorted that Marie Antoinette was a marvel of strength and solidity, famously adding, 'The King has only one man: his wife.' Some fifteen years later, this same compliment would echo eerily when Napoleon referred to Marie-Thérèse with awe as 'the only man in the family', after she had fearlessly defied him.

The celebrations for the fourteenth, the first anniversary of the storming of the Bastille, were orchestrated by the National Assembly. The spectacle was held on the Champ de Mars, a field named for the god of war, which faced the École Militaire.[4] Although it was planned to be a 'reconciliation of the people of France', it proved to be an odd affair – more a military parade evoking threat than a historic tableau celebrating fourteen centuries of a nation. Each department of France was allowed to send a certain number of soldiers, lieutenants, marshals and police; each battalion so many leaders. The Swiss Guard, their numbers small, was allowed to send most of their men, the navy its representatives. The evening before the celebrations, the King inspected soldiers from every division at the Tuileries, while the Queen introduced the soldiers to the Children of France.

According to an account by the Queen's childhood friend, Joseph Weber, that same day a particularly unwelcome guest presented himself at the Tuileries. Despite General Lafayette's warning to him not to return, the Duc d'Orléans had crept back into France. Monsieur de Simolin, ambassador to France from Russia, was so disgusted he dashed off a letter to the Empress informing her that although the King had not given permission, Orléans had had the audacity to travel to Paris. The Queen received him with good grace, however, which stunned him. The Duchesse de Tourzel wrote that the discomfited Duke could only mumble bits of conversation in her presence. The following day, when the Duc d'Orléans attended the Fête de la Fédération he heard cries of 'Vive le Roi!', and realized that his cousin, the King, although humbled, was not yet vanquished.

The delegates and soldiers gathered at four o'clock in the morning at the site of the old Bastille. They proceeded across the right bank of the Seine to the neighborhood of the Champs-Élysées where a bridge of boats spanned the river. The procession made its way to the Champ de Mars, where a few days before over 3,000 workers had constructed an amphitheater around the sides of the arena. The seating proved insufficient for the nearly 600,000 people who had come from all over France to observe their military leaders, the clergy and their political representatives swear an oath of allegiance to the King and the country's brand new constitution. Those who did not arrive at the Champ de Mars before dawn were left to line the streets of Paris where they stood in the pouring rain for the entire day. Twelve hundred musicians filled the air with patriotic songs and military marches. The royal family appeared at noon and assembled on the balcony of the military school, which had been festooned with fabrics to create an enormous tent. Although thrones had been provided, for most of the day the King, Queen, Marie-Thérèse and the little Dauphin – dressed in his National Guard uniform – remained standing, stirred from their seats by the powerful performances that evoked equally powerful emotions.

In the center of the circus rose the 'Altar of the Fatherland' where at four in the afternoon Talleyrand, in his role as the Bishop of Autun, led Mass and blessed the eighty-three banners that flew, one for each of the new departments of France. As he did so the sun came out. With General Lafayette on his white horse at the head of the National Guard, the oath was sworn, swords were raised aloft, and the Queen elevated her son in her arms to the crowd. She too affirmed the oath and when the crowds returned with 'Vive le Dauphin!' the little boy smiled and waved to the multitude. Shortly afterwards the rain started again, and the Queen wrapped her son in a shawl. Many who had doubted the Queen's sincerity saw this tender and motherly gesture as proof that she was in fact genuine. Marie Antoinette felt the crowd's shift in sentiment and for a moment felt reassured.

The celebrations went on for days. The royal family rode in an open calèche to inspect the troops around the Étoile. Cheered by the enthusiastic reception, the King told the officers that he would visit each and every one of their provinces. Although the King was not able to keep his promise, his daughter would not forget the idea and would later use it as a brilliant public relations move. She would also never forget that, although it was General Lafayette who was slated to be the center of attention, it was her father upon whom all eyes gazed. Most people had never seen their King before; they wanted to see him and touch him. According to the newspaper and eyewitness accounts, the masses were simply dazzled by his presence and many were overcome with emotion.

After the fourteenth the royal family went back to Saint-Cloud to sit out the rest of the summer. On October 30, they begrudgingly returned to the Tuileries to find themselves once more confined to the battleground of Paris, where the political situation had grown worse. Two days before the Fête de la Fédération in July, the National Assembly had passed a significant and inflammatory law, the Civil Constitution of the Clergy, which placed all clerics living in France under the authority of the new French government, forcing its priests to take an oath of loyalty to the constitutional government of France and forbidding any foreign sovereignty over religion in France. This law immediately split papists and secularists – the King squarely on the side of the former. The streets of Paris filled with crowds who burned effigies of the Pope, and anyone in clerical garb was attacked. As the pressure mounted to sign the decree, Louis eventually gave in. In response to the order that eradicated papal power in France, the Pope retaliated with his own dictum that any priest who complied with the law would be suspended from his parish. Even the Americans living in Paris, proud of their own new government founded on the basis of the separation of Church and State, expressed shock at the violence perpetrated against priests ostensibly in the name of democracy.

That winter, pamphlets appeared all over France accusing the Queen of adultery and questioning the legitimacy of the five-year-old Dauphin. The National Assembly passed a law stating that the Princes of the Blood and the two Children of France could no longer inherit the feudal lands or any other items belonging to the Crown, including property and furniture. The Queen was accused of having slept with everyone from her brother-in-law to General Lafayette, and the reappearance of another enemy in Paris, the infamous Madame de la Motte, perpetrator of the diamond necklace swindle, fuelled even more insidious lies about the Queen.

After the New Year, the King's two elderly aunts, living at the Château de Bellevue just outside Paris, decided that all of the commotion was too much for them and that they wished to leave France. In early 1791, the

National Assembly met to debate the future of the King's aunts. The ladies were initially given permission to leave the country but shortly after their departure on February 19, while their home was being ransacked, they were arrested at Arnay-le-Duc and detained for days while the Assembly once again discussed their future. The debate went on for days and was so intense that General de Menou joked that all of Europe held their breath to see if two old ladies were going to go to church in Paris or Rome. Finally, it was agreed that although the Assembly had the power to refuse their release, it did not want blood on its hands should some harm befall the women; King Louis XV's aged daughters were thus freed and permitted to leave the country.

The Jacobins had been gathering momentum in the Assembly and were becoming intoxicated with their newfound power. On March 22, 1791, the Assembly issued a diktat stating that the Queen would no longer have parental rights over the Dauphin and the State was to be his regent. On March 28, fearing civil war, the Assembly decreed that the King could not venture more than 50 miles beyond Paris. In early April, the Queen received word of the death of her ally and collaborator, the Marquis de Mirabeau, whose hard-living had finally caught up with him. At noon on April 18, Holy Monday, the royal family boarded a carriage in eager anticipation of a prearranged two-week break at Saint-Cloud. As the coach approached the gates to exit the palace, the National Guard blocked their path and bolted the doors shut. For Louis, who had faced the events of the past two years with patience and dignity, this was the last straw.

The Comte de Provence, who was with the party, wrote that as the dispirited group returned to the Tuileries Palace and alighted from their coach he was awestruck by the strength and stoicism of his niece. As her entire family crumbled around her, the twelve-year-old Princess maintained her composure. She passed from her father to her mother to her aunts and uncle, tearful, but with a gentle smile on her lips, hugging each of them in turn and offering soft words of comfort. The Count, finally able to utter a word, stood before his niece and offered this extraordinary girl a blessing: 'Oh, my child. May Heaven rain the happiness on you it refuses your family.'

CHAPTER VIII
A DANGEROUS GAME

THE MUTINY OF the guards at the Tuileries reflected the advent of a more sinister, anti-monarchical mood in the capital. The events of Holy Monday had revealed just how vulnerable the royal family was without their advocate, Mirabeau, and the King at last accepted that his family was in grave danger and that they must leave Paris, though he still had no desire to abandon France.

Marie Antoinette, however, had long been convinced of the need to get out of France altogether. Unbeknown to her husband, she had been formulating detailed escape plans with the complicity of her brother, Emperor Leopold II, Comte Mercy, Comte Fersen, and a French General, the Marquis de Bouillé. The previous November the Queen had contacted de Bouillé, commander of the Metz region, to ask for help. In late December 1790, Fersen had commissioned a berlin for a 'Madame de Korff' and obtained false passports for the royal family and their immediate staff. Before any departure, the Queen needed to ensure that her brother, Leopold, would provide money, soldiers and protection. To that end, Mercy, back again in Brussels, facilitated the depositing of money from Leopold to Marie Antoinette in England and Belgium. As early as February 3, 1791, the Queen wrote Mercy that an escape plan was now under way: the royal family would leave in the evening and head in an easterly direction toward Montmédy. Although the Queen had voluntarily returned the crown jewels to the Assembly along with the Mazarin diamonds, some rose-cut diamonds and a priceless string of pearls brought to France by Anne of Austria – which the Queen nonetheless considered French national property – she sent some of her personal diamonds to Mercy with instructions that if she did not survive the jewelry should be given to her daughter, Marie-Thérèse.

Inside the Tuileries the Queen had the loyal assistance of her lady-in-waiting, Madame Campan. In March, Campan recalled that the Queen told Campan to have an unusually large quantity of children's clothing made, presumably for the royal family's life in exile. Campan, afraid that the sudden and rather large quantity of clothing would attract attention, commented to Marie Antoinette that the Queen of France could buy her linen and gowns anywhere she wanted. The Queen persisted and Madame Campan, rightly convinced that there were spies at the Tuileries, nonetheless proceeded at great risk to fulfill every command issued to her. She used her own son as a model for the Dauphin's clothes and a niece for Madame Royale's. Once complete, the wardrobes were dispatched to a Madame Cardon, now drawn into the conspiracy. Cardon, one of Madame Campan's aunts, was a widow who lived in Arras and who owned property in Austrian Flanders, which she would visit from time to time. Should she decide to visit her own estates, she would have aroused little suspicion. Campan's aunt was now ready to depart at a moment's notice.

In early May 1791, the Queen wrote to her brother-in-law, the Comte d'Artois, poised for battle along with his German and émigré allies along the eastern frontier, that he should halt all plans of attack on France until the royal family reached safety. The King was only made aware of the escape plan in late May, when he was required to send the French General, the Marquis de Bouillé, 1 million *livres* worth of promissory notes for the General's army. While frantic letters arrived at the Hofburg from the Queen of France to her brother, the Emperor, Louis and Marie Antoinette continued to behave as if they were resigned to whatever outcome the people determined.

On May 30, as Madame Campan finished her duties for the Queen and was about to begin a vacation in Auvergne, Marie Antoinette confided to her that the royal family would depart between June 15 and 20, when Campan was not on duty. The Queen told Campan that she could only take one woman with her and, as it was imperative that no one had advance warning or could be accused of complicity, that servant would be whoever was on duty at the time. Marie Antoinette instructed Campan to head for Lyon the moment she heard that the royal family had escaped and that the Queen would send for her from there. Before she left, Campan notified Madame Cardon to send the children's clothing to Brussels immediately. Campan told the Queen that she was worried that the number of people aware of the royal family's imminent departure was growing and that not all of these people could be trusted. It was true: there was a growing list of foreign ambassadors at the various courts of Europe who had learned that an escape plan had been hatched. General de Bouillé, who waited in Montmédy with 15,000 men and 4,800 horses, was hardly inconspicuous, and Léonard, the Queen's hairdresser, who aimed to meet up with his royal patron once clear of Paris, was known to enjoy gossip and often told many of his client's secrets.

At the beginning of June, the Queen's *parfumier*, Jean-Louis Fargeon, received a note asking him to come immediately to the Tuileries but to enter by the side door at the Pavillon de Flore. Fargeon duly arrived and was surprised when the Queen placed an extraordinarily large order of her favorite scents and pomades. Fargeon quickly realized the reason. Madame de Tourzel also learned of the secret plan. In February the Queen had told Comte Mercy that she intended to take Madame de Tourzel with the family on their flight of escape, but then had a change of heart. According to Madame de Tourzel, one morning the Queen suggested to the governess that she ought to travel to Plombières to take the waters there. The Queen then whispered that the royal family was about to leave Paris, but she felt that Madame de Tourzel was too old to withstand such an adventure. Madame de Tourzel declined, refusing to leave the children, though she did send her daughter Pauline to stay with cousins in the country. The elderly Madame de Mackau, also informed, took refuge at a convent.

The intention was that the family would leave in one carriage on the night of June 19. However, Madame de Rochereuil, a chambermaid in the service of the Dauphin and one of Lafayette's spies, went on duty that night, so the royal family waited one extra day. Unfortunately, that day was the longest of the year; the evening, the shortest.

It seems that very few people who were close to the royal family did not know of the escape plan. One of those was Ernestine, who was sent to the country on Monday morning, June 20, 1791, to visit Monsieur de Lambriquet, her 'father'. The Queen's friend, the Comtesse d'Ossun, received a last-minute letter on that Monday. In it, the Queen apologized for not warning the Countess, as she knew that it would be dangerous for anyone to have been implicated in the plot. The other two kept in the dark were the Queen's own children. On the same Monday, the 20th, Marie-Thérèse noticed that her parents seemed agitated, but she did not know why. At five o'clock in the afternoon the Queen took the children for a very public walk in the Tivoli Gardens (located at the site which is today

the Gare Saint-Lazare). Owned by financier Monsieur Boutin, the beautiful gardens, designed after the spectacular Villa d'Este's Renaissance
paradise in Tivoli near Rome, were commonly referred to as the 'Folie-
Boutin'. While Marie Antoinette performed as if she had not a care in the
world, she whispered to her daughter that things were going to happen,
and they might be separated for a while, but that Marie-Thérèse was not
to be uneasy. Although Marie-Thérèse had only a limited understanding
of this cryptic message, she knew by now to trust her mother.

On returning to the Tuileries the Queen maintained the pretense and
informed the commander of her guards that she would be going out the
following day and would require a bodyguard. Meanwhile, Madame de
Tourzel, following the Queen's lead 'to throw my own people off the
scent of departure', told her own maid that she wanted a bath drawn for
her the next day. The evening of the 20th appeared to be very ordinary:
the Comte de Provence and his wife joined the family for dinner, though
at the dinner table the King whispered to his younger brother that they
were all to depart Paris that very night. His Majesty ordered his brother to
head toward Longwy and the Austrian lowlands. The Comte de Provence, who was scheduled to leave at the same time but by a different
route, helped the King write a declaration to be left behind explaining the
reasons for his departure. Provence and his wife took two separate
carriages into exile that evening traveling, as the King had ordered,
toward Longwy. The count arrived safely in the Netherlands where he
would remain until events would force him to join his youngest brother,
d'Artois, and his army of counter-revolutionaries in Coblenz.

The Tuileries Palace was surrounded by over six hundred National
Guards. Inside, everything appeared as usual. The Dauphin went to bed
at nine; Madame Royale at ten. A few minutes after she had climbed
into her bed, Marie-Thérèse was stirred by her mother. The Queen
ordered the children, helped by their governess, to dress immediately.
Marie-Thérèse put on a simple calico dress. The Dauphin was disguised
in girl's clothing and told that he was going to a great castle where there
would be soldiers for him to play-fight with. Surveying the feminine
clothing, he remarked that his apparel was clearly meant for a comedy
and not for a battle. The children, accompanied by Mesdames Brunier,
de Neuville and de Tourzel, made their way with the Queen to a private
exit near the ground floor apartments recently vacated by the Duc de
Villequier. A bodyguard smuggled into the palace by Comte Fersen, and
three more men disguised as couriers, shepherded the group of women
and children.

At about 10.30, the Queen placed her children in Fersen's hands at the Cour des Princes. Fersen, dressed as a coachman, had been waiting in the courtyard with a small carriage ready to take the royal children to safety. When she saw that she was going to leave without her mother, Marie-Thérèse started to cry, sobbing silently. Fersen later wrote of the pathos of this lovely young girl, her face bathed in tears as she boarded his carriage in the dark. He and Madame de Tourzel, who was in possession of a note signed by the King authorizing her to travel with his children, knew that they were risking their own lives in their attempt to save the royal children.

Fersen, an experienced soldier, performed his duty. He drove the carriage at a slow pace around the neighborhood to avoid suspicion. He then stationed the coach at the Petit Carrousel near the Tuileries to wait for the King and Queen. Inside the coach, the passengers waited nervously. The Dauphin hid on the floor under Madame de Tourzel's skirt. Marie-Thérèse saw General Lafayette pass very near to the carriage on his way to the King's *coucher*. An hour later, a woman approached the carriage and Marie-Thérèse held her breath in fear until the door opened and the person was revealed to be her aunt, Madame Elisabeth, who had made her way to the coach alone on foot. When Madame Elisabeth entered the carriage, she accidentally stepped on the foot of the little boy who, realizing the seriousness of the situation, and that they were not, in fact, playing a game, stifled a cry. Madame Elisabeth reassured the children that their parents were fine and that they would be with them soon.

The Queen waited until her servants were asleep and then changed into simple clothes – a plain taupe dress and a black hat with a thick violet veil. It was impossible for the King to get away until his *coucher* had finished, and even then Louis would be tied by a cord round his wrist to that of his valet – a tradition in case His Most Christian Majesty should need anything during the night. After the *coucher*, General Lafayette once again made his rounds and all seemed quiet. The King waited until his valet was asleep and then slipped the cord from his wrist. Dressed in the wig and costume of a lackey – a dark green jacket with mother-of-pearl buttons, a white satin vest, black silk pantaloons, white stockings and shoes with silver oval buckles – Louis escaped, as had the Queen, to meet a guard provided by Comte Fersen. The King then made his way to rendezvous with his family at midnight, and once the Queen was assured that the King had escaped the palace, she, accompanied by a member of the loyal *gardes du corps,* made her way to the Petit Carrousel also. En route, Marie Antoinette spied General Lafayette, who had been assigned by the National Assembly to keep a close eye on the royal family and who was making another tour of the palace grounds. As soon as he was out of sight she continued to the coach. Marie-Thérèse remembered watching her parents reunite, the King declaring: 'How happy I am that you are here,' as he embraced his wife. Madame de Tourzel recalled that the King and Queen then both embraced her.

Finally together, the carriage bearing the royal party began to proceed through Paris slowly and cautiously. Madame Brunier and Madame de Neuville followed behind in a calèche. Two very tense hours later and well behind schedule, their caravan reached the city gates. Once outside Paris, at Bondy, they looked for the second carriage to take the family to safety – the berlin that had been ordered for 'Madame de Korff' six months earlier. When Fersen finally discovered the carriage, liveried in bottle green with black trim, lemon-yellow axle and wheels, he found that it had only four horses rather than the necessary six and so hooked up two horses from the smaller carriage. The King, aware that Fersen was in love with the Queen, graciously thanked the Swede for his help. Fersen insisted that he wanted to remain with the royal family to guide them to freedom. The King, however, declined Fersen's offer, and the two men bade each other adieu. Marie-Thérèse did not understand the significance of that moment until she was much older, but recalled that Fersen mounted his horse and set off for Holland at full gallop at the same time the royal family's coach began its own flight.

The papers carried by the party identified them as: a valet by the name of 'Durand' (the King), a 'Madame Bonnet' (the Queen), 'Aglaë' – a girl of about twelve (Madame Royale), her younger 'sister' 'Amélie' (the Dauphin), and their nurse 'Rosalie' (Madame Elisabeth). Madame de Tourzel was primed to be the 'Baronne de Korff', a middle-aged woman and the alleged owner of the coach. There was, in fact, a real Madame de Korff, a Russian woman whose passport had been handed by the ambassador Simolin to Fersen. Three of the King's most loyal *gardes du corps* posed as drivers.

The interior of the coach, equipped as a traveling home, was lined in white velvet, and contained a larder, a cooker, a canteen big enough for eight bottles of water and spirits, a table that could be raised for eating, and a leather chamber pot. Stories told after the ill-fated journey often exaggerated the carriage's cumbersomeness. However, it had been constructed well for its purpose, and its top traveling speed – about 6 miles per hour – was no slower than a typical cabriolet pulled by two horses.

Marie-Thérèse recalled that the journey was at first uneventful, though its outcome would haunt her for the rest of her life. Town after town passed as the royals raced toward the eastern border. The careful planning of the Queen, Comte Fersen and their co-conspirators seemed to be working well. Posing as servants, the royal family stopped and changed horses at ramshackle inns. They reached Meaux at six in the morning and changed horses. At ten in the morning they stopped in the tiny village of Viels-Maisons, where the King relaxed for a few moments. The Queen, nervous that he was taking too long and was being too cavalier about timing, prayed that nothing would prevent them from reaching Pont-de-Somme-Vesle, a little over an hour from Châlons. There, the Duc de Choiseul would be waiting for them with his own cavalry of mercenaries and royalists.

Though due to arrive at Châlons between 12.30 and 1.30 in the afternoon of the following day, June 21, the King's carriage passed through the town hours later, at some time between 3 and 4 p.m. At Pont-de-Somme-Vesle, the Duc de Choiseul and his men, thinking that the King's delay meant that he had changed his route, were nowhere to be seen. The cavalry had also received confusing information from the Queen's hairdresser, who was hours ahead, near Verdun.

In the meantime, the disappearance of the royal family had been discovered in Paris in the early hours of the morning. The National Assembly had ordered Lafayette to dispatch soldiers on horseback to catch the escaping berlin, or at least spread word throughout the provinces that the King was on the run. The Comte d'Hézecques claimed that Lafayette had been forewarned by one of his spies at the Tuileries that the royal family was going to take flight. Hézecques was also certain that on the evening of June 20, the General had, in fact, seen Madame Royale in her carriage. It was also noted that Baillon, one of General Lafayette's aides de camp, had arrived in Châlons long before the King. Although when he appeared before the National Assembly on the morning of June 21, Lafayette claimed he could not have anticipated the escape plan, it seems that he had, in fact, set a trap for the King. After all, the General's reputation, badly tarnished from his blunders during the invasion of Versailles in October 1789, could once again sparkle with the well-timed capture of the fugitive King.

Marie-Thérèse wrote in her account that when the party arrived at Châlons-sur-Marne they were recognized immediately. There had been a series of sightings along the way in various towns and the royal family believed that their disguises had failed them and that they had been identified owing to their fame. In truth, the King bore little resemblance in real life to the slim and handsome engraving of his face on the coins of the realm, and he had in fact been apprehended because the postmasters and gatekeepers in many of the towns had been alerted to watch for the carriage, a detailed description of which had been circulated. The son of the local postmaster in Sainte-Menehould, a Jacobin leader named Drouet, received a note from a man named Viet, the postman from Châlons, which read, 'On behalf of the National Assembly, it is hereby ordered that all good citizens make every attempt to stop the berlin with six horses in which, suspected of traveling is the King, the Queen, Madame Elisabeth, the Dauphin and Madame Royale.' The local populace noticed a green berlin led by six horses. In addition, its three coachmen wore the livery of the Prince de Condé, the famous military hero of the Seven Years War, who was now poised in Coblenz with an army. Marie-Thérèse remembered that one of the officers in Clermont whispered to the King that His Majesty had been betrayed.

The royal family proceeded with great anxiety through Sainte-Menehould. Drouet was determined to be the man to personally apprehend the King, but should royalist troops of the Prince de Condé be nearby ready for combat, he had insufficient militia at his disposal for battle. Instead, Drouet ordered his local compatriots to keep watch on the vehicle, while he and the innkeeper, Guillaume La Hure, galloped on to Varennes, a town divided by the River Aire, to warn of the King's approach. Everyone knew that in Varennes the King would have to stop and change horses, and while the King's carriage was disabled, the townspeople could strike.

At Varennes, Drouet supervised the overturning of a furniture cart in the road so that the King could not reach the royalist soldiers waiting on the other side of the bridge. Young revolutionaries bearing torches surrounded the King's carriage. A small group of armed men seized their horses' heads and conducted the carriage slowly through town. Marie-Thérèse recalled having heard a salvo of shrieks, 'Stop! Stop!' as their carriage proceeded. The rebels ignited fires and rang bells to announce the capture of the royal family.

The royal party was taken to the home of the Mayor, a man named Sauce who sold candles, where they were to spend the night. Marie-Thérèse explained that her father 'kept himself in the farthest corner of the room, but unfortunately his portrait was there'. However, it took quite some time for the people to be convinced that, based on the portrait on Sauce's wall, the overweight, middle-aged man in their midst was indeed His Majesty and not some mere aristocrat. All through the night, unruly peasants with pitchforks stood guard outside the Mayor's home. Madame Sauce feared that her neighbors would take retribution against her and her husband for 'harboring' the royal family, and so she felt great relief when, at about three o'clock in the morning, Lafayette's aide de camp, Baillon, and another officer arrived to escort the King and his family back to Paris. Certain that his well-paid-for cavalry would arrive to rescue them, Louis tried to stall for time, asking Baillon not to disturb his children, who were sleeping. Baillon informed the King that if he thought he could prevent the soldier from doing his job, His Majesty was mistaken.

The cavalry, however, was nowhere to be seen. General Bouillé's son and his army had been stranded the other side of the bridge for hours and, while the King was being taken prisoner, the young Bouillé had fallen asleep. The young Duc de Choiseul, son of the minister to the late King Louis XV, meanwhile, directed his forces toward Varennes but had become lost in the woods and did not arrive until daylight.

When Choiseul at last arrived in town, he was directed to the Mayor's house and was allowed to meet with the King. Choiseul then presented Louis with a harebrained plan of escape. He could provide the royal family with seven horses and they could all ride away! The King, worried that one of his children in flight might fall or be hit by a bullet, refused the scheme. Louis had no choice but to surrender and to face the crowds of Varennes. The local rebels ordered the royal family back into their carriage and back to Paris. Having neither changed clothes nor slept, and traveling in stifling heat, the royal family prepared to return to the capital. The carriage wended its way back through the same towns it had traveled through on its way east, the very towns whose monuments had been erected to honor the marriage of their King and Queen some twenty years earlier.

Word of the King's attempted escape had, it seemed, traveled much faster than the royal berlin. The perception that the King was abandoning France inspired anger and contempt among the citizens all along the route back to Paris. In Sainte-Menehould, a local aristocrat named Dampierre, a royalist who had come to see the King's carriage, was flung to the ground, trampled by a horse and hacked to bits by a saber-wielding Jacobin. The coach traveled back through Châlons, where Marie-Thérèse felt they were treated kindly, and through Épernay, where they were intercepted by representatives of the National Assembly sent to escort the royal family back to Paris. The representatives – Pétion, Barnave, Mau-bourg, Dumas, and his nephew, La Rue – stopped the carriage and accused the King of trying to escape the country. The King replied that they were mistaken; his destination was Montmédy, and he had had no intention of leaving his kingdom. The men then ordered Marie-Thérèse and Madame Elisabeth out of their carriage so that they could travel in another one while the men shared their watch between two coaches. When Madame Royale refused to budge, Antoine Barnave and Jérôme Pétion climbed in the royal berlin. Barnave inserted himself between the King and Queen, who put the Dauphin on her lap. Pétion positioned himself between Madame de Tourzel and the King's sister, both women taking turns to have Marie-Thérèse on their laps.

Barnave and Pétion wrote reports for the National Assembly about their journey with the royal family. Both men commented that they found the royal family surprisingly likeable and ordinary. Pétion's account is, however, risible and wholly unreliable. He fantasized that the pious twenty-seven-year-old Madame Elisabeth found him so attractive that they flirted with one another during the journey and that as she began to doze, she rested her head on his shoulder, and that they exchanged glances in the moonlight. Pétion wrote that as soon as Marie-Thérèse fell asleep, he stretched out his arm and Madame Elisabeth slipped her arm through his and he 'felt the movements of the body and the warmth which passed through her clothing . . . I believe that if we had been alone, that if, by some enchantment, the others had vanished, she would have slipped into my arms and would have given herself up to the promptings of nature.' When he was thirsty, the vulgar Pétion asked Madame Royale for a drink and on the final day of the journey he placed a horrified Marie-Thérèse on his lap, writing that she must have enjoyed herself because he was so handsome. One of the less likely outcomes of the journey was the bond that developed between the Queen and Barnave, who would shortly serve as her advisor.

The children were terrified as crowds tried to overturn the carriage and poke lances through its sides. All along the road peasants brandished rifles and scythes, and bloody incidents continued throughout the haul back to Paris. When the family stopped for a moment in the village of Chouilly, the crowd spat in the King's face and some tore at Marie Antoinette's dress. In Épernay, the children heard someone cry that she would eat the heart of the Queen. Another woman screamed that she would see the Queen go to the scaffold. The Dauphin began to suffer from a form of stress-induced delirium. At Dormans, he dreamed that he was in a forest and that a pack of wolves was trying to eat his mother. He woke up sobbing and would not stop until he had sight of her.

The royal family did not have the opportunity to change clothing until they reached Meaux, where the King borrowed a shirt from the bailiff ahead of his re-entry into Paris. On Saturday, June 25, they arrived in Bondy on the capital's outskirts where mobs of people hurled themselves onto the berlin in an attempt to harm its passengers. Marie-Thérèse heard the crowd scream 'Whore!' at her mother, and of her brother, 'We know very well he is not the son of fat Louis!'

The flight eastwards, ending at Varennes, had taken less than twenty-four hours; the return journey lasted an interminable three and a half days. Nearly five days after their departure, the royal family was once again inside the gates of Paris. Although an edict had been passed in the capital forbidding violence, there was no guarantee that the populace would behave peacefully, and officials knew they were placing the family at great risk. Instead of heading directly to the Tuileries upon its return, the King's carriage was paraded around Paris so that its citizens could see the face of their humiliated King, like a defeated enemy. Lafayette, expecting large crowds, had authorized placards to be placed on the walls of buildings that read, 'Anyone who applauds the King will be beaten; anyone who insults him will be hung.'

Madame de Staël observed that the royal children looked stunned as they traveled through the crowd-filled streets of the capital. From her unbearably stuffy and claustrophobic carriage, Marie-Thérèse searched the faces of the angry crowds for molecules of sympathy and found but one. A well-dressed woman whose tears reflected the emotion that the Princess longed to see stood out in Marie-Thérèse's memory as one small comfort. Marie-Thérèse, with great pain, recalled seeing General Lafay-ette, seated on his great white horse at the Place Louis XV, enjoying his moment in the sun. Since his return to France after the American War of Independence, Lafayette's star had faded and the military hero had shown that he could be less than brilliant. Now that France's most-wanted fugitives had been recaptured, Lafayette's star was once again on the rise. In contrast, the King had suffered an immense loss of prestige even in the eyes of the moderates who previously had wanted to place him at the head of a constitutional monarchy. As Louis XVI said himself, from that moment on he was politically impotent and there was no longer a king of France.

CHAPTER IX
THE LOSING SIDE

IN THE STATEMENT the King left for his subjects to read after his escape, he avowed that he had no intention of leaving the country; rather he was merely, as he titled the document, 'Leaving Paris'. He explained in his proclamation to 'all Frenchmen', that, as his own family had been so thoroughly denied their own '*liberté*', and he, their monarch, was presently caught in the kind of stranglehold that made it impossible to perform his duties, he felt it necessary to remove his family from the hotbed of the 'Île de France'. Louis firmly believed that most of the politicians were, at heart, monarchists, and he was convinced that if he could operate from Montmédy in northeastern France, he would be able to regain a measure of control over the torrent of reforms emanating from the radical faction in the Assembly.

The Queen had demonstrated time and again that she would not be separated from her husband. They were a family; the children would stay with their parents and their parents would stay together. And so the royal family and its entourage returned to the Tuileries late into the evening of June 25, 1791. When Marie-Thérèse got to her room and removed her clothing the laundress noticed that the princess had a large tear in her dress that had been inflicted by the crowds. After disrobing, Marie-Thérèse opened the drawer to her desk and discovered that the money she had tucked away for charity had been stolen.

The next morning, June 26, the Dauphin awoke having had another nightmare. He confided to Monsieur Hüe he had dreamt that ferocious wolves, tigers and other wild animals were devouring him. He tried to tell his servant more, but the Baron, aware that the guards surrounding the boy in his own bedroom were listening, told the Dauphin to be quiet, fearing that the boy might innocently divulge other information. Marie-Thérèse and her faithful aunt, Elisabeth, were the only members of the family whose bedrooms were not infiltrated by hostile guards. The Dauphin continued to have nightmares, and, while he could not control his tears and nervousness, Marie-Thérèse, sensitive to her parents' profound depression after their unsuccessful escape attempt, once again dutifully feigned a cheerfulness that fooled no one.

It was not long before government officials arrived to interview the King, his family and servants, including Mesdames Brunier, de Neuville and de Tourzel, about the aborted escape. Some others who may not have accompanied the royal family but who were suspected of having information, like Diet and Camot, who served the Queen, were also questioned. A handful of courtiers including Madame de Tourzel were thrown in the Abbaye Prison for the greater part of the summer. Many servants later testified that the trauma of recent events had turned the Queen's hair from strawberry blonde to white. Upon her return to the Tuileries, Marie Antoinette attempted to contact her dearest friends to assure them that she was in fact all right. To the Princesse de Lamballe the Queen sent a lock of her hair in a ring accompanied by a note in which she, herself, described the sample as 'blanché'. On June 28, Marie Antoinette wrote to Comte Fersen, 'we live'; and, on the 29th, 'I exist'.

In early July, a faction led by Antoine Barnave, with whom the Queen had established a rapport during the solemn return to Paris, split from the Jacobins and formed their own political club called the Feuillants, named for the Couvent des Feuillants, a sixteenth-century convent situated between the Tuileries, along the rue St Honoré near the Place Vendôme and the Jacobin friary. This group stood for a constitutional monarchy and steadfastly against the dethronement of the King – which was now the topic of debate before the National Assembly. The prospects for Louis and his family had clearly worsened after their attempted flight to the border; but on July 7, just weeks after the King's arrest, the situation for the royal family became ever more perilous with news that the King's brothers were acting independently and against his orders. When Louis asked his younger brother, Provence, to help him word the document 'Leaving Paris', he also appointed him 'Regent of France' in the event of his own death or disablement. After the King's arrest at Varennes, Provence declared that his brother was now 'disabled' from performing his role as King and he declared himself Regent. Provence enjoyed the support of many royalists in exile as well as some European monarchs who agreed that Louis XVI was indeed impotent and now he and his brother d'Artois joined the Prince de Condé and his armies in Coblenz and declared their intention to invade France.

In Paris, knowledge of this growing threat from the exiles propelled the National Assembly to draft a new constitution giving the Assembly the power to pass legislation but retaining the King's right to veto. Louis believed – and he would later make it known to his family and friends in exile – that he had no choice but to sign the new document. For Marie-Thérèse this very public act had very personal repercussions. She had witnessed tensions between her father and his cousin, the Duc d'Orléans; she was now about to experience the growing friction among the members of the family to whom she was closest.

The Comte de Provence dispatched ambassadors to Vienna, St Petersburg, London and Madrid to ask for men, arms and financial support. The word from the English Parliament was that Britain would not involve itself in war: it would remain neutral and not impede a royalist invasion. Provence, acting as Regent of France, and his brother, d'Artois, set up a court in exile at Schönbornlust Castle – the ancestral seat of the Saxon sovereigns – lent to them by their uncle, the Elector of Treves. On August 25, the crowned heads of Europe, including the Holy Roman Emperor, Leopold II, and King Frederick William II of Prussia, convened at the castle in Pillnitz, near Dresden, and issued a statement. 'The Declaration of Pillnitz' called on all European powers to intervene in the internal struggle in France. Leopold, as Emperor of Austria, declared that his country would go to war against France if it received the backing of the rest of Europe, though as Leopold well knew, the English had already declined to intervene and for that reason the manifesto was an idle threat. The French people believed that their King was sanctioning foreign invasion and now any vestiges of sympathy for Louis and his family completely evaporated.

When Marie Antoinette saw the signatures of her brothers-in-law on the Declaration of Pillnitz, she uttered just one word: 'Cain'. For Madame Elisabeth, whose loyalty to the King had hitherto been steadfast, and for whom defiance of the monarch was an unthinkable act, the Queen's pronouncement caused divided affections. For the first time in her life Madame Elisabeth openly disagreed with the King, and wrote her émigré brothers supportive notes. Never before had Marie-Thérèse witnessed tensions between her parents and her beloved aunt.

The Dauphin was now forced to spend his days and nights under lock and key – even the Queen had to ask the guard for permission to see her son. When Madame de Tourzel was released from jail she returned to the

Tuileries to find that the Dauphin had been brainwashed by servants employed by the new regime into believing that his own beloved governess had committed a crime. When she asked him why he was angry with her, the Dauphin replied that she had 'done something bad'. Madame de Tourzel then asked if it was a bad thing to respect the King. The little boy apologized, burst into tears and asked her never to tell his dear Pauline that he had thought ill of her mother because Pauline might not love him anymore. Madame de Tourzel wrote that she despised the guards for poisoning the boy's mind, and found their decision to prohibit the children from attending religious services – on the grounds that the chapel of the Tuileries was too far from their bedrooms – 'amoral'.

Monsieur – later Baron – Hüe recalled in his memoir that one of the few pleasures left to the Queen was the chance to join her children for their studies. They had not had their lessons for some time and when Louis Charles's tutor resumed their schedule he suggested to the boy that he would not be at all surprised if the young Prince had forgotten his language studies on the degrees of comparison. 'Not at all,' replied the five-year-old:

> The positive, the comparative, the superlative . . . The positive is when I say, 'My abbé is a good abbé.' The comparative is when I say 'My abbé is better than another abbé.' The superlative (he continued, fixing his eyes on the Queen) is when I say 'Mummy is the kindest and most loving of all mothers.'

As ever, few seemed immune to the boy's winning ways. It was said that even the soldiers and crowds who marched on the Tuileries smiled when Louis Charles saluted them. One of the officers stationed to guard the royal family at the palace demanded that Louis Charles surrender his gun. The little boy refused, telling the guard, 'If you had said, "Give it to me", I would have, but you said, "Surrender".' The officer was impressed.

On September 3, the boy's father made demands of his own when the National Assembly presented the King with the finalized new constitution. Louis would only agree to sign if two conditions were met. First, all those who had taken part in the flight to Varennes would have to be pardoned; second, all émigrés would receive amnesty and would be welcomed back in France without consequence. When his two conditions were agreed to, the King and the National Assembly scheduled a formal signing. First, a delegation of sixty representatives of the National Assembly appeared together at the Tuileries to confirm that the King had agreed to sign the new constitution. Then the Queen brought Madame Royale and the Dauphin to the King's chambers where she and her husband, watched by their children, swore that they would all respect the new government of France. On September 12, the Queen said goodbye to her dearest and most loyal friend, the Princesse de Lamballe. According to Lamballe's own lady-in-waiting, the Baronne de Courtot, Marie Antoinette dispatched her friend on a mission of 'utmost importance and secrecy'. Lamballe was to go to England to try to persuade George III to invade France by sea. In London, Lamballe did indeed meet with both the King and Prime Minister Pitt; however, she did not succeed in convincing them to launch an attack.

Marie-Thérèse was very aware that both of her parents were engaged in hushed meetings; she understood their personalities – the Queen, engaging, clever, decisive and brave; the King, gentle and thoughtful – and that by their very natures, her parents often operated very differently. While the Queen insisted on taking a firm stand against the revolutionary movement and hoped to engage foreign help to quash it, the King tried to tread a more moderate and conciliatory path, always hoping to avoid spilling the blood of his countrymen. On September 13, the King wrote to the legislature that he would sign the new constitution in public, and the following day the royal family traveled from the Tuileries to the Assembly. Although the Assembly, like the États-Généraux, was largely composed of aristocrats, this alliance was not at all similar to the 'Fronde', the rebellion of a coalition of privileged local nobility and *sénéchals* who, a century earlier, had demanded of King Louis XIV increased entitlements. The legislators who forged the new constitution in 1791 had deliberately abolished all of the honors and prerogatives so dear to many of their own forebears. At noon, Louis XVI, without his crown and accompanied by his family, appeared before the Assembly and signed the document that, in effect, dethroned the Bourbons.

The Jacobins and Feuillants swiftly put aside their differences and agreed on one thing: it was essential that the nation perceive the new constitution to be the result of their joint efforts and therefore a show of political unity was required. The Assembly arranged for the royal family to attend public events to celebrate France's new constitution, including a Te Deum at the cathedral of Notre Dame and illuminations and festivities – the Queen remarking that all of the jubilation made her miserable. On Saturday, October 8, the King, Queen, Marie-Thérèse and the Dauphin attended a performance at the Théâtre Italien where the little boy, sitting on his mother's lap, charmed the crowd with his animated reactions to the play. The King, Queen, Marie-Thérèse and Madame Elisabeth went to the Opéra where they saw *Castor and Pollux* by Jean-Philippe Rameau, to the Théâtre Français for a performance of *La Gouvernante* by Pierre Claude Nivelle de La Chaussée and again to the Théâtre Italien for Grétry's *Les Evénements Imprévus*. Unfortunately this last performance was interrupted when fighting broke out between royalists and republicans, and the National Guard had to be brought in to subdue the crowd. It was almost impossible for the King and Queen and their children to attempt to go anywhere in public without emotions running high and in all directions.

Society had been turned upside down. No longer was the word 'sovereign' associated with the King; rather it was a right belonging to the masses, and while the royal Bourbons were suffering a total lack of freedom, the press enjoyed an unbridled lack of censorship. The King was now completely powerless in protecting his wife from libel, and pamphleteers took aim at Marie Antoinette with extraordinary liberty and viciousness. Pornographic illustrations appeared depicting the Queen engaged in bestiality. Poetry and plays such as *The Triumph of the Damned* were printed, which detailed the Queen's alleged sexual escapades with a variety of male and female lovers. Forged letters appeared as the Queen's 'true confessions'. In these sometimes melodramatic musings, the Queen would 'confess' to having lived a wanton life and to have wronged the people of France. One opera libretto featured a *ménage à trois* comprising the Queen of France, the Comte d'Artois and the Duchesse de Polignac.

A number of very vocal women had hoped for a new order in France, where all citizens would indeed be equal. They were sadly disappointed, however, when it turned out that they would remain voiceless in the formation of this new society. Although there were salons controlled by liberal thinkers such as Madame Roland, Pauline Léon, and the dramatist Olympe de Gouges – who wrote her own 'Declarations of the Rights of Women' in response to the proclamation hammered out by the representatives of the National Assembly – their assertions were ignored. De Gouges would later be tried and executed for treason as a result of her outspoken criticism of the Revolution's unequal treatment of women.

The Queen's new friend, Barnave, encouraged her to send for the Princesse de Lamballe, who was still in England. Barnave advised the Queen that since Lamballe had been head of the Queen's household, it would show good faith on the Queen's part to openly encourage her friend and other prominent émigrés to return to Paris. The King agreed with Barnave and wrote letters to his brothers telling them to return to the capital for the sake of the family, explaining that their reluctance to return would cause suspicion among the masses. Unsurprisingly the royal princes disobeyed their brother's wishes, claiming that they believed the King had been coerced into writing the letters. As for the Queen, despite advice from Barnave, she wrote asking her dear friend, Madame de Polignac, to 'stay away from the mouth of the tiger'.

On October 1 1791, reflecting the increasing radicalization of French politics, the Assembly was restyled 'the Legislative' and it immediately expelled the members of the former Constitutional Assembly. On October 31, the new legislators, having dismissed the moderate Feuillant group, proposed that émigrés who did not immediately return would have their land confiscated and the same would apply to their family members who remained in France. The King was able to veto this bill; nonetheless, under continuing pressure from Barnave, the Queen relented and wrote to the Princesse de Lamballe asking her to return. She knew that Lamballe, the most loyal of friends, would do as she was asked the moment she was asked. Ironically, at the same time that Lamballe returned to France, in November, Barnave, having been accused by the Jacobins of being a crony of the Queen, implemented his own escape plans and exiled himself to Grenoble.

On December 19, Marie-Thérèse turned thirteen and on New Year's Day, 1792, the King was forced to declare that all émigrés, many of whom Madame Royale had known and loved dearly since birth, were officially condemned as traitors to France. In the meantime, the émigrés made their own plans. It was rumored that the King's nephew, the Duc d'Angoulême, once the main contender for Madame Royale's hand in marriage, was to marry without the King's consent an Austrian archduchess whose dowry was the Austrian Lowlands. The marriage, however, did not take place. Marie-Thérèse was acutely aware that her immediate family was divided. She also became aware that the other rulers of Europe – also family – were ridiculing her father for his acquiescence and that he was now regarded as the shame of European sovereigns. The Swedish king, Gustav III, stood alone as an empathetic ally. With Fersen as his emissary, Gustav worked feverishly toward a European alliance that would actually effect change for the King and Queen of France.

The Queen spent her days cloistered with her children and writing desperate letters in cipher to European monarchs including her brother Leopold, Gustav III, and Catherine of Russia. To her childhood friend,

Louise of Hesse, whose sister Charlotte had died in childbirth in 1785, Marie Antoinette wrote that her only solace was her children. On January 7, the Queen, who always wrote to her friend, Madame de Polignac, of the children, reported that their lives were miserable. They could not go out for fresh air without being physically threatened. They could not go to the windows without being shouted at. The family tried to create their own cocoon inside the palace: writing to friends, recounting fond memories and hoping for better times. 'My daughter speaks to me of you often . . . your little note has given her infinite pleasure,' the Queen told de Polignac on March 17.

It was widely known in Paris that Comte Fersen had been involved in the King's escape attempt. Despite this, on February 13, Fersen returned to the capital disguised as a courier. Claiming that he had a letter from his King as well as the support of Catherine of Russia, Fersen begged the King and Queen to follow him to Quiberon on the coast of Brittany where a ship would be waiting for them. However, two days later Fersen was recognized and was forced to flee.

On New Year's Day, 1792, the French Legislative Assembly denounced Provence, d'Artois and their cousins as traitors and had them stripped of their lands and titles. Tensions already existed between France's new constitutional government and the Holy Roman Empire due to the Emperor of Austria's support for the émigré army in Coblenz. Now, the elderly Austrian Chancellor, Kaunitz, presented a letter of demands to the French Assembly that included the immediate liberation of King Louis XVI and his family and the restoration of German lands in Alsace. On March 1, Emperor Leopold II died and his son, Franz (Francis) II, became the new Holy Roman Emperor. As Marie Antoinette's nephew, he might have been even less inclined to come to the aid of the Queen of France than his father; but Franz was young and brash, and encouraged by reports that France's armies were disorganized and poorly equipped, he began to taunt the Jacobins into war.

Comte Fersen, now in Brussels, reported to his own King in March that, as Gustav III had predicted, the Jacobins had seized total power, reporting 'their triumph is complete'. Fersen was gone, Leopold II dead and on March 16, Gustav III was shot in the back at a masked ball and died a fortnight later. The Swedish King's tragic assassination would inspire Giuseppe Verdi's opera, *Un Ballo in Maschera*.

The French royal family mourned the murdered King and suffered his loss deeply. Marie Antoinette gently told her daughter of Gustav's assassination, and Marie-Thérèse, who had fond memories of the Swedish king, sobbed to her father that the new King, Gustavus IV Adolphus, was so young. Louis XVI explained to Marie-Thérèse that he was well aware of the new King's age because the boy had been born just weeks before her. He then told her that before she was born he knew that he was going to have a daughter since he believed no two kings were born in the same year. Marie-Thérèse then asked her father if her birth had disappointed him. 'Certainly not,' the King replied, hugging her. It was clear that he had meant every word. He had not for one moment cherished his firstborn child any less for not having been born his son and heir.

Madame Tussaud's recalled Madame Royale as a vibrant young lady dressed in a white muslin dress with a blue sash, whose beautiful blonde hair flowed in rich profusion against her lovely fair skin. Sadly, at thirteen years old, Marie-Thérèse, a witness to unspeakable acts of violence, had grown wan and prematurely serious, and was barely recognizable as the child frolicking at the Trianon. There were to be no parties, no rides on horseback in the country, no silly madcap escapades, and certainly no merry teenage times. The murder of one king close to her resonated and filled her with dread as the anniversary of the aborted escape and capture at Varennes drew near. Every moment she feared for the lives of her parents and brother her melancholy deepened.

Both Madame Royale and the Dauphin were extremely sensitive to their parents' emotions; they could read the pain on their parents' faces. Although the King and Queen tried to protect their children, the restricted living arrangements made it inevitable that the children would learn of the growing tensions between the King and the Assembly and between France and Austria. In addition to encouraging exiled Frenchmen to invade their own country, the Austrians were openly harboring French émigrés and providing them with funds. The French government protested but the equally hotheaded Franz II had no desire to bow to the demands of the Legislative. In the spring of 1792, France felt it had no choice but to declare war on Austria. With most of the Continent involved in the imbroglio, Louis XVI was grateful that George III of England and his Parliament once again decided not to become involved. The two kings maintained a cordial correspondence: the French King thanked his English 'brother' for his resolve in remaining patient in the face of France's internal disputes; the English King addressed the now fallen French King with great respect, deferring to Louis's wishes and offering him his friendship.

Now at war with Austria, the French boiled with hatred for 'l'Autrichienne'. After the King refused to sign a decree that ordered, among other things, the deportation of priests, the citizenry disdainfully gave the royal couple a new sobriquet, 'Madame et Monsieur Veto'. Madame Campan reported that as the anniversary of the flight to Varennes approached, the King became increasingly morose and barely said 'one word' for ten days except when his sister tried to jolly him up by playing card games with him or when the Queen employed 'every affectionate expression'.

Just as the royal family and their courtiers had feared, the anniversary of the flight to Varennes brought with it more violence. Marie-Thérèse later described events at the Tuileries as a 'massacre'. She wrote that it all began when a 'mania' for planting 'liberty trees' swept Paris. A group of citizens had asked the King for permission to plant a tree and have a small celebration in the garden at the Tuileries Palace. Although the King suspected that this was a ploy to gain access to the palace and harm the royal family, he acquiesced and granted permission for the people to have their ceremony. By the time the group had wound its way from the Carrousel to the palace, most of them were, according to Marie-Thérèse, drunk and unruly. The anti-royalist soldiers stationed to guard the palace made little effort to repel the crowd and the royal family was left protected by just a few loyal courtiers and grenadiers who were unable to keep the 'desperadoes', as Campan referred to them, from entering the palace and penetrating the royal family's personal chambers.

Some in the crowd who had made their way to the door of the King's chambers screamed for the head of the Queen. A number among them mistook the King's sister, Madame Elisabeth, for Marie Antoinette. As the intruders lunged at the King's sister, someone shouted that they had the wrong woman, to which Madame Elisabeth replied defiantly: 'Do not undeceive them!', declaring that she was willing to lay down her life for her sister-in-law.

Marie-Thérèse managed to grab her brother and flee through a secret exit in his bedroom just as the invaders started to hack at the bedroom door. They soon found their mother and the three of them hid in the Cabinet du Conseil surrounded by a group that included the Princesse de Lamballe, Madame de Tourzel, Madame de Mackau and the Princesse de Tarente. The bloodbath, in which many of the royal family's most faithful household troops were slaughtered, continued until the evening. As the hours worn on, the Queen became increasingly frantic from being separated from the King. Madame Campan wrote that one 'barbarian' who made his way into the Cabinet du Conseil carried a dirty rag doll suspended from a pole with the words, 'Marie Antoinette to the lantern' written on it. Another had pinned an ox's heart to a board with the words 'heart of the King' encircling it. Obscene placards referred to the King as a cuckold. One man pointed at a shaking Marie-Thérèse and asked the Queen, 'How old is the girl?' Marie Antoinette replied: 'Old enough to always remember these scenes with horror.'

In order to humiliate the royal family further, the invaders had forced the King and Queen each to put on the *bonnet rouge* – the red cap of the revolutionaries, but late in the evening officials of the National Assembly were able to restore order and the family was reunited. The next day it was found that all of the doors to the family's apartments had been broken down. One servant, Merlin de Thionville, wrote that grown men in the service to the King openly wept at the violation of the King's home and family.

Pauline de Tourzel observed that from this day on Marie-Thérèse's demeanor mirrored that of her mother's, assuming a mantle of bravery over a 'presentiment of doom'. Louis Charles, in contrast, too young and impressionable to pretend, simply stopped speaking and continuously clung to his mother. Every night for weeks thereafter, disturbances and loud noises emanated from the streets outside the Queen's rooms on the ground floor of the Tuileries. Afraid for her safety, the Queen's staff and the King begged her to sleep on the second floor, and eventually she acquiesced. One evening in July, a servant spy removed a set of keys from the King's pocket while he slept and set out to kill the Queen. Madame Campan, who had been asleep in the bed alongside the Queen, recalled that at one o'clock in the morning they were woken by the intruder. As the Queen stood frozen with fear, locked in Madame Campan's arms, another servant fought off and killed the would-be assassin.

On 14 July, the royal family was again required to appear for the national celebrations. Madame de Staël was among those present. Necker's daughter had always defended her father and often openly criticized the Queen; but on this occasion she was impressed by Marie Antoinette's courage, realizing that the Queen and her children must have been terrified to be among the crowd. De Staël reported that despite the fact that the Queen's eyes were red and swollen from crying, she appeared to all to be serene and pretended to be enjoying the pomp and circumstance. The King earnestly played his part as well and after he took his oath to the nation for the second time he rejoined his family on the dais.

Just eleven days later, on July 25, on the anniversary of the Declaration of Pillnitz, Charles William Ferdinand, the Duke of Brunswick, commander of the Allied Army of the Austrian and Prussian Armies, issued a new threat, later known as the Brunswick Manifesto. His declaration warned the French rebels that an army had been marshaled by the Holy Roman Empire and was on its way to rescue the beleaguered French King and his family. His statement gave notice that if, by the time the army arrived, it had been discovered that Louis and his family had been harmed in any way, the army would level, loot and take unimaginable vengeance against Paris. When news of the manifesto reached Paris on August 1, the masses reacted with fury and the streets were filled with cries for vengeance. French citizens were now certain that their King and 'l'Au-trichienne' were collaborating with the Germans, and when the army of more than 75,000 Germans and French émigrés – the army of princes who marched 'for God and King' – crossed the Rhine, the Legislative Assembly issued an order to prepare for war.

The royal family waited for the inevitable. The Queen burned papers and dispersed quantities of money to her surviving members of staff. The King, with the help of a locksmith – who unfortunately turned out to be a Jacobin – constructed a safe inside a wall in which to preserve papers of a sensitive nature. The safe opening was then painted to make it appear part of the stonework. Amongst these papers were minutes of a private meeting that the King had held with his ministers during which he had expressed his objections to the war with Austria; a war that he had been forced to declare the previous spring.

In early August, the Legislative Assembly closed the gates to the Tuileries, hung a banner of tri-colored ribbons over the Terrasse des Feuillants, and designated a demarcation between what was considered 'national property' and the Tuileries Palace – now mockingly called the 'property of Coblenz'. It was now not a matter of if but when the Tuileries would be assailed again.

CHAPTER X
TWO ORPHANS

ON AUGUST 9, 1792, the King, the Queen, Marie-Thérèse and Madame Elisabeth attended Mass as usual. One person present noticed that the ladies did not once raise their eyes from their prayer books. This pious scene was subsequently painted by Hubert Robert. For weeks everyone at the Tuileries had been extremely tense, poised for an invasion of the palace. For the first time in living memory, the King's *coucher* was cancelled. The King routinely wore his bulletproof breastplate, and that evening, after supper, the entire family convened in the Cabinet du Conseil with a handful of ministers to wait, as Madame de Tourzel described it, with 'funereal anxiety'.

After putting the Dauphin to bed, his *valet de chambre,* Jean-Baptiste Cléry, slipped outside the palace gates to learn that an attack on the palace had been planned for midnight at which time a tocsin would ring. Forty-eight alarm bells representing each section of Paris began to toll and continued throughout the night. The King, the Queen, Madame Elisabeth and Madame Campan did not allow themselves to sleep. At 4 a.m. the Queen discovered that the Marquis de Mandat, the new head of the National Guard forces defending the Tuileries, had gone to seek instructions from the Assembly. Unbeknown to him, a radical splinter group had taken over the Hôtel de Ville. The insurgents accused him of authorizing his troops to fire on the people, ordered him to the Abbaye Prison and dispatched a new commander, Santerre, to the Tuileries. Mandat did not even make it to the prison. On his way out of the Hôtel de Ville, he was attacked and murdered by a mob. His head was skewered on a pike and paraded around the streets.

Just two hours later, at 6 a.m. on the morning of August 10, Marie-Thérèse accompanied her parents, her aunt and her brother, to inspect the guard in the courtyard of the palace. François Armand Frédéric, Comte de La Rochefoucauld, a military man who stood near the King, was stunned that His Majesty could not utter one word of encouragement to the soldiers. The Queen also told Madame Campan that the King had displayed no energy and she felt that all was lost.

From about 7 to 10 a.m., the sound of cannon fire blasted through the air in the city. Nine hundred Swiss Guard had been assigned to the Tuileries but their numbers were minuscule compared to the 20,000 citizens who, after having broken into the Arsenal, were on the march from Saint-Antoine on the Rive Droit and Saint Marceau on the Rive Gauche. Armies of sans-culottes – citizen revolutionaries – flooded the Place du Carrousel and the vicinity of the palace. The cannons were turned toward the Tuileries in anticipation of a skirmish. Marie Antoinette begged her husband to order the troops to arms, but the King would not, refusing once again to spill the blood of Frenchmen.

With that decision most of the National Guard defected, leaving the royal family stranded except for their Swiss Guard troops. Pierre-Louis Roederer, a municipal officer, encouraged the King to take his family and seek refuge nearby at the National Assembly. The King refused. Roederer argued that the legislative body was far more sympathetic to the King than the new extremist group and would protect him. At last, the King conceded and sent word to members of the Assembly, requesting that they rescue his family; but the legislators did not respond. Instead, a handful of government officials arrived at the Tuileries and urged the King to take his family to the Assembly's convention hall. Joseph Weber, the Queen's childhood friend, served as a grenadier in the Filles-de-St Thomas brigade, a battalion that remained loyal to the royal family. Weber and many of his comrades abandoned their positions in the city and in the palace grounds to guard the Queen's body personally. When he arrived inside the palace the Queen was surprised to see him and begged him to take care; he, however, insisted that he would 'not forsake her', and advised the royal couple not to separate under any circumstances.

While thousands fought on the streets of Paris, the politicians debated the fate of the King and his family. Hours later, they agreed that the royal family should be escorted to the convention hall. There is a discrepancy in the accounts of August 10 concerning the presence of the Princesse de Lamballe. Both Hüe and Madame Campan claimed that Lamballe was with the royal family at the Tuileries the entire summer. Campan wrote that, while she was told to wait in the Queen's apartments, Marie Antoinette quietly requested that the Princesse de Lamballe and Madame de Tourzel accompany the royal family to the Assembly. Hüe also placed Lamballe with the Queen at every moment. De Tourzel only mentioned that she left behind her own daughter, Pauline, at the Tuileries to follow the King. The Baronne de Courtot, the woman who was with the Princess at all times, contradicted both of their accounts. She wrote that she and Lamballe had returned once again to England and were there during the events of August 10. Courtot produced a letter that she had 'preserved' written by Marie Antoinette to Lamballe. Dated '10 aout 1792, Paris', the letter explicitly warned Lamballe, according to Courtot in England on that day, 'NE RETOURNEZ PAS' (do not return) . . . 'VOUS RESTEREZ LÀ' (remain where you are).

The royal family proceeded through the courtyard to the Assembly. Joseph Weber was true to his word and placed himself among the soldiers who offered protection as the family made its way through the palace gardens past the Feuillants and throngs of hostile onlookers to the convention hall. Pauline de Tourzel recalled it as 'a convoy of the death of royalty'. The crowd pressed the royal family so closely that someone was able to rob the Queen of her purse and a watch.

At the Assembly they found the doors barred shut, as some of the deputies inside maintained their resistance to accepting the royal family. Outside, the soldiers threatened to break down the doors if the royal family was not permitted to enter. After half an hour, the King, Queen and their entourage were taken to a narrow corridor, described by Marie-Thérèse as so dark that she could not see. There, she was held by a man she did not know and who she thought was going to kill her. Another half-hour went by and still she could not see her parents in the darkness. Finally, they all were brought into the main assembly hall at which point the King pronounced loudly that he had come to ask refuge for himself and his family. The ensuing commotion necessitated that soldiers stand guard around the royal family until the lawmakers found a place for them to stand at the bar. After that, the royal family was escorted to the press box, which Marie-Thérèse described as a 'cage'. She could hear the sounds of musket and cannon fire and screams emanating from the direction of the Tuileries. At the palace, two-thirds of the 900-strong Swiss Guard, and many loyal friends and servants, were being slaughtered by the mob. The Dauphin, fearful that his adored Pauline had been killed, ran shrieking and sobbing to Madame de Tourzel, which momentarily silenced the politicians. The royal family stood without food or water from morning until late in the evening while the deputies hurled accusations of treason at the King and Queen.

While the family was among the Assembly, Cléry, still at the Tuileries, saw four heads on spikes placed on the terrace of the Feuillants, which he believed to be a signal to attack the palace. He was correct. Immediately afterward, bullets and cannonballs riddled the walls of the palace. Constant gunfire from the Pont Royal closed it off as an avenue of escape so Cléry crawled through the Dauphin's garden by the Seine where he saw a man looting the bodies of freshly murdered Swiss Guard. The Tuileries Palace was sacked, and the friends who had remained began to hide or flee for their lives. The Princesse de Tarente managed to help Pauline to safety, taking her to the house of the Duchesse de LaVallière, the Princess's grandmother. Madame de Soucy was under strict instructions from the Queen to get Ernestine to safety, and the two began a dangerous escape through cadaver-strewn alleyways. Their skirts soaked in blood, the pair stopped at the Carrousel as they felt they could go no further. Madame de Soucy tried to find a carriage and while she was gone someone mistook Ernestine for Marie-Thérèse and hurled a half-burned Swiss Guard, who was still on fire, at her feet. The girl began to swoon but managed to walk a few steps toward a small boutique. The owner of the shop, also convinced that the young girl was Marie-Thérèse, ran to her aid just as Madame de Soucy arrived in a carriage. Madame Campan was also making her way to safety and, as she headed past the Louvre to her sister's house, stripped off her blood-soaked gown and took flight in her petticoats.

The Tuileries Palace briefly caught fire as angry mobs looted the royal apartments and searched for evidence against the King and Queen. Marie Antoinette had had the foresight to send to Comte Mercy in Brussels some of the 400,000 *livres* of the 800,000 which she had saved (out of her annual pension of 300,000 *livres*, the 120,000 she had received on the birth of Madame Royale, the 300,000 she had received upon the birth of the first Dauphin and the monies she had received upon the births of Louis Charles and Sophie). She had previously turned over some priceless gems to the care of the Assembly; however, many of these were subsequently looted from the Royal Treasury, including the pearls that had belonged to Anne of Austria and three fabled diamonds: the Regent, the Sancy, and the French blue diamond from which the Hope Diamond was carved. The Queen had sent her personal gems to Belgium with her hairdresser, Monsieur Léonard. The King had also taken a measure of precaution and asked the American Gouverneur Morris to send a great deal of money out of France with instructions to deliver the funds to Marie Antoinette and their children in the event of his death.

Women on the streets who had raided the Queen's personal effects were now mockingly adorned in her dresses and accessories. Her tiny bibelots were stolen and *poissardes* bragged about their spoils. Valuable objets d'art that had belonged to the kings of France for centuries disappeared. Even the royal children's toys and schoolbooks were seized and defaced by citizens who believed that the two children were guilty of crimes against France simply by virtue of their birth.

The royal family had been standing in the unbearably hot auditorium of the assembly hall for over twelve hours when, at last, it was decided that they would spend the night at the Couvent des Feuillants. Four rooms were readied for the royal family to sleep in until the next morning when they were to be brought back to the Assembly for another day of haranguing and abuse. Only the children could manage to eat their supper that evening. The Dauphin cried repeatedly, 'Where is my dog?' No one could answer him. The King was granted permission to send for Pauline de Tourzel in the hope that she might comfort his son, and she arrived at the convent at eight the following morning. Pauline recalled that Marie-Thérèse embraced her with great emotion and the words, 'My dear Pauline, let us never separate again.'

The Assembly decided that the royal family should now be moved to the Temple Enclosure, an ancient conglomeration comprising a chapel, a castle and a prison. Originally built by the Knights Templar in the twelfth century, it formed a small walled city. At the turn of the fourteenth century, King Philippe le Bel ordered the place to be burned to the ground along with most of the powerful Knights Templar. The men were tortured and left to burn alive; however, the majority of the buildings remained intact and became home to a succession of occupants including the Knights of Malta. Louis XVI's youngest brother, the Comte d'Artois, acquired the property and often hosted lavish parties there. The Queen had always hated the place, however, and perhaps with some prescience, had often urged her brother-in-law to tear it down, dungeons and all. When the King was told that he was going to be moved to the Temple Enclosure, he imagined his family was going to be housed in the castle structure; the Queen guessed otherwise.

On Monday, August 13, 1792, the King, the Queen and the children were driven through the streets of Paris through jeering crowds. The drivers grew so scared of retribution that they stopped frequently to regain their composure. At seven o'clock in the evening, the somber cortège arrived at the Temple Enclosure, which had been illuminated in anticipation of its new 'guests'. Madame and Pauline de Tourzel,

Madame de Chamilly, the King's valet Hüe, and other servants were told that they would be allowed to remain with the family. Pauline de Tourzel recalled seeing the prison aglow, as if a great ball were going on inside. The family ate dinner and rooms were prepared for them, not in the castle, as the King had imagined, but in the smaller of two towers, as the Queen had predicted.

Marie-Thérèse and Hüe both attested to the fact that the Princesse de Lamballe was among the royal retinue in that 'fatal place', as she later described it; however, the Baronne de Courtot, detailing another drama that took place far away in London, specified that the Princess did not arrive until at least one week after the incarceration of the royal family. Courtot claimed that days after the invasion of the Tuileries in August, Lamballe, still in London, received another letter dated '14 aout' also from Paris, believed to be signed by the Queen. This missive was a short one, written in shaky handwriting, and pleading, 'Come to me at once. I am in the greatest of danger.' Without concern for her own life, Lamballe and her lady-in-waiting 'started that same day for Cherbourg with our three serving-women and two men . . . We reached Paris on the 25th day of August'. The very next morning, she and the Princesse de Lamballe, who had spent the night with the Duchesse de Laiancourt 'and was now half-distraught with terror, having with the utmost difficulty escaped from a gang of infuriated ruffians who pursued her through several streets', decided to make their way to the Temple Prison to be with the Queen. According to her lady-in-waiting, Lamballe 'implored me to join her in seeking refuge with the Queen in the Temple; prison walls offered better security than this mad whirlpool of a city, where bands of ravening monsters hunted down every decently dressed person they caught sight of'.

When they arrived, a guard laughingly told them that he was happy that they had 'saved us the trouble' of coming to arrest them, and he brought them to see the Queen. When Marie Antoinette saw her favorite, she was stunned and asked Lamballe why she had returned to Paris. The women then all realized that the note had been a forgery. They surmised that the person who would most profit from Lamballe's death and who had most likely been behind it was the Duc d'Orléans, smugly ensconced at the Palais-Royal. Lamballe, as the widow of the only son of the fabulously wealthy Duc de Penthièvre, would have shared in an enormous inheritance with the duke's only other child – Orléans's wife. Courtot recalled muttering to herself, 'Philippe d'Orléans, this is your handiwork!'

Among the most detailed accounts of the royal family's detention in the Temple Prison are those penned by Marie-Thérèse and the King's servant, Monsieur Hüe. Marie-Thérèse recalled that, at the request of the King, indecent engravings were removed from the walls of her room. However, what pained the King's daughter more was the insulting way in which her father was being treated. The jailers called him by his first name instead of 'Sire' or 'Your Majesty'. Marie-Thérèse hated one harsh jailer in particular, a man named Rocher, whom the children recognized from their capture at Varennes, and whom, she felt, took perverse pleasure in humiliating the family. She recalled that Rocher sang an offensive song around the family and would puff the smoke from his pipe right into the King's face as he passed, knowing that the King hated the smell of tobacco.

Hüe wrote that as the days went by the King borrowed a prodigious amount of books from the 1,400-volume library collection left by the Knights of Malta. He would read early in the morning before his family joined him in his room for breakfast at 9 a.m. According to Hüe, the Queen kept a copy of Thomas à Kempis's *Imitation of Christ*, which she read 'night and day', and he wrote that the King one day, reflecting on the books around him, pointed at those by Voltaire and Rousseau and charged, 'Those two men have been the ruin of France.'

The Queen taught Marie-Thérèse to fix her own hair before seeing her father, and the mornings were spent *en famille* while the King taught the Dauphin Latin, French literature, history and geography. The Queen instructed Marie-Thérèse in Bible studies and music, and the ladies spent hours at their needlework. Hüe requested that some busts be brought from Marie-Thérèse's drawing master, Van Blarenberghe, to enable the Princess to continue her lessons in portraiture. The revolutionary functionaries on duty at the prison did not recognize the busts as copies of famous ancient sculptures and believed them to be models of the heads of the Kings who were at war with France; they also suspected that the busts had been used to smuggle secret messages to the King.

Madame Elisabeth taught mathematics to both the children. When the illiterate, innumerate guards spied the children's arithmetic, they thought that the children were writing in a secret code. The King read some Racine and Corneille to his son and when it was the Queen's turn to read the tragedies of Racine aloud, the guards listened closely, proclaiming her 'bloodthirsty'. At first, the family was allowed into the courtyard in the afternoons. The Dauphin played ball and quoits, and sister and brother sometimes engaged in teetotum, a spinning-top game Pauline had given the boy, and shuttlecocks. To pass the time, the King devised riddles for them all from old issues of the *Mercure de France*, and he and the Queen played backgammon and piquet.

The King also taught the Dauphin a new prayer, which the boy said every night before going to bed:

> God, all-powerful, You who have created me and redeemed me. I adore you. Preserve the days of the King, my father, and those of my family. Protect us against our enemies. Give Madame de Tourzel the strength she needs to sustain herself through the pain she endures because of us.

After the Dauphin was put to bed, the King, the Queen, Marie-Thérèse, and Madame Elisabeth would have dinner. Before retiring for the night, Marie-Thérèse would say goodnight to her father and he would kiss her hand. She would often affectionately jump on him, her arms around his neck, while he hugged her and bid her goodnight.

Marie-Thérèse recalled that her father 'was lodged above on the third floor of the building adjacent to the main body of the Tower; having a municipal guard in his room'. Madame Elisabeth 'occupied a kitchen' with Pauline de Tourzel and Madame Navarre, another servant, and the Queen was stationed 'below in a salon with me and afterward with Madame de Lamballe'. The fact that Lamballe was 'afterward' may corroborate Courtot's story that the Princess arrived at the Temple Prison at a later date and was not with the royal family at the Tuileries at the time of the invasion.

The chaos of events makes it difficult to pinpoint the accuracy of some accounts. Again, while the Baronne de Courtot claims that she and the Princesse de Lamballe were not in Paris until the end of August, she also corroborates Hüe's account that the royal retinue was removed from the Temple Prison and she was there when it happened.

Hüe claimed that it was on August 19, after the French learned that the Duke of Brunswick's armies had enjoyed some victories over the rebels, that the Princesse de Lamballe, among others in the royal entourage, was taken to the prison of La Force. Courtot described the heartrending scene on that day when the Queen and Lamballe were forced to part: 'they literally tore my sobbing Princess from the arms of the Queen so roughly that her Majesty nearly fell. One more kiss, one last fond look, and the two friends parted never to meet again in this life.' Courtot accompanied Lamballe and was relegated to a crowded dungeon at La Force, before being released shortly afterward. Hüe, also taken away and questioned, was permitted to return to the Temple Prison to serve his king.

Back at the Temple, Hüe recalled that the family only learnt of events in the outside world when they were allowed to walk in the gardens where they could hear the shouts of newsboys. By this means the royal family learned that Lafayette, once the nation's greatest hero, had been declared a traitor by the Commune – the revolutionary metropolitan government of the city of Paris – and that he had escaped for neutral Liège. Marie-Thérèse recalled that on the morning of the day of Saint Louis, August 25, she heard the revolutionaries loudly singing their new anthem 'Ça Ira', a song of victory by the people over the aristocrats and the clergy. Hüe was also with the royal family when they heard news of the victory of the army of princes at Verdun.

Marie-Thérèse recalled that the King and Queen continued to be threatened in front of their children. Her brother would cry and tremble when he heard the jailers describe the ways in which they were going to torture and kill the King. Marie-Thérèse wrote that her father would respond with 'calm and contemptuous silence'. Her mother had always maintained her dignity and poise in front of the guards, but on September 2, a three-day massacre began in the city that broke the Queen's resolve.

On day two of the slaughter the Princesse de Lamballe was taken from La Force on to the streets of Paris, decapitated, disemboweled and her breasts cut off. The Baronne de Courtot was convinced that the murder had been carried out on the orders of the Duc d'Orléans in order to taunt the Queen and benefit his wife. The Princess's head was placed on one pole, her mutilated body on another. A mob bearing the two pikes then marched to the Temple Prison where the prison guards let them into the courtyard and paraded Lamballe's head under the Queen's window. According to Marie-Thérèse, the jailer, Rocher, shouted with joy upon seeing the head. Although the mob screamed for the Queen to appear at her window, she did not. When questioned by the King as to what was going on outside, a young officer replied: 'Well, if you want to know, it is the head of Mme de Lamballe they wish to show you.' The Queen was overcome with terror and Marie-Thérèse recalled that her mother cried all night.

The following day, Hüe, who had been with the family when they learned of Lamballe's tragic fate, was removed from the Temple Prison and placed in the jail at City Hall. As Hüe was being evicted, the King gave him a farewell token of esteem – a lock of hair, which His Majesty cut from his head himself. 'This is the only present I can give you now,' apologized the King as he handed it to his faithful servant. Hüe would always consider it his greatest treasure.

Outside the jail, indiscriminate massacres continued, sometimes resulting in the deaths of children. The Commune began collecting evidence against the King at the Tuileries and at the homes of the royal family's loyal friends and servants. Anyone who was suspected of possessing letters that had been written by the royal couple was denounced and had his or her house ransacked.

The Queen had entered the prison with only 25 *louis*, a sewing kit, a small hand mirror, two tiny packets filled with locks of her children's hair (the ones living and dead), a ring also containing locks of hair of her husband and all four of the children she bore, and portraits of the Princesse de Lamballe, and her two German childhood friends, Charlotte and Louise of Hesse. Friends of the royal family, including the British ambassador's wife, found clandestine ways to get linens and money for provisions passed to the King and his family. Marie-Thérèse was permitted to send for some clothing, including handkerchiefs of cotton batiste, blouses, a skirt, two corsets, a percale dress, napkins, two linen caps, seven cotton batiste scarves for her neck, and gray and black stockings.

The royalists were all hopeful that the family would soon be rescued; but even though Brunswick had had some successes in Verdun and Longwy, and French émigrés were working hard at gathering momentum abroad to rescue the King, the roads to the capital were so crowded and the progress so slow that the attempt was shortly called off. The armies of émigrés and their royalist allies were passionate about their cause, but most were inexperienced and they proceeded in unwieldy carriages with bystanders as if on parade, not in battle. In addition, the September massacres had dented their morale, allowing the French revolutionary forces to prevail. Heady with victory, on September 21 the Commune declared the monarchy and all aristocracy officially dead, and the government of France was officially renamed the National Convention. The Commune's words resounded, plastered everywhere on posters and pamphlets. The old elite in France had been abolished, and to make their point, the Convention ordered construction workers to raise the Temple Prison walls to 'obliterate the presence of the King'. On September 26, the King was moved into the great tower. On the 29th, all writing utensils, wax and paper were removed from all members of the royal family.

The prison officials allowed the family to reunite with the King for dinner, but for the rest of the day the King remained in solitary confinement in the dungeon. On October 26, the Queen, Marie-Thérèse, the Dauphin and Madame Elisabeth were moved to the same tower and a routine much like they had had in the small tower was resumed. The family, who once presided over France's greatest palaces, now lived in damp, dark quarters with bars on the windows and centuries of residue and filth on the walls and floors. The ground floor and second story of the tower contained offices and lodging space for the prison officials and guards. The King, the Dauphin and Cléry, who was allowed to serve him, were placed on the third floor and the women on the fourth. The fifth floor contained an open-air gallery where the family could walk as they were no longer permitted to stroll in the gardens.

Marie-Thérèse now shared a room with her mother directly above the King's, and similar to his in layout. She wrote that the walls of her room were covered in shabby blue and green striped wallpaper and on one wall there was a marble chimney-piece. A clock with a bronze figure of 'Fortune' sat on the mantle. The Queen slept in a canopied bed covered in green damask; Marie-Thérèse in a tiny bed near her mother. Cléry had requested a more comfortable bed for the teenage Princess, but his request was ignored. Cotton curtains and valances framed the windows and there was one chest of drawers, two chairs and a screen behind which the women could dress.

Every nod, every motion, every conversation was scrutinized by the guards. The group was forced to speak loudly so that their jailers could understand their words. On November 6, after dinner, the family heard screams from the street calling for the King's head. On November 14, the King became ill with pains and a high fever, but the officials would not permit a doctor to visit him for a week. In the meantime, the rest of the family began to exhibit similar symptoms, and the little Dauphin contracted whooping cough. When Louis Charles cried out in the night for his mother, the guards did not permit the Queen to comfort him. On December 3, the Queen requested bouillon but her cook was not allowed to prepare it, and the ailing Queen went to bed without eating.

On December 11, King Louis XVI was placed on trial. He was no longer allowed to see his family and the Dauphin was moved to his mother's room. Although the King was forbidden contact with his loved ones, Cléry managed to get messages to and from the man now disrespectfully called 'Louis Capet', after his ancestor King Hugues Capet, who reigned from 987 to 996. No longer permitted a title of nobility, Louis was, however, allowed pen and paper to prepare for his trial. He also used these utensils to write notes to his family. In a brilliant piece of subterfuge, the family communicated thus: Cléry would tie a string around the King's note, forming it into a little ball. The little ball would be hidden in a cabinet and would then be collected by a loyal servant named Turgy. Turgy would pass the note to Madame Elisabeth. Madame Elisabeth would answer the note, and put it in a small ball of wool. She would then give the little ball of wool to Turgy who would throw it under Cléry's bed when he walked by. Next, Cléry would pass it to the King. This way, when, for instance, Marie-Thérèse suffered continuous pains in her legs, the King could be secretly informed of her malady, and on December 19, her fourteenth birthday, it was Cléry who brought Marie-Thérèse a birthday present from her father. It was an almanac for the year 1793 – the year in which both her parents would be guillotined.

On Christmas Day, the King wrote his last will and testament. He asked his children to remain united, to obey their mother and to think of his sister, Madame Elisabeth, as their second mother. His advice to his son, should he 'have the unhappiness of becoming King' was:

to dream that he must devote himself entirely to the happiness of his people, that he must forget all hate and resentment . . . that he cannot provide for the people's happiness unless he rules according to the laws, but at the same time, he cannot make the people respect him and know the good that is in his heart unless he has the necessary authority.

Louis XVI now prepared to die. In January 1793, out of 719 possible votes, 366 members – a slim majority – of the Jacobin assembly ordered the execution of the King. His own cousin, the Duc d'Orléans, was among those who voted for the regicide. When word of Orléans's treachery reached England, the Prince of Wales ordered his friend's portrait to be removed from the wall of their men's club and his name scratched off the membership roster. European aristocracy as a whole shunned the Duke for the rest of his life – which was not for much longer, for on November 6, 1793, he too would go to the guillotine.

At the revolutionaries' convention, the Americans Thomas Paine and Gouverneur Morris condemned the brutality of regicide and made eloquent, impassioned speeches pleading for the King's life. There ensued a discussion of the notion of sending the King and his family to America where they would live as ordinary citizens. In fact, a small group of royalists were already on their way to an idyllic piece of land on the Susquehanna River in Pennsylvania, which they would call 'Azilum' – asylum. In the town, which became known as French Azilum, the émigrés built a house, 'Grande Maison', with the hope that the royal family would be allowed to live there in peace. Another group near the town of Wiscasset, Maine also joined together to build a home for the King and his family harboring the same hope. Although the French admired the young country and its colonists who had battled for their own democracy, the Assembly voted to reject the Americans' pleas.

On Sunday, January 20, a crier walked by the Temple Prison, beneath the royal family's quarters, announcing that King Louis XVI had been given the death sentence. That is how the Queen and her children found out that the King was going to die. Cléry was with the royal family when the King came to them and, from seven until after ten that night, he watched the distressing farewell. Marie Antoinette and Louis Charles clung to the King, but it was Marie-Thérèse who became hysterical. In his memoir, Cléry recalled how the usually composed Marie-Thérèse wailed so uncontrollably that she fell onto the floor in a state of near unconsciousness. Later, the Queen's favorite portrait painter, Madame Vigée Le Brun, asked Cléry to recount what had happened so that she could paint the family one last time, but when Madame Le Brun heard the details she was too upset to paint the scene. Another artist, Jean-Baptiste Mallet, did, however, attempt to capture it in a watercolor based on the recollections of a guard on duty. Other artists would follow with their own interpretations.

Before he bid his family goodnight, the King told them that he would see them in the morning. The Queen, who did not even have the strength to undress herself, lay in her bed, weeping and trembling with grief all night. Marie-Thérèse lay on the floor beside her. It snowed until daybreak, when the snow turned to mud. The King was permitted to have a priest with him during his last hours and he requested the Abbé Edgeworth, who also accompanied him to the scaffold. As the King could not bear to again face his family's suffering, he did not keep his word to his wife and children. On January 21, Louis XVI went to the guillotine without a final adieu. Over 80,000 National Guards were mobilized; 3,600 soldiers were stationed strategically around Paris, and 1,500 soldiers protected the prisons. The Dauphin heard the sound of drums and, flailing his arms at his guard, screamed, 'Let me out! Let me out!' The jailer asked the sobbing boy where he planned to go. 'To talk to the people so they don't kill my father!'

By 10.30 a.m., the Queen knew that her husband was dead. She kneeled on the floor in front of her son and said, 'The King is dead. Long live the King!' She then rose, and all three women – Marie

Antoinette, Marie-Thérèse and Madame Elisabeth – curtsied deeply before Louis Charles.

Marie Antoinette, Marie-Thérèse and Madame Elisabeth and the new seven-year-old King waited for news. They hoped that Cléry would return and tell them about Louis XVI's last hours. After the King's execution, however, government officials refused to allow Cléry to meet with the Queen, and shortly afterward, he left the Temple Prison. Cléry was especially troubled at not being able to speak with Marie Antoinette because the King had given him an important final mission: before going to the scaffold, the King had removed his wedding ring and signet ring and placed them together in a packet with locks of his children's hair. He handed it all to Cléry to take to the Queen with a message: the King asked Cléry to deliver the packet to the Queen and tell Marie Antoinette that he would only have removed his cherished wedding band in death.

The packet containing the ring, the locks of hair and the King's seal was found and confiscated by prison officials. Two months after the King's death, a kind-hearted official named Toulon secretly slipped the packet to the Queen, and for this gesture to the widow he was guillotined. The Queen managed to smuggle the packet to her former secretary, Jarjayes. On the fifth anniversary of the death of Louis XVI, Cléry was in Blakenberg with the late King's brother, the Comte de Provence, and he offered to let Provence read the journal that he had kept of his time in the Temple Prison. When Provence got to the passage about his late brother's personal effects, he went to a drawer and pulled out a note signed by Marie Antoinette, the Dauphin and Marie-Thérèse along with the signet ring, and asked Cléry if he recognized the items. Cléry was overcome.

On January 28, one week after the death of Louis XVI, the Comte de Provence and a group of émigrés, now in Westphalia, held a memorial service for the King and proclaimed the Dauphin, Louis XVII, King of France. The Count, in exile, declared himself Regent until the boy's majority in a little more than five years' time. Both the young King and his teenage sister, quite ill after their father's execution, remained without medical care. Marie-Thérèse had persistent leg pains and boils from an infection she had contracted from being confined in her filthy quarters. It took over a month for her to recover and she believed that it was only her own sad state that kept her mother preoccupied and from going mad with grief. The Queen refused to walk upstairs to the outdoor gallery because she simply could not bear walking past the King's room.

As the months wore on, life in the prison for the Queen and her children became even more punitive. In early May, the little King was again ill with a very high fever and a pain in his side. Despite the Queen's continual requests for Dr Brunier, the boy was denied medical treatment. At last, a doctor was allowed to see him, and he had the good sense to consult the boy's own physician. The fever subsided, but the pain in his side did not. Marie-Thérèse insisted that her brother's health was never the same after that.

On July 3, the guards arrived to separate Louis Charles from his mother. Terrified, the eight-year-old boy threw himself at his mother and she refused to let go of him. Threats against her own life did not frighten Marie Antoinette; it was only when the jailers threatened to kill her son that she at last acquiesced. She was so distraught that she could not dress him, so Marie-Thérèse readied her younger brother for solitary confinement. Louis Charles kissed his mother, sister and aunt goodbye and was dragged away in tears by the prison guards. For days and nights, Marie-Thérèse and her mother could hear his cries and then his screams when the guards beat him for crying. There was a small chink through which the Queen could watch her son pass in the distance, and she lived for those moments, 'her sole hope, her sole occupation' wrote Marie-Thérèse.

The jailers' instructions, apparently issued by the National Convention, were to remove all traces of 'arrogance and royalty' in the boy, and to prepare him to testify against Marie Antoinette. His own harsh jailer, a shoemaker named Antoine Simon, took his orders from Jacques Hébert, a powerful member of the Commune and publisher of the radical newspaper, Le Père Duchesne. Hébert, a former monk, masterminded the torment perpetrated on the boy, according to Marie-Thérèse. Hébert's minions taught the young king obscene language and poured alcohol down his throat until he became ill. Simon would tell the little boy that they were going to guillotine him, as they had his father, until Louis Charles passed out with fright. The boy was forced to wear the clothing of the revolutionaries and was coerced into signing a document stating that his mother, his sister and his aunt had all sexually molested him. Both the Spanish and English Foreign Secretaries received information from their spies at the Temple Prison that prostitutes had been brought to the prison to rape and infect the eight-year-old boy with sexual diseases so that the Commune could manufacture 'evidence' against the Queen. Louis Charles developed constant diarrhea yet nothing was done to treat his illness.[1]

On July 31, the National Convention approved a proposal to destroy the royal necropolis at Saint-Denis. The lead and bronze caskets of a thousand years of Kings, Queens and Princes of the Blood was to be melted down to make bullets. At the beginning of August, the Committee of Public Safety began its program of emptying the coffins and dumping the bones of France's rulers into a mound of quicklime. At the same time, their living Queen, Marie Antoinette, was moved to the Conciergerie, a medieval prison on the Île de la Cité, which would be her last 'home'. When the officials arrived to remove the Queen from her daughter, Marie-Thérèse begged them to allow her to go as well, but they refused. The Queen embraced her daughter and told her to have courage, and, as her father had instructed, to obey her aunt as a second mother. On leaving the tower, the Queen hit her head on the lintel of the door. A government official asked her if she had hurt herself. 'No. Nothing can hurt me now,' were the last words her daughter heard her say.

Marie-Thérèse and her aunt Elisabeth cried themselves to sleep for weeks. Every time Marie-Thérèse heard the beating of drums she feared that it might signal her mother's execution or another massacre. She was relieved to find that she and her aunt were mostly ignored except when servants brought in food and water. Marie-Thérèse made her own bed, swept her floors and saw almost no one. She and her aunt were searched every day and they were no longer allowed to walk along the tower gallery.

While Marie-Thérèse anxiously awaited news of her mother, on August 25, a poster nailed on the door of Marie Antoinette's beloved Petit Trianon at Versailles announced an estate sale like no other. From 10 a.m. to 4 p.m. and every day thereafter all furniture, paintings, *objets*, pots and pans, clothing, books and any and all personal and intimate belongings of the royal family – even the wardrobe, schoolbooks and toys that had belonged to the children – would be sold to the highest bidder. A note on the announcement stated that goods to be exported would be exempt from taxes. Thus began the incomprehensible dismantling of the entire complex of the Palace of Versailles. Architectural structures, sculptures, priceless antiques, as well as tokens of mere sentimental value, were stripped from the premises. While serving as US Minister to France between 1794 and 1797, James Monroe would make many purchases of furniture, porcelain and plate in France, which he would bring back to America, including, from Versailles, a desk on which he would in 1823 craft the document known as the 'Monroe Doctrine', as well as a china scent bottle decorated with cabbage roses and the initials 'MA' etched on it in gold.

As pieces of her life were making their way to Parisian antiques dealers, Marie Antoinette waited in her cell at the Conciergerie expecting to die, though holding on to a fragment of hope that she and her children might yet be rescued.

There had, in fact, been a number of well-intentioned but ill-fated attempts to rescue the Queen including one that became known as 'the carnation plot' when a flower bearing a note was dropped at the Queen's foot in order to forewarn her of the attempt. Another involved an eccentric Englishwoman, a former actress called Mrs Charlotte Atkyns. The highly determined and slightly delusional Atkyns traveled to Paris and managed to slip into the prison disguised as a National Guardsman. Here she hoped to change places with the Queen and thus save her. According to Atkyns, although she was able to see Marie Antoinette, she was only able to hand the imprisoned Queen a posy of flowers – and in the process create a legend concerning her own exploits.

While Marie Antoinette's friends were trying desperately to free her, her enemies were preparing to put her to death, and they would use her own children toward that purpose. On October 8, Marie-Thérèse was taken downstairs to her brother's cell. She was alarmed by how ill and bloated he had become in the short time since they had been separated. She also noticed that the boy whom the Queen had once playfully described as 'a peasant child . . . big . . . fresh-faced and fat' had hardly grown in height at all since he had entered the prison. The government officials questioned her about Varennes, her prison guards, and 'a great many vile things of which they accused my mother and my aunt. I was aghast at such horrors, and so indignant that, in spite of the fear I felt, I could not keep myself from saying it was an infamy'.

Some commentators have claimed, with great melodrama, that Marie-Thérèse's spirit was broken by these proceedings; that at some point under interrogation she collapsed and suffered a nervous breakdown. According to her own journal, however, although she cried with shock when she understood the perversity of the officials' questions, and when they tried to make her dishonor her mother, Marie-Thérèse stood her ground for hours. She refused to name anyone involved in the flight to Varennes or any sympathetic prison officials. She wrote later that her parents had always taught her that 'it was better to die than to compromise anyone, no matter whom'. Marie-Thérèse noted that although they examined Madame Elisabeth for one hour, they questioned her for three. She believed that the men assumed that because she was young, she would be intimidated. She clearly was not.

At the Conciergerie the Queen was interrogated for days, and on

Monday, October 14, she was put on trial. Unlike the King, she was not permitted to mount a defense. At the last minute, two lawyers arrived and asked to have the proceedings delayed so that they could read all of the 'evidence' that had been collected against her. They were denied their request. Marie Antoinette's trial was a sham; but, as usual, she impressed everyone with her dignity. As she sat on an unimposing armchair that had been placed on a small platform, the clerk read out the accusations against her, calling her the 'new Agrippina' – a reference to the infamous sister of Caligula, who was said to have enjoyed incestuous relations with her brother, to have had undue influence over her son, Nero, and was accused of plotting the downfall of Rome.

The charges against Marie Antoinette included crimes against France stemming as far back as her arrival as a fourteen-year-old Dauphine. She was accused of spying for her brother, the Holy Roman Emperor Joseph II, and of giving him vast amounts of money from the French treasury. She was charged with masterminding the trip to Varennes and, worst of all, of sexually abusing her son. When she heard the testimonies of Simon and Hébert that her son had accused her and her sister-in-law of molestation, the Queen became distressed, realizing that they must have first harmed or tortured Louis Charles in some way. Incredulous and struck dumb, Marie Antoinette eventually found her voice and replied: 'If I have said nothing, it is because nature refused to respond to such a question posed to a mother.' She then made an appeal to all mothers, refuting the charges as grotesque and, although her courage and her words garnered sympathy from even those who disliked her, she was nonetheless sentenced to death.

At 4.30 in the morning on October 16, 1793, hours before she was to be guillotined, Marie Antoinette wrote her final thoughts in a letter to her sister-in-law Madame Elisabeth. Mistakenly believing that Marie-Thérèse had been separated from her aunt, the Queen addressed her note only to her sister-in-law and not her daughter. Her only regret, wrote Marie Antoinette, was that she was abandoning her children. She asked for-giveness from her enemies, and from Madame Elisabeth for the time she persuaded the King not to let Madame Elisabeth join a convent as she had wished. The Queen wrote that she regretted her interference and begged pardon from the woman to whom she would commend her children. Marie Antoinette also begged the virtuous Madame Elisabeth to forgive little Louis Charles for his ignorant allegations. She implored her sister-in-law to understand his terrible situation and his innocence. The Queen asked her to kiss her 'poor and dear children' and say goodbye to them, and, as her husband had before her, she expressed her final hope that they would reunite and love each other, always help each other, and forgive the people of France.

After sunrise, the Queen, who had been denied a non-juror priest[2] and refused mourning clothes, dressed in white and asked God to forgive her sins without benefit of a clergyman. The executioner arrived and bound her wrists. When she informed her guard that she needed some privacy to relieve herself, he would not consent to leave her side, claiming that his duty was to keep an eye on her at all times. Even during her final moments the Queen of France was not accorded the privacy that ordinary citizens enjoyed: Marie Antoinette suffered the humiliation of having to squat in a corner with a guard and executioner immediately nearby. She was then taken from the Conciergerie in an ordinary cart to endure the final taunts and insults of crowds lining the streets to the Place du Carrousel. Twenty-three years earlier, she had made her way in a gilded carriage from the Rhine to the Palace of Versailles, and the masses had excitedly hailed her as their beautiful Dauphine who would carry the future of France in her womb. On this day, as she made her way from the Conciergerie, near the Place Dauphine on the Île de la Cité, she symbolized the gloaming of the ancien régime – the past.

The Queen carefully ascended the scaffold, but accidentally stepped on the executioner's foot. 'I did not do it on purpose,' she reportedly said, her apology her last words on earth. At two weeks shy of her thirty-eighth birthday, Marie Antoinette was guillotined. Later that morning, the Queen's enemies violated the grave of her beloved son, the first Dauphin, Louis Joseph and, in celebration, disinterred the boy's remains and tossed them into a mass grave.

Marie Antoinette's letter never reached Madame Elisabeth. It was intercepted and given to Robespierre, and at the time, Marie-Thérèse, isolated in her cell, doors bolted, had no inkling of her mother's death. Nor did Louis Charles. Locked in his own room with only a bell to ring for his needs, the boy was so afraid of his jailers that he avoided all contact with them, often going without food for days rather than face potential abuse. Marie-Thérèse wrote that she continued to have no knowledge of the outside world besides the announcements of passing newsboys. It was by this means that she learnt that the Duc d'Orléans, now called a traitor simply by virtue of his aristocratic bloodline, had been executed. According to eyewitnesses, the populist Duke went to the scaffold dressed lavishly and, in contrast to the King and Queen, met his end with cowardice and fear.

By the autumn of 1793, the capricious and bloody Reign of Terror was under way. Girondists, Jacobins, Cordeliers and other factions all had to answer to the ultimate authority: the Committee for Public Safety. Determined to break with the past, the Committee established a new, revolutionary calendar. The new regime was so rancorous, so randomly brutal that, with the Law of Suspects enacted on September 17, which created a tribunal specifically to condemn to death those it found guilty of treason, it turned neighbor against neighbor, and would shortly turn against its own leaders.

From November 25–30, the Committee debated the notion that because Marie-Thérèse contained the vile blood of the Bourbons, she too should face the 'national razor'. Some objected to this plan because of her age. Another idea was suggested: Why not poison the girl? Robespierre, the brilliant orator known as 'L'Incorruptible', and one of the leaders of the Committee for Public Safety, had always been antithetic to the royal family; this time, however, Robespierre showed some sympathy for a Bourbon and devised a plan that would spare the Princess. He argued that a law should be passed ordering all girls over the age of fifteen to marry, and if they did not within six months, they would be brought to public justice. Robespierre was aware that Marie-Thérèse would be fifteen in about three weeks' time, and he thought that if he could find a husband outside France for 'Mademoiselle Capet', as the Commune referred to her, he could save her. Or, in 'an act of equality . . . one could marry her off with a young sans-culotte who had been wounded in the army'. One argument that even made its way to her uncle, the Comte de Provence, in exile, was that 'the odious Robespierre' had designs on his 'unfortunate niece'.

On December 28, 1793, English spies reported to their contact in Italy that the discussion of the murder of Marie-Thérèse had been tabled. Before the execution of the Queen, Madame de Staël, who had not, in the past, thought highly of Marie Antoinette, decided to write an impassioned plea for the life of the Queen and her children. Staël argued that the revolutionary government in France should allow Marie Antoinette to return to Austria, claiming that all of Europe was watching. She referred to the children as unfortunate victims, and warned that not only would France be judged harshly for its barbaric treatment of the children, but also a country that enacted such punishment was not destined for liberty.

Unaware of the debate in France regarding her future, Marie-Thérèse felt abandoned, not least by her European cousins. Around Christmas, some two months after the Queen had gone to the scaffold, Marie-

Thérèse heard repeated condemnations of her mother and assumed her still to be alive.

The execution of Louis XVI and his Queen had done nothing to assuage the intense enmity felt for the aristocracy in France. The blood-letting merely increased and spread from Paris throughout the country. Now *La Terreur* reigned. Young children parroted their parents and were taught that the royal children were wicked, and indoctrinated into believing that Marie-Thérèse and her little brother were in league with the devil. One girl, a bourgeoise named Michelet whose father served as a guard at the Temple Prison, wrote to a friend that:

> The young princess, despite the charm of her age . . . is more Austrian than her mother . . . her looks are filled with pride and scorn . . . The nature of these crowned persons is truly different than our own. They are without soul.[3]

In the tower, sixteen-year-old Marie-Thérèse prayed for deliverance. She and her aunt were refused ointments for sores, caps to keep their heads warm, and were even accused of making counterfeit money.

On January 19, 1794, Marie-Thérèse heard a great deal of noise in the prison tower and wrote that it sounded as if things were being dragged. When she peeked through a keyhole and saw a great many large parcels she thought that perhaps preparations were being made for her brother to leave the prison. She imagined that a German prisoner of war or someone else was to take his place, and in her mind she baptized the unknown prisoner 'Melchisedech', after the biblical figure who had brought bread and wine to a victorious Abraham. She found out, however, that it was the jailer, Simon, who was moving out and she later described the decision to leave her ailing little brother alone and without anyone to care for him as 'barbaric'.

By spring, the Terror had turned inward. On March 24, Hébert, the man who had perpetrated so many evils against Louis Charles, was sent to the guillotine for having become an outspoken critic of the powerful Robespierre faction within the Committee for Public Safety. The Committee itself then turned its attentions to Madame Elisabeth, Marie-Thérèse's 'second mother'. On March 29, Madame Elisabeth petitioned the jailers for clean underwear for her niece. They responded that if she wanted clean underwear, she should wash it herself; the nation was sick of her demands. On May 9, just as Marie-Thérèse and Madame Elisabeth were going to bed, there was a loud knock at the door. Officials ordered

Madame Elisabeth downstairs without Marie-Thérèse. The two kissed goodbye and Madame Elisabeth told her niece to have courage, firmness, always to have faith in God, to practice the principles of the religion given to her by her parents and to follow the last instructions that the late King and Queen had wished her to follow.

Marie-Thérèse was once again left without information. She had no idea what had happened to her aunt. Much later she would learn that within a few hours of their separation, Madame Elisabeth, just thirty years old, had gone to the scaffold with the same dignity as her parents. At the foot of the guillotine, the women with whom Madame Elisabeth shared a cart asked to kiss her before they died. The executioners then made her aunt wait in the cart until last so that she could watch the execution of the other women.

Madame Elisabeth had assisted in raising her niece toward the goal that, as a Bourbon princess destined always to be in the public eye, she should serve as a model for all women. Madame Elisabeth could have left the country with her aunts or brothers; however, she chose instead to stay with the King and his children. Marie-Thérèse recognized her young aunt's sacrifice and remembered her as pious, good, gentle and modest. 'It is said that we resembled each other in face: I feel that I have her nature,' she once wrote. She acknowledged that her aunt 'considered me and cared for me as her daughter, and I, I honored her as a second mother'.

The only two members of the royal family now left in the prison, separated by walls, a staircase and rebel guards, and unaware of each other's condition, were the two children, Louis Charles, who had just turned nine, and his one-time protectress, his sister, Marie-Thérèse.

CHAPTER XI
SOLE SURVIVOR

BEFORE HER EXECUTION, Madame Elisabeth had instructed Marie-Thérèse that if she were to be left alone in the prison she should ask for a female companion. The guards were often drunk, and rumors abounded that the young girl had already been raped in prison.[1] Marie-Thérèse obeyed her aunt, but she was denied anything and everything she asked for. She asked the guards where her aunt was and received the sarcastic reply 'getting some air'. She asked to be taken from the prison to see her mother, and was met with silence. She begged to see her brother, but was denied contact due to an official order from the Committee of Public Safety.

Two days after Madame Elisabeth's death, Marie-Thérèse received a surprise visitor. A man appeared in her cell. Neither Marie-Thérèse nor many of the guards knew his identity; his visit was obviously a secret. She wrote that the officials with him showed him great deference and she believed the man who looked at her with such insolence to be none other than Robespierre. He examined her reading materials and her cell and then left. Onlookers wrote of Marie-Thérèse's composure during the visit. She had informed the prison officials that she would not speak one word to her guards or visitors unless they told her the whereabouts of her mother and aunt, and she made no exception for this particular visitor. Instead of speaking, she handed him a note addressed to the Convention, unaware that the Committee of Public Safety was now in control. The note read: 'My brother is sick. I have written to the Convention for permission to nurse him. The Convention has not yet responded. I reiterate my demand.'

English spies recorded that on the evening of May 23, 1794, Robespierre returned to the prison, this time to kidnap Marie-Thérèse's brother. It was claimed this was to test palace security and that he brought the boy back to his cell a day later. According to the spies, the Committee of Public Safety had no knowledge of this escapade, if it indeed occurred at all.

Each morning, Marie-Thérèse swept her room and ate her breakfast quietly. Government officials refused to supply her with new books to read and she had grown bored of the ones she had: *Voyages* by La Harpe, and a prayer book, which she had read over and over. She no longer knew the names of the people who brought her food, and she no longer spoke with anyone unless a formal interrogation was demanded, and in that case she answered in as few words as possible.

Louis Charles also suffered alone. His sheets were left unchanged for months and he remained in the same clothes for over a year. His excrement remained in his room; no one bothered to remove it. He was severely light deprived and suffered from rickets. For a long while Marie-Thérèse had heard his cries for his mother and his screams when he was beaten. He was permitted neither fresh air nor medical care and eventually he lost the ability to walk.

Marie-Thérèse was completely isolated not only from her brother but also from the events of the Revolution still ravaging France. Cut off from news, she measured the political winds – a change of power or a change of mood – by the arrival of new officials in her room. She also knew that something significant had occurred if she heard the beat of drums and the ringing of church bells. She knew nothing, for instance, of the insurrection of royalists in the Vendée. In one of the bloodiest massacres in history, over 100,000 men, women and children died in that western region of France when the local citizens took up arms to defend their faith and, by extension, the monarchy, against the Revolution.

On June 10, the Law of 22 Prairial (the date of the revolutionary calendar) was enacted. This law empowered every citizen to turn in any person believed to be an 'enemy of the Revolution'. This draconian ordinance limited the ability of the accused to defend themselves, guaranteeing almost certain death merely on the word of one's neighbor or enemy. One month later, on July 27 (the revolutionary date 9 Thermidor) the Committee of Public Safety ordered the execution of Robespierre without trial. Among the accusations hurled against 'L'Incorruptible' by his political enemy, Barère, was the charge that he had plans to marry Marie-Thérèse and place himself on the throne. On the morning of July 28, Robespierre and more than twenty of his comrades were guillotined. Found among Robespierre's possessions and under his mattress after his death were some very personal mementos of the late Queen – a lock of hair that Marie Antoinette had cut from Louis Charles's head, locks of the Queen's own hair, and the last letter that Marie Antoinette had written to her sister-in-law, Madame Elisabeth, on the morning of her execution – stolen as grisly tokens and proof of his own power. One day after his execution, the Dauphin's sadistic former warden, Antoine Simon, was also guillotined.

Paul François Jean Nicolas Barras, a soldier and Jacobin nobleman who had risen to prominence in the Convention, had, with the help of his young protégé, Napoleon Bonaparte, successfully suppressed insurrections in the south of France, fighting loyalist and English forces, most notably at the siege of Toulon where Napoleon had been artillery commander. Barras was subsequently appointed Commander of the Army in Paris. Napoleon, meanwhile, showed that he was equally skillful in the conquest of women when, upon returning to the capital, he stole Barras's mistress, the widow Josephine de Beauharnais. Barras showed little animosity toward his henchman for his actions and continued to support his advancement. Barras openly explained to friends that he was, in fact, quite relieved because Madame Josephine had been proving to be an expensive distraction.

Marie-Thérèse recalled that at six o'clock on the morning of July 28 (10 Thermidor) she heard the guards' cry to arms, the drums beat, the gates to the prison open then close and shortly afterwards the bolts of her brother's cell door being drawn back. She dressed hurriedly. It was Barras. He had decided to visit the royal children in the prison. Despite his active participation among the Jacobins and in the Revolution, Barras respectfully addressed the children as 'Prince' and 'Madame'. Barras recorded in his memoirs the pitiable conditions he witnessed. On entering the little boy's chamber, he reported that he could barely breathe owing to the noxious smell. There he found the nine-year-old lying in a tiny bed, little more than a cradle, in the middle of an intolerably filthy room. The boy was drowsy and weak and he kept glancing nervously at his jailers. When Barras asked to speak with Louis Charles, the boy said that he was fine and that he just wanted to sleep. It was clear that the child did not want to say anything critical of his conditions for fear of retribution. Barras next climbed the stairway to see Madame Royale, whose room he found in a better state. When Barras questioned Marie-Thérèse she refused to answer him.

Barras ordered that the children be allowed to walk every day in the courtyard in order to get some exercise and fresh air. He reported to the

Committee of Public Safety that the boy needed to see a doctor. His request was ignored. However, three days after his visit, a new guard – a twenty-four-year-old man from Martinique named Laurent – appeared in Marie-Thérèse's room and asked if she needed anything. He addressed her politely and removed a bed from her room to give to her brother, whose bug-infested bed was to be disposed of. She learned that a new government, with Barras and his group at the helm, was responsible for the more humane treatment.

Laurent too was overwhelmed by the stench and horrific sight of the boy's room. Louis Charles lay inert on the cot-bed, his skin green-gray, his stomach bloated, his eyes enormous and his face hollow from malnutrition. He had black, blue and yellow welts all over his body and his nails were excessively long. Laurent immediately ordered that the child should be bathed, the vermin that covered his body removed and all the furnishings and curtains in the room removed and burnt. He asked for there to be an inquiry into the Dauphin's condition and that very same day members of the Committee of Public Safety came to inspect the boy's cell. Unlike Simon, who had scornfully called the boy 'Capet', Laurent always referred to him as 'Monsieur Charles'. Occasionally, Laurent would carry Louis Charles up to the tower gallery so that he could look at birds and trees and stars. The quality of the prison food did not improve, however, and Louis Charles remained too debilitated by malnourishment and other ailments to walk by himself. While talk of liberty pervaded France, the two children remained cruelly incarcerated.

One child vanquished; one defiant. Marie-Thérèse still refused to speak with anyone but she sensed that Laurent might be more willing to give her information about her mother and aunt, and so she finally decided to speak with him. He was, however, under strict orders not to divulge the fates of Marie Antoinette or Madame Elisabeth. At all other times, Laurent followed orders but performed his duties with kindness and compassion. Previous guards had taken away all candles and matchboxes from their royal charges, leaving them to endure long periods in darkness. One day, after the powder magazine at nearby Grenelle exploded, terrifying Marie-Thérèse, Laurent returned her box of matches and candles to her. Now, noises in the dark would be less frightening.

There had been multiple tales of Louis Charles's escape and death. At the beginning of November a civil commission came to the prison, staying for twenty-four hours, to verify the fact that the boy in the cell was indeed Louis Charles. On the 8th, the Committee of Public Safety appointed a man named Gomin to join Laurent in the care of Louis Charles. Laurent introduced Gomin to Marie-Thérèse but, predictably, she refused to speak with him. Gomin, like his colleague, Laurent, and Barras before them, was shaken when he saw the little boy and he asked the commission to visit the children once more. At the end of November, another official named Delboy came to see Louis Charles. Delboy tried to speak to the boy but received no answer as Louis Charles was by now far too weak to speak. Delboy reflected on how a country that hailed fraternity could treat a child in such a cruel way: the sun was for everyone, he declared to the guards, and had the bars from the cell's window removed. Louis Charles's eyes lit up. 'You would like to be outside playing with your sister?' Delboy enquired. Turning to Laurent and Gomin, he apparently said: 'It is not his fault if he is the son of his father . . . we have here no more than an unhappy little boy; so, do not be harsh with him: unhappiness is the master of all humanity, but the country is the mother of all children.'

Louis Charles now had more light in his room and Gomin spent hours every day with the boy. When Louis Charles became feverish, Gomin petitioned the Committee to visit the boy and see his condition for themselves. Gomin and Laurent were allowed to carry the child outdoors for fresh air and, one day in late November, Marie-Thérèse caught a glimpse of her brother on his way up to the tower. Louis Charles was so sick, however, that he could not spend much time outside, and mostly remained in his cell by the fire.

On December 19, Madame Royale's sixteenth birthday, three commissioners, Harmand de la Meuse, Matthieu, and Reverchon came to the prison to see the royal children. Harmand de la Meuse, who published his account over twenty years later after the Bourbons had been returned to power, set himself in a very good light. He stated that after having seen the little boy, he climbed the stairs to visit Marie-Thérèse. He had been warned that she would not speak to him. It was a cold, rainy day, and the tower was particularly damp and glacial. The teenage girl wore a gray cotton toile dress, which, he noted, could not possibly keep her warm, and a tired little cap. She was knitting and seemed uneasy. He saw that her hands were swollen and nearly purple from the cold and that her fingers appeared chilblained. As she turned her head toward him, he recalled that he saw her disquiet and asked 'Her Highness' why, with such excessive cold, did she sit so far from the fire? Marie-Thérèse answered that the light was better where she was sitting. He told her that a fire would throw off light. She said that she had insufficient wood to keep the fire going. Harmand de la Meuse alleged that he offered to tune her piano, obtain for her clean underclothes and anything else that she desired. When he saw that she had a copy of the prayer book *The Imitation of Jesus Christ* and religious works, he wondered aloud if these books were enough diversion for the imprisoned teenage girl. 'These books are precisely the ones that suit my situation,' Marie-Thérèse is said to have replied.

Harmand de la Meuse, who, again, published his version of this encounter when Marie-Thérèse was in a position of power, found her response 'sublime' and 'edified', adding that this young woman was suffering the most unjust captivity. He said he assured Marie-Thérèse that he would allow her to see her brother. Then, said Harmand de la Meuse, he and his colleagues left these two children – 'of the most august family in Europe' – in tears, adding that he would have kept his promises to Marie-Thérèse had he not been sent immediately on a mission to the Indies.

Harmand de la Meuse's actual report to the Committee of Public Safety in 1794, however, was far less effusive and complimentary about the royal children.[2] As Harmand de la Meuse himself had written, he had been forewarned that Marie-Thérèse would not speak with him. The more truthful version of the account was surely Marie-Thérèse's own version in which she stated that Harmand de la Meuse did not say one word to her.

On February 23, 1795, another civil servant, named Leroux, who was an admirer of the late Robespierre, toured the prison. When he entered Marie-Thérèse's room she completely ignored him, failed to even raise her head, and continued with her needlework. Leroux, a self-important functionary, insisted: 'Does one not rise before the People?' Marie-Thérèse remained mute and immobile. She would not communicate her feelings or needs to any visiting municipals. Instead she chose to record her 'hopes' and 'fears' in rhyming couplets in her private diary:

Sans discourir, ouvrez dit-on	Without discourse, 'Open' one says
Je me lève mon coeur balance	I wake my heart balanced
Entre la crainte et l'espérance	Between fear and hope
Je croyais que j'allais partir	I believed that I was going to leave
De la tour j'espérais sortir	The tower I hoped to depart

The fact that these officials felt they could just visit her at any hour of the day or night distressed her:

Fiers sans doute d'un tel exploit	Proud, no doubt, of such exploits
Contents d'avoir fait leur emploi	Content to have done their work
que pour me venir voir	that come to see me
Ils abusèrent de leur pouvoir	They abuse their power
En choisissant une heure indue	In choosing an undue hour
Pour se présenter à ma vue . . .	To present themselves in my sight . . .

Whenever there was a knock at the door her emotions rocked 'between fear and hope'. She hoped each time for liberty, but then the doors would be slammed and bolted once again and she would return to her needlework, or her bed.

Despite their wretched lives, the Children of France had not been forgotten. The new government saw in its treatment of them an opportunity to disassociate itself from the Terror. There was also a revival of foreign interest in the 'Orphans of the Temple', as they now became known, that led the republican government to see the children as useful pawns. In an attempt to portray the new regime as more humane, the republican newspaper, *Courrier Universel,* published a story stating that the royal children in the tower, like everybody in France, had also benefited from the coup that had deposed Robespierre. The article pointed to the improved treatment the children were receiving. Others took this 'newfound humanity' as a sign to step up their efforts to get the children released. The very same Mrs Atkyns who had tried to smuggle the Queen out of the Conciergerie spent a considerable amount of time and money formulating plans to kidnap the little King and his sister from the tower. Others continued to try to ensure that the children had better medical care and nutrition. François Hüe, just released after a long period of incarceration, approached the Committee of Public Safety and asked if he could move in with Louis Charles in order to care for him, but his request was refused.

The young government of France had been at war for almost as long as it had been in existence. As early as January 1795, representatives of Franz II, the Holy Roman Emperor, and the Spanish King, Charles IV, began conducting negotiations with the French Foreign Minister, François Barthélemy, in Switzerland. The Spanish King, via his experienced ambassador, Domingo d'Yriarte, set forth his conditions: in order for Spain to recognize the new government of France, the royal children must be released. In addition, the son of Louis XVI was to be given Navarre, his inherited right, to govern as his own country. Although a formal treaty with Spain was greatly desired by the revolutionary government of

France, they would not agree to turning over any territories. Franz II tried to offer money in exchange for the children. Another French minister in Switzerland, Théobald Jacques Justin Bacher, wrote to the Committee of Public Safety asking if he could stall for more time until he could obtain the best offer. All parties understood that the two monarchs hoped to annex lands. The Spanish King coveted the Low Navarre. Franz II had a subtler plan: if Marie-Thérèse could be brought to Vienna and to the altar with one of his brothers, the Emperor would have a reason to reclaim Lorraine. Throughout these negotiations both monarchs demanded and received up-to-date reports on the health and welfare of the royal children.

Others began to ask questions as well. Journalists who dared to write of the inhumane treatment of the children were thrown in jail. Reports began to circulate that the Dauphin had been rescued or kidnapped and another boy had been placed in his cell. It was an easy story to believe as vermin, bugs, fleas and scabies now covered the boy and rendered him unrecognizable. On March 31, 1795, Laurent was replaced by a man named Etienne Lasne who now joined Gomin in guarding and caring for the ten-year-old boy and his sister. Lasne remembered Marie-Thérèse as strong and full of courage. She woke early, dressed, combed her hair, made her bed and cleaned her room as if she had been born to servitude. She was, he observed, an example of 'resignation and will'.

When, at last, on May 6, Dr Pierre-Joseph Desault was permitted to treat Louis Charles, the doctor reported the atrocious details of the boy's mistreatment. A month later Dr Desault was dead, killed by a sudden mysterious illness – some believed he had been poisoned. Two further doctors, Jean-Baptiste-Eugénie Dumangin and Philippe-Jean Pelletan, came to treat Louis Charles, but to no avail. At about 2.30 in the afternoon on June 8, 1795, the ten-year-old King Louis XVII died. The cause of death was given as tuberculosis, but the child had languished and suffered from so many pernicious infections that the exact cause of death was almost irrelevant. Lasne and Gomin both witnessed the cadaver and the next day government officials came to see it as well. It took four days for the officials to announce the child's demise to the public. The autopsy was performed by Dr Pelletan who secretly wrapped the boy's heart in a handkerchief and took it home with him.

The horrendous treatment of the child had taken its toll even on those who had had a hand in the cruelty. Some could no longer bear the responsibility for their own participation in the unconscionable torment of a child. One woman, a Madame Tison, who worked in the jail alongside her husband, suffered a mental breakdown and for years thereafter insisted that she had helped the Dauphin escape. Over twenty years after the boy's death, another woman, Madame Simon, who had assisted her husband in the torture of Louis XVII, insisted that Louis Charles had visited her in her hospital room. Haunted by memories, some later offered deathbed confessions. With the passage of time the conspirators in torture would one by one offer up shriven apologies, their tales re-igniting passionate interest in the disappearance of the boy King. Some cried that he had been poisoned, but Pelletan, the doctor who performed the autopsy, denied this. Later, when Marie-Thérèse learned of her brother's death, she confronted such rumors by stating that the only poison that killed her brother was the brutality of his captors.

While all of Europe learned the pitiable details of the little boy's death, his own sister remained completely ignorant. On June 16, French émigrés in Germany declared the Comte de Provence 'King Louis XVIII of France', and a week later in Verona, Provence accepted the crown in exile.

Meanwhile, a group of citizens from the town of Orléans, so horrified by news of the boy's demise, appeared before the Convention and made a touching and impassioned plea for the deliverance of the 'orphan girl' from the Temple Prison. The officials ignored their request; but it was becoming clear that there was growing attention focused on Marie-Thérèse and her plight and that this was causing the populace to pity her. It was essential that the French people did not learn the details of Marie-Thérèse's incarceration and the Convention determined to get her out of the country. On June 30, 1795, the republican government agreed in principle to releasing the only surviving child of Marie Antoinette to her Habsburg family in Vienna in exchange for nine French prisoners of war. Among the prisoners requested was Drouet, the man responsible for capturing the royal family in Varennes.

The Committee for Public Safety decreed that it would place a female companion with Marie-Thérèse. Madame Hüe, Madame de Tourzel, Pauline de Tourzel and Madame de Frémonville, who had been in service to the late Queen, all stepped forward to ask for the position. Instead the Committee chose a woman named Madeleine-Élisabeth-Renée-Hilaire Bocquet de Chanterenne, the thirty-year-old wife of a police department administrator and daughter of an Alsatian shipowner who had lost his money before the Revolution. Renée, although provincial, was literate and well educated. She also spoke some Italian and English, had studied history, geography, music, drawing, and was an adept needlewoman. She was pretty and blonde, and considered intelligent and sensible.

When Madame de Chanterenne arrived at the tower, Marie-Thérèse decided to try to speak to the woman. The teenager had barely spoken for over a year and at first found it hard to summon a noise, but on trying a second time managed to ask in a scratchy and quavering voice if her new guardian had news of her family. Madame de Chanterenne had been ordered, like the others, to say nothing, and told the girl that as she had just arrived in Paris she was uninformed.

Madame de Chanterenne pitied Marie-Thérèse and saw that she had little to occupy her, so she obtained new books, clothing, materials for drawing and writing, knitting and needlework, and resumed her lessons, spending hours every day with the teenager. To help the girl regain her voice, she requested that Marie-Thérèse read aloud. She was also pained that she could not divulge the news that Marie-Thérèse so urgently needed to know.

Early in July, Madame de Chanterenne received permission to take Marie-Thérèse into the Temple Prison's gardens, her first chance to breathe fresh air in years. Marie-Thérèse was also delighted that her brother's dog, Coco, a red mixed-breed spaniel, was able to join her. And when the guards gave her a baby goat as a pet, she began to smile again.

As soon as word got out that Marie-Thérèse had been seen walking in the prison gardens, many came to catch a glimpse of the Princess who had been locked in the tower for over three years. In that time she had changed from an adolescent girl of thirteen to a young woman of nearly seventeen years of age. Her father's loyal valet, Hüe, rented an apartment in a nearby building called La Rotonde. From there he could watch the Princess on her promenades and sang songs loudly from his apartment in the hope that she could hear them. Marie-Thérèse would have recognized their romantic lyrics: 'Young, unfortunate one . . . soon the doors will open.' He also brought a Mademoiselle Brévannes to sing and play songs including 'The Young Prisoner', with Madame Hüe accompanying on the harp. Monsieur Hüe, one of the very few people mentioned by name in King Louis XVI's last will and testament, signaled to Marie-Thérèse using their old secret code that he had received a letter from her uncle, the new King, Louis XVIII.

Others, such as Madame de La Briche, came to watch the teenage prisoner. She recalled spying Marie-Thérèse, dressed in white with a fichu tied low around her head, accompanied by her female guardian and the little red dog. Madame de La Briche observed that Marie-Thérèse appeared taller than she actually was because she carried her head high, like her late mother.

Soon the rue de Beaujolais on the southeastern side of the Temple complex near the gardens was filled with spectators at open windows. Marie-Thérèse heard the music and songs being played for her and no longer felt abandoned. One artist set up a telescope and sketched her in the courtyard, while another, Jean Philippe Guy Le Gentil, the Marquis de Paroy, painted the Princess drawing in the garden with her eyes turned toward the tower. Paroy gave the portrait to Madame de Tourzel, who had been repeatedly asking officials for permission to visit her former charge, to give to Marie-Thérèse as a present in case she should be granted her request. The Comte d'Allonville paid a great deal of money to rent a room on the rue de la Corderie, which bordered the entire southern garden walk, so that he, too, could watch the Princess. Although there were many who saw Marie-Thérèse in the garden at the Temple Prison in 1795, later, when rumors circulated that she had switched places with an impostor, those who had seen her from afar could provide only imprecise descriptions.

There was also, as would be expected, interest expressed from fortune seekers. One day a woman arrived at the Temple Prison claiming to be one 'Stéphanie Louise de Bourbon-Conti', the illegitimate daughter of the Prince de Conti and the Duchesse de Mazarin, and therefore Marie-Thérèse's cousin. Although this alleged Bourbon princess had repeatedly made this claim in public, Marie-Thérèse had no idea who the woman was and refused to meet with her. The woman was found to be one Marie Mornand, who later died in an institution for the insane.

On July 30, the Holy Roman Emperor agreed to the terms offered by the French republican government. He would trade French prisoners of war in exchange for his cousin, Marie-Thérèse. His aunt and mother-in-law, Maria Carolina, Queen of Naples, had grown tired of the wrangling and knew that Franz had a political motive in rescuing the Orphan of the Temple. She wrote to him stating that she wanted custody of her niece, that she, in contrast, had no political agenda and that she only wanted to raise her dead sister's child as her own. On August 11, the Queen of Naples reiterated her sentiments to her daughter in Vienna, and suggested it would be a good idea if Marie-Thérèse married her cousin, the Duc d'Angoulême, eldest son of the Comte d'Artois, and she offered them both the hospitality of the Neapolitan court. The Queen of Naples also wrote to her imprisoned niece offering to be her loving mother. Marie-Thérèse replied saying simply: 'My mother had often spoken of you, she loved you more than all her other sisters.'[3]

All summer long French ministers Barthélemy and Bacher remained in Basel negotiating the finer points of the exchange with the Austrian Foreign Minister Degelmann. Franz II insisted that all protocol was to be observed toward the daughter of the late King. This would be no simple matter. There had to be complete agreement on who would accompany her out of France, how the exchange would take place, and where this would happen. Louis XVIII, aware of the exchange, mobilized. He sent letters to the Austrian Emperor stating that the minute his niece was off French soil, he wanted her. He sent his cousin the Prince de Condé and his army closer to the border, and notes to royalists in Paris to pass on loving words to Marie-Thérèse, reassuring her that she would soon be free and that he would act as her new father.

Marie-Thérèse, captive for so long and so unused to kindness, had grown genuinely fond of and emotionally dependent on Madame de Chanterenne and now referred to her as 'my dear Renète'. When she was not with her, the teenager would pen little notes and rhyming couplets to her guardian telling her how much she missed her: '*Qui près de moi dans ces moments/Revient adoucir mes tourments?*' – 'Who is near me in these moments/Returns to soothe my torments?'

On August 17, the *Gazette de France* reported that Marie-Thérèse still did not know of the fate of her mother, aunt and brother. On August 31, the *Journal de Paris* reported the same information; however, by that time, the situation had changed. In the latter part of August, Madame de Chanterenne, unable to stand her friend's torment any longer, broke the news to Marie-Thérèse. One by one, as she told the girl that each member of her family was dead, Marie-Thérèse emitted sobs of anguish and pain. Renée de Chanterenne then wrote to the Committee of Public Safety begging their pardon and explaining that she had not been able to bear the inhumanity of keeping such important information from the girl.

In early September, the Committee at last allowed Madame de Tourzel, Pauline and the elderly Madame Mackau to visit Marie-Thérèse in prison. Madame de Tourzel had anxiously prepared herself to tell Marie-Thérèse that her family was dead until informed by Renée de Chanterenne that Marie-Thérèse had already been told. Madame de Tourzel took an immediate dislike to the Princess's 'companions'. She thought de Chanterenne too coarse and unfit to be in the royal Princess's company, and when Gomin stopped her from looking at the prison register she wondered what he was trying to hide. Marie-Thérèse hugged Pauline and her mother fondly. She told them of the last time she saw her father before he died, and the women all cried together. She then showed them the room in which her brother had died. Pauline was impressed by how strong Marie-Thérèse remained throughout and thought the girl resembled all three of her parents – the King, the Queen, and her 'second mother', Madame Elisabeth. Marie-Thérèse revealed to her old friends that she had scribbled on her cell wall:

> I am the unhappiest of creatures. She can obtain no news of her Mother, nor be reunited to her, though she has asked it a thousand times. Live, my good mother! Whom I love well, but of whom I can hear no tidings. O, my father! Watch over me from heaven above. O, my God! Forgive those who have made my family die.

On the wall of her late brother's empty room, the women saw that he had written in charcoal an unfinished message to his mother, which read '*Maman, je vous pr . . .*' – 'Mummy, I beg you/promise you . . .' On another wall, he had drawn a flower.

Madame de Tourzel, Pauline and Madame de Mackau wept as they envisioned the sadness experienced by the King and his family within the walls of the Temple Prison. De Tourzel asked her how she had withstood the hardships of her incarceration, to which the Princess replied: 'Without religion, it would have been impossible. It was my sole resource and the only consolation that assuaged my heart.' She explained that her feelings of trust for Madame de Chanterenne and Gomin were natural ones given her situation because having been treated so horrifically for so long she would love anyone who showed her kindness. After having seen something of the misery in which Marie-Thérèse had lived the ladies were astonished when the Princess confessed to them that she still loved her country and did not hold the French responsible for her plight.

Madame de Tourzel then broke the news that Marie-Thérèse would shortly be leaving France to live with her mother's family in Vienna and that Franz II had agreed that she accompany her. Marie-Thérèse expressed relief that her incarceration was coming to an end but explained that she would rather have stayed in the country where her family had died, arguing that it would have been better to share in their deaths than to live 'condemned to cry'. She added that if she had to leave France, she wanted to join her father's aunts in Rome. She bore no affection for her Austrian family, who she felt had abandoned her mother.

Madame de Tourzel wrote to the new King, Louis XVIII, of her visit. He responded that he would like the former governess to present an idea to Marie-Thérèse. The Princess already suspected that her trip to Vienna might culminate in her being married to Franz II's brother, the handsome Archduke Karl. Louis XVIII, as her sovereign, her 'father', and her uncle, wanted her to marry his nephew and presumptive heir to the throne, the Duc d'Angoulême. He asked de Tourzel to tell Marie-Thérèse that this union would have been what her parents had wanted. Marie-Thérèse considered obedience to His Majesty as her primary duty and although she could not remember her parents ever suggesting such a thing, from that time forth she would say that she would marry no other man than the one her uncle had chosen for her.

Madame de Tourzel did not want to jeopardize the extradition to Vienna or her own place among the Princess's entourage, so she proceeded delicately, acting as the go-between for the King's emissaries and the Princess. The King thought it important that Marie-Thérèse bring herself up to date with political events and so piles of pamphlets and newspapers were brought in to the prison under cover. And as soon as she was allowed paper and pencil, Marie-Thérèse began her memoir of her time in the Temple Prison. She also wrote poetry, usually creating verses filled with affection for Renète and expressing how grateful she was to the woman who was able to restore to her the simple pleasures so long denied.

The royal family's former courtiers would arrive at the Temple Prison to visit Marie-Thérèse at noon and depart at eight in the evening. On one occasion they brought a ring made for her by the Marquis de Paroy. Apparently, Marie-Thérèse had asked him to create a ring similar to the one he had made for her mother, with images of her husband and children engraved on it. Paroy asked Pauline to measure Marie-Thérèse's finger using a ring of her own, and happily fashioned one for the teenage girl. Marie-Thérèse was thrilled with the ring and hoped to thank him in person soon.

One day, Marie-Thérèse placed a small piece of paper in Pauline de Tourzel's hand. Pauline opened it as soon as she got back to her accommodation. It read, 'I will be attached to you for life.' On other occasions Marie-Thérèse gave Pauline some very personal mementos – the little backgammon set that Louis Charles had played with, and the gold, enamel and amber watch and chain that her mother had given her. The watch had formerly belonged to her grandmother, Maria Theresa, and was the one the Empress had given 'Maria Antonia' upon her departure from Vienna.

All through September, visits from her friends continued. On October 5, 1795 (Vendémiaire 13), there was a mutiny in Paris of pro-monarchy sympathizers that was suppressed by Barras and Napoleon but which, once again, resulted in a change of government and a change in the conditions under which Marie-Thérèse was held. After the insurrection was put down, the Directory, headed by a group of five men including Barras, was formed. On November 8, officials of the new government arrested Madame de Tourzel after she was found to have letters from Louis XVIII in her possession. When Franz II learned that Madame de Tourzel had been working in concert with Louis XVIII he decided to reverse his decision and bar the former governess from entering Austria.

Marie-Thérèse was asked to submit names of people whom she would find suitable as alternative traveling companions. Marie-Thérèse suspected that Renète would never be acceptable to the Austrians because 'the Republic' had appointed her. Nonetheless, Madame de Chanterenne wrote three letters to the Directory and two to the Minister of the Interior, Pierre Bénézech, requesting that she accompany the Princess to Vienna. Marie-Thérèse personally asked for Monsieur and Madame Hüe and her aunt Elisabeth's lady-in-waiting, Madame de Sérent, although she did not know if the latter had survived the Terror. She also suggested that if the Committee required a guard to accompany her, then Gomin would be acceptable to her. Another on the Princess's list was Madame de Mackau, but Mackau, at over seventy years of age, was simply too frail for the trip. Ultimately the Directory chose someone not on the Princess's list: Madame de Mackau's daughter, Madame de Soucy. Marie-Thérèse, like her mother, did not especially like Madame de Soucy and when she learned that de Soucy was permitted a maid for the trip, while she was not, she protested. De Soucy was also allowed to bring along a son, which Marie-Thérèse also found presumptuous.

In November, the Austrian minister Degelmann wrote to Bacher that Franz II had personally requested that the Princess's childhood playmate, Ernestine de Lambriquet, accompany Marie-Thérèse to Vienna and Bacher forwarded that wish to the French Minister of the Interior. Bénézech claimed that this was not possible as he had no idea where the girl was. Madame de Soucy knew exactly where she was, after all she had been instructed by the Queen to take care of her 'daughter'. We do not know if Ernestine was among the friends who visited Marie-Thérèse in the tower prison, but we do know that she had been kept in hiding by the Mackau family from the date of the invasion of the Tuileries Palace in August 1792.

The two sides of the exchange tried to keep the route of Marie-Thérèse's journey from Paris to Vienna a secret and disseminated misinformation to that effect. The Prince de Gavre, chosen by the Emperor to meet Marie-Thérèse in Switzerland, was well aware that Louis XVIII had his men positioned to snatch his niece: the Prince de Condé, erroneously believing that Marie-Thérèse would follow the same route in reverse that her mother had taken as a new bride, was waiting in Germany. Franz II believed that the Spanish King might also try the same thing and that there were others who might try to kill the Princess.

On December 4, *La Gazette Nationale* reported that Marie-Thérèse had left France the previous month. According to the newspaper, a communiqué dated November 23 from Basel stated that 'the daughter of Louis XVI is expected tomorrow' and that she was already on her way from Belfort. The story, however, was incorrect and premature.

Meanwhile, the Directory had been taking great pains to create a lavish trousseau for Marie-Thérèse to underscore the impression that the teenager had been treated well. While the couturiers were putting the finishing touches to the much-discussed wardrobe, the actual plan of escape was hatched. It was decided that, because of the dangers of transporting a Bourbon across France, Marie-Thérèse would travel incognito as a girl named 'Sophie'. Madame de Soucy, Gomin, and a soldier named Méchin, who was to pose as 'Sophie's' father, were to travel with her in the same carriage. The party was afraid that Coco would bark and draw attention to the travelers, so they agreed to send him in another carriage with Monsieur Hüe, a servant named Monsieur Baron, Meunier the cook, Madame de Soucy's son and her maid.

At 11.30 in the evening on December 18, Marie-Thérèse hugged Renète de Chanterenne goodbye and handed her a batch of papers, her account of her life in the Temple Prison, which she wanted her to keep safe in the event that she did not survive her journey, and a tender note of farewell, which she had written the day before. Fifteen minutes later, two knocks, the pre-arranged signal between the Directory's Minister of the Interior, Pierre Bénézech, and prison official Etienne Lasne, were heard at the prison's side door. At precisely midnight on her seventeenth birthday, December 19, 1795, Marie-Thérèse quietly slipped out of Temple Prison accompanied by Bénézech, who led her to a waiting carriage in the adjacent rue Meslay. As the church bells chimed the hour, she remarked to her companion that she had been in the prison for three years, four months and five days.

PART TWO

SAINT

La Royne Ergaste voyant sa fille blesme
Par un regret dans l'estomach enclose
Crys lamentables seront lors d'Angolesme
Et au germain marriage forclos

Nostradamus, Century X,
Quatrain 17

(The Murdered Queen seeing her daughter pale
From a deep sorrow internally enclosed
Lamentable cries will be those of the Duc d'Angoulême
Whose marriage to his first cousin foreclosed)

CHAPTER XII
EVERY INCH A PRINCESS

I N FLEEING FRANCE, Marie-Thérèse was unwittingly running right into the arms of warring factions, many of whom wanted to either kill or kidnap her. First, there were the obvious: the anti-royalists who wanted her dead. Next, there were those who had far less overt reasons, those who wished to influence her choice of husbands so as to alter the map of an already turbulent Europe. While the French-funded experiment in democracy in America was enjoying the second term of its peacefully elected first President, George Washington, France was emerging out of a series of bloody and violent coups d'état and into an uncertain future. Causing further chaos for France was the Holy Roman Emperor's anti-republican coalition on the continent and skirmishes with England on the open seas in the Mediterranean and in the Caribbean. While its armies were able to claim victories in Belgium, Spain, the Netherlands and on the west bank of the Rhine, forcing Prussia, Spain and Hessen-Kassel to sign three separate treaties collectively known as the Peace of Basel, France remained embroiled in battles with Austria and England.

In these Franz II had his own agenda. He wanted to reclaim Lorraine, lost to France in 1766, and if, in these unstable times for France, he could place a Habsburg on the country's throne that would be an even sweeter victory. Although the rebel government of France had already ignored Franz's petition for the return of Lorraine, the Holy Roman Emperor hoped that once his coalition of allies prevailed and his brother, Archduke Karl, was married to Marie-Thérèse, Austria could place the pair on the throne, and, in effect, subsume France. Charles IV of Spain and Louis XVIII in exile suspected their cousin's motives and determined to quash any such scheme. Louis XVIII saw himself on the throne of a restored

France, and Charles, despite the recently signed peace treaty with France, still hoped to obtain lands adjacent to Spain. At the center of each of these schemes and bound for Basel and, she imagined, freedom was Marie-Thérèse, the intended bride of two of the most powerful men in Europe: Archduke Karl of Austria and Louis XVIII's nephew, Louis-Antoine, the Duc d'Angoulême of France.

Bénézech had explained to Marie-Thérèse before leaving Temple Prison that she was going to have to travel incognito and that she could face many dangers; however, she thought the minister was exaggerating and, for now, remained unintimidated. Bénézech and the blonde young woman were driven at pace to the rue de Bondy behind the derelict Opéra, where a post chaise, more suitable for the long journey into exile, awaited them. Marie-Thérèse later learnt that during her imprisonment the Opéra, where she had spent so many happy evenings with her parents, had closed down and a new opera house on the rue de la Loi had opened just four months earlier. Madame de Soucy, a gendarme named Méchin, and Gomin, waited nervously in the carriage. Méchin helped Marie-Thérèse board the coach and Bénézech bid the party farewell. As they made their way toward the outer edge of Paris, it became clear to Marie-Thérèse that Gomin, de Soucy, and Méchin were petrified, fearing that at any moment anti-monarchists might halt the carriage and abduct or murder any or all of them. At the city gates, guards examined their fake passports and allowed them to pass. Positioned along the route were spies – and mercenaries – in the pay of Franz II, Charles IV of Spain and Louis XVIII in exile. After all, this particular coach contained a very precious commodity – a seventeen-year-old woman whose hand in marriage could lead to vast lands, wealth and the throne of France.

Out on the open road, the carriage reached its first staging post, the little village of Charenton, where it was necessary to bribe the local officials in order to press onwards. At nine the next morning, they arrived in Guignes where they breakfasted quickly and within half an hour were on their way once again. Marie-Thérèse, who understood better than her companions that an uneventful beginning did not necessarily assure smooth passage, was still noticeably tranquil when, at two o'clock in the afternoon in the town of Provins, her true identity was uncovered. The royal party had stopped to change horses, and as 'Sophie' alighted from her carriage an officer guessed her true identity. Marie-Thérèse's calm reaction suggested that she almost expected the charade to fail.

It did not take long before locals arrived hoping to get a glimpse of the daughter of the martyred King. This time, there were no angry shouts, no swords thrust at the carriage, no bloody heads on spikes, and no arrests. Instead, with a show of silent respect, the officer, on horseback, escorted the entourage to the next staging post, the town of Nogent-sur-Seine. When the travelers stopped to refresh themselves at an auberge, the innkeeper's wife greeted Marie-Thérèse with great deference. News of the Princess's arrival had spread fast and crowds formed outside. As Marie-Thérèse made her way gingerly from the inn to her carriage, uncertain as to whether the crowd was hostile, she was showered with blessings and cries of support. Cheered by this reception, Marie-Thérèse decided they should dine and stay overnight at the next town, Gray in the Haute-Saône. Although Méchin remained nervous, he deferred to the Princess's wishes.

In Gray, Marie-Thérèse learned that the Tuscan ambassador, Carletti, had been lying in wait for them but that he had now left. Dispatched by Emperor Franz's brother, Ferdinand III, the Grand Duke of Tuscany, to spy on the caravan, Carletti had actually been pretty close to his target, but missed his mark because he had asked the local townspeople only to watch for two carriages traveling in convoy. As she made her way to the French border towns, Marie-Thérèse realized that her safe delivery outside France might be thwarted not so much by revolutionaries as by the machinations of soldiers, ambassadors and spies sent by squabbling monarchs.

On August 21, shortly after the Holy Roman Emperor and the Directory had agreed to the exchange, Louis XVIII had written a note of thanks to the Austrian monarch. In the note Louis pretended that he hoped Marie-Thérèse would be sent to Rome to live with his elderly aunts. The Emperor was not fooled: he knew very well that Louis wanted nothing more than for Marie-Thérèse to marry the Duc d'Angoulême. For her part, Marie-Thérèse believed her uncle's lie that it was her parents' dearest wish that she should marry d'Angoulême, and she had decided that she would marry no one but him. She understood that the Emperor had made plans for her, but in her own mind she had resolved to live in Vienna only until she was allowed to go to Rome and live with her father's aunts, or, if the people of France tired of revolution and begged the Bourbons to return, join her uncle, the exiled King of France.

The following morning, the royal group departed for Troyes where once again Carletti just missed them. This time, he had tried to interfere with their progress by taking the last of their fresh horses. Marie-Thérèse called the Tuscan ambassador 'that villain' and laughed when she heard a courier refer to Carletti as 'that toile merchant', apparently because his coach was lined with toile. The Princess's group determined to get ahead of Carletti so that he could no longer cause any mischief. In the next town, Méchin presented his copy of official orders to the authorities and was able to get preferential treatment and fresh horses, and the party was back on the road by eleven that night. This time Carletti, still on the prowl, missed them by two hours. In a letter dated January 12, 1796, the US Minister to France and future President, James Monroe, wrote to the then Congressman James Madison that the Directory was so outraged by what they perceived to be Carletti's aggressive and unwarranted behavior in his attempts to 'visit the unfortunate daughter' of Louis XVI, that the French government demanded the Italians recall him.

Early the next morning, December 21, the royal party arrived at Chaumont where they breakfasted whilst onlookers watched them through the windows of the dining room. Marie-Thérèse was gamely making her way through the large crowds toward her post chaise when a great cry of 'God Bless You!' penetrated the silence and once more effusive shouts filled the air. The group resumed their journey toward Fayl-Billot where they had to wait for new horses. All along the route to exile, Marie-Thérèse impressed the populace with her dignity and gra- ciousness, just as her parents had. The little girl who had haughtily disdained her public role had turned into a young woman who under- stood her duty and that sense of duty would be her guiding light and motivating force for the rest of her life.

While Louis XVIII's cousin, the Prince de Condé, and his army lined the roads of German towns along the Rhine, Marie-Thérèse headed toward the Swiss border: on to Vesoul, Ronchamp, past Frahier, through Belfort and finally, on Christmas Eve, after six days of traveling, they arrived at six o'clock at the French border town of Huningue. The other carriage, bearing Hüe, Madame de Soucy's son and maid, Meunier, Baron and Coco the dog, had arrived there hours earlier despite the fact that it had left Paris an hour after Marie-Thérèse's. The minute she arrived, the gates of the fortress city were locked and would not be re-opened until her departure.

The carriage pulled up at the steps of the Hôtel du Corbeau ('raven') with its black sheet metal raven hanging ominously over the door. Marie- Thérèse made her way to the third floor, as instructed, and closed the door to room number 10 behind her. She was exhausted, but there was something she felt she must do. Remembering the words of her father's last will and testament – to 'forget all hate and resentment' – she began a letter to her uncle, Louis XVIII, imploring him to forgive the French people. 'Yes, uncle, it is she whose father, mother and aunt have been made to perish by them, who, on her knees, begs you for their grace and for peace!' she wrote.

In another room in the auberge, a relieved Méchin promptly dispatched his own letter to Foreign Secretary Bacher in Basel:

> I have just arrived this evening in Huningue with the deposit with which I am charged to deliver in Basel. I remain here and wait for the objects of exchange to arrive in Basel. Please advise me and send me your instructions immediately.

At ten o'clock that evening, Hüe called on the Princess and brought Coco with him. Although the King's servant had seen Marie-Thérèse from a distance when she had strolled about the garden of the Temple Prison that summer, it had been three years since they had been in the same room together. At last, they were able to meet in person and speak with one another. Marie-Thérèse asked Hüe to deliver the note she had written to her uncle, and, honored to have her trust, he was overjoyed when she told him that he could read it.

The next day, Christmas Day, a crowd of curiosity seekers turned up at the inn. The Corbeau's proprietors, François-Joseph and Anne-Marie Schultz, afraid of an onslaught that would cause damage to their hotel and harm to their esteemed guest, bolted the doors and shut all the windows. Despite these precautions, a local woman named Madame Spindler, the wife of the captain of the town's civil engineers, disguised as a servant, bypassed security and brought a pitcher of water to the Princess's room in a desperate attempt to see the Child of France. Later, the proprietress brought the couple's two children, a girl and their adopted son, to meet the famous Princess. The children, seeing the commotion outside their home, thought that Marie-Thérèse must be a saint. They presented a bouquet of flowers – hard to find in winter – kissed her hand, and shyly ogled the teenager. The blond little boy, about ten years old, reminded Marie-Thérèse of her beloved Louis Charles, and she wistfully told Madame Schultz how much she would like to take the boy with her to Vienna. The innkeeper's wife seemed genuinely distressed. Although she hesitatingly told Marie-Thérèse that she had, the night before, prayed to God that he grant all of the Princess's wishes, and that she would be honored to fulfill any desire of her esteemed guest, she did not wish to comply with that particular request. Before she could complete her sentence, Marie-Thérèse interrupted with an apology, telling Madame Schultz how wrong it was for any child to be separated from his parents. The woman, grateful for the Princess's understanding, asked Marie-Thérèse if she required anything else. Marie-Thérèse, who had noticed the woman's pregnant belly, smiled and said that she would be honored if the couple would name their baby after her if it were a girl. A few months later, Marie-Thérèse-Charlotte Schultz was born.

At the hotel, Marie-Thérèse and her entourage gathered in a salon where they wrote letters and talked. Marie-Thérèse wrote to Mesdames de Mackau and de Tourzel and began a very long, detailed account of her journey for Madame de Chanterenne. The Princess had met her friend Renète when she was called simply 'Marie Capet', and the two had a somewhat less formal and more intimate relationship than she had known with her courtiers of the ancien régime. In her note to Renète, she wrote not only of the journey's petty annoyances, like nails in the road that caused delay, she also expressed her most intimate feelings and concerns. She told her friend how much she already missed her, and how she wished they could have traveled together to Vienna. She wrote that when her identity was discovered: 'You could not imagine how they ran to see me. Some called me "their good lady", others "their good princess". Some cried with joy . . . how different from Paris!' And she expressed her anguish at leaving France: 'Everywhere I felt my pain augment as I faced leaving my compatriots who shouted a thousand vows to heaven for my happiness.'

She also offered her most private opinions on her traveling companions. She explained to Renète that the soldier Méchin was jumpy the entire time as he was convinced that they would be attacked by assassins or kidnappers and that he persisted in the charade even after the party's true identity had been recognized, which she found tedious. Marie-Thérèse, who had never particularly liked Madame de Soucy, liked her even less in Huningue. 'She often causes quarrels . . . I do not like her, she annoys me.' Marie-Thérèse added that although she knew that Bénézech liked Madame de Soucy (because her brother had joined the Revolution and now had an important post with the Directory), she hoped that the tiresome woman and her entourage – 'her son' and 'her maid', no names mentioned – would return to Paris and not accompany her to Vienna. She wrote to Renète that she was going to meet with officials that afternoon and confided that she was nervous because she had heard the rumors that she would be married within eight days to 'her lover', the Archduke Karl.

Méchin received a communiqué from Bacher in Basel giving details of the exchange that was to take place the day after Christmas Day. Méchin replied that the Princess had been informed and was ready to conform to the plans. Gomin added his own note to the minister asking him to forward to the Hôtel du Corbeau any correspondence addressed to him. Madame de Soucy and Marie-Thérèse both expected that Madame de Mackau may have written to them care of Gomin. As a Directory employee, Gomin was not allowed to accompany Marie-Thérèse to Vienna, and when he expressed his sadness to Marie-Thérèse that they would soon part company, she told him that before they parted she would give him a memento of their time together.

At 4.30 in the afternoon, Foreign Secretary Bacher arrived at the Corbeau. He and Marie-Thérèse discussed the trousseau, which had been prepared at great expense for the Princess.[1] Marie-Thérèse declared that she would not accept the gift from the Directory and asked Bacher to find a seamstress in Basel who could make her some simple clothing. Gomin asked the minister if he would perform a small task: post a packet of letters, addressed to himself in Paris. Inside the packet were other sealed letters addressed to Mesdames de Mackau and de Tourzel, the letters written by Madame de Soucy and Marie-Thérèse. Bacher later opened the packet and reported to Foreign Minister Charles Delacroix in Paris that he had been asked to send the letters written by Madame de Soucy and the Princess. He did not confiscate the notes, however, and the letters were allowed to reach their intended recipients. Marie-Thérèse, who guessed that her letters might be intercepted, did not include her note to Madame de Chanterenne in the parcel because she trusted no one other than Gomin to deliver it in person. This note, which arrived safely, remains the only account in the Princess's handwriting detailing her release from Temple Prison and journey to France's borders.

Although her confident demeanor fooled many, Marie-Thérèse sent another letter to Madame de Chanterenne in which she described her inner sadness and anxieties. Calling herself 'an unhappy expatriate', Marie-Thérèse wrote a heartfelt goodbye to her cherished friend. She explained that at that moment she was sitting in a room with Madame de Soucy, her son, Hüe and Gomin; the two men were chatting near the doorway with 'my dear Coco' lying cozily asleep in the corner near the stove. She would be seeing Foreign Secretary Bacher again the next morning,

and tomorrow evening at the end of the day, at the very moment when they lock the gates [to the city], I leave for Basel where the exchange will immediately take place, and then I will straight away leave for Vienna, where perhaps I will be when you receive this letter. One speaks much about my marriage, that it will take place soon, I hope not; finally, I do not know what I say. I promise to always think fondly of you; I neither can nor do I wish to forget you. Please take care of this poor M. Gomin who is in pain about our separation . . . Adieu, my dear Renète, peace, peace is what I desire . . . May it arrive . . . and may I see you in Rome and not in Vienna! Adieu, good, charming, tender Renète, my beautiful lady.

Bacher returned to Basel to write a report on his meeting with the Princess for Delacroix. 'The daughter of the last King of France arrived in Huningue without incident, as I had advised yesterday,' he wrote. He filled the rest of the report with falsehoods that conflicted with his personal experience: the Princess's arrival had caused little in the way of sensation in the town, he wrote, and her stay was regarded as no more than an 'inconvenient curiosity'. Finally, he informed the Minister that a 'detachment of cavalry' was on its way to the hotel to escort the Princess to the border. A few days later, when the exchange had been completed and Marie-Thérèse was out of reach of the French government, Bacher expressed his admiration to Delacroix for the teenage girl. He said he realized that behind her bravado she was, in fact, just a teenage girl, uncertain about her future. He recalled a conversation that took place at the hotel between Madame de Soucy and the Princess. Marie-Thérèse asked de Soucy what she thought awaited her in Vienna. De Soucy replied that she thought the Princess would probably marry the Archduke. Marie-Thérèse reacted with incredulity: 'But don't you know that we are at war?' to which Madame de Soucy replied: 'Then you might be an angel of peace.' Marie-Thérèse responded: 'On that condition, I will make the sacrifice for my country.'

Bacher kept his promise to Marie-Thérèse, and on the morning of Saturday December 26, a modiste from Basel named Mademoiselle Serini arrived at the hotel. The dressmaker came bearing a selection of dresses and bonnets from which Marie-Thérèse could choose her traveling wardrobe. As Bacher had offered to pay for whatever Marie-Thérèse desired, Madame de Soucy took advantage of the situation and grabbed stockings, handkerchiefs, hats, fichus, and other sundries for herself. Marie-Thérèse spent an hour in her room with Serini, but was far less greedy.

When Marie-Thérèse was almost ready to leave, the entire Schultz family appeared at the door of her room and asked her to give them a special benediction. As they lay prostrate on the floor before her, she offered them her blessing and handed out presents – fichus to the children and a handkerchief to their mother. When Madame Schultz began to weep, Marie-Thérèse gently reminded the pregnant woman that she needed to remain calm. Each member thanked the Princess and kissed her hand.

In the afternoon, Bacher arrived to get the group on the road to Switzerland, and when Marie-Thérèse asked the diplomat if Gomin could come with them after all, he told her that it was, unfortunately, not in his power; those who were to accompany Marie-Thérèse to Vienna had already been decided on. Marie-Thérèse then turned to Gomin and said, 'I do not know if I will see you in Basel, or if I will ever speak with you again. I want to keep my promise,' and she handed him a memento. It was a note containing her expression of devotion to the man who had, at first, served as her captor at the Temple Prison, and who had since become her trusted friend. In it, she wrote that she would not ask Gomin to think of her because she knew that he would, and that she would always think of him. As she bid him goodbye she said: 'Do not cry, and above all, have faith in God.'

It was dark and the gates to the city remained shut. Marie-Thérèse was ready, though unhappy, to go. Méchin led the way toward the carriage, and Bacher walked by the Princess's side. Monsieur Schultz closed the door of the carriage and it pulled away escorted by a brigade of revolutionary dragoons. The gates of Huningue were opened. As the carriage picked up speed, so did the soldiers' horses. This was no ordinary visitor en route to the border. Here was political currency. As her coach approached the Rhine, Marie-Thérèse declared to her companions, 'I leave France with regret. I will never cease to regard it as my country.' As the carriage crossed the tiny bridge that spanned the river, shouts of '*Vive la Princesse!*' filled the air. Marie-Thérèse waved at the local Swiss citizens who had lined the bridge, each holding lanterns to catch a glimpse of her. Word had spread from Huningue that the French were 'losing an angel' – an eerie echo of her grandmother's words to Maria Antonia as she left Austria to become Dauphine of France.

The carriage headed not south toward Basel, but southeast toward the countryside. Both sides of the exchange were afraid that if they met in the city it might cause further commotion and jeopardize the proceedings. The Prince de Gavre and Minister Degelmann waited for Marie-Thérèse at the Villa Reber, the private home of a rich Swiss businessman. Barely a few miles beyond the bridge, the carriage stopped before high gates. Small groups of people waited near the house to see Her Highness, among them the persistent Carletti, who had arrived in Basel that afternoon, an officer of the Prince de Condé, and spies who were surveying the scene for the English ambassador Wickham. The local *Burgermeister*, a Monsieur Bourcart, kept a diary of the unusual goings-on.

The gates opened and the carriage proceeded toward the Villa Reber. The path was muddy and Bacher proposed that he obtain a chair to carry the Princess to the door. Marie-Thérèse declined, saying that it was not necessary. Those who watched her alight at the villa wrote of an inhumanly pale, malnourished little waif who looked sad and exhausted; she appeared to have suffered from some kind of trauma as her eyes were red-rimmed and she startled very easily.

It was about seven o'clock in the evening when the Child of France walked up the path toward the waiting Prince de Gavre. The Prince introduced himself as the emissary of her cousin, the Emperor, and then introduced the Austrian minister Degelmann. Marie-Thérèse testified to the two men that she was Marie-Thérèse-Charlotte of France at which point Bacher stated with great formality to the two men: 'I am charged with placing in your hands Madame of France.' Maintaining her composure, Marie-Thérèse told Bacher, 'Monsieur, I will never forget that I am French.' Moved, the Prince de Gavre softly told her: 'Madame, I am charged to receive Your Royal Highness to conduct you to His Imperial Majesty who is impatient to see you, to embrace you, and to give you, Madame, his marks of tenderness and his best wishes.' She responded that she was aware of His Imperial Majesty's kindness and that the same blood ran through each of their veins.

At the villa, Marie-Thérèse ate some bread, drank some water tinged with wine and rested until nearly nine o'clock. Bacher and Degelmann, meanwhile, ironed out their agreement. Monsieur Hüe advised Marie-Thérèse that the trunks containing the trousseau prepared for her had arrived should she decide to now accept the wardrobe.[2] Once again, she declined. Despite the fact that Bacher reported to Delacroix that the young girl clearly did not want any gifts from the revolutionary government, the Directory shrugged off her refusal, excusing it as a decision made for her by the Austrians. Traditionally, a princess who was to go to a foreign country and marry would be symbolically disrobed and transformed into the identity of her new nation, just as Marie Antoinette had been when she arrived in France in 1770. The Directory assumed that the Austrians were preparing Marie-Thérèse to become Austrian, and that the choice to refuse the extensive trousseau was made not by Marie-

Thérèse herself, who was in desperate need of fresh clothing, but by the Austrian dignitaries on behalf of the teenager.

Degelmann was a shrewd diplomat. Although he and the Austrian court had had spies in Paris and had been fully aware that Madame de Tourzel was not to accompany Marie-Thérèse to Vienna, Degelmann feigned ignorance and lodged a complaint to Bacher stating that the Emperor expected to see de Tourzel among the Princess's party. Despite the Austrians' protests that the French were not participating in their agreement in good faith, the prisoners were released and subsequently dined at the home of the French ambassador. Bacher, who was responsible for escorting the group of prisoners back to France, concluded his own business. He gave Méchin his discharge papers stating that the man had fulfilled his duties; he received a certificate from the Prince de Gavre in which the Prince testified that he had received the daughter of the last King of France. Marie-Thérèse, kept far apart from the revolutionary prisoners of war, had the opportunity to say goodbye to those who had accompanied her thus far. The Austrians refused to allow any other French émigrés permission to meet with Marie-Thérèse for fear of a kidnapping plot.

The official handover complete, Marie-Thérèse, under the protection of His Imperial Majesty, Franz II, departed into the night toward Rheinfelden. To protect her from the crowds (among whom was one Herr Fesch, Napoleon Bonaparte's uncle), the Austrian Emperor had dispatched a cavalry unit and a Major Kolb to remain by the Princess's window. The entire party headed east, away from France, along the Rhine toward Vienna with strict instructions not to trespass on foreign territory. Both Bacher and Méchin wrote detailed accounts of the exchange. Whereas Bacher was an experienced diplomat with the confidence to pepper his report with a certain flavor, Méchin, whom Marie-Thérèse had described as afraid of his own shadow, had neither the self-assurance nor the skill to report anything other than the bare facts.[3] Both men attested to the fact that Marie-Thérèse-Charlotte, the daughter of the late King of France, was now in the possession of the Austrian government.

The carriage carrying Marie-Thérèse made haste until, late into the night, it reached Laufenburg. On the morning of December 27, Marie-Thérèse awoke for the first time in her life not on French soil. She then attended a simple Mass in her parents' honor, the first time she had been in a church in over three years. After the service, she and her party resumed the journey east, still surrounded by Austrian cavalry. In Füssen,

Marie-Thérèse stopped to visit her father's aunt and uncle, the Elector of
Trèves and his sister, Princess Cunegonde of Saxe, with whom she
entrusted a letter for her own uncle, King Louis XVIII. In the letter,
she wrote that his will would be her own, and that whatever he wished her
to do she would do gladly. She sent him her deepest affection and begged
the King to send her instructions. She again asked him to pardon the
French people. She had clearly forgotten neither her manners nor her
education during her incarceration. Although the King's elderly aunt and
uncle were, in fact, quite aloof with her, Marie-Thérèse, suspecting that
they would later read her letter, flattered her hosts and assured her uncle
that the elderly brother and sister were treating her with every kindness.
She also sent every compliment to the King from his subject, Madame de
Soucy, even though she had thoroughly tired of the woman.

Along the road, Hüe spotted Condé's soldiers. On January 2, 1796, the
cortège arrived in Innsbruck and stayed for two days to meet with Her
Imperial Highness, the Archduchess Maria Elisabeth, a sister of the late
Queen Marie Antoinette. Marie-Thérèse found the infirm and severe old
abbess difficult and 'repulsive'. She was so uncomfortable in the presence
of Maria Elisabeth that she even considered agreeing to marry the
Archduke Karl just to be left alone. In the meantime, King Louis XVIII
had placed his own emissaries in Innsbruck, among them the Prince de
Condé and the Comte d'Avaray, his closest minister. The Prince de Gavre,
however, would not permit any of the French émigrés to approach Marie-
Thérèse.

As they neared Vienna, in the town of Wels, Marie-Thérèse was finally
able to see a familiar face. The ever-faithful and persistent valet Jean-
Baptiste Cléry had made his own way to the town to wait for the Princess.
She was overjoyed to see him, and she asked him to deliver a note she had
written to her uncle. Cléry informed Marie-Thérèse that the exiled King's
emissaries had been trying to reach her but that they had been denied
access to her. She then wrote another note to her uncle, expressing her
growing annoyance with what she now understood as the Emperor's
deliberate attempt to keep her away from any French émigrés. She
stressed to her uncle that she in no way consented to this plan: 'I would
prefer to be unhappy with my family as they are than to be at the court of
a prince who is an enemy to my family and my country.' Again, concerned
that her other letters might not have reached His Majesty, she reiterated
her plea that he forgive the people of France and asked for forgiveness for
herself in advance. 'Sire, I will arrive in Vienna where I will await orders
from Your Majesty. But I sense, although I have a great desire to send

news, I fear that I will not be able to write often, as I will be closely observed.' She reassured her uncle that although the Emperor wanted her to marry his brother, she would defy neither her parents' wishes nor those of her King: 'My position is very difficult and delicate, but I have confidence in the God who has rescued me and brought me out of so many dangers.'

In Verona, the exiled French King received both the letter sent via Cunegonde of Saxe and the one hand-delivered by Cléry. Louis read the notes with his minister, d'Avaray, and both were impressed by Marie-Thérèse's courage and steadfastness. The King, determined to maintain control over his niece, answered her letters and dispatched Cléry to Vienna to deliver his answers. Louis, fully aware that these letters might not reach his niece, devised a ploy to facilitate their delivery. Cléry should seek a public audience with the Holy Roman Emperor and declare to all present that he had letters in his possession for Marie-Thérèse from her uncle. Louis calculated that Franz, hailed by his subjects as well as the other monarchs of Europe as the magnanimous savior of the poor Orphan of the Temple Prison, would not want to appear otherwise and would allow the Princess the letters.

Louis remained fearful that Marie-Thérèse, just seventeen and without anyone to advise and protect her, would submit to Franz's will and ruin his own plans. In the notes that Cléry carried, Louis responded to his niece's pleas for the people of France. He told her that although peace was in his heart, it was not in his hands. He advised Marie-Thérèse to tell anyone who tried to marry her to Archduke Karl that she must state that, before their unfortunate deaths, her parents had promised her to another. Lastly, understanding that although she might be wise beyond her years in many ways, she would be innocent in the ways of romance, he began to wage a campaign to convince Marie-Thérèse that his nephew, the Duc d'Angoulême, was pining for her. Emperor Franz was equally certain that the anemic d'Angoulême would pale in her eyes once she saw the dashing Archduke Karl.

CHAPTER XIII
VIENNA

O N JANUARY 9, 1796, a fair-haired girl, hailed as Marie-Thérèse-Charlotte of France, traveled the Route La Dauphine, the road taken by the late Queen Marie Antoinette upon her departure from Vienna twenty-six years previously to the Hofburg Palace. Although members of the imperial family had seen paintings of the girl when she was younger, it was the first time that the Austrian court had ever laid eyes on her in person. This teenager, presumed to be the only surviving child of the late King Louis XVI and Queen Marie Antoinette, would live in private royal apartments befitting a child of an Austrian Archduchess and a King of France.

Not long after the gates of the Hofburg had been closed behind her, Marie-Thérèse sensed that she might have escaped one prison for another. She was met by her first cousin, Franz II, and his wife, Maria Theresa of Sicily, another first cousin. The two women disliked each other from the start. Marie-Thérèse found her cold and believed that the Sicilian-born Princess thought herself superior to the daughter of the King of France, who ought to be grateful for her husband's handouts. The Emperor, for his part, anticipated being rewarded for rescuing Marie-Thérèse from her French captors. He and his minister, Thugut, had assumed that Marie-Thérèse would wish to exact revenge on the people of France and had prepared a document for her to sign on her arrival. The document asserted her hereditary rights to Burgundy, Brittany, Lorraine, Alsace and Franche-Comté – pivotal territories for both the Holy Roman Empire and France. However, the fragile-looking teenager read it and stubbornly declared that she would not sign it.

Hours later, Marie-Thérèse wrote to her uncle assuring him that she, a subject of His Most Christian Majesty, the King of France, would obey his command only. She held onto the note until she could be sure of its delivery by hand to him in Verona.

The next morning, January 10, Joseph Weber, a childhood friend of Marie Antoinette who had followed the late Queen to France to serve her, was allowed to visit Marie-Thérèse at the Hofburg. Weber reflected that he had been transported there by a 'sensation of overwhelming emotion'. Thrilled to see her again, he described Marie-Thérèse as having the 'grace of Marie Antoinette, and the goodness of Louis XVI'. He came away from the meeting feeling as though he had 'spoken with an angel'.

Weber was not the only one to ascribe to Marie-Thérèse a heavenly aura; the girl with the 'celestial eyes' was acquiring something of an iconic status across much of Europe. She was no longer simply the daughter of the late King, but an 'angel on earth', someone whose very survival contained some grander meaning. In Paris, people made pilgrimages to the Temple Prison to view the abandoned cell of the young woman who had slipped out of Paris mysteriously into the night. Curiosity seekers waited in queues to see the walls on which Marie-Thérèse had, using a needle, scratched her prayers and her testament to misery. Along with the solitary musings left by the Princess, visitors saw the Queen's own wall markings. On March 27, 1793, Marie Antoinette had etched: 'Four feet, ten . . . Three feet, two . . .' – the height of each of her children.

As had been the case when she was alive, fictional stories about Marie Antoinette began to creep into factual accounts. Sightseers could now step onto the balcony from which Marie Antoinette was supposed to have witnessed the mob carrying the bloody head of her friend, the Princesse de Lamballe – despite the fact that, according to Marie-Thérèse and Hüe, this incident never happened. The contemporary historian Montjoye visited the Temple Prison and witnessed people selling rings, locks of hair, and other mementos said to have belonged to the royal family. Montjoye was offered drawings claimed to have been done by Marie-Thérèse. Impressed by their professional appearance, he wondered if the Princess was that talented an artist. He showed the sketches to an expert, who explained that they had been executed in a very sophisticated manner with copperplate and could not possibly have been done by the Princess in her prison cell. Such issues seemed to matter little, however. The people were hungry for some bit of the teenage girl, real or not – souvenirs of the child who had such royal pedigree that two of Europe's most exalted princes were contending for her hand in marriage.

For weeks, the editors of the *Gazette Nationale de France* intentionally underplayed and misreported Marie-Thérèse's journey from Paris, hoping that readers would lose interest in the story. On Monday, December 21, two days *after* Marie-Thérèse left Temple Prison, the *Gazette* reported that 'the noise is because the daughter of Louis XVI has left the Temple . . . one knows that representatives from Austria have been in Fribourg for days'. Another report from Basel, dated December 26, which appeared in the *Gazette* on January 8, 1796, claimed to offer the curious reader 'details on the exchange of the French deputies and the daughter of Louis XVI, scheduled for the evening of December 27th or December 28th'.[1]

Journals and reports written by Directory officials also offered deliberately conflicting dates, places and times – which inadvertently stoked the public's fascination and added to the mystique of the story. Wherever she was, the accounts agreed on one thing: along the way she had seen a boy who reminded her of her brother and this had made her cry. It was not until Marie-Thérèse was sequestered in the Hofburg that the French press finally printed a somewhat accurate account of her journey. On January 13, four days after Marie-Thérèse arrived in Vienna, the *Gazette* acquiesced to public desire. The article led with the return of the French prisoners, declaring it to be a great victory for the Directory. It then gave an account of the crowds of people who had come out to see the daughter of the late King during her passage to Vienna and the large quantity of soldiers that had been required to keep the peace during the proceedings in Basel.

The inaccurate reports and newspaper articles became typical of what was to be the beginning of the mythification of the banished Princess. It was at this time that wild stories began to circulate about Marie-Thérèse, her brother, and their experiences in prison. Rumors abounded that she had been drugged, raped, and was now an imbecile. Another popular story claimed that the King's daughter had fallen in love with a guard and had escaped on his arm, and that her place in prison was taken by a lookalike. Tales also resurfaced that royal sympathizers had removed her brother from his prison cell, substituted another very ill little boy, and that Louis Charles and Marie-Thérèse were planning to reunite in Vienna – or even America. People speculated about how and where, en route to the Hofburg, she might have switched places with another – and who was involved in the plot. Had she changed places with someone in Huningue before her arrival in Basel? Maybe it had happened in Germany? Had she escaped to America? Was she on a ship bound for the Caribbean? Fueling the fascination, a novel called *Ninon* appeared shortly after the Princess left Paris, and it became a sensation. The story, which would later be presented as a play in Strasbourg, a city dangerously close to enemy territory, has as its main character 'Ninon', the young Queen of France who changes places with a servant girl at an auberge and wears a veil to hide her identity.

Indeed, many keen observers believed that there was something suspicious about Marie-Thérèse's release. The English ambassador, Wickham, confessed in his report on the exchange to Foreign Minister Baron Grenville that 'there is something so very mysterious in this whole transaction and I am so entirely destitute of real information upon the subject'. He also confirmed to Grenville that he had received a note from Burgermeister Bourcart, in which Bourcart claimed he had been party to discussions regarding a kidnap attempt by the Prince of Condé, declaring: 'The Prince of Condé once asked me whether the Canton of Berne would give her protection in case she escaped . . . I afterward overheard some part of a conversation between the Comte d'Avaray and M. Degelmann in my own house here within, they talked of the possibility of carrying the princess to the Vendée.' News of such a plot would have most certainly alarmed the British. Months earlier, in an echo of the uprising in the Vendée, about 3,000 French royalists succeeded in convincing the British to ferry them to the peninsula of Quiberon in northwest France in order to overthrow the French government. Bad weather subsequently prevented the British navy from supporting the insurrection and nearly half of the invaders were executed. No one wanted a repeat of such a tragedy.

The disparate newspaper reports and Marie-Thérèse's own account, delivered to Madame de Chanterenne, also offer intriguing inconsistencies. In her letter to Chanterenne, she referred to the men by their names – Gomin, Méchin, and the servant, Monsieur Baron – but she never mentioned the names of either Madame de Soucy's son or that of de Soucy's maid. Was it possible Marie-Thérèse was hiding something from Renée de Chanterenne? Did she omit information because she simply was unable to lie to her friend or feared compromising her with explosive information?

According to historians, the passports issued for these two 'unnamed' people were for a teenage boy named 'Pierre de Soucy' and a woman traveling under the name of 'Catherine de Varenne'. But Madame de Soucy did not have a son by that name (her children were: Louis Xavier, Charles Philippe, and Philippe Charles, and in December, 1795, they were twenty, nineteen and fourteen years old respectively). Madame de Soucy also had two daughters. One was eleven at that time and one was the same age as Marie-Thérèse. Were the passports issued to either 'Catherine de Varenne' or 'Pierre de Soucy' fraudulent? Was 'Pierre', dressed in boy's clothing, really one of Madame de Soucy's daughters who would serve as a decoy? Or was, as some historians have posited, 'Pierre' really Ernestine – Marie-Thérèse's look-alike and possible half-sister? Could 'Catherine de Varenne' have been a pseudonym for the late King's putative daughter? Others claim it was the young seamstress, Mademoiselle Serini (diminutive of 'Serenissima' – 'Highness' – a code name perhaps?), who changed places with Marie-Thérèse at the hotel in Huningue moments before (and after the letters to Madame de Chanterenne had been written and dispatched) the Child of France was due to meet with the Austrians in Basel. Even the notes received by Chanterenne have been suspected of being forgeries, as some suspect that the 'Marie-Thérèse' who arrived in Huningue had already changed places with the real Princess, who had been spirited away even before she reached the border town.

Whatever the suspicions, the young woman who arrived at the Hofburg that January displayed gumption. She quickly stunned the Emperor and his advisors with her tenacity, and Franz soon realized that if he were to gain any influence over the girl he would have to break her resolve. His first tactic was to pry the Princess loose from all French influences. He allowed her unlimited access to her Austrian imperial family, while banning Madame de Soucy, Monsiuer Hüe and Cléry from the Hofburg. Loyal and persistent, however, they remained in Vienna and all managed to slip letters to her, and she found ways to reply.

The Emperor proceeded on his course and Marie-Thérèse on hers. As she informed Madame de Soucy, in her first two weeks at the Hofburg she had been in the company of Archduke Karl on a number of occasions; however, she reassured her uncle, she would not be swayed from her desire to marry d'Angoulême. Marie-Thérèse instructed de Soucy to write to Louis XVIII and tell him that although she thought the Austrian Archduke Karl was amiable, she found him 'ugly'. On January 20, she wrote to her cousin, the Prince de Condé:

> I was extremely touched and flattered by your letter . . . I am filled with pleasure to have a Cousin so gloriously wearing the name of Bourbon, a name so virtuous that history will speak of it always; your love for God and for your King makes you admired everywhere . . . I have had the pleasure of seeing some of your gentlemen that gave me great pleasure

because I will always be happy seeing Frenchmen so attached to their
Duty . . . I admire and envy very much your role . . . I hope that
Messieurs the Ducs de Bourbon [the Prince de Condé's son] and
d'Enghien [de Condé's grandson] are well . . . someone told me that
the Princess Louise [de Condé's daughter] is in Piedmont . . . she must
be very unhappy to be separated from her father for such a long
time . . . Your affectionate cousin.

Denied the right to write letters for so long, Marie-Thérèse found paper
and pen a privilege and took full advantage of the luxury. She wrote to
her family in Naples, her uncle in Verona, a cousin in Milan, her cousins
at the German front, her aunts in Rome, and a very touching letter to her
Aunt Clothilde, the Princess of Piedmont, who sent her a portrait of
Marie-Thérèse's beloved late aunt, Madame Elisabeth. And out of sheer
politeness she corresponded with Archduchess Elisabeth, the aunt she had
found repugnant when she had stopped in Innsbruck. On January 21, the
Archduchess wrote to Marie-Thérèse that she had received two letters
from her and that she was very happy to hear that her niece had been
welcomed with open arms by her Austrian family.

Copies of Marie-Thérèse's letters flurried around Europe offering
tidbits of news to the Princess's anxious relatives. However, the only
physical contact she had with a French man or woman that month was
momentary and with someone she secretly despised. It was with Monseigneur de la Fare, the Bishop of Nancy – the priest who had excoriated
her mother at the opening prayers of the 1789 États-Généraux. The
Bishop, who had fled the new secular France, was now the leader of the
French émigré community in Vienna. On January 21, Marie-Thérèse,
dressed incognito, attended a Mass marking the third anniversary of her
father's death. She had come to the church armed with letters and a
miniature portrait of herself, painted by Fuger, in case she was able to
make contact with any senior French émigrés. Putting to one side her
dislike for the man, she slipped into de la Fare's hand a letter addressed to
her uncle, Louis XVIII, along with the miniature and the letter to the
Prince de Condé. The Bishop, anticipating that Marie-Thérèse might try
to attend the Mass, had also come forearmed – with letters from her
uncle, another from the Prince de Condé, and a note from her cousin, the
Comte d'Artois's younger son, the Duc de Berry. While de Berry's letter
showered her with gallantries, she heard nothing from his brother, the
Duc d'Angoulême – the man she was supposed to marry.

Marie-Thérèse, who had been deprived of news and company for over three years, was ecstatic to hear from her family. She responded to the flood of letters, imploring Bishop de la Fare to ensure their safe delivery. On January 22, she wrote excitedly to her childhood playmate, the Duc de Berry, telling him to refrain from paying homage to her as she was nothing more than his cousin, imploring him: 'Please write to me often and without ceremony.' On February 5, de Berry responded:

> I received yesterday your charming letter of January 22nd. It is impossible to express to you the pleasure it gave me: it was the only consolation that I could receive not having permission to see you. I assure you that nothing gave me more pain than the Prince de Gavre's refusal.

On February 3, the *Gazette Nationale de France* carried an inflammatory article claiming that Marie-Thérèse was now an official member of the Austrian court and that as part of the process of being 'Austrified', she now wore the formal court dress of the Austrians. The truth, however, was very different. To the Emperor's dismay, Marie-Thérèse had refused to wear anything other than black mourning dress. From the moment of her arrival at the Hofburg, she had been treated as an esteemed member of the family: she was invited to attend court functions and included in all family dinners and parties. And she arrived at them all dressed in mourning for her parents, her brother, and for the death of the ancien régime.

By the end of January, Franz was losing patience with what he saw as Marie-Thérèse's uncooperativeness. He had imagined her at his side, smiling, grateful and engaged to Archduke Karl. Suspecting that the French coterie was advocating subversion, the Emperor expelled her entire French entourage from his realm. Madame de Soucy was given a final audience with the Emperor before her departure, during which he presented her with a parting 'tip' of 1,500 ducats. De Soucy, wrongly believing that it was her place to speak for the teenager, responded by telling His Imperial Highness of King Louis XVIII's wedding plans for his niece.

Marie-Thérèse was stunned by what she perceived to be de Soucy's disloyal and high-handed behavior. De Soucy had already upset the Hües by telling Madame Hüe – recently arrived in Vienna – that her husband had made a pass at her during the journey from Paris. Marie-Thérèse, disgusted by the governess's behavior, began to encourage de Soucy to return quickly to France. Although Marie-Thérèse would bear a grudge against the woman for many years to come, she managed to write her former servant three very polite letters before her departure. In one, she asked de Soucy to 'please kiss' Madame de Mackau (de Soucy's mother), and Madame de Chanterenne when she arrived in Paris. Marie-Thérèse requested twice that Madame de Soucy send her a particular tapestry from Paris that her mother had worked on and portraits that were with a Madame Thibaud, which Marie Antoinette had commissioned before her death. Her final request was that Madame de Soucy should tell everyone to contact her through the Hofburg court servant, Madame de Chanclos.

Josépha de Chanclos, appointed by the Emperor to serve as head of household to Marie-Thérèse, was proving to be an astute choice. A French-born woman who had been married to an Austrian, Chanclos had served in the court of Franz's first wife and had also known Marie Antoinette as a child. This immediately endeared her to Marie-Thérèse. Madame de Chanclos understood that the Emperor's intention was to turn Marie-Thérèse into an Austrian Archduchess and prepare her for marriage to Archduke Karl. Franz would have loved to eliminate all of the French-speaking aristocrats from having contact with Marie-Thérèse, as many of them believed, like Marie-Thérèse, that the Austrians had abandoned the French royal family. However, to sever that tie would be impractical: although Marie-Thérèse had been taught German as a child, owing to her lack of education in the Temple Prison, she had simply forgotten most of it. Chanclos knew that her role, while grooming Marie-Thérèse for life at the Hofburg, was to keep a very close watch on her charge, and this included all communications coming in or going out from Marie-Thérèse. The Princess would be kept firmly under palace protection and starved of external contacts – including the highly un-desirable news of Napoleon's victories over the Imperial Austrian army in Italy.

In addition to the seemingly invisible surveillance at the Hofburg, Vienna's infamous Black Cabinet kept a lookout for any letters addressed to friends of the French Princess. Their spies made copies of all of Marie-Thérèse's letters, which, having lived surrounded by informants and enemies, and astute beyond her years, she expected. She proceeded to write to her uncle and her friends on a regular basis as if she suspected nothing; however, she made a point of coloring her letters with glowing reports of the *gemütlichkeit* at the Hofburg – the cozy atmosphere she said her mother often spoke of with great sentimentality – and she always remembered to write of her gratitude to the Emperor.

While the Emperor endeavored to keep Marie-Thérèse isolated from people and news that conflicted with his purpose, the public remained fascinated. A 'Letter from Vienna', written on January 17, just a week after her arrival at the Hofburg, and published on February 8 in the *Gazette*, reported that the only surviving daughter of Louis XVI had arrived on January 9, causing 'as much sensation as a general regarded as the first man of war of the Empire'. This same letter also contained an unsettling piece of news: a young blonde woman had arrived at an auberge near Vienna insisting that she was Marie-Thérèse-Charlotte of France. The townspeople, completely credulous and in awe, welcomed her and showered her with honors. The police were called; the young woman was pronounced an impostor and arrested, though she subsequently, somehow, escaped their custody.

Not long after Marie-Thérèse's arrival in Vienna, her mother's great friend, the Princesse de Chimay, had written to Hüe to ask what news he had of the Princess. French émigrés were concerned about the circumstances in which Marie-Thérèse was being kept; they feared she was imprisoned again, albeit this time in a gilded cell. The Princesse de Chimay, who lived in the province of Thuringia, Germany, had heard rumors that Marie-Thérèse had begun to hate the sound of music and showed signs of terror every time she saw a barred window. Thuringia was believed to be the place where the legend of 'Barbarossa' had occurred hundreds of years earlier. According to the myth, the ferocious Holy Roman Emperor, Frederick I – known as 'Barbarossa' because of his red beard – had fallen asleep in a cave in the Kyffäuser Mountains and would wake, the folk tale continued, when the ravens ceased to fly. Thuringia, steeped in romantic lore, became the epicenter of the new Romantic movement, whose philosophy, literature, art and music attempted to appropriate the ideals of the French Revolution.

Within Thuringia, towns like Jena and Hildburghausen became home to writers such as Novalis, the Schlegel brothers, Schiller and Goethe, who had met in 1794 at the University of Jena. Another writer who studied in Jena was Clemens Brentano, who would later co-author, with his brother-in-law, Achim von Arnim, a collection of poetic German folk tales called *Des Knaben Wunderhorn* (The Boy's Magic Horn). These stories inspired another pair of brothers to write similar tales – the brothers Grimm. *Des Knaben Wunderhorn* was so influential among the German Romanticists that portions of it were later set to music by composers such as Mendelssohn, Schumann, Brahms, Mahler and others.

And it was not long before Thuringia was in a fever over Marie-Thérèse, the tragic Princess who had been held captive in the tower.

Madame de Chimay had written to Hüe to ask if there was anything she could do to help the Princess. Still in Vienna, Hüe was finding it increasingly difficult to communicate with Marie-Thérèse. He would send her letters written in lemon juice, which she could read by firelight, or, knowing that Hüe would watch for her when she walked Coco in the gardens of the Hofburg, she would make signs that she and Hüe had previously concocted. Although Hüe had been told to leave Austria, he delayed his departure until he could get word to Marie-Thérèse through Madame de Chanclos that he was going to join King Louis XVIII in Italy. She was heartbroken, but she did not complain at all to Franz. She did complain, however, when the Hofburg staff tried to take away her dog. Coco had bitten the Prince de Gavre and the Emperor's advisor insisted the dog had to go. Marie-Thérèse stood firm and argued that the dog was the only thing she had left of her brother's. Franz knew better than to fight her in this battle and let the dog stay.

On February 19, her spirits were buoyed when she spied an old family friend while on her way to Mass. It was Comte Fersen, the man who had tried, unlike her Austrian cousins, to rescue her family. As she passed him, she blushed and offered salutation. Upon leaving the service, she turned to look at him once more. Fersen wrote in his memoir that he thought she had grown to look more like her aunt Madame Elisabeth than her mother, though she nonetheless evoked the memory of the late Queen. The man who had known Marie-Thérèse as a little girl in happier times and who had accompanied the Princess and her family to the outskirts of Paris on the night of the ill-fated flight to Varennes, decided that, apart from her face being more fully formed, the Princess appeared unchanged.

She had, of course, changed in many ways. She had come also to represent so much. There had been those at Versailles who remembered her as an insufferably haughty child and those throughout France who, because of her bloodline, believed her to be the incarnation of evil. By 1796, however, as her uncle Louis XVIII wrote on February 18, she had become to many: 'the angel which God has sent to erase Evil'. Certain that this angel would change the course of events, Louis wrote in the same letter: 'your union with my nephew' will bring about the Bourbon restoration to the throne of France. Still, however, Marie-Thérèse, in close quarters to the charming Archduke Karl, had failed to hear one word from d'Angoulême.

CHAPTER XIV
THE ÉMIGRÉS

W HILE MARIE-THÉRÈSE was learning to re-adjust to a life of opulence after three years in prison, many ancien régime courtiers were learning to live by their wits in exile. Some had remained on continental Europe; others had sailed to England, Sweden and America. They found a variety of careers and sympathetic helping hands from disparate places. Some, who were lucky enough to have been able to transport silver and porcelain, sold their family heirlooms discreetly at auction. Others tried to use hobbies they had learnt in France, such as painting and embroidery, to earn a living. The Comtesse de Saisseval, having arrived in London after a harrowing sea voyage with her thirteen-day-old baby, took to making straw hats. Fortunately, the bonnets caught on among the fashionable women of British society, and she was able, at last, to support herself. Others engaged in trades such as bookbinding and manufacturing.

While the English were at first sympathetic to the arrival of French aristocrats who had escaped the scaffold, England had been at war with France for a number of years and a growing mistrust forced Parliament, in 1796, to renew the Alien Act, a law which forbade foreigners to live near the coast in case of invasion. A number of the French émigrés were moved from the Channel Islands and mainland coastal towns and relocated to London.

After the Baronne de Courtot was released from Paris's La Force prison she fled to Germany. When she had been in England as the Princesse de Lamballe's lady-in-waiting, she had had the foresight to leave much of her jewelry there and in Germany was able to sell much of it for cash. In Germany, she was treated with great kindness, especially by the daughters of Marie Antoinette's deceased friends, the Princesses of Hesse. She was invited to their castles, her favorite being on the border of the 'green forests of Thuringen . . . and picturesque ruins'. She recalled that they all enjoyed playing a party game called 'Boston'. Courtot was also included in family weddings and baptisms and was especially touched when, on one occasion, Queen Louise of Prussia stepped out of protocol, kissed her, and exclaimed, 'I hope to see you frequently here.' The Queen also asked Courtot to recount the details of the Princesse de Lamballe's sad end.

Madame de la Tour du Pin had moved with her family to a farm near Albany, New York, where she churned and sold her own butter. Another who survived reversals was the cunning Charles Maurice de Talleyrand. The Bishop, whose own mother had professed that her son was too immoral to be a cleric, initially went to England. He was not, however, accepted in British society as he had hoped and left in disgrace. Talleyrand then made the journey to Philadelphia where he fared better. In the Quaker 'City of Brotherly Love', he was entertained by the socially prominent Binghams, Alexander Hamilton and Aaron Burr. He profited in exile, selling property for a time in New Jersey as well as secret British documents, obtained in London, to the Spanish envoy in America. Moreau de St Méry, the son of a rich colonialist who had embroiled himself in Parisian politics, also fled to Philadelphia. He opened a bookstore, where many of the émigrés congregated to discuss events. In the 1790s, one out of every ten Philadelphians was a French émigré. Many others migrated to Boston, New York, the Caribbean and the American frontier.

Shunned by the aristocracy in Europe, the son of Philippe Égalité, who had become the new Duc d'Orléans, made his way from small town to small town using pseudonyms, and leaving a trail of illegitimate children from Switzerland to Scandinavia. Finally, he too made his way to the United States, settling in Boston. There, he taught French and lived above the famous Union Oyster House.

Some courtiers remained in France, displaying the chameleon's knack, serving, and in some cases, profiting, under the new political administration. Madame de Chanterenne, who had suffered terrible financial reversals when her husband became incapacitated and they had had to relocate to a home in the country, was offered a job with the family of Napoleon Bonaparte. She wrote to Marie-Thérèse to ask permission to accept the post, though without mentioning her straitened circumstances, and she ultimately went to Naples to live at court with Napoleon's sister. Living under the new Directory, Marie Antoinette's former First Lady-in-Waiting, Madame Campan, opened a school for girls in Saint-Germain-en-Laye. Among her students were Napoleon's stepdaughter, Hortense, and Eliza Monroe, daughter of America's Minister to France and future President, James Monroe.

By early spring 1796, the Directory had decided its position on the subject of nobility: unless an aristocrat was proven a traitor to the new government through specific and chargeable actions, the second *état* was welcome to live peacefully in France and work alongside the bourgeoisie. The government had already set a certain tone by sparing the life of the King's surviving daughter, Marie-Thérèse. Twenty-six-year-old Napoleon Bonaparte, who had been elevated from General of the Interior Army to Commander-in-Chief of the French expedition in Italy, believed that many of the émigrés could prove useful, and he offered many of the former courtiers an olive branch – coveted posts in his army. Some aristocrats returned to their homeland to serve the new and seemingly more forgiving government. Some, however, refused to return to France, preferring poverty and deprivation to living under the rule of one regarded by many as 'the Usurper'.

For most émigrés, Marie-Thérèse represented a beacon of hope for the future and the embodiment of France's glorious past. She received a daily stream of letters at the Hofburg from priests asking for asylum in Austria, from citizens in Switzerland, Germany and Italy who had harbored émigrés and asked Marie-Thérèse to reimburse them for their trouble, and from women unknown to her asking for positions in her household. For some individuals, to be able to serve Marie-Thérèse of France presented a nostalgic link to the ancien régime; for others, employment on the staff of the 'Orphan of the Temple' would, they imagined, result in handsome remuneration.

Although she had instructed Monseigneur de la Fare to reply to the multitude of émigrés who had written her at the Hofburg, they, despite often writing of great hardship, received no financial relief from the Princess. Many were shocked and insulted and deemed her uncharitable. Among those who had written Marie-Thérèse offering her services was her mother's dear friend, the Princesse de Tarente. Tarente believed that Marie-Thérèse would most certainly beg her to come and live at the Hofburg. When Tarente did not receive an effusive reply from Marie-Thérèse, she dispatched an angry note to Monsieur Hüe accusing Marie-Thérèse of being cold-hearted. The Marquise de Favras, now living in Bohemia, was another who wrote a poignant note and received an unsatisfactory reply.

While Franz lavished Marie-Thérèse with shelter, clothing and an allowance fit for an archduchess, he was not entirely forthcoming about what she was entitled to receive. Others set out to secure for Marie-Thérèse what was rightfully hers. Before arriving in Vienna in late January, Comte Fersen had traveled from court to court across Europe in an attempt to retrieve the money and jewels Marie Antoinette had so carefully set aside for her daughter in the event of her own death. Still loyal to the memory of the late Queen, Fersen had gone first to question Mercy on the whereabouts of the money – hundreds of thousands of *livres* – and jewels that Marie Antoinette had entrusted to him. Mercy replied that he had given them to the late Queen's sister, Marie Christine (Princess Albert of Saxe-Teschen). He wrote to the Princess, who explained that she had sent everything to Emperor Franz II in Vienna. Fersen also wondered what had happened to the money that Marie Antoinette had sent to her sister in Naples. Upon that inquiry, he was told that the money had never made it to Naples. Neither did anyone seem to know the whereabouts of Monsieur Léonard, who had slipped out of France with a case full of the Queen's diamonds.

Fersen, suspecting that most of the money and at least some of the jewels had, somehow, made their way to the Holy Roman Emperor, was determined to force Franz II to relinquish them to Marie-Thérèse. However, at an audience with Franz on February 24, Fersen was horrified to learn that although the Emperor admitted that he had much of his cousin's inheritance, he intended to hold onto it and use it as her dowry. He also informed Fersen that Marie-Thérèse ought not to have any complaints as she was being treated on an equal footing with his own sisters. Besides, the Emperor added, she was only seventeen and not old enough to manage her own money. Fersen countered with the fact that in France seventeen was considered of age, but this was something the Emperor already knew.

Fersen was in Vienna not only on behalf of Marie-Thérèse, who he now realized had no idea of the fortune due her, but also in the hopes of collecting something from the estate of Marie Antoinette to assist Madame de Korff, the woman who had risked her own life in order to provide Marie Antoinette with her false passport for her ill-fated trip to Varennes. In late March, Comte Fersen was able to see Marie-Thérèse during an official visit to the Hofburg; however, there were so many people around the Princess that he simply could not speak with her on confidential matters.

Marie-Thérèse continued to believe that the Emperor was, at heart, a good man and that he had her best interests at heart. She understood that he wanted her to marry Archduke Karl. She thought, however, that he would eventually allow her to be reunited with her French family and abide by what she had been told were her parents' wishes and marry the Duc d'Angoulême. That plan was further stalled, however, when, on March 27, Easter Sunday, 1796, Napoleon was victorious on the Italian front and Louis XVIII was ordered to leave Verona immediately. In rare accord, Franz and Louis agreed that it was an inauspicious time for the Princess to join her Bourbon uncle, who was now in search of another safe haven.

Franz was delighted to be rid of the man who had been such a thorn in his side. Although Louis was a King without a country and his machinations could be largely ignored, the Emperor also knew that Louis was capable of going behind his back and causing trouble. The previous year Louis had expressed his desire to join the Prince of Condé's forces in Germany. When the Emperor denied him permission, Louis, circumventing his then host, wrote to Empress Catherine of Russia, who enthusiastically encouraged Louis to join the army of exiles. Franz ignored the Czarina, stood firm and insisted that Louis remain in Italy, out of trouble. The Emperor also knew that Louis was intent on sabotaging his marriage plans for Marie-Thérèse and manipulating her into marriage to d'Angoulême.

Before Louis left Verona, Marie-Thérèse surreptitiously sent her uncle a note giving him absolute assurance of her intentions:

> My uncle, I am extremely touched by your goodness and how you concern yourself with my establishment. You have chosen the Duc d'Angoulême for my husband; I accept with all my heart and I prefer this establishment to all, even an imperial crown if it is offered . . . I accept, then, with greatest joy, my cousin Angoulême . . . I very much desire that this marriage happens quickly.

She would marry the Duc d'Angoulême because at the bottom of her heart she hoped that the Bourbon monarchy would return to France, and she knew that her marriage to the Duc d'Angoulême would indicate to millions that she believed in that dream.

Louis took this letter as her official acceptance of his nephew's hand in marriage and he adopted a much more aggressive stance toward achieving 'their shared dream' once he left Verona. To gain a higher profile as the King of France, he proceeded with his original plan to join the royalist army of the Duc d'Enghien on the banks of the Rhine, which infuriated Franz. Louis angered the Habsburg monarch even further when he enlisted the help of another Habsburg King, Charles IV of Spain. In order for Marie-Thérèse to marry her first cousin, a papal dispensation was required. Louis wrote to Charles IV asking him to use his influence with the Pope in order to obtain the special consideration. At the same time, Louis contacted the Spanish King's ambassador to the Vatican, Señor d'Azara. The Spanish were obsessed with the notion that, in an effort to dismember France, Franz II would use Marie-Thérèse's inherited rights to lay claim on Navarre, where, it could be argued, Salic law did not apply. D'Azara, acting precipitately and in the belief that Charles would have been violently against an Austrian alliance for the French Princess, approached the Pope and received his permission and blessing for the two first cousins to marry, thus giving Louis carte blanche to move forward with his plans. Unbeknown to d'Azara, Charles IV's reply to Louis was that he would *not* intervene and approach the Pope.

The Emperor suffered yet another blow to his scheme when Archduke Karl, who at twenty-four was the youngest general in the Emperor's army, was called away to lead imperial forces against Napoleon's army along the Rhine. Marie-Thérèse wrote to Louis that with the Archduke away in battle, he ought to be reassured: 'When he returns, surely I will no longer be here . . . therefore, you see, you have nothing to fear.'

Having outfoxed the Emperor, Louis then had the nerve to remind Franz that since Marie Antoinette's dowry had not been paid back to France, it should be paid directly to Marie-Thérèse. Franz was incensed and responded that he was treating Marie-Thérèse appropriately, like a princess. Louis wrote to his niece on May 3, explaining that relations with the Emperor had soured somewhat and that she would have to act as their go-between. 'You are, my dear child, the link of friendship between the Emperor and me', he wrote, before telling her how thrilled she would have been by the reception he received from the émigré army along the Rhine.

With the advent of summer, the Emperor moved his entire family to the Schönbrunn Palace and for the first time since that final summer with her parents at Saint-Cloud, Marie-Thérèse was in a bucolic setting that gave her happiness. She was able to walk the gardens and breathe in the sweet-smelling aromas her mother had known as a child. She was allowed to visit the Convent of the Visitation near Belvedere Palace on the outskirts of Vienna and receive visits from some young French friends, including the two nieces of Monseigneur de la Fare. One of these, Alexandrine, later the Baronne du Montet, recalled that the first time she saw Marie-Thérèse she appeared in black, a 'celestial beauty, blue eyes with a grandeur and unique expression, a svelte and well-formed figure, beautiful, radiant skin'. Alexandrine began to receive frequent visits from Marie-Thérèse and noted her azure-colored eyes and fresh and youthful beauty. In the countryside, Marie-Thérèse changed from her mourning clothes, often favoring cloths of vivid royal blue – the very color of the centuries-old Bourbon family banner. Marie-Thérèse had learned from her mother the impact that her choice of dress could have. Her calculation proved successful. Du Montet recalled that people were overcome at the very sight of the royal orphan.

While Marie-Thérèse succeeded in making the statement she desired, she was personally uncomfortable with the emotions she evoked, so she developed a rapid walk to avoid the tears and adulation. Du Montet remembered that Madame de France, as she was referred to in Austria, inspired sentiments of veneration, admiration and love. Before his departure for the Rhine, Archduke Karl made it obvious to all that he too felt those sentiments for his cousin. In fact, it appears that his appreciation had blossomed into romantic feelings for Marie-Thérèse. When rumors suggested that the attraction was mutual, the émigré community alerted Louis XVIII. Despite the reassuring missives from his niece, Louis was right to be concerned. Before Karl left for battle, he had been most attentive to Marie-Thérèse while the Duc d'Angoulême had not written to her once. Louis, anxious not to lose momentum, wrote to Marie-Thérèse implying that d'Angoulême had romantic feelings for her but that he was so painfully shy that he needed her encouragement.

Marie-Thérèse, hitherto innocent of any such sentiments, obediently wrote to her cousin. At last, in a letter dated July 5, 1796, Louis-Antoine responded from his home in exile in Edinburgh. He was happy to learn that she wanted him to write to her often. He wrote about the weather: the Scottish climate was miserable, but the people were nice. He wrote that his future was uncertain and that he did not know how long he would remain in Scotland. He wrote that, like Marie-Thérèse, his overwhelming desire was to serve the King of France. The letter was friendly, at best. He may have understood his duty, but he certainly did not understand women, displaying neither the charm nor the gallantry of his father, the Comte d'Artois, or his eighteen-year-old brother, the Duc de Berry, who was already winning women's hearts.

That summer, Archduke Karl scored impressive victories against Napoleon's army on the Rhine. He became the idol of not only the entire Habsburg Empire but also of most French émigrés and thousands of young women who thought him dashing. The Duchesse d'Abrantès recorded in her memoir that four years after Karl's expedition to the Rhine even Napoleon could not hide his admiration for the valiant Austrian Prince, remarking: 'Here is a man who will never incur a syllable of reproach! Archduke Charles [Karl]. That man has a soul, a golden heart. He is a virtuous man.'[2]

It was while Karl's star was rising, and while Marie-Thérèse was content at the Schönbrunn, that she received a letter from Louis asking her to be 'persuasive' with the Emperor concerning a new idea. Louis wanted her to travel to the border between Germany and France, where, under the protection of the Emperor's army, she could be married in secret to d'Angoulême. Although Marie-Thérèse had every intention of performing her duty, she most definitely did not want to rush into the marriage without her own conditions being met. She had recently met with Comte Fersen and learned of her mother's legacy, and she now wrote to her uncle informing him that she did not intend to leave Vienna without some substantial part of it. She understood that life in exile among her wandering family members would require funds and she wanted to be in charge of her own money.

In the meantime, she enjoyed herself with Madame de Chanclos's two nieces, made friends with her Austrian cousins, Franz's sisters, the Archduchesses Amelia and Maria Clementina, and renewed acquaintances with some French members of her family, who also sought her out as their go-between with the Holy Roman Emperor. One of those who arrived on her doorstep was Louise de Condé, daughter of the Prince de Condé. Louise had been boarding in a convent throughout the Terror and the Prince thought the time was now right for his daughter to join her cousin at the tranquil country home of the Habsburgs. The brilliant military tactician advised his daughter to write to Marie-Thérèse for permission to visit and to leave right away whether she received an answer or not. In the late summer of 1796, Louise arrived in Vienna. She reported to both her father and her brother that everyone had nothing but praise for the daughter of Marie Antoinette and that Marie-Thérèse in Vienna, after years of deprivation, had grown

> pretty, fat (a little too). She speaks well and said with grace what one ought to, but with more gravity than the Queen. She spoke with me of you and your children, very nicely; she is truly loved here, everyone praises her, says she is extremely pious.

To her brother, Louise wrote of a series of misadventures on her way to Vienna, and offered her opinion that she thought Marie-Thérèse looked very like the late Queen of France. Louise also informed her family that Marie-Thérèse appeared to her to have suffered much and that she had confided to her that her real desire was to live quietly in a convent.

Marie-Thérèse, had, through Monseigneur de la Fare, only just begun to learn of the difficulties facing many of her parents' former courtiers in exile. She wanted to help them, but she was not yet in control of her money, so she surreptitiously sent small sums from her allowance through de la Fare and instructed him to send her deepest expressions of gratitude with an explanation of her situation to those in despair.

With Napoleon's forces gaining in Italy, Marie-Thérèse's Bourbon cousins increasingly began to seek asylum elsewhere. Although Louis XVIII detested his wife, Marie Joséphine, it had been his father-in-law who had offered Louis XVIII shelter in Verona when he had escaped France. In return for that act of kindness, Louis had asked Marie-Thérèse to approach the Emperor and ask him to allow Marie Joséphine, unable to remain in her father's conquered territory, as well as French clergy, exiled from Switzerland by Napoleon, to take refuge in Austria. Still just seventeen years old, Marie-Thérèse was placed in a pivotal position whereby she would act as the unofficial ambassador of the Bourbon government in exile to the Holy Roman Empire. Marie-Thérèse accordingly spent the entire summer pleading the case of family, extended family, friends and clergy until Franz grew even wearier of his Bourbon cousins and the intransigent Madame de France.

While in Riegel with Condé's army along the Rhine, Louis XVIII suffered a bullet wound to the head from an assassination attempt. The shot only grazed his scalp, and he recovered in a few days. He decided, however, to get far away from the battle front and traveled to the Prussian town of Blankenburg, where under the protection of the Duke of Brunswick he found accommodation, two rooms above a shop, for himself, his minister d'Avaray and a servant named Guignet. From there he hoped to make contact with a sympathetic ruler and re-establish his court in exile. At the same time he kept up the pressure on his nephew, Louis-Antoine, instructing the young man to court his niece. D'Angoulême complied and wrote to Marie-Thérèse on September 3, that since she had given him permission to write her frequently, he would, and that he wished he could spend all day every day writing her. 'The sentiments that my amiable and very dear cousin inspire in me are at once my happiness and my torment.' Toward the end of this note, which, in fact, did reveal a shy nature, he bid her 'Adieu', and wrote that he hoped her heart could read in his 'the tender homage and eternal attachment of your very affectionate cousin'.

In mid-September, the imperial family returned to the Hofburg. Franz remained convinced that he could arrange a marriage between his much-sought-after brother and Marie-Thérèse. The Emperor and his staff devised a plan based on the notion that if Marie-Thérèse could discover that pleasure was more appealing than duty, she might embrace life at the Hofburg. They surrounded her with a group of young women whom she genuinely liked and invited her to a constant stream of parties and balls, encouraging her to experience the normal life for a seventeen-year-old princess. For a while she appeared to be enjoying herself.

On September 16, 1796, Gouverneur Morris, the American to whom the late King Louis XVI had entrusted a great deal of money before his execution, happened to be wandering the Prater, Vienna's lively amusement park. There, Morris came upon:

M. Hüe, the valet-de-chambre of Louis XVI . . . I have a good deal of conversation with him. He is highly discontented with the treatment he meets with here . . . With a false mysteriousness he lets me know that he conceives they have the idea of marrying the young princess to one of her cousins, brother to the Emperor, and setting up in that way a claim to the throne of France. This may be, but it is a very remote speculation, and if I were to guess, such marriage would form an insuperable bar to her success. He speaks very highly of her, and I see her passing by. She is much improved in her appearance since I saw her in France.'[3]

Morris expanded on his objections to the scheme:

I have long suspected something still more important to the peace of Europe; viz, that the heir of the Spanish monarchy [Ferdinand] should be placed on the French throne . . . This idea I was always cautious not to publish . . . To consolidate it, they contrive to get the French princess . . . for his wife.[4]

Despite Franz's considerable efforts to persuade Marie-Thérèse of the benefits of staying in Vienna, Marie-Thérèse remained firm in her desire to fulfill her role as Child of France. Like her grandmother, the Empress, Marie-Thérèse was serious-minded, interested in politics and hungered for news of events in Europe. When she heard that Catherine of Russia had died on November 6, Marie-Thérèse contemplated what this might mean for French royalists and expressed her most private, and quite astute, thoughts to her uncle that the new Czar, Paul I, Grand Duke Paul – whom she had met at Versailles when she was a child – would be a comparatively weak successor; but she hoped he would continue to support her uncle as his mother had done before him.

For her own survival, Marie-Thérèse had long mastered the 'act of compliance', as her uncle had assessed in a letter to her in March, 1796. Whilst still receiving a steady stream of communiqués from her uncle and Bourbon cousins, she continued to attend parties and balls and socialize alongside the Emperor's sisters and wife. On November 13, Gouverneur Morris once again saw Marie-Thérèse at a party: it was his opinion that she was the picture of her late father.

Sir M. Eden presents me to the archduchesses, sisters of the Emperor, and Madame of France. The elder archduchess, who is betrothed to the heir apparent of Naples, has a striking resemblance to the Queen of France, which I mention to her, and she tells me that others have observed it . . . Madame of France strikes me by the strong resemblance she bears to her father, Louis XVI, and I cannot help observing, when we leave her presence, on the malignity which pursued her poor mother, and would have persuaded the world that this was an offspring produced by her gallantries. Every trait gives the lie to that aspersion.[5]

Of course, among those who had been first in line to insinuate that Marie-Thérèse had not been fathered by Louis XVI, and he did so at her baptism, was the late King's own brother, the Comte de Provence, now King Louis XVIII, the man who had become Marie-Thérèse's adopted father, the man whose lie she also adopted when she told the Emperor that she had to marry her cousin, d'Angoulême, because her parents had wished it.

Gouverneur Morris, who had thought the late King Louis XVI a fine man, felt honor-bound to deliver the late King's money with which he had been entrusted directly into the hands of his surviving child. Here, Louis XVI had demonstrated sound judgment. Unlike the friends and family of Marie Antoinette who took advantage of the late Queen's trust, Morris proved completely reliable. He knew that the whole affair would be a delicate operation because the Emperor – or the late King's brother – might try to intercept the money. Morris waited until he could arrange a method of payment that would circumvent those parties. Once he had made contact with Marie-Thérèse, the two were able to arrange the transactions. Marie-Thérèse also understood the need for discretion regarding the funds, which began to arrive via credit memos and notes from Switzerland and England.

Instead of spending the money on party dresses or trinkets, Marie-Thérèse decided to use the funds to help the Bourbon cause, and she immediately forwarded sums to émigrés in need. On January 25, 1797, she wrote to her uncle:

> I have received with great pleasure your two letters of December 19 and January 3. I am very grateful that you have thought of me on my birthday, it is a happy day for me, because owing to the goodness of the Emperor, I recovered my liberty [from prison] . . . the note and memo herewith, I have from M. Morris, Minister of the United States to the Court of France during the early years of the Revolution, you will understand what I mean.

She had begun her journey down the path of her own choosing: she would live her life devoted to the memory of her parents and to serving and promoting the Bourbon cause.

CHAPTER XV
THE BIRTH OF
A STRATEGIST

ON JANUARY 21, 1797, the fourth anniversary of the death of King Louis XVI, Louis XVIII wrote to his niece stating that he had met with the Abbé Edgeworth, the priest who had been with her late father at the scaffold. Louis XVIII, who rarely missed a public relations opportunity, asked Marie-Thérèse if she would write the priest a letter of gratitude for publication, and backdate it to the day she crossed the border. Marie-Thérèse, who had publicly declared that she was on earth to obey her King, privately declined to do so, claiming sweetly that she was too young for such a letter to have any import. She also begged her uncle to forgive her 'resistance to your wish', claiming that she did not want to call attention to herself for fear of irritating the Emperor. Louis wrote a second time; and, once more, she refused him. She was extremely uncomfortable using her parents' tragedy in such a fraudulent way, and was angry that her uncle had asked her to do this. She enquired whether her father had left any secret instructions for her with the Abbé. He had not. Her uncle then referred to his own sad days in exile. She thanked him for confiding in her, and reciprocated by telling him of her own experiences:

since the 10th of August 1792 until the month of August, 1795, I had known of nothing concerning my family, of politics, we only knew of the injuries that overwhelmed us. You have no idea of the harshness of our prison. Those who have not seen it with their own eyes could not have imagined it. I, who greatly suffered, could hardly believe it. My mother, ignorant of the existence of my brother, who lived below her.

My aunt and I ignorant of the transport of my mother to the Conciergerie and after that her death. In vain I demanded to know why we
were separated. They closed the doors without answering me. My
brother died in the room beneath mine; they kept me in ignorance . . .
   I swear that during that time I had begun to lose all hope, and I feared
that I would spend all my life imprisoned. Having lived alone in my
room for a whole year, I had the time to reflect, and I could only
imagine the worst about my parents, but as the unhappy love to delude
themselves, there were moments when I had hope.

Although Louis had previously thought of his niece mostly as his
political ally, he felt genuine compassion as a result of her words and was
impressed by her grace and kindness. The Duc d'Angoulême too seemed
more enthusiastic as the tone of his letters changed from pleasant to
ardent. On January 3, 1797, d'Angoulême wrote that on reading her
letter of December 26 he had his

   lips pressed to the lines which your hands had traced . . . and I wonder
   how long I will be separated from she who occupies all my thoughts . . .
   who gives life to my own existence . . . the King has given me the hope
   that I will soon rejoin Condé's army. I will be on the same continent
   where my cousin breathes, and I will fight for her.

In early 1797, Archduke Karl was forced to leave for the Italian front.
His military successes in Germany were not repeated in Italy, however,
and after heavy defeats his troops fled his command. Louis seized the
moment and summoned d'Angoulême to Blankenburg in the hope that
the closer proximity to Marie-Thérèse would seal matters. The young
Prince traveled there from Edinburgh on April 27, 1797, just as Napoleon's army was gaining ground in northern Italy. It appeared as though
the French armies would arrive at the steps of the Hofburg at any moment
and the Emperor decided to move his family far away from Vienna for
their own safety. Marie-Thérèse was relocated to a convent near Prague
where her mother's sister, Maria Anna, would look after her. Monseigneur de la Fare wrote to the nun for an update on the French Princess,
and she responded on June 2 that Marie-Thérèse was 'very well . . . I am
persuaded, like you, that she is destined for greatness . . . she has perfect
submission to Divine Will'.
   By late summer 1797, with Napoleon victorious in Italy and peace
negotiations between France and Austria imminent, Marie-Thérèse

expressed her desire to return to Vienna. She wrote to her uncle, 'I greatly love my aunt Maria Anna, but I do not know if you know what state she is in. She has consumption and has been sick for many years . . . she must drink women's milk . . . I vow that if I stay here, I will be constantly with her, and to be with someone in this state, I am certain that I will become ill.' She did, however, like the tranquility of the convent and hoped that she could live similarly in Vienna.

On August 22, the Duc d'Angoulême fell off his horse and broke his clavicle. Marie-Thérèse read about the accident in a newspaper and was annoyed that her uncle had not written to her about it. Her Austrian family chorused that it was obvious from this that the Bourbons cared little for her. Louis had, in fact, written to his niece about the mishap and included the reassuring information that her fiancé was recovering nicely, but the letter did not reach Marie-Thérèse until weeks later. In the letter, Louis also wrote that d'Angoulême was only able to maintain good spirits because of the thought of Marie-Thérèse's uplifting letters. She, herself, hurt by the fact that she was forced to find out about her own fiancé in the newspapers, made a mental note that she had not heard at all from the Comte d'Artois nor from his wife, her aunt and uncle and future in-laws, and she was beginning to feel ignored by her Bourbon family.

In France, the coup of 18 Fructidor (September 4, 1797), which placed the Jacobins in supreme command, sent the moderates into exile and dashed any hope of reconciliation with the monarchists. The time had come for the Holy Roman Emperor to negotiate with 'the Usurper'. Once peace negotiations with Napoleon were under way, the Emperor recalled his family from Prague, this time to the Belvedere Palace on the outskirts of Vienna. Marie-Thérèse liked the Belvedere, with its beautiful gardens designed in the French style by Dominique Girard who had trained in the gardens at Versailles, much more than the fortress-like Hofburg, and she returned to Vienna most willingly. She read of Napoleon's successes and followed the peace talks leading up to the signing of the Treaty of Campo Formio in October, in which Austria forfeited possessions in Burgundy and Lombardy, Belgium and the Ionian Islands and Franz received part of Venetia, among other parcels of land, as small compensation.

Archduke Karl also returned to Vienna, and told Jacques Matthieu Augeard, the late Marie Antoinette's secretary, that he had seen Marie-Thérèse and was infatuated with her. Receiving reports in Blankenburg, Louis decided that d'Angoulême needed to make an appearance at the Belvedere as well and instructed d'Angoulême to go to Vienna 'incognito'. Once again, Marie-Thérèse vetoed the King's plan, strategically arguing that the Emperor would certainly learn of the French Prince's arrival, that Franz was in no mood to receive a Frenchman at court and that it would be an insult to d'Angoulême if he arrived without fanfare. Once again Louis XVIII could not outwit his young niece in such a game of nerves.

Marie-Thérèse then wrote to her uncle underlining the precariousness of the Bourbons' position and stressing, 'It is a great problem to know if the peace will bring happiness or sadness for us, that is to say, for France, because these words are synonymous.' Equally, she insisted that she would not leave Austria until she had financial independence – until her uncle had arranged for the Emperor to 'do something' for her – as she did not need to be in a prison to be miserable and without her own funds she would not be happy. In November, King Frederick William II of Prussia died, and the new King, Frederick William III, informed Louis that he would have to leave his realm. Marie-Thérèse understood that for the moment the plan to reunite with her uncle and marry her cousin was impractical. In the meantime, she played the game, made the best of her situation and sat back and waited.

Worn down by his dealings with the French, Emperor Franz loosened surveillance on Marie-Thérèse at the Belvedere and allowed her greater freedom to meet with her countrymen. Among her visitors was the Duc d'Enghien, grandson of her Bourbon cousin, the Prince de Condé. D'Enghien wrote to his grandfather that Marie-Thérèse was enchanting and lively – 'you will be charmed when you see her'. Marie-Thérèse wrote to Louis that she had seen her cousin, 'My God! It had such a profound effect upon me – at last, to once again see a member of my family.' She told her uncle that she hoped someday soon to see the Prince de Condé and, in a change of heart about her 'neglectful' Bourbon cousins, thanked him for all he had done for their cause. Convinced that it might now be safe to send Marie-Thérèse items of value, Louis forwarded something he had been promising for a long time: a ring with the portrait of her mother carved on its stone.

Marie-Thérèse also enjoyed more contact with the French émigré community as a whole and Madame de Chanclos and Monseigneur de la Fare worked in concert to introduce her to more people of her own age, including some French girls. During this time she made friends she would hold dear for life – Madame de Chanclos's niece, Marie-Françoise de Roisins, daughter of the Marshal de Roisins, who later became Comtesse Esterhazy, a girl from Lorraine named Anne-Charlotte-Henriette de Choisy, whose family had had a long history serving France with honor, and Comtesse Marie-Wilhelmine Ferraris. Madame de Chanclos arranged for the three young women to join Marie-Thérèse's household, and the four became inseparable. Marie-Thérèse was delighted when she was once again permitted to receive both Monsieur and Madame Hüe and Jean-Baptiste Cléry who asked her to read a journal he had written of his time in prison with her late father. She read it and gave him her permission to publish it. Cléry then left for Blankenburg to seek the blessing of Louis XVIII.

The Treaty of Campo Formio had been a disaster for the German Princes, forcing them to cede lands to France on the eastern bank of the Rhine to the French Directory. In December, the Congress of Rastatt convened in order to placate the Princes, and among the ambassadors was the Swedish Count, Axel Fersen, who represented his own King in the compensation discussions. The French Directory, declaring him a friend of the late King and an enemy of France, refused to allow him to participate and sent him on his way. Fersen traveled to Vienna to see Marie-Thérèse with news that he wanted to deliver in person. He had asked the Directory to relinquish the crown jewels that her mother had returned to the State so that Marie-Thérèse could have them, but Napoleon had refused his request.

Fersen had other news. A boy had been found wandering aimlessly in the countryside near Châlons-sur-Marne in northeast France. It was said he could not remember his own identity. Rumors spread that he was Louis XVII, and that his jailers had taken him out of the Temple Prison in a basket. A few months later, it was revealed that the boy was one Jean-Marie Hervagault. Fersen uncovered the fact that Comte Louis de Frotté, with whom he spoke, had been involved in a rescue attempt orchestrated by the late royalist General Charette. According to Frotté, at one point the Directory had desired peace at all costs and had agreed to release the boy King. On the evening of June 13, 1794, Frotté and a woman waited in a carriage outside the Temple. A man appeared with a little boy. The boy was handed over to Frotté and the woman. They changed the child into girl's clothing and their carriage took off. When they arrived at Fontenay, where Charette's troops had temporarily relocated, they presented the boy to the General, who informed them that they had the wrong child. Frotté told Fersen that he was not sure who had been duped, themselves, or the Directory. Frotté and many others believed that Louis Charles was alive and being kept hidden until Napoleon and the Directory could be overthrown. This story, as with almost every other new story concerning Marie-Thérèse's beloved brother, received confirmation from some loyal courtiers and was reported widely. The possibility that Louis XVII still lived fascinated everyone, and pained no one more than his own sister.

One man, of course, dismissed all of the stories as implausible. From his two-roomed apartment in Blankenburg, Louis XVIII sent an emissary, the Marquis de Bonnay, to Vienna to meet with his niece. Louis prefaced the visit by writing to Marie-Thérèse on December 19, her nineteenth birthday, assuring her that her happiness was of the utmost importance to him, and that he was working feverishly to ensure it. Five days later, Bonnay wrote to the King from Vienna that he had met with Marie-Thérèse and that she remained steadfastly committed to her King and to marrying no one other than d'Angoulême. Bonnay declared that he was astonished by her clarity of judgment and 'sang-froid' – as he put it – in her commitment to her duty. He cautioned, however, that she could be willful and defiant. Bonnay advised that the King and d'Angoulême put some effort into their relationship with this extraordinary young woman; he suggested that Louis should write to her often, encourage other members of the family to do so, send her family portraits and ensure that she felt loved. As d'Avaray had already pointed out, Marie-Thérèse, like most women, needed to be wooed and to know her fiancé's character and innermost thoughts. Bonnay advised that as Marie-Thérèse took devotion quite seriously, it would be a good idea for d'Angoulême to stress his own churchgoing in his letters to her. Finally, he suggested Louis find a way for the Princess to have significant money of her own; win her 'young heart by any method'; marry her off to d'Angoulême as quickly as possible; find a more permanent home for his own court in exile; and obtain the cooperation of the other crowned heads of Europe.

Louis had already started on the crowned heads of Europe by playing on their fears of mass insurrection. There had been seeds of revolution and copycat uprisings in Hungary, the Netherlands and Germany and Louis reminded his cousins that they must continue to support his cause for their own good. Finally, in early 1798, Louis received word from Czar Paul that the French court in exile would be welcome to establish itself in Mitau ('Jelgava'), on the Baltic Sea. The Czar offered Louis a generous allowance, a palace, and complete protection. The palace, formerly the home to the Dukes of Courland, was lavish. Mitau itself, like Lorraine, was a region that had been fought over and passed back and forth in peace settlements. The town, a place of refinement, was filled with Russian noblemen and German Jewish intellectuals, and as far as Czar Paul was concerned, Mitau, a border region only recently repossessed by Russia, was the perfect solution as it placed the Bourbons at a comfortably good distance away.

In a packet containing letters from d'Angoulême, Marie-Thérèse received a letter from her uncle explaining that he and her fiancé would soon depart for Mitau and, although far, far way from France, he hoped that Mitau would provide a more settled and fitting home for the Princess. After a grueling month-long journey from eastern Germany, Louis and his retinue arrived at Mitau Castle to great fanfare from the local officials and militia. Awaiting Louis was Marie-Thérèse's noncommittal reply:

> My dear uncle, I have had the infinite pleasure of, at last, receiving your news, because I have acutely felt privation, these six weeks have been so long . . . I have already learned that you had departed Blankenburg . . . It is so sad to have obliged you to go so far; one must hope that in the end you will be at the least tranquil in Mitau . . . I had not sufficiently admired the Emperor of Russia: he distinguishes himself among all of the sovereigns and his actions do him honor . . .
>
> I thank you for the letters from my cousin. It is impossible for him to be any more attentive than he is, and it always gives me great pleasure when he gives me news of you. I flatter myself, that despite my distance from Mitau, I will receive from time to time your news; that will be one of my greatest consolations.

While Napoleon launched an ambitious military expedition to Egypt, his enemies plotted in Europe. The great allies reorganized to fight him once more and in Germany, England, and Russia, French émigrés, in contact with sympathizers in France, plotted to reinstate the Bourbons. A newspaper called *Le Spectateur du Nord*, published in Hamburg, provided propaganda for the royalists and their mission. From Mitau, Louis organized his court, his ministers, messengers and spies. He also attempted to increase pressure on Franz II to allow Marie-Thérèse to rejoin her family. Pleading his case with the Emperor's most valued allies, the Czar, Charles IV of Spain and the remaining Bourbons in Italy, Louis reminded them all that it had been the wish of the late King and Queen of France that their daughter marry his nephew, the Duc d'Angoulême, and that the marriage already had the blessing of the Pope.

With Lord Nelson's stunning defeat of Napoleon's navy at Aboukir Bay, the sovereigns of Europe saw a glimmer of hope that they could reclaim France from the Jacobins. Franz II needed his European allies, so he acquiesced: Marie-Thérèse would go to Mitau and she would marry the Duc d'Angoulême. Throughout the second half of 1798 and early

1799, Charles IV, Louis XVIII, the Holy Roman Emperor and Czar Paul haggled with the gravity and tenacity usually accorded to the most significant of affairs of State over the impending nuptials of Marie-Thérèse-Charlotte. In an effort to shame Franz II into releasing the money that was owed Marie-Thérèse from her mother's estate, Czar Paul insisted that the Holy Roman Emperor pay her traveling expenses. When Franz complained that he had already spent a good deal of money on his cousin, the other sovereigns retorted that she was supposed to have been his guest, and that he might recall that they themselves had offered to be her host. The Spanish Bourbon King Charles IV agreed to provide Marie-Thérèse with an annual income and, at last, Franz agreed to cover the cost of her journey, whose total amounted to only a part of the interest that he had earned on Marie Antoinette's monies. Just as Marie-Thérèse turned twenty, she was informed that she would, at last, be getting married to her cousin.

Anne-Charlotte-Henriette de Choisy, Hüe and Cléry would escort the bride-to-be to Mitau. Cléry had just returned from London where he had had his memoir published and whilst there had been approached by the incorrigible Mrs Atkyns who asked him to deliver a quantity of gifts to Marie-Thérèse. He accepted the presents on the Princess's behalf and wrote a gracious thank-you note to the Englishwoman, offering his opinion that 'there is no one better than she . . . no one would thank you with more attachment and zeal'. Also en route from Paris was Madame Hüe, whose good friend Joséphine Bonaparte had written a letter enabling Madame Hüe to leave France.

Louis continued to write to his niece, filling his letters with praise for her fiancé; but, for Marie-Thérèse, the storybook romance had become unimportant. That winter, Marie-Thérèse's cousin and friend, Archduchess Amelia, died, plunging the Austrian court into mourning. While grieving with her mother's family, she received a package from the Elector of Trèves containing a miniature portrait of her brother, Louis Joseph, the first Dauphin. Marie-Thérèse confided to her uncle her delight at receiving the little painting as it had been ten years since his death and, as she had only been ten years old when he had died, Louis Joseph's face had begun to fade in her memory. Also in the parcel from the Elector was an item even more shocking: the chemise her father had worn to the guillotine, which had mysteriously made its way out of France to the late King's uncle. The shirt, smeared with blood, would become her banner.

Marie-Thérèse had been in Vienna now for nearly three years and four months, about the same amount of time that she had been in the Temple

Prison, when she set out for Russia in early May. She traveled through Brno, Crakow, and Opatow and reached Terespol, at the border, on May 17.

Napoleon had spent nine months on the march after his defeat in the Battle of the Nile. In May, English naval hero Sir Sidney Smith crippled Napoleon's already ailing forces at Acre. The monarchs of Europe and the royalists in Paris were poised for a skirmish of their own, ready to rid France of Napoleon and his allies. Marie-Thérèse had always been acutely aware of the political factions pitting monarchists against revolutionaries in France and although she had been told of the fate of many French émigrés, she remained innocent of the infighting, the competition, the jealousy, and even insidious sabotage that had gone on, and would continue, among her own family and friends, scrambling, as they had at Versailles, for favors, promises and appointments from Louis XVIII.

His kingdom in 1799 was, however, a mirage – a tragic-comic piece of well-rehearsed pantomime, enacted over the ages, now in a foreign land, and in a borrowed castle. Waiting in the wings for a return to France was the daughter of the martyred King and Queen. And if anyone could perform as required, it was Marie-Thérèse of France. So uniquely trained and practiced, and so inculcated with the obligation of duty, Marie-Thérèse headed toward Mitau to rejoin what was left of the Bourbon family, carrying with her her father's bloodstained shirt, which, for the rest of her life, would never leave her side.

CHAPTER XVI
A BRIDE

MARIE-THÉRÈSE ALSO carried some wedding presents with her from Vienna to Mitau. It was widely known in the Austrian and Neapolitan courts that Marie-Thérèse and her Neapolitan-born first cousin, the Empress Maria Theresa, disliked each other. The Empress, however, was kind enough to give Marie-Thérèse a portrait of her imperial self in a diamond-studded frame as a parting gift. Marie-Thérèse also received a letter from the Comte d'Artois, her soon-to-be father-in-law. With the letter d'Artois sent a gift of an exotic East Indian-style dress, and his best wishes. He had no intention of attending his son's wedding. He was too happily ensconced in Edinburgh near his longtime mistress, Louise de Polastron, surrounded by his own coterie of courtiers and living on credit and a generous allowance from George III.

As the father of the groom, d'Artois did try to impose his own wishes on the marriage of his eldest son. He argued for months with his brother about who would serve his new daughter-in-law. D'Artois had his own favorites and recommended that the Polignacs be given that honor. Louis, understanding that granting favors to the controversial Polignacs would evoke unpleasant memories for some, suggested instead that they comply with traditional Bourbon etiquette and appoint the wife of d'Angoulême's former governor, the Marquis de Sérent. D'Artois acquiesced, and the Marquise de Sérent, a lifelong family friend, was appointed *dame d'honneur*. D'Artois, seizing the moment, wrote to his wife Marie-Thérèse of Sardinia, from whom he continued to be estranged on the grounds that she repulsed him, telling her that she could not attend her own son's wedding. Neither would their younger son, the Duc de Berry, be making an appearance: he, like his father, found the idea of a trip to the Baltic far too much of a bore.

In fact, Louis was beginning to have serious doubts about his brother's entire family. Although he had repeatedly sung d'Angoulême's praises to Marie-Thérèse, in truth, Louis found his nephew lazy, timid and unattractive. After having lived in England for many years, d'Angoulême had become an anglophile and openly embraced English clothing, the English way of life and, worse, he had become fond of the notion of constitutional monarchy. Understandably, Louis feared that if Marie-Thérèse, who was marrying her cousin out of a belief in the divine right of kings and hereditary obligation, discovered d'Angoulême's predilection for the power of the bicameral legislature, she would be horrified. He therefore planned for the wedding to take place almost immediately upon her arrival at Mitau, before she could learn too much about her husband-to-be.

With d'Artois, his wife and their younger son missing from the proceedings, Louis was desperate to muster a show of family solidarity. Although he had little interest and even less affection for his own wife, Marie Joséphine, who had been residing in Kiel with her companion, Madame de Gourbillon, Louis ordered his queen to appear in Mitau for the wedding and to leave her friend behind in Germany. Marie Joséphine was so upset at the thought of being parted from de Gourbillon that she circumvented her husband and wrote to the Czar asking for his help. The Czar chose not to intervene in this matrimonial matter, and ignored her letter.

Marie Joséphine departed Kiel and, ignoring her husband's orders, arrived in a carriage in Mitau with her friend and suspected paramour. As her carriage made its way to the Governor's house, police spotted it on the street, saw de Gourbillon and physically removed the woman from Marie Joséphine's coach. After what, to the local citizenry, appeared to be an *opera buffa* – with much flailing of arms, kicking and screaming – the Italian-born queen stormed off toward Mitau Castle to see her husband. In front of the entire household staff, ministers included, who had assembled to greet their Queen, she refused to change out of her traveling clothes and move into her quarters until Madame de Gourbillon was allowed to join her. Louis refused so Marie Joséphine locked herself in her room with a bottle of liquor and refused to come out. Madame de Gourbillon would later get revenge when she showed a letter penned by Louis's own friend and minister, d'Avaray, to one of the Czar's ministers, a letter that contained unflattering comments about Czar Paul. De

Gourbillon's spite would cause friction between Louis and the Czar, eventually being among the causes that would lead to Louis's expulsion from Mitau.

By morning, the royal spitfire had calmed down, and she agreed to travel with her husband and the Duc d'Angoulême to meet Marie-Thérèse. As their carriage approached the outskirts of Mitau, they spotted the royal coach. Marie-Thérèse ordered her coachman to stop, and, alighting quickly, ran toward her uncle. According to all present, the Princess threw herself at the feet of her King and sobbed: 'I see you at last. I am so happy. Here is your child; please be my father.' The portly and awkward King lifted her from the floor and embraced her, as did his wife. D'Angoulême, who had not seen Marie-Thérèse in ten years, shyly kissed her hand and stuttered his own greeting.

As she entered the main hall of Mitau Castle, Marie-Thérèse was greeted with cheers. She looked around at childhood friends and Bourbon faces and, at last, felt a sense of home. The King presented her to the Abbé Edgeworth but he was so overcome with tears that he could not speak. Louis then gestured toward the hundred or so reunited *gardes du corps*, who, before individually escaping France, had protected the royal family at Versailles, and declared: 'Their wounds and their tears state everything that I wish I could express.'

Also in the crowd was one of Louis's foremost spies, the Marquis de la Maisonfort, who had come from St Petersburg to present the bride with gifts from the Czar, which included a stunning suite of diamonds, a purse filled with money, a collection of hats and gowns, her marriage contract (signed by the Czar), and a note praising her for her courage and inviting her to stay in Russia until the day when she would be able to return to France. Marie-Thérèse was shown to her apartment where she changed and wrote a letter of thanks to the Czar, calling herself his 'very affectionate sister, cousin and servant'. She then spoke privately and at length with the Abbé Edgeworth, the man who had been with her father in his last moments. He entreated her: 'Allow me to cry with you . . . tears in your presence soothe me.'

At five o'clock Marie-Thérèse joined the King, Queen, her fiancé, and their court in exile for dinner. In the salon, she was reunited with her beloved governess, Madame de Tourzel, who recorded in her memoirs that Marie-Thérèse resembled her mother, her father and Madame Elisabeth and therefore her appearance 'seemed to unite the earth and the sky'.

On the evening of June 9, the bride-to-be and d'Angoulême quietly signed an abbreviated nuptial document befitting a royal couple without a kingdom. The next morning Marie-Thérèse of France married her cousin, Louis-Antoine, Duc d'Angoulême in the home of the Dukes of Courland in a makeshift chapel decorated with bowers of greens and lilacs, entwined with roses and white lilies – symbolizing royalty and the Bourbon dynasty. Courtiers of the ancien régime and the hundred or so *gardes du corps* attended alongside senior residents of Mitau. Marie-Thérèse wore the diamonds given to her by Czar Paul and the couple knelt before the elderly Cardinal de Montmorency, who blessed their union. The King gave the pair his own present. It was the ring his brother, King Louis XVI, had removed from his wedding finger and given to Cléry before mounting the scaffold. Engraved inside were the initials 'M.A.A.A.' – for 'Marie Antoinette Archduchesse d'Autriche' – and the date May 16, 1770. Louis-Antoine placed the ring on Marie-Thérèse's hand and both 'cried tears of joy'. De la Maisonfort, who attended the wedding, wrote that it was 'the most touching, the most interesting I had ever seen'.

D'Angoulême, overwhelmed by his new role center stage, penned Czar Paul an effusive letter expressing his gratitude for all that the Emperor had done for his family, and for orchestrating his happiness. He mentioned the fact that he was aware of the exploits of the dashing Archduke Karl and of the courage of his own bride and asked Paul, and separately his uncle, permission to leave Mitau to join the Czar's army, as many other French émigrés had. Russia along with England, Austria, the Ottoman Empire and some small German and Italian states had just regrouped, forming the Second Coalition of allied forces against the French. Only days after the wedding of the d'Angoulêmes, the sixty-nine-year-old Russian General, Alexander Suvorov, whose troops had recaptured Milan and Turin, scored another victory at Trebbia forcing a French retreat into the Alps. With Napoleon focused in the Middle East, Archduke Karl led Austrian troops to victory near the Rhine. D'Angoulême explained to the Czar that he thirsted for glory and, unlike many of his ancestors, had no desire to be idle and unemployed. Louis, exasperated that Louis-Antoine would want to leave his new bride – especially now the eyes of Europe were turned toward the new couple, and the hopes of French royalists pinned on their ability to procreate – dismissed his nephew's request as a moment of uncharacteristic ebullience.

Louis, meanwhile, wrote to d'Artois extolling his niece's many virtues. 'Portraits you have seen of our daughter' did not do her justice; she was charming, precociously sage and resembled at the same time her father and her mother, to the point of reminding us of both of them perfectly, together and each separately . . . she is not as tall as her mother, and a little taller than our poor sister . . . she holds her head marvelously and walks with ease and grace. When she speaks of her misfortunes, tears do not come easily, from habit, as she contained herself to not give her jailers the barbaric pleasure of seeing her cry . . . Nevertheless, her natural gaiety has not been subdued . . . she smiles with a good heart and is amiable. She is sweet, good, tender; she has, without a doubt good reason . . . she is modest . . . innocent as the day of her birth . . . finally, I recognize in her the angel for which we have cried.

Louis was not just uttering pleasantries to impress the family. He found Marie-Thérèse delightful, as did his advisor, the Duc d'Avaray, who wrote to his friends in Italy that Marie-Thérèse was everything the French people could want in a princess. Inestimably buoyed by the union, Louis wrote to d'Artois that 'we will soon ourselves be reborn with their children'. Louis, a prodigious reader who, among his literary accomplishments had written a dissertation on Horace and had translated Horace Walpole's *Historic Doubts on the Life and Reign of Richard III*, had hopes of turning his nephew into a thinker, but had found d'Angoulême's intellect lacking. He had tried to instill some enthusiasm in his nephew, but found the young man without vigor. Before Marie-Thérèse had arrived in Mitau, Louis had written to his niece advising her that it would be up to her to make a man of her husband, though he strongly suspected that this was going to be a difficult task.

The King's wife, Marie Joséphine, departed Mitau as quickly and energetically as she had arrived, leaving Marie-Thérèse, new bride and new Duchesse d'Angoulême, to preside as first lady at her uncle's court. It was clear to Marie-Thérèse from the moment of her arrival that Mitau was to be an attempt to mimic court life at Versailles, over which this Louis had never reigned. Excluding the soldiers, there were 180 people in the Mitau *maison du roi*. Louis was quick to establish the ceremonies of the *lever* and *coucher*, and the ceremonial public meal, the *couvert*, but with the King at his own table surrounded by bodyguards. When the royal family attended Mass, the soldiers stood at arms. The castle, which had suffered damage from fire, had been partially used as a hospital and barracks, and, although it was grand, the family and their household only had access to certain parts of it.

Ritual and close quarters gave Marie-Thérèse, who hoped to conceive a child very soon, precious little time alone with her new husband. The royal family, like most families in rural areas, breakfasted and went to Mass early in the morning. After lunch at eleven in the morning, Marie-Thérèse would stroll and talk with Henriette de Choisy, Madame de Sérent and a few others in the household. Except for Henriette, who had come with Marie-Thérèse from Vienna, there were no other young people at the court. She took long walks, did needlework, and wrote letters to Pauline de Tourzel and her friends from Vienna, the Countesses Zichy and Esterhazy. Marie-Thérèse found that she had to mother elderly courtiers and priests, like the Cardinal de Montmorency, who often sat beside her at mealtimes and was stone deaf. Most of the distinguished figures to whom she played hostess, like General Suvorov, when he returned to Russia, were old, many infirm, leaving Marie-Thérèse little opportunity for fun.

Visitors soon noticed that the Princess did not look happy. Many close to her commented that she had begun to lose the joyful freshness and remarkable spirit, which, despite deep loss and her time in prison, had seemed to lend her personality its distinctiveness. Franklin Darlington, an American who traveled among Louis XVIII's coterie of spies, recalled in his memoirs that when he arrived in Mitau, he

> bowed before Madame Royale, the daughter of Marie Antoinette, and saw in her eyes the shadow of those terrors of her girlhood which, they say, never left her; the Duc d'Angoulême complained to me that the cold spoiled the hunting . . . gentlemen of the bed chamber, aides-de camp, equerries, almoners in ordinary, officers of the guard, all the functionaries of a court, intent upon the ritual of their duties, elbowed and jostled me with exquisite indifference to my comfort. It was like a nightmare in the palace of *La Belle du Bois Dormant*.[1]

Some saw an irritability in Marie-Thérèse that echoed the days of her girlhood, when instead of being able to play with her brother in the gardens she was forced to sit for hours in public under the strain of heavy wigs and massive hooped skirts. Others noted that Marie-Thérèse simply 'did not seem herself'. Madame de Chanterenne and her former charge continued to write to one another. Renète had given birth to a son in 1797. She had still not given him a name in the eyes of the Church and she wrote to Marie-Thérèse asking her to name her son and serve as his godmother. Marie-Thérèse agreed, suggesting that, since part of her name was Charlotte, why not name him Charles? She also granted Madame de Chanterenne's wish that she would be the boy's godmother, but the tone of her response was subdued and not at all what Renète had expected.

Monsieur Hüe was also surprised by Marie-Thérèse's tone. Jean-Baptiste Cléry had published his memoirs in England with the sanction and blessing of Marie-Thérèse and her uncle. The memoirs had sold well throughout Europe and America and had elicited a good deal of sympathy for Marie-Thérèse and the surviving Bourbon family. Hüe, who had served the late King for many years and who had been mentioned in his will as 'the loyal Hüe', told Marie-Thérèse that he hoped to publish his own account, and that he, like Cléry, would like her public approval for this venture. When she refused, Hüe was mystified. Whereas Hüe had been a cherished servant of the murdered king, Cléry had only joined the royal family in service while they were in the Temple Prison. Hüe, who had actually suspected Cléry of initially being an informant, felt that he had a superior right to tell his story and struggled to understand why Marie-Thérèse had reacted in such a way.

Many others were beginning to pen their own recollections of court life at Versailles and of the Revolution. Louis XVIII had already, in the winter of 1798–99 after arriving in Mitau, written *Réflexions historiques sur Marie Antoinette*. Understanding the current climate of interest in his niece, he decided that a heartrending story written by the Orphan of the Temple herself would be helpful to the Bourbon cause and encouraged Marie-Thérèse to write her own version of events. So, instead of enjoying her days as a newlywed, anticipating the birth of a child or simply enjoying the attentiveness of her new husband, Marie-Thérèse spent the summer reliving the traumas of the past, from the invasion of Versailles in October 1789, to the ill-fated flight to Varennes, to the day in August when her family was taken to Temple Prison. As she had been only ten years old at the time her family was forced from Versailles, Louis assisted her with names and explanations. It was a grueling task and the memoir reads as if its author is struggling to maintain self-control. Eight years after the flight from Varennes, she recalled with indelible clarity and specificity the murder of Dampierre on the route back to Paris from Varennes:

> he was flung to the ground, and a man on horseback rode over him and struck him several blows with a saber; others did the same, and soon killed him. The scene, which took place close to our carriage and under our eyes, was horrible for us . . .

While attempting to keep her account clear-eyed and to be generous with the details of the events that 'convulsed all France', her pain would often resurface, as she averts her glance to recall: 'My brother, especially, enchanted everyone by his amiability.'

Her uncle persisted in making difficult demands on her, repeatedly pressuring her to perform her duty for the Bourbon cause. That summer, General Dumouriez, a nobleman who had turned Jacobin, came to see the Bourbons in Mitau. Having no desire to see a man who she felt had betrayed her father, Marie-Thérèse made a point of telling her uncle that she planned to be indisposed for the General's entire visit. The King then informed his niece that the General would join them every day for dinner. Marie-Thérèse knew that she could not avoid her entire family for a week, so she agreed to face Dumouriez. Her uncle noticed that upon seeing the revolutionary soldier Marie-Thérèse grew pale and her expression glacial. The King understood the values that Marie-Thérèse had been inculcated with and from which she had proved she would not depart. If he, her King, were to formally pardon Dumouriez, Marie-Thérèse would have to do likewise. The King extended forgiveness and this seemed to calm her; but she could not resist challenging the military man, demanding: 'Return my uncle to his subjects. God will do the rest.' Dumouriez placed his hand on his heart and replied: 'Ah, Madame! I could not save your father, and Providence does not let me take revenge.'

Marie-Thérèse remained hopeful. Her uncle continued to receive assurances from the Czar and King George III of England that when Napoleon stumbled they would be there to return the Bourbons to the throne of France. Louis asked them to ensure that the Holy Roman Emperor would not dismember France. English ambassador Wickham had been replaced in Switzerland by a Mr Talbot, who in turn was removed from his post for being too embroiled with Louis's spies. Wickham was then returned to Switzerland to deal with the émigrés on the continent while the English Parliament hammered out details for the return of the Bourbons to France. Feeling it imperative that he play a role in the negotiations, the Comte d'Artois moved from Edinburgh to London to represent his family's interests. In a meeting with Foreign Minister Lord Grenville, d'Artois offered to lead an expedition to seize Lorient and Saint-Malo. According to d'Artois, the English agreed to provide men and money. On July 16, Louis received a proposal from the allies that stated they would invade France and leave the borders of France as they were before the Revolution. The proposal, however, contained the proviso that although the allies believed the restoration of the Bourbon monarchy would be best for France, as foreign powers they could not enforce a particular regime on the people of France.

D'Artois, less conciliatory and farsighted than his elder brother, was furious. He stalled negotiations and angrily returned to Edinburgh. By the time Louis had been apprized of his brother's actions, the small window of opportunity had closed: Napoleon was on his way back from the Middle East, and by that winter, he had successfully engineered a coup d'état and proclaimed himself First Consul of France.

Louis made one more desperate attempt. He wrote to Napoleon, groveling before the General's feet by calling him a 'great general'. Next, he offered Bonaparte advice: he must decide whether to be 'Cesar or Monk' (a reference to George Monk, the English General responsible for putting Charles II on the throne of England after its Civil War). Louis claimed that should Napoleon try to assume the mantle of sovereign of France, he would always be perceived by the world as a usurper. It was time for the Bourbons to come home, he wrote, and when he, Louis, ascended the throne, Napoleon could stay on as First Consul. On February 19, 1800, Napoleon installed himself at the Tuileries Palace.

Two months later, as Napoleon began a second campaign into Italy, Louis gave in to the Duc d'Angoulême's desire for glory, realizing too that the heir to the throne of France (after his uncle and father) should not appear to be disengaged from battle. His nephew would not fight in the Czar's army but alongside Condé, whose troops were now in Italy with the Austrian army. When her husband left Mitau, Marie-Thérèse was still without child, and with Napoleon gaining ground by the minute, the chances of a Bourbon restoration were beginning to look bleak.

In May, Comte Fersen arrived in Mitau and was stunned by the Princess's appearance. She seemed stifled and genuinely drained of life. Fersen believed she had seen through her uncle's ruse and was broken-hearted to discover that her husband had never really been interested in her at all. Fersen then delivered what he thought would be happy news for Marie-Thérèse. He informed her that it was his belief that her brother had been safely brought to Philadelphia. Once again, he misunderstood the pain this story would cause her. An additional assault, this time from, at last, a young person who came to Mitau, compounded her misery. It was Louis-Philippe, the son of the late 'Philippe Égalité', who, with his siblings, had been living a nomadic life in America. The new Duc d'Orléans was the very boy who had been put forth by his father as a marriage partner for Marie-Thérèse, and whom Marie Antoinette had rejected out of hand. He hoped to make amends with his uncle and reunify the different branches of the Bourbon family. Louis was willing, but this was one émigré for whom Marie-Thérèse found it impossible to feel any compassion, and she refused even to meet with him.

By the summer of 1800, Napoleon's army seemed invincible, having won the pivotal battle of Marengo in Piedmont; yet the people of France remained fascinated by the Bourbons. A book by the popular writer J. J. Regnault-Warin called *Le Cimetière de la Madeleine* became all the rage. It was claimed this was a true account of the escape of Louis Charles from the Temple Prison, told to the author by an unimpeachable source. In the book, Regnault-Warin mentioned the journal of Cléry, which everyone knew had been verified by Marie-Thérèse, implying that even she believed that her brother had survived. The book caused another groundswell of interest in the Royal Children, and, riding the wave of his success, four years later, Regnault-Warin followed that book with another royal mystery – the story of the masked prisoner in the Bastille that had so fascinated Marie Antoinette – *L'Homme au masque de fer* (The Man in the Iron Mask). Forty years later Alexandre Dumas would also recount this captivating tale.

As a result of the overwhelming success of *Le Cimetière de la Madeleine,* Madame de Chanterenne wrote to Marie-Thérèse requesting permission to publish the memoir that she had handed her upon her departure from Temple Prison. Once again Marie-Thérèse refused a cherished friend, instructing Chanterenne to burn the papers, hide them, but, 'above all, do not publish them'.

On January 20, 1801, Louis received an order from the Czar stating that he was to leave Russia immediately. Paul had turned his back on the allies, and had grown tired of the quantity of couriers and political networking going on in Mitau. He had also learned of d'Avaray's outspoken criticism of his decisions. Although the Czar wanted Louis gone from his realm, he showed no such hostility to Marie-Thérèse and invited her to stay with him at his palace in St Petersburg. She was furious that the Czar would importune her uncle in so humiliating a manner and she refused the invitation.

Without a known destination and without warning, the King would be forced to travel in the dead of winter. The Czar had also neglected to make his latest payment to Louis, compelling him to travel with very little money. The Bourbons held a sale of some furniture and belongings at Mitau to raise funds, but the items reached low prices. Stepping into the breach, Marie-Thérèse ordered Madame de Sérent to sell the stunning suite of diamonds that Czar Paul had given her as a wedding present, and then announced that she would follow her uncle wherever he would go. Overwhelmed by her devotion and sense of duty, Louis likened his niece to the faithful daughter of Oedipus, another exiled king, who appeared in Sophocles' *Oedipus at Colonus*, and proclaimed her 'The New Antigone' – an epithet that would follow her wherever she went.

CHAPTER XVII
THE NEW ANTIGONE

T HE SNOW WAS deep and the blizzards fierce. Their carriage had turned on its side and Marie-Thérèse's face was bruised from having hit the window glass. It took three hours to turn the coach back over on to its wheels. For five days, much of it on foot because the horses were too frightened by the storms to continue, Marie-Thérèse accompanied her uncle across the plains of Lithuania to Memel, at the mouth of the Niemen River. They had hoped to return to France in glory; instead, one year into the new century, their entire caravan consisted of two carriages and for one night, when no inn would receive them, they had to bed down in a cabaret hall that stank of tobacco and alcohol.

The Comte de Hautefort wrote that before she left Mitau, Marie-Thérèse, in possession of little cash herself, gave the Vicomte d'Agoult 100 ducats to disperse among the faithful *gardes du corps* with the instruction that he was not to reveal the source of the gift. Hautefort explained that d'Agoult did as he was told, but that everyone knew who the benefactress was. As she assisted her overweight uncle through the snow, the Comte d'Avaray, the Marquise de Sérent, Philippe Louis César d'Hardoisneau, Abbé Edgeworth and two domestics managed the coaches and dragged the horses. Along the way, things became so desperate that one of Louis's secretaries and sometimes priest to Marie-Thérèse, Abbé Marie, committed suicide. At his last words 'Mademoiselle de Choisy', Marie-Thérèse suffered the shock of realizing that her confessor was in love with her best friend and *demoiselle d'honneur*.

Louis had sent ahead a messenger to deliver letters to Frederick William II, the King of Prussia, asking permission for the exiled French royal family and their retinue to reside somewhere in his realm. The messenger, who waited for Louis in Memel, had received a reply that the King of Prussia, who did not want to irritate Bonaparte, was first waiting to hear if the First Consul of France would allow him to do so. From Memel, Louis wrote again to his brother, praising their niece (and d'Artois's daughter-in-law) for her unparalleled bravery, and calling her 'our admirable daughter' and 'the New Antigone'. Marie-Thérèse wrote her own letter from Memel – to Queen Louise of Prussia, daughter of Marie Antoinette's close friend, Fredericka of Hesse. In the note she too requested a place to live for herself and her uncle. Marie-Thérèse and the Queen, who was famous for her beauty, had received constant reports on each other from the time they were girls and they had always felt a close connection. In her note, Marie-Thérèse explained to Queen Louise that although she had been offered asylum in St Petersburg, she could never abandon her uncle. 'He is everything to me, he takes the place of all that I have lost,' she told her. And it was Marie-Thérèse who received word from Queen Louise that Napoleon had agreed to allow the French royal family and their entourage to stay in Warsaw on the condition that Louis abandon his title and be known as the 'Comte de l'Isle' (a reference to property he had owned in Armagnac before the Revolution) and that Marie-Thérèse be known as the 'Marquise de la Meilleraye' (after the Château de la Meilleraye, a property owned before the Revolution by the Comte d'Artois).

On March 6, Louis, Marie-Thérèse and their attendants arrived in Warsaw where they were shown to the Vassilovitch House on Krakow Street. Marie-Thérèse wrote to her husband that he should stay with the army; he wrote to the Prince de Condé that he was going to take leave of the military and join her. 'I am so angry that my wife is obliged to take such a course in this season,' he explained to his cousin. A couple of weeks later, d'Angoulême arrived in Warsaw to rejoin his wife and uncle. On March 30, English statesman Lord Glenbervie wrote in his journal that a Mr Routh from the War Office had come to see him regarding rumors in Paris that Napoleon had plans to appoint the Duc d'Angoulême as his successor. The story that had circulated was that Napoleon's wife preferred the old nobility to the social climbers around her. Members of the French police dispatched spies to Warsaw to watch the exiled royals.

Shortly after d'Angoulême's appearance, the party learned that Czar Paul had been assassinated in his bedchamber by a small group of allegedly drunken aristocrats, disgusted with what they believed to be Paul's erratic decision-making. His son, Alexander, although implicated in the plot, was now proclaimed Alexander I. Louis declared that he harbored no hostility toward the murdered sovereign, who had, in fact, for a while showed great generosity of spirit toward the exiled French royal family. D'Angoulême and Marie-Thérèse all hoped that the new Czar would prove to be an ally, but Alexander showed little interest in the Bourbon cause. The local Polish nobility, however, demonstrated considerable deference to the French royal family. After all, King Louis XVIII of France was a great-grandson of their late King, Stanislas Leszczynski. Although Louis appreciated their affection, he told Marie-Thérèse that his intention was to soon leave Warsaw and go to the court of Naples. Once again, she responded that she would go wherever he went. When Louis informed his brother of his desire to head for Italy, d'Artois replied that he wanted his son and daughter-in-law with him in Scotland. Louis was stunned by his brother's sudden patriarchal interest in the couple, and he wrote to him explaining to d'Artois that, while he clearly had other comforts – his mistress and the allowance from George III – Marie-Thérèse and d'Angoulême were all that he had – his 'everything'.

She may very well have been his 'everything', but as the object of worldwide curiosity and fascination, she was also of great use to Louis. Prints from an engraving of Marie-Thérèse walking somberly in the snow, memorializing her journey from Mitau, quickly appeared all over Europe. In France, the drawing became so popular and ubiquitous that Napoleon banned it. The French police had dispatched spies to Warsaw not only to spy on Louis but also to keep watch on the d'Angoulêmes. Marie-Thérèse, now a little older and wiser, also realized, as did her uncle, the propaganda value of the prison memoir she had written and knew that there were discrepancies between the two accounts. Determining that she needed to get it back from Madame de Chanterenne, to whom she had entrusted it upon her departure from the Temple Prison, she asked Cléry to write requesting its return. In addition to providing the authentic testament of her family's suffering, Marie-Thérèse, as an advocate for a Bourbon restoration, needed to affirm her uncle's claim as the sole legitimate heir to the throne. Despite a real and constant gnawing at her conscience that she was unsure if her brother had truly perished in his prison cell, she publicly affirmed in her own statements that her brother had died in the Temple Prison and that she was the sole surviving 'Orphan of the Temple'.

Outwardly, the French royal family in exile complied with Napoleon's dictum: on the streets of Warsaw, the King of France was called the 'Comte de l'Isle' and his niece the 'Marquise de la Meilleraye'. Within the walls of their home in Warsaw, where they could not be seen, it was business as usual with court etiquette enacted, their roles performed as if at Versailles. Louis spent his days writing and reading: in one letter, he mentioned that Marie-Thérèse's beloved dog, Coco, had been killed in an accident and that since it was the last link between her and her brother, she was bereft. It was turning into a stunning game of charades and together, Louis XVIII, Marie-Thérèse and the Duc d'Angoulême made a formidable team, their private doubts subsumed for a public role. Louis had more faith in his niece as a monarch than in his own nephew, and, when it came to political plotting, the King relied on the opinion of his niece rather than the man who might someday be king. Marie-Thérèse consistently sent any surplus funds to help French émigrés. She visited convents and the poor, as her mother and her aunt had taught her. Word spread immediately of the kindness and goodness of the 'Marquise de La Meilleraye', and she was hailed, as her uncle had proclaimed her time and again, as a gift from God.

Marie-Thérèse had become the focus of cult-like adoration among the Polish nobility. In tribute to the 'New Antigone', Comtesse Branicka arranged for the French royal family to spend the summer at the Palace Leszczynski – a bold and clear statement of sympathy for the Bourbons. Despite the rumors that Napoleon would extend an olive branch to the younger generation of Bourbons, Napoleon decided to act otherwise. At the ancestral home of their Polish forebear, the French royal family learned that Napoleon had made peace with the Pope. They now knew that not only were their plans for Italy dashed, but, with a pact that ensured the safe return of the clergy to France, their own role as defenders of the Christian faith would be usurped by the new accord between Napoleon and the Pope. Yet, for Louis and his family there was no other option but to continue to maintain their belief in their inherited right to rule France.

Funding their court in exile continued to be a challenge. Salaries had to be paid and meals and lodging provided for the King's attendants and their own servants. Once the King had established himself in Warsaw, an extended retinue of courtiers began to turn up from Mitau to serve their King. Others appeared from all over Europe, once again, to receive remuneration for various services they had performed for the cause. Louis received some money from his cousin, Charles IV of Spain, who continued to provide an allowance, and later that year Czar Alexander agreed to restore less than half of what his father had paid the Bourbons in exile. They also continued to receive about 50,000 florins from Franz –

interest on the money that Marie Antoinette had smuggled out of France, which the Emperor rightfully owed Marie-Thérèse, while the Comte d'Artois managed to arrange for some money to be sent from Britain.

Indeed, d'Artois continued to live a carefree and comfortable existence. The painter, Madame Vigée-Lebrun, recalled in her memoir that, while she was in London in 1802, it seemed that d'Artois and his son the Duc de Berry were quite able to enjoy themselves despite the difficult lives of their family members. She remembered the evening that de Berry and his cousin, the Duc de Bourbon, accompanied her to the home of the scandalous Lady Emma Hamilton. Lady Emma, who, onlookers claimed, downed three bottles of port that evening, entertained her French guests by posing inside a life-sized frame offering her visitors an array of live tableaux.

Still, d'Artois ensured that Louis would receive an immediate payment of £5,000 and an additional £6,000 per year from Parliament. Louis felt that his family was coming together. It had been Marie-Thérèse – by offering to sell the gift of diamonds from Czar Paul – who had saved them initially. In addition they had managed to cut expenditure quite dramatically: Monsieur Hüe was given a list of cost-cutting measures to implement, down to the number of candles permitted to each courtier. In his memoir, published later without Marie-Thérèse's permission, but still with great sympathy for the Princess, Hüe recalled that the winter of 1801–02 was a particularly harsh one causing great deprivation, but that Marie-Thérèse performed stoically throughout, though she often appeared to have been crying and she, of course, remained childless.

Her strength was continually tested. Jean-Marie Hervagault, the young man who had pretended to be Louis Charles, had made quite an impression on influential people around Europe. He had even met with the Pope and twenty cardinals. A prominent bishop, the now republican Charles de la Font de Savine, who had met Louis Charles at Versailles, traveled to meet Hervagault and when he insisted that the man was indeed Louis XVII there was public uproar. Napoleon tried to quash the story, but that failed owing to the public's continuing fascination. When his attempts to quiet public interest failed, Napoleon's prosecutors charged the pretender with fraud and brought Hervagault to trial. Jean-Marie was sentenced to four years in prison, which caused another outcry.

Hervagault was moved to the prison of Bicêtre, and as Napoleon had hoped, the public lost interest in him over time. However, others would come forward with their claims and stories; each one would be reported and cause Marie-Thérèse distress. She had to quell her doubts, in public at least, for the sake of the Bourbon monarchy, but her heart was conflicted. When asked if she were truly certain that her brother had died, she would answer firmly that she, more than anyone, would never support a king who was not the rightful one.

On March 25, 1802, France and Britain signed the Peace of Amiens, in which Britain formally recognized the French Republic – a treaty that, for the moment, halted hostilities and allowed Napoleon to channel his energies into his domestic agenda, which included creating public schools and a new constitution. On August 2, Napoleon was named 'First Consul for Life'. In February 1803, upon the orders of the King of Prussia – but at the instigation of Napoleon – Louis XVIII was presented with a decree that stated that he, Napoleon, had not been responsible for the fall of the monarchy in France, that the First Consul for Life was not a regicide. The document claimed that Napoleon had reinstated a strong government in France and therefore it was necessary for the Bourbons to renounce their hereditary claims to the throne of France. Three days later, on February 22, 1803, with Marie-Thérèse at his side, Louis XVIII presented his answer to the King of Prussia (and Napoleon). It read that although he had great respect for the military talents of the First Consul, he would not relinquish his right to the throne. At the bottom of the page on the same letter was a statement signed by the Duc d'Angoulême declaring that he, too, refused to renounce his own claim. On March 22, Marie-Thérèse's cousin, the Duc d'Enghien – Louis-Antoine Henri de Bourbon-Condé – sent one of his own from Ettenheim, in case Napoleon did not understand Louis XVIII's message. Another letter 'dated April 23, Wanstead House Essex', arrived from the Ducs de Berry, d'Orléans and his brothers, which echoed their joint affirmation that they would not renounce their respective hereditary rights to the throne of France.

On April 30, Napoleon sold the Louisiana Territory to the United States, thus ending French sovereignty there, and in mid-May, a little over a year after it had been signed, the Treaty of Amiens was broken. The French charged that the British had not evacuated Malta; the British responded by claiming that Napoleon's most recent aggressions had violated both the Treaties of Campo Formio and Lunéville. After both governments accused each other of having improperly seized ships, Napoleon ordered the imprisonment of all English male citizens currently in France, making Britain and France enemies once again.

Britain had been kind to the Bourbons. Louis, d'Angoulême and Marie-Thérèse were all firmly convinced that the British would vanquish 'the

Usurper'. Napoleon, however, was no longer amused by Parliament's tolerance of the French royal family, and he determined to send his own message to the Bourbons. And it was to be a message of the most personal, vicious kind.

In the autumn of 1803, an unusual couple arrived in the tiny German town of Ingelfingen in Württemberg, bordering the Rhine, attracting great interest from the townspeople. The young woman – blonde-haired, blue-eyed, and estimated to be in her early twenties – wore a veil to cover her face. The man, considerably older than the young woman, seemed aristocratic and foreign. The man received post addressed to 'Herr Vavel de Versay'. Locals overheard them speaking in French and took to calling them the Dark Count and Countess. The couple employed an obviously high-caliber servant, the kind who might have been trained at a royal palace, which, local residents concluded, meant that the couple must be important. One of the servants in the town had gossiped that she had worked on the young woman's laundry and that all of it was embroidered with the Bourbon fleur-de-lys; while the son of a town councilman named Kraus claimed he had managed to catch a glimpse of the young woman's face without her veil on. At one point, after the couple's departure, the young man had been shown a picture of Marie-Thérèse-Charlotte of France and exclaimed: 'But that is my Comtesse de Vavel!' Their sudden and mysterious departure from the town at two o'clock in the morning, toward the end of March 1804, was equally stupefying.

'Vavel de Versay' and his young, blonde companion had fled immediately on receiving terrible news. It had all started when Napoleon's chief spy, Karl Schulmeister, had forged a note from the Princess Charlotte de Rohan-Rochefort, claiming that she had been kidnapped. When her lover, the Duc d'Enghien, came to her aid, Napoleon's men seized him. D'Enghien was accused on trumped-up charges of having taken part in a conspiracy against Napoleon and sentenced to death. He was executed by a firing squad on the night of March 21, 1804. As d'Enghien held a lantern against the dark to guide his executioners, Napoleon's soldiers shot him in the heart. A young Bourbon Prince – and the last Prince of the House of Condé – had been murdered on the direct orders of the First Consul. Napoleon's message to the Bourbons in exile could not have been clearer.

No one could quite explain the link between the execution of the Duc d'Enghien and the abrupt and hasty departure of the 'Dark Count and Countess' from Ingelfingen. Suspected to have been any number of men, some speculated that 'Vavel de Versay' was an alias for the illegitimate son rumored to have been born of an alleged liaison between Count John Albert Bentinck and Georgiana, Duchess of Devonshire. Another story at the time claimed that Vavel de Versay had been appointed to protect his companion by Napoleon's Foreign Minister, Talleyrand. Others believed he was an agent of King Louis XVIII, and still others thought he was one of Franz II's loyal minions.

In the 1920s, Elizabeth Hawkinson Whitshed, an author known professionally as 'Mrs Aubrey Le Blond', revealed that much of the story about the Dark Count and Countess had been culled from private Bentinck family papers. She explained that Charlotte Sophie, the daughter of the Count of Altenburg, who had married William Bentinck, a younger son of the Earl of Portland, in 1733, had left a cache of letters that gave detailed portraits of 'famous contemporary personalities' of the latter half of the eighteenth century. Among the Bentinck family's own skeletons was the belief that their son, John Albert, had been the lover of Georgiana, Duchess of Devonshire in the early 1770s. Mrs Le Blond admitted that it was widely suspected that the pair had produced an illegitimate son who would grow up to be the man known as the Dark Count. In 1954, a member of that same German noble family, Frédéric de Saxe-Altenburg, penned the book *L'Énigme de Madame Royale*, in which he disclosed that various members of his family had inherited possessions that had belonged to the Dark Countess along with a pledge to never reveal the secret story that there had, indeed, been a switch.

Le Blond had, herself, traveled to Germany to try to uncover the truth about the identity of the mysterious man, but it was ultimately O. V. Maeckel, in his 1926 book *Das Rätsel von Hildburghausen*, who had been able to trace the path of the man behind the mystery. Maeckel disclosed at last that the man, traveling incognito under the name 'Vavel de Versay', was in fact Leonardus Cornelius Van der Valck, a man of Dutch origin who had served both as a soldier in the army of French exiles and as a minister to France. In 1799, Van der Valck was in Paris and in 1800 he was in Linz at the same time as the Duc d'Enghien. From there, he went to Schweinfurt, and, in October 1801, Cornelius Van der Valck appeared in Regensburg, Germany, in order to renew his passport. He was then traveling with a young, blonde-haired, blue-eyed woman, who appeared to be about twenty years of age.

Van der Valck's passport renewal was approved and his passport signed by the local French Consul General, Théobald Jacques Justin Bacher – the very man who had received instructions from Franz II to bring Ernestine de Lambriquet with Marie-Thérèse to Vienna when he was French Minister in Switzerland; the man who had negotiated Marie-Thérèse's release; and the man who visited her in her hotel room in Huningue and turned her over to the Austrian delegation in Basel. Was there a special relationship between the Dutchman Cornelius Van der Valck and the Bourbon family? He was, indeed, an ardent supporter of the Bourbons, and, according to Saxe-Altenburg, Van der Valck, who assumed the alias 'Vavel de Versay' at his convenience, had corresponded regularly with Princess Charlotte de Rohan-Rochefort. Finally, Saxe-Altenburg claimed that shortly after the assassination of the Duc d'En-ghien, Prince Friedrich Ludwig von Hohenlohe-Ingelfingen received a top-secret report from an employee that on March 31, 1804, 'Herr Vavel arrived safely with the unlucky daughter of the late King Louis XVI'.

In Warsaw on April 9, King Louis XVIII and his court were informed of the Duc d'Enghien's assassination. The Duchesse d'Angoulême and the Abbé Edgeworth went to the Convent of the Benedictions in Warsaw to tell Louise de Condé about her nephew's murder. That afternoon, Marie-Thérèse wrote to the slain soldier's inconsolable grandfather, the Prince de Condé.

> I take the pain that you are feeling and my heart shares in it sincerely. Despite all that I have suffered, I never could have imagined the hideous event which places us all in mourning. This morning, I went to see Louise whom I found calm in her pain that Religion and Resignation to the will of Providence can give . . . she was only concerned with you . . . I beg you, I vow that your courage sustains me . . . your health . . . resist . . . the too justly dolor of our cruel and common loss . . .

The stunned Bourbons now understood that their lives were in grave danger. And they were horrified when just a few days after the young Duke's assassination, the Spanish King, his Bourbon cousin, awarded Napoleon the Order of the Golden Fleece. Louis, who, as a Bourbon cousin, had also been given this same honor, wrapped up his own medal and put it away with a note that included the comment that he refused to share such an honor with 'a great criminal':

> Religion could engage me to forgive an assassin, but the tyrant over my people will always be my enemy . . . Providence, in its mysterious secretiveness, may condemn me to finish my days in exile, but neither

The formidable Habsburg Empress, Maria Theresa, mother of Queen Marie Antoinette of France and grandmother of Marie-Thérèse-Charlotte.

In keeping with the Habsburg family motto, 'Let other nations wage war; you, happy Austria, achieve your ends through marriage', the beautiful young Austrian Archduchess, Maria Antonia, married the future King Louis XVI of France at age fourteen and became known as 'Marie Antoinette'.

The official coronation portrait of King Louis XVI. Although he was ruler of a vast empire, for seven and a half years after taking a bride he was ignorant as to how to consummate the marriage.

There were many illegally published pornographic cartoons that poked fun at the King and Queen. This particular illustration, showing a phallic-shaped ostrich, makes use of a pun on the word for ostrich – *autruche* – an unsubtle reference to '*Autriche*', Austria.

After eight and a half years of marriage, Queen Marie Antoinette gave birth, in front of crowds of onlookers, to a daughter: Marie-Thérèse-Charlotte. To the right of the bed is the secret panel through which the Queen fled to find her children and the King when the Palace of Versailles was overrun in 1789.

This portrait of Marie-Thérèse was sent to her grandmother (and godmother), Empress Maria Theresa, for whom she was named. The Austrian Empress proclaimed that her granddaughter resembled King Louis XVI and instructed her daughter to try immediately for a playmate (and heir to the throne) for the little girl.

Marie-Thérèse and Louis Charles in front of the Temple d'Amour at the Petit Trianon, by Ludwig Guttenbrunn, painted during the family's last halcyon days at Versailles.

On October 6, 1789, the royal family was forcibly removed from Versailles. That night, they slept on rugs and chairs at the barely habitable Tuileries Palace in Paris. This cartoon depicts the first public appearance in Paris of the royal family the day after their arrival. The artist's caption, stating that the King and his family were delighted to be among their people in Paris, was clearly untrue.

On the first anniversary of the storming of the Bastille, a great celebration called the 'Fête de la Fédération' was held on the Champs-de-Mars. The royal family is seated above the audience on the far right.

The King's last night in Temple Prison, as depicted by Mather Brown. Although he promised his family that he would come back to say farewell the following morning, he could not bear to do so. As her father left, Marie-Thérèse wept so uncontrollably that she collapsed on the floor 'in a state of near unconsciousness'.

Weeks after Marie-Thérèse fled the Temple Prison, these two portraits displaying facial discrepancies, and by the same engraver, were published. Such varying images fueled the speculation that there had been a 'switch'.

Her mother's daughter, Marie-Thérèse knew
how to make a political statement with her
fashion choices. While at the Hofburg in Vienna,
the 'Orphan of the Temple' discarded her mourning
clothes, often in favor of cloths of vivid royal blue
– the color of her ancestral Bourbon banner.

The Comte d'Artois, later
Charles X, Marie-Thérèse's
uncle and father-in-law.

The dashing Duc de
Berry, Marie-Thérèse's
brother-in-law. He
was a favorite with
the ladies and was
tragically assassinated
before the birth of his
son, Henri.

King Louis XVIII
referred to his niece as
'The New Antigone'.

Marie-Thérèse insisted on nursing Abbé Edgeworth, who had
contracted typhoid. Edgeworth, the priest who had accompanied
Louis XVI to the scaffold, died on May 22, 1807.

Marie-Thérèse claimed to have forgiven all the French people; however, upon the Bourbons' return to France, she was not as charitable toward her mother's First Lady-in-Waiting, Madame Campan, with whom she refused to speak. During the Bourbons' exile, Campan had educated Napoleon's stepdaughter and other daughters of the Empire.

King Louis XVIII ordered the immediate removal of the bodies of the late King Louis XVI and Queen Marie Antoinette from their graves in Paris to the royal crypt at Saint-Denis. This sculpture, which marks the couple's grave in the crypt, depicts the Queen without a crown, as Marie Antoinette was never allowed a formal coronation.

Marie-Thérèse, the most powerful woman during the Bourbon restoration, resolved not to repeat her parents' mistakes, and frequently traveled throughout France to meet the people. At the beginning of March 1815, she and her husband, the Duc d'Angoulême, arrived to cheering crowds in Bordeaux. Their elation was short-lived as they learned that Napoleon had escaped exile and was marching on Paris.

After her failed attempt to orchestrate the defeat of Napoleon's troops at Bordeaux, Marie-Thérèse bid farewell to adoring crowds at Pauillac and boarded the *Wanderer* for exile once more.

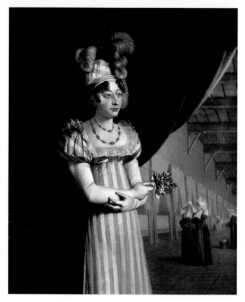

Upon the second return of the Bourbons, Marie-Thérèse resumed her travels throughout France. In the summer of 1815, she journeyed to Toulouse, where Joseph Rocques painted this portrait of her.

Mistakenly believing that she was pregnant in 1820, Marie-Thérèse posed for this portrait, reminiscent of the pregnant Gabrielle d'Estrées.

S. A. ROYALE MADAME, DUCHESSE D'ANGOULÊME,
Née le 19 Décembre 1778.

DÉDIÉ A SA MAJESTÉ LOUIS XVIII
Roi de France & de Navarre.

The face of the Bourbon family and restoration: Marie-Thérèse is depicted in a diadem, her mother's pearls and white Bourbon plumes.

After learning that her childbearing days were behind her, Marie-Thérèse focused her attention on her niece and nephew, Louise and Henri, loving them as if they were her own.

Villeneuve-l'Étang became the country retreat for Marie-Thérèse and the children. This idyllic refuge, which had an Orangerie, evoked fond memories of Versailles and inspired her to assemble a menagerie like the one her mother had had at the Hameau.

Hartwell in
Buckinghamshire,
the English country
estate where the
Bourbons resided until
Napoleon's defeat.

Frohsdorf Castle, outside Vienna, where Marie-Thérèse spent her last years.

The young Comte de Chambord, who, as
Henri V, elected to remain in exile rather than
accept the tri-colored flag.

In June 2004, after a long and mysterious journey, the
heart of little Louis Charles was at last laid to rest in
the royal crypt at Saint-Denis, outside of Paris.

posterity nor my contemporaries has the right to say that in adversity was I, for one instant, unworthy of inheriting the throne of my ancestors.

Marie-Thérèse echoed her uncle's sentiments, but was dismayed when, on April 25, 'the Criminal' – as she now referred to Napoleon – had the French Senate pass a new law once again permitting hereditary monarchy, allowing him, on May 18, to proclaim himself Hereditary Emperor of the French. Louis wrote a letter of protest, asking the monarchs of Europe to join against the man who had appointed himself ruler of France. Not one sovereign responded. Franz, fearing that Napoleon would try to seize control of the Holy Roman Empire, created a new title for himself, as if he were conceding in advance to the Corsican-born General. Franz's titles included the Emperor of the Holy Roman Empire and King of Hungary and Bohemia. Aware that Napoleon, if victorious, would attempt to carve up the Holy Roman Empire to his own design, Franz took the pre-emptive step of declaring himself 'First Emperor of Austria', a less expansive, less threatening title.

The American Franklin Darlington recalled that, while traveling with Louis's spies from Kehl on the Rhine across a wooden bridge of boats, he saw a sign on entering Strasbourg that read '*Ici Commence le Pays de la Liberté*' ('Here begins the Land of Freedom') and another that read '*République Française, Une et Indivisible*' ('The Republic of France, One and Indivisible'). He, who had accompanied Princess Charlotte de Rohan-Rochefort to meet her doomed lover, sadly noted the irony of the placards that greeted him upon his return to France.

On July 30, 1804, Louis and the Duc d'Angoulême left Marie-Thérèse behind in Warsaw while they traveled to Sweden to convene with all of the French Bourbon Princes at Kalmar Castle in Sweden. Before they left Vassilovitch House, there was an attempt made to poison the three of them that was intercepted by the cook. Marie-Thérèse was understandably anxious as her uncle and husband set out on their journey. She and Louis-Antoine had developed a deep attachment and respect for each other and she wrote to her uncle requesting that he allow her husband to return to her for three days while they waited for news of the other Bourbons. He responded that she was sweet to ask his permission and, as usual, she had charmed him. Louis, who had been a stern critic of Marie Antoinette, was greatly impressed by her daughter, declaring her 'French, as I am' – the greatest compliment he would pay anyone, and a comment that was intended to disavow her Habsburg roots. From Sweden he wrote to her of the complications that had arisen surrounding the intended reunion of Bourbon Princes, relying once more on Marie-Thérèse's sage counsel and discretion.

> Well, now I must confide a secret . . . It is for you alone . . . there is not one person in the world to which I have given the slightest indication. Yesterday, I received news of my brother. The British government . . . whatever motive . . . formally opposes the departure of my brother and the princes. This was the point of the reunion. I do not know whether to head for Riga or Liebgau, because I do not yet know from which of these two ports I will embark. There, only, I will learn if my relatives are coming.

As England had once again severed diplomatic relations with France and the Treaty of Amiens had been broken, Parliament decided that it would now grant a passport to the Comte d'Artois, but only to him, to join his brother and nephew in Kalmar. D'Artois had not seen his brother in over fifteen years. Once assembled, the first, second and third in line to the throne of France issued a joint protest against Napoleon's actions. King Gustavus IV Adolphus of Sweden had intended to meet the Bourbon brothers in Kalmar to give his support; however, at the last minute he decided to send his emissary and longtime Bourbon ally, Comte Fersen, in his place. While in Sweden, Louis learned that the King of Prussia, terrified of antagonizing Napoleon, had issued his own proclamation ordering the Bourbons to leave Warsaw. Louis petitioned both Czar Alexander and the King of Sweden for asylum: the Czar did not respond; Gustavus Adolphus offered asylum but Louis decided to remain on the continent, and wait.

Napoleon continued to violate Prussian treaty rights, but the King of Prussia was powerless to respond. Queen Louise of Prussia took matters into her own hands. She circumvented her husband and once again, displaying great moral courage, came to the rescue of her friend, Marie-Thérèse. As the Duchesse d'Angoulême prepared to leave Warsaw, Queen Louise wrote to the Czar and to 'Franz I of Austria', begging them to take a stand against Napoleon. This was the beginning of what would, one year later, result in the Potsdam Treaty, an alliance that joined Prussia with Russia and Austria against France. For her efforts, Napoleon would call Louise 'my beautiful enemy'; but, to Marie-Thérèse, whose mother had been like an aunt to the Queen when she was a girl, Louise remained a steadfast friend. Louise of Prussia had also managed to soften the heart of the Czar and in the autumn of 1804 he offered the French royal family refuge once again in Mitau. Although Louis gratefully accepted the offer from the Czar, he and his brother made a pact that they would reunite in England. Before the brothers said goodbye to each other, Louis asked d'Artois to negotiate with George III and the British government toward that end.

In Mitau, the French royal family would not, as they had in 1799–1801, live in the castle of the Dukes of Courland. Instead they would reside in a smaller house with a much smaller pension. King Charles IV of Spain had ceased his payments to Louis, and the Holy Roman Emperor only paid irregularly. Without these allowances it was impossible for Louis to pay for the upkeep of a household. With great sadness, Louis instructed Hüe to cut costs with absolute severity and tell many of their friends that they would have to strike out on their own. Louis, who made it clear to his wife that he could no longer support two households, summoned Marie Joséphine to join him in Mitau.

King Louis XVIII and his nephew traveled back to mainland Europe through a violent storm. Once they disembarked at Riga, the Duc d'Angoulême, who had been ill most of the time while on board, asked his uncle for permission to visit his wife before the men headed off to Russia. Louis, forbidden to enter Warsaw, remained near the coast while his nephew headed south to see Marie-Thérèse. At the beginning of December, the couple said their farewells and d'Angoulême rejoined his uncle for Mitau. In Paris, on December 2, using the Holy Ampulla containing the chrism that had anointed the Kings of France for over a millennium, Napoleon crowned himself 'Hereditary Emperor of the French'. Marie-Thérèse, like all royalists, was outraged. She felt that Napoleon's action was the defilement of all of her ancestors, but it also strengthened her sense of purpose. After the New Year, with the Abbé Edgeworth and a handful of courtiers to accompany her, Marie-Thérèse set out on the perilous journey in the middle of the Russian winter to join her uncle and husband in Mitau. It was the same journey in reverse that she had taken three years ago. As she told doubters, she was intent on continuing the fight.

The journey had been arduous once again, and Marie-Thérèse arrived at Mitau in April 1805. On the 29th she wrote to Czar Alexander's mother, Sophie Dorothea of Württemberg (called Maria Fedorovna by the Russians) 'Madame, my sister and cousin . . . The moment when, thanks to the friendship of your august son, I am at last reunited with my husband, with my uncle, is that which I chose to thank Your Imperial

Majesty.' Their household now included the King, Queen, the Duc d'Angoulême, his Duchess and a skeleton staff. In the summer of 1805, the court in Mitau was once again in mourning, this time for the death of Marie-Thérèse's mother-in-law, Marie-Thérèse de Savoie, the Comtesse d'Artois, who had been living in Germany, far away from her own husband and his mistress.

In Paris, the remains of Marie Antoinette and King Louis XVI had been found, placed together and marked. Pauline de Tourzel, the adored friend of both Marie-Thérèse and Louis Charles, had visited the Madeleine cemetery (near the site of the guillotine on the recently named Place de la Concorde) and plucked a flower from the graveside. In Mitau, Marie-Thérèse received a long letter from Pauline and with it the flower. Marie-Thérèse was unutterably grateful and wrote that she would never forget Pauline's act of kindness.

Marie-Thérèse-Charlotte of France was now truly European. She had lived in Vienna, Russia, and Poland. She learned that her particular fate more than most was closely tied to whichever way the political winds blew. One day, a king would offer them a castle and allowance. The next day that same king might be deposed or in exile himself. Departures would be sudden and great adaptability was required. For much of the time, her husband went off to join some regiment for the cause of the Bourbons and he would find her in a new home upon his return. Their marriage was one of friendship, tenderness and mutual respect, but it was certainly not one of passion.

From the time of her daring flight from the Temple Prison aged seventeen, like the biblical Esther, Marie-Thérèse had followed her adopted parent. She had sacrificed her own personal needs for the principle of divine right. She saw it as a statement to the world that the King of France was sovereign over all of his subjects, and although her devotion to that principle made her a living symbol of reactionary politics, and thus dangerous to many, it was her firm stance that legitimized Louis XVIII, and he knew it. When she was a little girl, she had longed to be the most significant person in her father's heart, and for a while she, typically, resented her own mother. Now, as the adopted daughter of the new King in exile, her uncle, she had achieved that position, at the center of the heart of the King of France. They were father and daughter, political allies as well as conspirators, and for all intents and purposes, there were three in her marriage. And she was still childless.

Rumors abounded that her husband was homosexual; others claimed he had mistresses. Some explained his inability to father a child was due to a medical condition. There was a dark story that had circulated, which Louise de Condé had written of to her father, that Marie-Thérèse had been drugged in prison and that these poisons had made her sterile. Louise said the Temple Prison guards had bragged about it and claimed that they had once and for all put an end to the Bourbons. Most put these stories down to mere braggadocio; others remained convinced they were true.

Marie-Thérèse longed for a child. She also longed for an end to the steady stream of petitioners claiming to be her beloved little brother, Louis Charles. Some were so persuasive, having knowledge of the details of life at Versailles, that even women who had lived at court were convinced and they would beg Marie-Thérèse to see 'her brother'. Although she desperately missed her brother, and longed to believe he was still alive, she knew that there would be dire political consequences if she agreed to meet with any of them. Their stories, printed in newspapers around the world, created a fever of uncertainty and speculation, all of which continued to take a tremendous psychological toll on Marie-Thérèse. She suffered mental anguish in private; but, in public, she stayed steadfast to her uncle's purpose.

Marie-Thérèse remained in Mitau, turning twenty-six, twenty-seven, twenty-eight as events unfurled in Europe that changed the continent's geography with breakneck speed. In 1805, Archduke Karl had become the Holy Roman Empire's Minister of War and, although he led his troops valiantly, it was futile. Napoleon occupied Vienna, was crowned King of Italy and bludgeoned the armies of both Russia and Austria at Austerlitz. In 1806, Napoleon placed his brothers Joseph and Louis on the thrones of Naples and Holland respectively. On August 6, 1806, after losing some Germanic states to the newly formed Confederation of the Rhine, Emperor Franz was forced to abdicate his imperial throne, ending the thousand-year-old Holy Roman Empire. In the autumn of 1806, Napoleon and his Marshals Ney, Augereau, Soult, Murat and Bernadotte humiliated Prussia with their successful campaigns through Jena, whose intellectuals had engendered the early phase of German Romanticism. After the decimation of Jena, Napoleon began his march toward Eastern Prussia and the Russian frontier. Jena, Coburg and Meiningen were behind him.

In January 1807, in Thuringia, Germany, the Ducal Commissioner, Senator J. C. Andrae, arrived at the Englischer Hof hotel in the small town of Hildburghausen, not far from Jena, to tell its owner that important visitors would shortly be arriving. The proprietor, Frau Weber, inferred that the Senator had been sent by no less than Charlotte, Duchess of Hildburghausen, sister of Queen Louise of Prussia. Frau Weber was instructed to observe great secrecy and meet unusual demands. The visitors would arrive at midnight on February 7. They were to have their own manservant and would not require staff employed by the inn. Frau Weber was ordered to prepare the second floor, have all rooms as well as the staircase completely illuminated, though neither she nor any of her staff were to be present to greet their guests. Andrae, with great firmness, insisted that the guests be accorded privacy. Frau Weber asked how long they intended to stay, but she obtained no fixed date. She would be apprized weekly.

At midnight on February 7, as scheduled, an elegant coach arrived at the Englischer Hof. Inside sat a man in livery, a middle-aged, seemingly aristocratic man, and a woman in her twenties. They presented no passports, which suggested to the inn's owner that their visit had been arranged by the ducal court. Sometimes during the day, the man would emerge from the inn with the younger lady on his arm. She was always heavily veiled. When they went driving in their coach, the curtains on their windows were always drawn. The local citizenry was intrigued. A few letters addressed to 'Vavel de Versay' were delivered to the inn, but an even larger quantity were made out to 'Philip Scharre', their manservant. As gossip spread, townspeople compared notes. They had heard of a similarly described mysterious couple who had fled Ingelfingen four years earlier. Their descriptions tallied, and it was determined that these visitors were the very same wanderers now residing in the Englischer Hof.

People began to stroll by to try to catch a glimpse of the mysteriously veiled woman. Attached to the inn was a butcher's shop, and on a few occasions, the middle-aged traveler was alarmed to see a hotel servant and the butcher, with blood on his hands, staring up at the second-floor windows. In August, the man and his young companion left that hotel, moved to another in the town called the Herzogliches Gästehaus, and after a while moved again, with the assistance of Commissioner Andrae, to another guesthouse called 'Radefeld House'. Frau Radefeld, however, claimed that she would not allow anyone in her house whose identity she did not know, at which point Frau Radefeld was summoned to a meeting with Duchess Charlotte of Hildburghausen. When the couple's landlady emerged from her meeting with the Duchess, she had been persuaded of the necessity of keeping the couple's identity a secret.

Frau Radefeld was instructed that there must be no noise at Radefeld House. The mysterious visitors adopted a mundane routine while there.

Vavel de Versay accompanied his young companion on walks. She never removed her veil. When they went driving in their coach, the curtains were always drawn. They employed a cook, a local woman, Johanna Weber, who was forbidden to enter any of the quarters except for the kitchen, and each night, instead of living at Radefeld, the cook went home. From her conversations with the man of the couple, Frau Radefeld determined that he was a cultured man but that his German was not that of a native-born. Once, she asked a question about the young woman and the man simply ignored her. She was never allowed to speak with the young lady, and she realized that she was not even permitted to mention the young woman's existence. In order to comply with the directives of the Duchess of Hildburghausen, Frau Radefeld housed her own sons, during their vacation from school, in other accommodation so that they would not disturb the young woman. Sometimes, Frau Radefeld would hear the man's voice through the walls in the house, and she understood that he was not speaking in German. Sometimes, late in the evening, she would also hear another sound through the walls: the young woman sobbing.

The casualties inflicted by Napoleon's armies in Prussia and on the Russian front were staggering and many of the injured and infirm soldiers arrived daily in Mitau. Marie-Thérèse and the Abbé Edgeworth ministered to the unfortunate men. As a result of his service, Edgeworth contracted typhoid. Despite warnings from her uncle and husband that she could catch the disease, Marie-Thérèse nursed the priest who had been with her father during his last hours until she was exhausted. She insisted that she had no concern for her own health, but that she owed the Abbé a great debt. Abbé Edgeworth died with Marie-Thérèse by his side on May 22, 1807. Dorothea, the Duchess of Courland, who would later become the Duchess of Dino – and live in Paris with her great-uncle-by-marriage and lover, Talleyrand – wrote in her journal that everyone in Mitau social circles remarked that sadness made Marie-Thérèse even more beautiful, and that despite her own grief, she continued to visit friends and to be extremely considerate to all.

That spring, the Czar arrived in Mitau to discuss his own sad news with King Louis XVIII. He was on his way to Tilsit, he said, to meet with Napoleon, who had been victorious in Eylau and Friedland. As defeat for the Russian Empire seemed imminent, he was going to make concessions to the Emperor of the French. The Czar informed Louis that it was no longer safe to be a Bourbon anywhere on continental Europe and the

King of Sweden would give Louis and his family asylum. On July 7, 1807, the Czar of Russia signed the Peace of Tilsit; and, in August, King Louis XVIII and the Duc d'Angoulême, leaving their wives barely supported in Mitau, hurriedly boarded a frigate, the *Troja*, placed at their disposal by King Gustavus IV Adolphus, and crossed the seas to Stockholm. A storm lasted for days, forcing the *Troja* to dock much farther south in Karl-skrona. Marie-Thérèse was frantic to hear of their safe arrival and wrote to her uncle's minister, Saint-Priest, begging for news. One small detail in this letter reveals an unusual level of emotional intimacy between husband and wife. Marie-Thérèse repeatedly refers to Louis-Antoine as 'my husband', instead of addressing him by the title 'the Duc d'Angoulême' or 'the Prince', as was the custom for members of the nobility. In their six years of marriage, the extraordinarily trying circumstances in which they had been forced to live as man and wife, together and apart, had, it seems, drawn them closer.

Although the King of Sweden was, as ever, very hospitable to his French guests, Louis and d'Artois were still determined to go to England, where they felt they could recruit powerful support for their cause. The Duc de Berry arrived at Kalmar, surprising his uncle and brother, and the three men together boarded a packet boat called the *Troya* for England. Although Louis had written to his 'cousin', George III, he had not received formal permission to reside in England. In fact, the King had sent officials up and down the east coast of England with orders to refuse the boat that contained the King of France. When the boat was about three miles off Great Yarmouth in East Anglia, British officials boarded the *Troya* and informed Louis, who had imagined himself in London, that his boat would be permitted to land with the proviso that he and his party head straightaway for Scotland where Holyrood Palace in Edinburgh had been made ready for their arrival. Louis angrily informed the English envoys that he would ask neither his wife nor the Duchesse d'Angoulême to live in Scotland. Fortuitously, the Marquis (later Duke) of Buckingham intervened and offered the 'French colony' residence at his ancestral home, Gosfield Hall, about forty-five miles northeast of London.

On November 2, 1807, Louis XVIII, the Duc d'Angoulême and the Duc de Berry landed at Great Yarmouth, where they were met by the young Duc d'Orléans and the Prince de Condé. They discovered that on learning of his cousins' difficult situation, d'Orléans had approached his good friend the Prince of Wales – 'Prinny' – and received permission for the French royal family to disembark at Great Yarmouth. Despite their traveling aliases, they were greeted warmly by the local townspeople who

shouted: 'It's the King of France! It is Louis XVIII, brother of Louis XVI.'
Louis stated that he was genuinely touched by their homage and generosity. He had a very good feeling about his prospects in England, and
after touring the English countryside and being fêted by the English
aristocracy, he felt persuaded that his wife and niece ought to join him in
England.

In late spring of 1808, the Duc d'Angoulême boarded a ship for Libau,
not far from Mitau, to escort his wife and Marie Joséphine to England.
On a bright, sunny day in July, they set sail. Marie-Thérèse, a very ill
Marie Joséphine, who was suffering from dropsy, and the Duc d'Angoulême arrived at Gosfield Hall in Essex on August 24.

In April of the following year the French court in exile relocated to
Hartwell House in Buckinghamshire. Before their departure from Gosfield Hall, the Bourbons cooperated on a tribute to their benefactor, the
Marquis of Buckingham. The French royal family erected a round, stone
altar at Gosfield, which was then placed in the renamed 'Bourbon Tower'
in the grounds of Stowe House, Buckinghamshire. Around the tower they
planted five oak trees, one for each of them, and, with the help of one of
the men in service to the Comte d'Artois, the royal Bourbons in exile
compiled a collection of flowery speeches which they placed with their
portraits and locks of their hair into a beautifully decorated blue and gold
volume. This book is now in the British Library.[1]

CHAPTER XVIII
COUNTRY LIFE

H ARTWELL HOUSE HAD, since the sixteenth century, been the home of the Hampden and Lee families, from whom the American General Robert E. Lee was descended. Louis rented the place for a mere £500 per annum, a favorable price arranged by his new friend, the Marquis of Buckingham. The house boasted an impressive entrance hall where carved oak figures of Hercules, the Furies and knights in armor stood sentry on either side of the grand stairwell. Queen Marie Joséphine was so terrified by the shadows formed by the statues that she had them all removed to the basement. Portraits of the Lee family by Vandyke, Reynolds and other notable artists hung on paneled walls, and the house contained the requisite ballroom and beautiful marble fireplaces. Located only forty miles northwest of London, Hartwell afforded Louis easy access to the capital, and proved a pleasant home for the French courtiers, who arrived in groups until their number swelled to over two hundred within a few months. Out of these, 140 émigrés lived in the house and in its extensive grounds. Outbuildings were used as shops and large chambers were divided into smaller apartments. There were reports of courtiers farming livestock and chickens everywhere, even on the rooftops. Many of these émigrés would leave behind them messages in French, carved on the beech trees in the grounds.

Marie-Thérèse was now surrounded by relatives: not only her husband and her uncle, the King, but also her father-in-law, a brother-in-law, and cousins including the Prince de Condé and the Orléans family – whom she still would not receive. Family dynamics began to change considerably.

For one thing, her father-in-law, the Comte d'Artois, remained in London on South Audley Street, enjoying the pleasures of gaming clubs, the theater and dinner parties. He encouraged his son and daughter-in-law to visit him often, which they did. In addition to attending social events, they also appeared together at the Church of St Louis, the chapel of the French émigrés on Little George Street, where a special chair, meant to symbolize a throne, had been installed for Louis XVIII, and a bench placed nearby for the rest of the royal family. The English were equally hungry to see the daughter of the martyred King, who had just turned thirty. The memoirs of both Hüe and Cléry, which had been published in London, had elicited such great sympathy for the Orphan of the Temple that once again another public had, sight unseen, predetermined her to be saintly. Marie-Thérèse was received in London as a visiting deity. *The Times*, when referring to 'Her Royal Highness, the daughter of the unfortunate Louis XVI', recorded almost every word she uttered in public and, on April 25, 1814, declared that 'every voice was exerted to announce the esteem and respect generally felt for the amiable daughter of Louis XVI'.

When, in May 1809, Archduke Karl defeated Napoleon in the battle of Aspern – the Emperor's first personal defeat in over a decade – and his name was on everybody's lips, it was noted that Marie-Thérèse appeared more red-eyed than usual. People whispered that she was unhappy. In contrast to the Austrian Archduke's growing reputation as an energetic, brilliant figure, the Duc d'Angoulême, like Marie-Thérèse's own late father, was reserved, liked to hunt, and seemed, to many, decidedly taciturn. Her uncle, the King, had acknowledged that she was definitely the smarter of the pair. It was the Comte d'Artois, who had suffered little since the Revolution, who knew how to lavish gaiety on his daughter-in-law. And, very much like her mother, Marie-Thérèse succumbed to d'Artois's natural charm.

Then there was the matter of her brother-in-law, the Duc de Berry, the renegade young Prince who had fought so valiantly alongside the Prince de Condé for the Bourbon cause. He was very much like his father and many people openly remarked that Marie-Thérèse had, sadly, married the wrong brother. Despite de Berry's reputation as a womanizer and his seeming disregard for dynasty, Marie-Thérèse adored her brother-in-law. She so enjoyed de Berry's company that she forgave him his many indiscretions. He had been more regular in his correspondence with her in Vienna than had her own then fiancé and they had developed a close but solidly platonic relationship.

For years, Louis and the Comte d'Artois had made attempts to marry the Duc de Berry to a number of European princesses, all of whom seemed

more than delighted with the captivating Bourbon Prince. In 1802, he was
sent off to Sicily to meet and marry one of Queen Maria Carolina's
daughters, but he instead seduced two of them and left in disgrace, having
married neither. As time marched on, Bourbons in exile – without funds,
their own castles or a country to rule – were increasingly considered bad
matches. De Berry seemed unperturbed by the slights and, when the entire
royal family arrived at Gosfield Park in 1808, and the Marquis of
Buckingham let it be known that he would be happy to mingle Bourbon
blood with that of his twenty-one-year-old daughter, Lady Mary Grenville, Berry seemed a willing conspirator. Buckingham gave a wild party
at Stowe House during which Lady Mary set out to hook de Berry.
Although the Bourbon Prince participated in the dancing, drinking and
flirting, he departed without a marriage contract. According to Lady
Mary's cousins, she was bereft, and the subject was dropped. Two years
earlier, de Berry had entered into what some have called a morganatic
marriage with an English commoner named Amy Brown. Although no
documents have ever been found that verified a wedding, by 1809, they
had had two daughters, Charlotte and Louise.

D'Angoulême was far less amusing and easygoing than his brother. He
could be pompous and demanding and for a long time he had expressed
his dislike for King Louis XVIII's long-time advisor, and some believed,
lover, the Duc d'Avaray. Once settled at Hartwell, tensions between
d'Angoulême and d'Avaray came to a head. When a public rupture
occurred between the two men, d'Angoulême called for the royal favorite
to be dismissed. Careful to appease the husband of the woman who had
come to symbolize his dynasty, the woman he called 'our angel' and 'my
charming star', Louis was forced to send his favorite away. To save face,
d'Avaray publicly announced that he needed to live elsewhere for his
health. With d'Angoulême's blessing, Louis replaced d'Avaray with the
Duc de Blacas. Although Marie-Thérèse had not been involved in the
contretemps, the mere fact that her husband might bring his complaints to
his wife made others realize they would have to tread carefully around the
Duc d'Angoulême in future.

Life at Hartwell suited Marie-Thérèse. As Queen Marie Joséphine
remained very ill with dropsy, it was, as in Mitau, Marie-Thérèse who
became lady of the house. She, her husband and her uncle adopted the
rhythms and patterns of English country living. Louis, Marie-Thérèse and
d'Angoulême rose early, went to church, planted and tended vegetable
and flower gardens and read books in the library. It was a very tranquil
life, and, for the first time in years, Marie-Thérèse felt safe. At 10.30 in the

morning, the Duc and Duchesse d'Angoulême would appear together in a salon to greet guests who would then join them for lunch. At 11 a.m. the King would be announced, a door would open, the King would enter, walk toward his niece and kiss her hand as she curtsied. They would then all head into the dining room where the table was usually set for about ten people. The meal would not be lavish, the ladies would re-wrap their napkins in ribbon to save on laundering expenses, and in half an hour, it would be over. For the rest of the day, until about 5 p.m., all of the family and their friends would do whatever they pleased. The King would grant audiences, or take a mid-afternoon promenade flanked by two *gardes du corps*. Marie-Thérèse frequently went horseback riding on one of only two horses in their stable into the nearby town of Aylesbury to visit a cluster of French émigrés, among them Jean René Asseline, the Bishop of Boulogne, who had relocated there to be near their King. She also enjoyed the company of her friend, Mademoiselle de Choisy, who had become the Vicomtesse d'Agoult, and the Marquise de Sérent.

At 5 p.m., they all would reconvene in a room that had previously been used as a library. The King would enter, the Duchesse d'Angoulême would follow, and soup would be served. After dinner, coffee would be served in another room. Marie-Thérèse liked playing billiards and would often pair up with her friend's husband, the Vicomte d'Agoult, against her husband and another player, often the Comte, later Duc, de Damas. They would play for about an hour at which time Marie-Thérèse would invite those who wished to join her to her own apartments. The ladies would sit to her left; they would chat and do needlework. The gentlemen would sit in chairs facing her. At 11.30, she would rise, say goodnight, and everyone would disperse until the following morning. For those visitors who had either experienced or read about the breathtaking spectacles at Versailles, the entertainment at Hartwell was exceedingly simple by comparison. Although judged dull by many, life at Hartwell was serene, and for Marie-Thérèse in particular, a welcome respite.

When Marie-Thérèse had lived at the Hofburg as a seventeen-year-old, she had not only made lasting friends with girls her own age, but she had also delighted in Franz II's young and growing family. His eldest daughter, Maria Louisa, was just four years old when Marie-Thérèse arrived in Vienna, and she was an adorable little girl with whom Marie-Thérèse would play games and read books. On March 11, 1810, eighteen-year-old Archduchess Maria Louisa was married by proxy to Napoleon Bonaparte. Napoleon, whose real love, Joséphine de Beauharnais, was no longer able to have children, had decided that he needed a royal heir, so he had negotiated with the Habsburg King for the hand of the beautiful young Maria Louisa.

Standing in for the groom in the Hofburg chapel was Archduke Karl, the man intended by his brother to marry Marie-Thérèse. The choice of Karl, the heroic battlefield champion, as Napoleon's representative caused horror in all of the royal houses of Europe, and occasioned many to go into mourning. Once the figure of victory, he now loomed in the minds of all of Europe as the tragic symbol of defeat, and Maria Louisa as its saddest victim. Both Marie-Thérèse and King Louis XVIII were visibly depressed by news of the marriage, because of its significance for the future of the Bourbons; but in Marie-Thérèse it also engendered a very personal sadness. Maria Louisa, like herself, had been obliged to sacrifice any chance of personal happiness for her country; the difference, as Marie-Thérèse well knew, was that whereas she had had a choice, Maria Louisa most certainly had not.

Not long after the wedding of Maria Louisa to 'the Criminal', Marie-Thérèse suffered another two very painful losses. In late June, news arrived that Comte Fersen had been murdered. Fersen, who had continued to investigate reports on the possibility that Marie-Thérèse's brother was alive and well in America, had visited her in England, and had gently informed Marie-Thérèse that he would pursue the stories in person on her behalf. He never made it to America. Upon his return to Sweden, he was assassinated by political enemies. More sad and unexpected news came in late July, when Marie-Thérèse learned that her friend and benefactress, the magnificent Queen Louise of Prussia, had died at the age of thirty-four in Strelitz while visiting her father. The valiant Queen, who, even when pregnant and suffering from typhus, had traveled with Prussian troops and with her husband to Memel, Tilsit, and St Petersburg on behalf of her people, had grown fragile and eventually died in her husband's arms.

The death of Queen Louise prompted her sister, Charlotte, Duchess of Hildburghausen, to immediately arrange for Vavel de Versay and his mysterious young companion to move from Radefeld House, in town, to the outskirts where they would reside in the shuttered and forbidding Castle Eishausen. The castle's system of underground tunnels and caves allowed for secret access to and from the adjacent forests; strict measures were put in place to ensure the couple's complete seclusion, and, in particular, to ensure that the identity of the young aristocratic woman remained concealed.

The couple perfected an unusual routine. They retired very early and began their day at about 3 a.m., before the locals could detect activity in the grounds. Herr Scharre continued as the couple's manservant. Johanna Schmidt was now required to accompany the 'Dark Countess' on her morning walks. Each day, Frau Schmidt would arrive at the castle, turn her back to the door and when she heard the Dark Countess leave the house, she would proceed to the garden and open the gate without turning around to see the woman's face. Frau Schmidt observed that the Count, who always watched from a window, pistol in hand, would wait for the woman to signal with her handkerchief that she was ready to return home. He would then permit his charge back into the house, the whole time Frau Schmidt never having seen the mysterious woman. 'De Versay' and his younger companion were so reclusive that local people speculated as to whether the pair was hiding out to protect the woman, or, if it was, in fact, the Dark Count who was in need of anonymity owing to some nefarious act he may have committed.

Johanna Weber, the couple's cook, had been moved into the castle and was rarely permitted to leave the premises. Provisions were sent to the castle door. The townspeople noticed that the couple received no less than the finest of everything. There was a piano delivered for the woman to play. French wines arrived from Frankfurt, as did clothing, designed in Paris. Money arrived, it was claimed, from Holland and Paris. Vegetables arrived from Bamberg in Bavaria. Herr Scharre received frequent communiqués from Charlotte, Duchess of Hildburghausen, herself. Many years later, after she no longer worked for the mysterious couple, Johanna Weber would tell others that the house was filled with expensive candles, that the mysterious woman's room contained many items embossed with fleur-de-lys, and that from the rare occasions she was able to see the face of her mistress, she had concluded that the mysterious woman was definitely the daughter of Marie Antoinette.

In England, another Queen of France had died. On November 13, Marie Joséphine, aged fifty-seven, succumbed to her long battle with dropsy. Her illness had softened her, and acknowledging the kind treatment that Marie-Thérèse, in her usual role of nurse, had lavished upon her aunt, the Queen, shortly before dying, told Marie-Thérèse and Louis-Antoine that she had always thought of them both as her own children. The funeral service for the Queen in exile took place in London's Church of St Louis, which, according to *The Times*, was 'hung with black and lighted with wax'. Her body was then moved to Westminster Abbey, and, ultimately, to Cagliari, Italy. Her husband, surprisingly grief-stricken, did not attend his wife's funeral; but Napoleon sent his spies, ordering them to write down every person's name who attended the ceremony so that they could be placed on the Emperor's 'enemy list'.

Ten days after Marie Joséphine was buried, the Prince of Wales received a note from the Marquis of Wellesley stating that King Gustavus IV Adolphus of Sweden, who had been forced from the throne by a coup d'état, had arrived in England. Traveling under the name the 'Comte de Gottorp', Gustavus had headed first, not to meet the English King, who was gravely ill, but to Hartwell, where he knew that he would be warmly welcomed and given shelter.

Another visitor to Hartwell was Madame de Staël. De Staël, long banished from France for her outspoken criticism of what she had correctly predicted were Napoleon's imperial ambitions, had had a series of adulterous affairs with various political radicals including Talleyrand, Louis de Narbonne, Benjamin Constant, and Comte Adolph-Louis Ribbing – the man believed to have been the mastermind behind the assassination of the Swedish King, Gustav III. She had come to Hartwell, she claimed, to pay homage to her King. However, her real motive was to ask Louis XVIII to promise to return to her a great deal of money that she believed the French government had owed her father. Louis agreed. In an ironic twist, it would be these monies that de Staël, who claimed sympathy for republican principles, would use to engineer the marriage of her daughter, Albertine, fathered by the fervent anti-royalist, Benjamin Contstant, to the Duc de Broglie, a member of one of the grandest families of courtiers of the ancien régime.

At Hartwell, de Staël had used flattery and charm in order to achieve her ends; however, once the duplicitous novelist departed and was in the company of others, she became a vicious, outspoken critic of the Bourbons. Princess Charlotte, daughter of the future King George IV, wrote, in a letter dated Tuesday, February 1, 1814 to her friend, Miss Mercer Elphinstone that, 'Staël is most violent against the Bourbons being placed on the throne.' De Staël's daughter, Albertine, would also bite the hand that fed her and openly derided the French royal family at every opportunity.

The English, once again at war with the French, were much kinder. With the recurring dementia of George III, in early February 1811 the Prince of Wales was named Prince Regent. It was not long before the Prince, the future King George IV, famous for his profligate spending and harsh treatment of his wife, became an unlikely favorite of Marie-

Thérèse. Ignoring the political ramifications and outrage expressed by his opponents, he offered the exiled French King and his wandering retinue permanent asylum, and in 1811 alone handed out approximately £154,752 in allowances to the French Princes of the Blood, their wives and daughters. The English Prince treated the French émigrés with great affection, always seating Marie-Thérèse, who was, as he was, the child of a king, in the place of honor to his right at his lavish parties and balls.

In March, Louis XVIII received word that Marie-Thérèse's former companion whilst in Vienna, Madame de Chanclos, had died. He admitted that as she had already been saddened by the deaths of her aunt and the Queen of Prussia, he did not have the heart to bring her more bad news, so he asked the Duc d'Angoulême to be his messenger. The French royal family received another blow that same month, which was especially painful to the childless Duchesse d'Angoulême: on March 20, Napoleon's royal bride gave birth to a son.

Marie-Thérèse decided to see some more of England, and in May she and her husband visited Bristol, Cheltenham and the famous spa town of Bath. Her mother, even at the Conciergerie, had insisted on drinking only Ville d'Avray mineral water. Marie-Thérèse's time at Bath was so restorative that she became a convert to the curative powers of mineral waters and the visit heralded a lifelong enthusiasm for spas. On June 3, 1811, *The Times* reported on the visit to Bath that once 'the public began to identify them . . . a vast concourse assembled round the White Hart, anxious to gratify their curiosity with a sight of these interesting personages. They went on a tour of pleasure from Hadfield House, through Oxford, Cheltenham and Gloucester; and returned through Marlborough.' Marie-Thérèse brought back to Hartwell a 'Guide to Bristol' for her uncle, with which he was reportedly delighted. The King had grown so fat that he was no longer able to walk without assistance and he suffered terribly with gout. Marie-Thérèse convinced the King that he needed to go to Bath and in the late summer and early autumn of 1813, the King joined his niece and 'took the cure'. Much as he enjoyed his own stay in Bath, the waters did little to remedy his ailments.

On June 19, 1811, the Prince Regent gave an extravagant ball at his London residence, Carlton House, for over two thousand guests – in honor of himself. On the top of his guest list were many prominent French émigrés, including the entire royal family. His wife, whom he loathed, was not invited; his mistress, however, was. Seated to the Prince Regent's right, however – the place of honor – was Marie-Thérèse. As a homage to the Duchesse d'Angoulême, the Prince Regent had instructed his staff to decorate a room, in which he would greet the daughter of the martyred King of France, draped floor to ceiling in blue silk and embellished with white fleurs-de-lys. When the Prince Regent appeared in this room later that evening he addressed King Louis XVIII not as the 'Comte de l'Isle', as the King had continued to be formally referred to in England, but as 'Your Majesty'. The guests finally sat down to dinner at 2.30 in the morning. The *Gentleman's Magazine* reported the dinner:

> Along the center of the table, about six inches above the surface, a canal of pure water continued flowing from a silver fountain, beautifully constructed at the head of the table. Its banks were covered with green moss and aquatic flowers; gold and silver fish swam and sported through the bubbling current, which produced a pleasing murmur where it fell, and formed a cascade at the outlet. At the head of the table, above the fountain, sat his Royal Highness . . . The most particular friends of the Prince were arranged on each side. They were attended by sixty *servitors;* seven waited on the Prince . . . in their state liveries, *with one man in a complete suit of ancient armour.* At the back of the Prince's seat appeared aureola tables, covered with crimson drapery, constructed to exhibit with the greatest effect, a profusion of the most exquisitely wrought silver-gild plate, consisting of fountains, tripods, epergnes, dishes and other ornaments.[1]

Another party guest, Lord Colchester, recorded in his diary entry for June 19 that he

> went to the fête at Carlton House . . . The great rooms lie all on the right side of the building; the smaller apartments on the left; and in them the Prince waited to receive the King of France, etc . . . [at the Prince's end of the table] it was oriental . . . for in that part the table widened, and the water also, and fell by a succession of cascades into a circular lake surrounded with architectural decorations, and small vases, burning perfumes, which stood under the arches of the colonnade round the lake. Behind the Prince's end of the table there was a magnificent sideboard of gilt plate three stories high. A band in the garden, not seen by the company, played the whole time.[2]

Not to be ignored, the Prince Regent's wife planned a luncheon party of her own for the French royal family on July 8. All of the French royals were, for the moment, visiting the Prince de Condé at his home in

Wimbledon. King Louis declined the invitation, claiming that he had suffered another attack of gout. His courtiers immediately followed his lead, some insisting that they were needed to care for the ailing King, some offering the excuse that King Louis had requested them to receive the visiting Duke of Cumberland. Three days before the scheduled party, Marie-Thérèse sent word that she was unwell, experiencing an inflammation in her head, and simply could not appear for the festivities. Shortly after her note was dispatched, her own courtiers sent the Princess their apologies explaining that they needed to remain with their mistress. At last, the Prince de Condé refused, explaining that since all of his houseguests were ill, he could not very well leave them all. An hour or so before the luncheon was to take place, the Duke of Brunswick told his mother not to bother to go to Kensington Palace because he had just seen the Duke of Cumberland in town, and he had heard that all of the French were staying away. To be somewhat polite to the banished Princess, in fact, the Ducs d'Angoulême, de Berry and de Bourbon made an appearance on behalf of the rest of their family. The entire party comprised these three men and about thirty-five English friends of the Princess.

At the same time that the Bourbons in exile were being fêted in England, a Pastor Kühner arrived in the village of Eishausen, to serve as priest for the village. He had been tutor to the children of the Duke and Duchess of Hildburghausen. Immediately upon his arrival in Eishausen in 1812, Kühner met with 'Vavel de Versay'. The men had a pleasant conversation, during which the Count offered to give the prelate some newspapers and other publications. One morning, a few days after their encounter, an elderly woman wearing white gloves slipped a parcel of printed material under Kühner's door. The two men began a frequent exchange of articles enclosing their own comments and notes on world events. When a mysterious bouquet of white lilies and roses, a symbol of bloody martyrdom, appeared at the door of the Dark Countess, her guardian, under the impression that the priest had sent them, had harsh words with the pastor. Kühner insisted that he had not nor would he ever do such a thing, and the two men resumed what, for 'Vavel de Versay', was his closest friendship in the town.

In Eishausen, there was a New Year's tradition whereby impassioned young men would try to impress their girlfriends by discharging many rounds of gunfire. The noise apparently upset the mysterious Countess. De Versay sent his cook to the parsonage to ask the pastor if there was a way he could get the men to stop. Kühner had no success, so de Versay persisted and sent Senator Andrae to speak with the Hildburghausen police. The police, understanding that the Senator would only appear before them on behalf of a highly distinguished person, placed two of the rowdy young men in jail. Although the townspeople were in an uproar, the Hildburghausen police, on orders of the Ducal Court, banned the exuberant gun show for the following year. This order, backed up by the appearance in Eishausen of the Landschaftsrat Fischer, head of a local security peacekeeping force, with a commando squad on the following New Year's Eve, backfired. Upset that local tradition had been undermined, the young men showed complete contempt for authority, rallying friends from nearby towns to join them in their marauding. The gunfire was even worse than the year before. Pastor Kühner then took matters into his own hands on behalf of the Countess. He spoke with the men and explained that the Count was willing to give a great deal of money for them all to enjoy a wonderful New Year's celebration, as long as no shooting took place. The matter was settled, and Vavel de Versay was grateful.

There were other occasions when the priest would come to the rescue of the Dark Countess, including the time when, during an appearance of Russian troops in the area, an officer of the Czar demanded to meet with the woman, insisting that he would use force to enter the castle. Kühner distracted the commander until his unit had orders to depart immediately. On another occasion, the couple's manservant, Scharre, wanted to confess secrets to the priest and asked Kühner to keep his confession a secret from his master. Kühner assured Scharre that his conscience was clear, but he did not want to promise confidentiality. Feeling a sense of obligation toward the Count and the Duchess of Hildburghausen, and although he corresponded for many years with Vavel de Versay, he never disclosed any information about the couple, other than to say that de Versay was cultured and well educated.

In late July 1812, the Duc d'Angoulême had written an impassioned letter to Czar Alexander asking for permission to join the Russian army. The Czar turned him down, advising him that it would be more appropriate for him to fight alongside British forces against Napoleon. In the autumn of 1812, Napoleon invaded Russia. When his army arrived in Moscow, they found that the city had been torched, the hospitals emptied. Frozen and starving, the French were forced to retreat.

In England, Louis sensed that the moment of Napoleon's defeat was near and started to gather troops, money, and political support for his family's return. There was some discussion among the allied powers as to whether the regency should be shared, with Napoleon's newborn son being placed on the throne; in essence, dividing France. The Bourbons, however, would not relent. Louis XVIII continued to place his niece center stage in order to evoke maximum sentiment and support for a Bourbon restoration; for her part, Marie-Thérèse, who had waited so long for this moment, proved a willing accomplice.

Louis strived to keep Marie-Thérèse's social comings and goings private, thereby preserving the image of Marie-Thérèse the Pious – Marie-Thérèse the Orphan of the Temple. In fact Marie-Thérèse often went to parties, enjoyed the spa and society of Bath – a place that some considered a hedonistic haunt – and relished the company of men like her brother-in-law, the Duc de Berry, and the Prince Regent, both widely known for their excesses. Newspapers, however, with Louis's encouragement, continued to portray her as the long-suffering embodiment of Christian perfection. People assumed that she never socialized, which was clearly incorrect, and that she was dour and somber, although those who knew her always spoke of her natural gaiety.

As she turned thirty-four, on December 19, 1812, Marie-Thérèse seemed overflowing with happiness. On January 27, 1813, Princess Charlotte gave a ball and noticed that d'Angoulême too was in high spirits. In a letter dated February 7 to her friend, Miss Mercer Elphinstone, the English Princess made a special note that at her grand fête, d'Angoulême proved to be a wonderful dance partner. Marie-Thérèse's doctor, Monsieur Lefebvre, knew the reason for the couple's ebullience, and as he would explain to Hüe that January: 'At this moment, I am tending to a woman who lives above me and who is pregnant for the first time after more than thirteen years of marriage.'

On January 30, Hüe wrote to his wife that Dr Lefebvre had given him the miraculous news that the Duc d'Angoulême would be a father in June. The doctor confirmed this in his own handwriting on the same letter. Madame Hüe received the note and added a formal sentence on the paper: 'Monsieur Hüe and Monsieur Lefebvre designate Madame the Duchesse d'Angoulême, announcing her pregnancy.'[3] On February 15, 1813, Louise de Condé wrote to her father that she was stunned to hear of the pregnancy as she had heard for years that, while Marie-Thérèse had been in the Temple Prison, the Jacobin guards had bragged about destroying her fertility with a combination of drugs.[4] Marie-Thérèse's joy was to be short-lived. Quite a few months into the pregnancy, she suffered a miscarriage and that summer left for Bath to recuperate.

In early 1813, the Prussians severed their alliance with France, joining the Russians against Napoleon. The tide was beginning to turn against the Emperor of the French, raising Bourbon hopes that they would soon return. On Saturday, October 16, Princess Charlotte wrote to her friend Miss Mercer Elphinstone that since the day Napoleon had married his Austrian Archduchess, he 'affects to call all crowned heads his relations, &, on someone talking of Revolution, he said, "If that happens again, do you think they will treat me like *my poor uncle?*",' referring to the late Louis XVI. Even his powerful ally, Talleyrand, participated in a plot against him. Talleyrand, who was often referred to as 'Prince Girouette' – 'Weathervane' – because his loyalty swung whichever way the wind blew, sensed that change was in the air. He dispatched the royalist Baron de Vitrolles to allied forces in eastern France with a letter written in invisible ink, advising Napoleon's enemies to attack Paris at that very moment. On March 31, 1814, the allies entered Paris. On April 6, Napoleon abdicated in favor of his son, abdicated unconditionally days later and was exiled to the small Mediterranean island of Elba.

Copies of Louis's 'Declaration of Hartwell', in which he promised the people of France peace and stability, were strewn about the streets of the French capital. On Sunday, April 10, the English newspaper, the *Examiner,* published the new French constitution – or Charter – in which five of the twenty-nine articles declared that the new French government would be 'monarchial, hereditary from male to male, in order of primogeniture . . . the French People call freely to the throne . . . the House of Bourbon, in the ancient order . . . the ancient Nobility resume their titles . . . the sanction of the King is necessary for the completion of a Law'. The newspaper also wryly commented that those who pointed to 'Saint Louis' and 'Henry the Great' as great kings of France needed to remember that the rest of the rulers of that country were 'wretched', adding that Saint Louis was 'a bigot'. The *Examiner* denounced the idea of the Bourbon restoration saying it would be a serious mistake and a retrograde step for liberty, while tacitly acknowledging that it had, in fact, been the allied monarchs who had placed their 'cousin' back on the throne and that, in the end, the people of France, now a vanquished nation, had little choice.

Paris was clearly a conquered city. The English soldiers enjoyed promenading in the Bois de Boulogne and the Austrians had taken over Saint-Cloud. It was an unusual coincidence that in 1814, both Catholic and Orthodox Easter fell on the same day, April 10. In Paris, an altar was built in the Place Louis XV where Louis XVI and Marie Antoinette had gone to the guillotine. The road to the Place Louis XV was filled with allied soldiers, who marched in triumph and unison toward the altar. There, the Czar of Russia and the King of Prussia stood for a *Te Deum* mass and benediction. At the end of the service, a hundred Russian cannon roared. The allied soldiers kneeled as the Czar Alexander and King Frederick William embraced the Marshals of France, their lifelong enemies, as a sign of Christian forgiveness. Both royalists and liberals celebrated.

The Marquis de la Maisonfort was at Hartwell when Marie-Thérèse celebrated Easter that Sunday, April 10. Louis XVIII wrote in his memoirs that he had never seen her as jubilant and that when his niece learned that she would be returning to France her usual 'impenetrable calm' cracked. She sobbed and sobbed, repeating over and over that she was once more going to see France. After a while, she spoke between her tears and told the King that he was to go ahead of her so that he could make an unforgettable entrance. The King refused, telling Marie-Thérèse that he would not set one foot on French soil without her and that she was their 'angel of forgetting and pardon'. He would later reflect in his journal on the tragic irony that she, who had suffered and sacrificed so much for France, should be denied the consolation of perpetuating their dynasty for posterity.

CHAPTER XIX
THE ONLY MAN
IN THE FAMILY

T HE PROSPECT OF Napoleon's wife as Regent of France, with the eventuality of his son becoming the next Emperor of the French, had proved unpalatable to Europe's monarchs (with the exception of Maria Louisa's father, Emperor Franz, whose idea it was). The story, however, could so easily have unfolded differently for Marie-Thérèse, and Louis XVIII knew it. Louis was consummately aware of the prevailing sympathy for Marie-Thérèse and believed that if his niece had married Archduke Karl his own chances of becoming King of France would have been destroyed. The Emperor would have achieved Habsburg domination over most of continental Europe as his brilliant Austrian Foreign Minister Metternich would no doubt have negotiated – with some give and take with Russia, Prussia and Spain – to place Marie-Thérèse and Karl on the throne of France as co-Regents, an arrangement that would have echoed the marriage of Empress Maria Theresa and Francis of Lorraine some seventy-eight years earlier.

It was true that Karl had proved to be a leader among men, but neither he nor his brother, the Emperor, had managed to control Marie-Thérèse. She had demonstrated time and again that she was a formidable opponent and that her loyalties were first and foremost to France. Even if she had accepted marriage to the Austrian Archduke she probably would have insisted on the removal of Salic law or, at the very least, something like the Pragmatic Sanction that had placed her (their) grandmother on the throne of her own empire. She was an accomplished strategist and knew that presented with these circumstances she would have been able to quite effortlessly become *de jure* ruler of France. However, because she had remained steadfast to what she believed was best for France, to her father's memory and her belief in divine right, she had rejected the Habsburg route. She would continue in her role as team player, with her Bourbon relatives poised to mobilize allies throughout Europe to put a portly and awkward fifty-nine-year-old man – the man she had regarded as her father since the death of her own father in January 1793 – on the throne of France.

With the defeat of Napoleon came a pervasive need to investigate the twenty-five years of convulsion in French society, as well as a flood of nostalgia for the past. Ministers like Francois Guizot, François-Auguste Mignet, Augustin Thierry, and Jules Michelet, who would serve in the France of the Restoration, would not only write their reflections on the Revolution but also exhibit a penchant for a romantic re-examination of such figures as Charlemagne, Abelard and Heloïse, and for translating heroic dramas from Latin into French, thereby popularizing a thirteenth-century text by Guillaume de Nangis on the House of Capet. Augustin Thierry also looked to the past, claiming that the defeat of Napoleon had created an opportunity to put into place a plan devised by the seventeenth-century Abbé Saint-Pierre, who had called for a European confederation – a union of monarchs.

While the historians began to explicate and deconstruct, the Bourbons sprang into action. The Comte d'Artois had embarked from Great Yarmouth at the end of January 1814 and journeyed to The Hague in order to pave the way for his brother's return to France. The Duc de Berry, the La Ferronnays and others made their way to Cherbourg. Marie-Thérèse's husband had joined the Duke of Wellington in the Pyrenees at the moment of triumph and had proved to be a good soldier, adding luster to the family's image.

Meanwhile, from the tiny town of Eishausen, Vavel de Versay dispatched three letters to the Comte d'Artois, the Duc de Berry and the Duc d'Angoulême, now all on the continent. 'De Versay' offered them his undying support and expressed his longing that he would soon 'experience the pleasure of knowing you personally'.

In England, the Prince Regent, who had so openly demonstrated his friendship for the exiled Bourbons, traveled from London to the country town of Stanmore, to meet with Louis XVIII and Marie-Thérèse at the Abercorn Arms. It was recorded that the crowd went wild and lifted his carriage in the air, and greeted the future George IV with effusive cheers.

This meeting was a preliminary to an official celebration to honor the Bourbons that the Prince of Wales had planned to take place in London in a few days, on April 20. The *Examiner* would later criticize events, complaining that it was extremely inappropriate that the King of France, 'huzzaed' by the people of England, had not been invited to stay at either Buckingham House or St James's Palace. Instead, Louis and his entourage were booked into the Grillon Hotel on Albemarle Street.

The Prince Regent, Louis XVIII and Marie-Thérèse arrived in Piccadilly at around 5 p.m. to enthusiastic crowds and orchestras playing 'God Save the King'. The Duchesse de Gontaut-Biron wrote that the whole city had been decorated for the day and its people were joyous. Even Madame de Staël conceded, 'All London is drunk with joy.' Devonshire House hoisted the colors of France. Flags embroidered in gold and silver bearing the arms of the Bourbons were waved in the streets while other revelers sported the Bourbon white cockade. King Louis XVIII gave the future English King the Order of St Esprit for his kindness. The Mayor of London, politicians of all political complexions and members of the English aristocracy came out to hail Marie-Thérèse, mindful no doubt that she would be the one in control of the invitation list at the new French court.

Fanny Burney, the author known socially as Madame d'Arblay, received a letter from Queen Charlotte of England inviting her to meet the Duchesse d'Angoulême. Unfortunately there was some kind of mix-up and when d'Arblay arrived at the hotel on Albermarle Street she instead came face to face with the King of France. She would, however, be one of those Englishwomen who would have the pleasure of receiving an invitation to meet with Marie-Thérèse later that year in Paris. D'Arblay recalled that she had studied a portrait of the Duchesse d'Angoulême, which depicted the daughter of the late King as a melancholy woman, but that when she had met with her later in the year at the Tuileries she thought her smile was so 'becoming, that it brightens her countenance into a look of youth and beauty'. When d'Arblay discovered that Marie-Thérèse had just finished reading her latest book in French because she could not find an English copy in Paris, the author insisted on sending the Duchess an English edition. Marie-Thérèse then delighted the author by promising that she would read the book again in English. Madame d'Arblay inquired whether Marie-Thérèse preferred to speak with her in English or French, and Marie-Thérèse, with great modesty, insisted that her English was not very good, although D'Arblay noted that the Duchess had understood every word she had said to her in English.

D'Arblay found her charming, with impeccable manners and no preten-
sion and more like an English aristocratic girl from the country than a
future Queen of France.

The day after the great celebration in London, the Prince Regent gave a
ball at Carlton House and invested Louis XVIII with the Order of the
Garter. Louis and Marie-Thérèse, with a small entourage that included
Hüe, who had remained in their service throughout the long years of
exile, sailed from Dover a few days later and arrived in Calais to hordes of
cheering people. Although she was moved by the reception, Marie-
Thérèse also felt agitated and disconcerted, recalling the scenes of violence
on the road from Varennes. On April 28, the royals arrived in Amiens to
the astonishing sight of the local townspeople's homes belted in black
fabric with their chimneys painted black. Louis and Marie-Thérèse
discovered that these displays of mourning had been put into effect upon
the execution of Louis XVI and had remained in place since that day.

On Friday, April 29, Louis XVIII and his niece arrived at the palace of
Compiègne, which they found to have been redecorated by Napoleon
with a dizzying plethora of 'N's, bees and eagles. Even the tableware had
been monogrammed in tribute to the former Emperor. Waiting to receive
Marie-Thérèse were beloved childhood friends, such as Madame de
Tourzel and her daughter, Pauline, now married and known as the
Comtesse de Béarn. It was an emotional and tearful reunion. Also at
Compiègne were those whom the Bourbons mistrusted, including Tal-
leyrand who in fact had played a major role in effecting their return.
Recognizing Napoleon's marshals among the groups waiting to greet the
Bourbons, Louis was conciliatory, calling them all 'good Frenchmen'. The
minions of the former Emperor of the French were impressed.

The King and Marie-Thérèse entered Paris on May 3 to be greeted by
deafening cries of 'Vive le Roi!' Marie-Thérèse wore a white gown
embroidered with silver leaves, essentially draping herself in her own
interpretation of the Bourbon banner. At her neckline was a ruff, which
made her seem rigid to the crowds. Worse, she appeared 'English',
wearing no jewelry and just a toque – a little rimless feathered hat –
described by Le Moniteur as 'à l'anglaise', which to the conquered French
was considered distasteful and a major fashion faux pas. Two years later
the historical novels of Walter Scott were translated into French and not
long after that a mania to look like Scott's heroines swept Paris and that
same style of toque would become the vogue. Upon her arrival, however,
Marie-Thérèse was judged too modest and severe by Parisian standards.
Although to the crowds Marie-Thérèse had appeared composed and

dignified, as soon as she arrived at the Notre Dame cathedral she collapsed on a prayer stool and wept.

After prayers, they drove again through the streets of Paris as great numbers of curious people turned out to see the only royal child to have survived the Reign of Terror. The King was thrilled to see that a statue of the heroic Bourbon king Henri IV had been restored to its place on the Pont-Neuf in his honor. Madame de Chastenay watched the royal cortège pass by on the rue Saint-Honoré and recalled that the street was so adorned that it resembled a theater. Her glimpse of the King's carriage, covered in bouquets of lilies, and the whole spectacle, the return of the royal livery after so long, reduced her to tears. While the King waved theatrically at the crowds, Marie-Thérèse sat rigid and lifeless. Madame de Genlis wrote that the people of Paris were shocked that Marie-Thérèse did not look happy in Paris and that she appeared to be in some sort of pain. Fortunately, Marie-Thérèse did not have to endure the further agony of passing by the Temple Prison on her route because Napoleon had torn it down over five years earlier, but she did pass the Conciergerie, where her mother had spent her last days. When at last the carriage arrived at the Tuileries Palace, Marie-Thérèse collapsed. When she came round she found that she had been placed in her new apartment, the Pavillon de Flore, the chambers facing the Seine in which her late mother had lived.

The following morning, a grand parade of troops formed on the banks of the Seine facing the Tuileries. In the afternoon, commanded by His Imperial Highness, Grand Duke Constantine, the soldiers stood under the open windows of the Tuileries Palace where the Emperors of Russia and Austria and the King of Prussia were joined by King Louis XVIII and his family. Seemingly recovered, the Duchesse d'Angoulême also greeted the crowds and that evening the royal party sat down to a splendid banquet.

The Comtesse de Boigne, daughter of the Marquis d'Osmond, a nobleman at court at Versailles, and an ex-mistress of the current Duc d'Orléans, wrote that Marie-Thérèse was the only person of the royal family people remembered in France. Over the past fifteen years, while the rest of the Bourbons had faded in the minds of many, Napoleon had created a new aristocracy with grand new titles and riches. Marie-Thérèse wanted nothing to do with them. During one evening at the Tuileries, Marie-Thérèse offended the wife of Napoleon's great Marshal Ney. His wife, a niece of Madame de Campan, was known to Marie-Thérèse as a girl. Instead of addressing Madame Ney by her formal name, Princesse de la Moscowa, in public, Marie-Thérèse greeted her by her Christian name,

Aglaé. Napoleon's appointees and their fashionable wives, some of whom had been shopkeepers and servants during the reign of Louis XVI, found that *déclassé*. They also ridiculed Marie-Thérèse for having arrived in Paris with a wardrobe of English country clothes. Now in her mid-thirties, her hair had gone from blonde to a dull, reddish brown, and, when she spoke, they found her voice unpleasant and raucous. (Often criticized as unpleasant, her voice was described by some as 'hoarse' and 'exceedingly high'. Because of the affliction strangers were often put off by what sounded like 'brusqueness'.) To the Parisian parvenus, being out of fashion was an unforgivable sin. They could not, however, fault her in her royal bearing. It was impeccable. She was so obviously regal that members of the ancien régime wept merely at the sight of her.

In addition to those ennobled by Napoleon, Marie-Thérèse bore a grudge against those old friends who had prospered under the Empire. When she learned that Madame Campan had presided over a successful school and had even tutored members of the Bonaparte family, she shut the door on their relationship. In order to try and regain the royal family's trust and favor, Madame de Campan began to write her memoirs, which were exceedingly loving and flattering toward her late mistress, Marie Antoinette. There was another person whom Marie-Thérèse continued to refuse to acknowledge. That was the son of the man whom she held responsible for her parents' death: her cousin, Louis-Philippe, the Duc d'Orléans. After he had been refused Marie-Thérèse's hand, he had married her first cousin, Marie Amélie, daughter of Marie Antoinette's favorite sister, Maria-Carolina, Queen of the Two Sicilies. Marie Amélie was the younger of the two sisters with whom the Duc de Berry had flirted but never married. Out of respect for her mother, Marie-Thérèse agreed to meet with Amélie, and despite Marie-Thérèse's contempt for Amélie's husband, the two women became the best of friends in an almost bittersweet echo of their mothers' friendship.

King Louis XVIII, however, was keen to demonstrate his family's forgiveness and one of his first actions was to return to Louis-Philippe the Orléans *apanages*, the income-producing fiefdoms given by the King of France to royalty that had been taken away by the revolutionary government in September 1792. It would not be until the end of the year that he would do the same for his own brother, d'Artois. Louis also immediately enacted measures for the Treasury to repay those kingdoms in which he had incurred expenses while in exile.

Once more wishing to set the new constitutional monarchy off on the right foot, Louis established his court not at Versailles – which stood

etched in the memories of Frenchmen as a palace of excess and lasci-
viousness and a place of isolation for the monarchy against the powerful
voice of Parisian politics and publishing – but at the Tuileries Palace, from
where Napoleon had enacted, in the minds of many Frenchmen, some
very worthwhile measures. He also selected his cabinet of ministers from
a broad political spectrum. Louis needed to convince French men and
women, those born after the end of the ancien régime and those with long
bitter memories, of France's glorious past and of their commonalities –
not their differences.

To this end, Louis needed Marie-Thérèse, both as a symbol of the new
regime and as an ally. He organized a series of ceremonies to pay homage
to her murdered family and in an effort to bring 'closure' for his long-
suffering niece and for the people of France, a requiem was sung in every
church in Paris to honor the late King, Queen, Dauphin and Madame
Elisabeth. At the cathedral of Notre Dame, the priest referred to Louis
Charles as 'an angel'. In June, on what was imagined to be the anniversary of his death, memorial services were held all around France commemorating 'the little king and martyr', but, because the Dauphin's body
could not be produced, gossip spread once again and Marie-Thérèse
continued to suffer. Noting the sentiment of the people who pitied his
young niece, and quite aware of his own precarious position, Louis
declared to all, that he, in the absence of her father, was acting in her best
interest, stating: 'If my crown were of roses, I would give it up to her; but
it is of thorns, and I keep it.'

Privately, however, they bickered over family assets. When the King
decided to make himself comfortable at Saint-Cloud, Marie-Thérèse
complained that she should at least receive the same consideration as
other returning émigrés and have the property returned to her. The King
explained that Saint-Cloud was the property of the Crown, but Marie-
Thérèse reminded her uncle that it was, by rights, hers because it had been
given by her father to her mother. The King relented, and asked his niece
if she could at least spare one little room for him if he decided to visit.
They also squabbled over her appearance. The King told her that he
wanted her to stop looking 'ghoulish' in public, cease wearing drab
clothes, and put on some rouge. Louis XVIII was also critical of her
general demeanor, which he felt might encourage their countrymen to feel
guilt and shame.

Louis reflected in his memoir that although it was Marie-Thérèse who
was the heart of the court, she had neither the taste nor the inclination for
celebrating at the Tuileries, where her family had suffered so much. She

actually found any kind of gaiety, especially the laughter of parties, within that particular palace sacrilegious. She preferred modest costume as she had worn simple clothing for so long. The household she established at the Tuileries would not be a gay *maison*. She banished the flashy clothing of the Napoleonic period, preferring that her ladies wear simple, narrow white silk dresses with trains and white lace mantillas, almost reminiscent of mourning veils – similar to the bridal costume that Antigone was meant to have worn to her death. The King, meanwhile, wore a dark blue morning coat with gold epaulettes; most of the men wore military garb, rather than the lavish costume of the ancien régime – though Louis continued to wear powdered wigs, which had long since gone out of fashion.

On May 17, the King took Marie-Thérèse to the Opéra to see *Oedipus at Colonus*. Many of the audience members wore white and had fastened white lilies on their clothing in honor of the restored Bourbons. The evening was a calculated attempt to place Marie-Thérèse in the hearts of the public as their Princess – and, this time, Marie-Thérèse acquiesced, adorning herself in crown jewels and a magnificent gown. The King's scheme worked. When a well-known verse – 'She has lavished upon me her affection and her care' – was sung, the King extended his hand for his niece to kiss. When she did, the audience jumped to its feet and began to shout, '*Vive le Roi! Vive la Duchesse d'Angoulême!*'

The Parisians may not have always appreciated her wardrobe or sullenness, but they admired this singular woman who had shown such fortitude in accompanying her uncle through the snow from Mitau to Warsaw in the winter of 1801. As the King had named her, the people of France now hailed her as 'the New Antigone', the courageous, loyal and most dignified of daughters. Her mythic presence in Paris would prove fascinating to esteemed literary figures such as Sainte-Beuve, Chateaubriand, and Lamartine, all of whom would receive court patronage. Poets and musicians wrote ballads in her honor. The American author James Fenimore Cooper wrote a charming book called *Autobiography of a Pocket Handkerchief*, in which the protagonist, a handkerchief, lives among royalty. Cooper's handkerchief testifies, in this account, that Marie-Thérèse was a wonderful woman known to have arranged for the exiled French noblemen to receive money.

A few days after her arrival in the capital, Marie-Thérèse contacted her former companion, Madame de Chanterenne, who had hurried back from Naples the moment she heard of the Bourbon restoration. Marie-Thérèse sent a note to her beloved childhood friend, Pauline, asking her to visit the Tuileries with her husband and children. Marie-Thérèse arranged for an annual income for her 'dear Renète' and invited her often to visit her at the Tuileries. She also intervened on behalf of Madame de Chanterenne's son (her godson), Charles, obtaining a position for him among the *gardes du corps*, despite his young age.

With every day in Paris, however, Marie-Thérèse's personal anguish was becoming more and more profound. It was at this time that she asked of Pauline a particularly difficult favor. Pauline had previously sent Marie-Thérèse mementos from the grave of her parents, and now the Duchess asked her childhood friend to take her to their burial ground in the Madeleine cemetery. Pauline arranged with the owner of the property for the two of them to visit the site in private. They left at seven in the morning, Marie-Thérèse dressed simply. Pauline described the scene. They arrived and approached the spot, marked by a black wooden cross. Marie-Thérèse, leaning on Pauline's arm and the arm of Pauline's son, began to involuntarily tremble. She then fell, first on her knees, and then prostrated, her face in the grass. Pauline lowered herself beside her friend. At last, Marie-Thérèse lifted her head, and Pauline saw that the Duchess's face was wet with tears. She recalled that she cried: 'Oh, my father! You who have obtained for me the grace of my first prayer, to return to France, please obtain the grace that I may see her happy.'

To assuage their own guilt for the crimes they had committed against the young Madame Royale, the French assumed a common posture that it was the Austrians who had robbed Marie-Thérèse of her happiness and that her 'captivity' at the Hofburg had been worse than her time at the Temple Prison. Despite having longed to be back in France for almost twenty years, Marie-Thérèse was not prepared for the memories that engulfed her once she returned. She hated the Tuileries, but Louis XVIII, learning from the mistakes of his brother, understood the importance of remaining in the capital. While his pain was more a twinge of nostalgia, for Marie-Thérèse the experience of living in her mother's rooms was almost unbearable. Either the King simply did not understand her grief after all of these years, or he chose to ignore it.

The King's continuing public relations campaign included daily press conferences during which he would offer the press men tidbits on his activities and stories illustrating the harmony among his ministers. Marie-Thérèse convinced the King that it would be good as part of this campaign if she were to visit other areas of France and toward the end of June she went to the spa at Vichy, where once again she took the cure. She remained there until the beginning of August when she traveled to Riom in the Auvergne region of central France. There, the mayor escorted her to the corn market. Little girls presented her with baskets of flowers and peasant women serenaded her with songs sung in the Auvergne dialect. She was warmly received at the town hall; more, she was enjoying herself. She journeyed on to Clermont-Ferrand and other small towns, their streets draped in white banners and fleurs-de-lys in her honor. In Clermont-Ferrand, sixty men dressed in white unharnessed her horses and carried her carriage to the cathedral. On August 6, she entered Lyon where the town teemed with dancing children, banners that exclaimed their 'Love to Madame', and tableaux recreating historic battles. She was next persuaded to visit the Île Barbe on the Rhône, where she was taken in a luxurious gondola, which was followed by a flotilla of tiny boats.

Soon she was back again in Paris, arriving at the Tuileries on the 13th. The King, however, chose this time to grant her her wish to visit her childhood home, Versailles, and on August 17, for the first time in twenty-five years Marie-Thérèse returned to the palace. During the Revolution it had been ravaged by looters, though Napoleon had begun restoring it with dreams of installing his young royal bride and their son in the spectacular royal residence. He had also begun repairs on Marie Antoinette's beloved Petit Trianon, and invited his sister, Pauline, to live there. Louis XVIII also, despite his public presence in Paris, had, upon his return to France, initiated and overseen a massive restoration of his childhood home, which even included additions to the legendary chateau. When Marie-Thérèse arrived at Versailles, she saw craftsmen everywhere: gilders, carpenters and masons, working away on scaffolds, attempting to bring back Versailles to its ancien régime splendor. She wandered the rooms where she had slept and played, into her mother's bedroom where she and her late brothers and sister had been born and visited the gardens of the Petit Trianon where she and Louis Charles had frolicked without care. And then, she returned to the Tuileries, the home she despised, in order to once again stand by her uncle's side.

She was required for the celebrations of the Fête Saint Louis on August 25, a significant state occasion. The Duke of Wellington, who was growing increasingly unpopular due to his outspoken and unsolicited advice to the new French government, was, nonetheless, invited to the dinner at the Tuileries. Afterwards there was a firework display for all the people of Paris to enjoy. Four days later, on August 29, it was the people's turn to honor the royal family. The King and his family attended a gala at the Hôtel de Ville where Marie-Thérèse was seated, according to her status as the daughter of the late King, next to her uncle. The Baronne de

Chabrol was given the honor of serving Marie-Thérèse her meal. After dinner, a cantata by the Italian-French composer Luigi Cherubini was performed.

It became apparent that the daughter of the House of Bourbon, which had ruled for centuries by divine right, was believed by many to possess some inherent quality of miraculous power. Marie-Thérèse was nearing thirty-six, almost the age her mother was when she was led, white-haired, to the guillotine. The provincial women of France now prayed for Marie-Thérèse to have a baby, a Child of France. On the very day of the Fête Saint Louis, the churchwardens of Nîmes vowed to make an offering of a solid silver statue, the weight of a baby, if Marie-Thérèse were to give birth to a boy. On September 24, in the *Journal de Nantes*, an article appeared stating:

> There is, in the Church of Saint-Eloi, a beautiful statue of the Virgin. All of the women of this parish congregate in front of this august image as the pastor has planted at her feet a great stalk of silver lilies. Five flowers express our recognition of what we possess, and a bud, for what we pray. The women of the parish have been celebrating a novena. One can read at the base of the white marble pedestal, underneath the bouquet of lilies: 'Offering to Mary for the happy fecundity of the daughter of Louis XVI, and the perpetuity of the Bourbons on the throne of France.'

It was in the provinces, and in the countryside in the company of 'good Frenchmen', that Marie-Thérèse was at her most comfortable. The Comte de Villèle noted in his journal that when Marie-Thérèse visited Toulouse in 1814, she received an enthusiastic and lavish welcome, though she later reproached Villèle for allowing the town to spend so much money on the reception. She was decidedly not happy in Paris surrounded by Bona-partists who required her to feign gaiety or among the members of the new 'fashionable society' who frowned on her sincere piety. She would often avoid women's functions in the capital altogether, preferring instead to go horseback riding in the Bois de Boulogne. Nor did she find the new parliamentary monarchy appealing. She firmly believed that the King ought to rule by divine right and that the new, so-called government by charter, a paean to the Revolution, was a sham, wherein only less than a quarter of 1 per cent of the country were actually eligible to vote, and only men over the age of forty who paid taxes over 1,000 francs a year were able to hold office. Rather than sit in on her uncle's political meetings, she chose to visit the poor and make gifts including little paper notebooks, which she sold for the benefit of the émigrés who still needed assistance. She treasured these friends who had suffered and would visit them privately. She also made very public tours, as her mother had done to show her support for French industry, to places like the Gobelins tapestry manufacturing facility at Sèvres.

Everywhere she went in Paris, Marie-Thérèse faced one agonizing memory after another. On the site of the former Temple Prison, where her family had spent their final days together, she ordered a cypress tree and a weeping willow tree to be planted. On the anniversary of her mother's death, she remained alone in her room at the Tuileries in prayer. Both she and the King were intent on having proper burials for their families killed in the Revolution. The bodies of Marie-Thérèse's parents, which had been identified in 1805, were exhumed from amongst the 3,000 corpses in the Madeleine cemetery so that they could be placed in the royal crypt at Saint-Denis. The gravediggers were also told to look for the remains of other royal corpses in the mass grave, which had been stolen in 1793 from the necropolis at Saint-Denis. Some were found and identified. Louis Charles's body, however, was not. It was rumored that his body had been taken to another mass grave at the cemetery of Sainte-Marguerite, where those who had been beheaded at the guillotine during the Terror had been laid. (That spot, today, is at the Place de la Nation.)

Privately, the King interviewed the widow of the man who had claimed to have secretly moved Louis Charles's body from one spot to another. On December 13, Marie-Thérèse went to the Hôpital des Incurables to meet with Madame Simon, a patient there, and the wife of her brother's sadistic jailer. Marie-Thérèse dressed very simply and went incognito so as to deflect gossip. Madame Simon was not expecting the visit and Marie-Thérèse, presenting herself as just some ordinary visitor, located the old woman, who regaled her with stories about Louis Charles. Madame Simon insisted that the boy did not perish in the prison, and, in fact, had come to visit her in 1802. When the Duchesse d'Angoulême asked Madame Simon how she had recognized the boy, the old woman replied: 'Well, I recognize you, Marie-Thérèse, despite your disguise.' Distressed by the encounter, Marie-Thérèse left immediately.

That winter an old report by former revolutionary Committee of Public Safety Commissioner Harmand de la Meuse began to be circulated. It claimed that when the members of the Assembly visited Louis Charles in prison he did not seem to be able to hear or speak. The revival of this account caused a resurgence of speculation that the little boy they saw had been a deaf mute substituted for Louis Charles while the real Louis XVII had escaped the Temple Prison and might still be alive.

On January 21, the twenty-second anniversary of the death of King Louis XVI, the exhumed bodies of the late King and Marie Antoinette were taken to the royal crypt at Saint-Denis. Marie-Thérèse, upholding the ancient tradition that the King and his family did not attend funerals, remained locked in her room at the Tuileries deep in prayer throughout the procession and burial ceremony at Saint-Denis, though she could hear the artillery discharges firing in the distance. When the body of her mother had been unearthed, the laborers had found some locks of hair, a ring and some garters that they felt they should give to the authorities to be passed on to the Duchesse d'Angoulême. It fell upon the Marquis de la Maisonfort to deliver these personal effects, and on January 22 he met with her at the Tuileries to do so.

Marie-Thérèse approved Louis XVIII's plans for the construction of a memorial building, the Chapelle Expiatoire, on the site of the mass grave at the Madeleine cemetery. The structure, designed in the grand neo-classical style by Pierre François Léonard Fontaine and Charles Percier, would take nearly ten years to complete and Marie-Thérèse would visit the site regularly to watch progress. It was also determined to erect another monument at the Place Louis XV, where Louis XVI, Marie Antoinette and Madame Elisabeth, whose body had been located at the Errancis cemetery, had all been guillotined. The shrine, which was never completed, was to be a three-sided sculpture raised on a plinth carrying testaments to each victim. On one side a statue of Louis XVI would be shown ascending to heaven assisted by an angel, with the words of the Abbé Edgeworth ('Son of Saint-Louis, Ascend to Heaven!') and the late King's own words forgiving the people of France. Another side was to contain a bust of Queen Marie Antoinette accompanied by her words, 'I have seen all, understood all, and forgotten all', and the third was to be a bas-relief of Madame Elisabeth with the quote 'Do not undeceive them', a reference to the incident at the Tuileries. This public project, the first stone of which would not be in place until 1826, would effectively be left abandoned four years later.

On January 27, while visiting the patients of a hospital, l'Hôtel-Dieu, Marie-Thérèse was introduced to its chief surgeon, a Dr Philippe Jean Pelletan. Dr Pelletan had been trying, through various contacts, to meet with Marie-Thérèse from the moment she had returned to France. In the doctor's unpublished memoirs, he recounted that she 'said with kindness that she had known me "from other days" and asked me, if, effectively, since I had cared for her brother, it were true that I could recognize his body by the cranial section that I had made. My answer was "yes" and Her Highness left.' The next day, he received a letter from the Duc d'Havré asking him to come to the Tuileries to meet with the Duchess. The following day he claims he had a very private meeting with Marie-Thérèse during which he told her how he had cut her brother's heart from his body and that he wanted her to have it. The doctor was never able to give her the heart because, very soon after their meeting, as he described it, 'all hell broke loose' in France.[1]

Despite her discomfort at being in Paris, Marie-Thérèse performed her duties impeccably, attending with her uncle the opera, theater, dinners, a party given by her jovial brother-in-law, the Duc de Berry; and in February, Marie-Thérèse hosted a party at the Tuileries during which there was a performance by actors from the Théâtre des Variétés. The American James Gallatin wrote in his diary how, one March morning, he and his father, Albert, were received privately by the King and the Duchesse d'Angoulême. 'She looked very sad,' he noted in his diary. James told Marie-Thérèse that he was going into politics, and the Duchess wondered aloud if he was a bit too young. When he protested that he was seventeen, she pronounced, 'But, he is a baby!' The Gallatins, who would enjoy a close relationship with Marie-Thérèse for nearly ten years, all admired her. James once described her in his diary as 'the most royal-looking personage one can possibly imagine'.

That March, the Duc d'Angoulême came to his wife's rescue. He proposed a month-long tour of central France, after which he would take his wife to visit his seat in Bordeaux, the first city to hail the return of the Bourbons. Because she was greeted so enthusiastically by crowds throughout her journey, Marie-Thérèse wrote to the King: 'I have concluded that the Bourbons are really affirmed on the throne.' She later recorded the visit in a twelve-page letter to her dear friend, Marie-Françoise – 'Fanny' – Roisins, now married to Prince Nicolas Esterhazy de Galantha and living between Budapest and Vienna.[2] Opening her letter 'Ma chère Fanny', Marie-Thérèse described her arrival in Bordeaux as 'the most lovely in the world' as the quay was covered with well-wishers. 'My husband and I loved it!' she effused. She rode in a calèche while the duke, on horseback, inspected the troops. On March 12, the anniversary of the date of her husband's arrival in the city of Bordeaux, she went to the very spot where he had received the keys to the city to the general admiration of all.

Their joy, however, was cut short by news that Napoleon had escaped from his island prison. Forces had been sent by Louis XVIII to intercept him but the 5th Regiment of the Line under Marshal Ney had turned and were now proceeding up the Rhône valley, led by their former commander, en route for the capital. The Duc d'Angoulême departed immediately to lead the King's 4,000 loyal volunteer troops in Nîmes. Marie-Thérèse remained in Bordeaux and with the 'courage of a lioness' took charge.

Each morning, after prayers, the Duchesse d'Angoulême described how she would face the barracks full of soldiers and speak to them of their duty to France. As she reviewed the troops, she would shout '*Vive le Roi!*' and thank them for their loyalty. She would then drive to the town hall where she would encourage the authorities to sign up more volunteers in the fight for the King. Napoleon, however, was able to swiftly re-ignite old loyalties and raise a regular army of over 140,000 and a volunteer army of almost double that. He re-entered Paris victorious on March 20. A day earlier Louis XVIII had fled to Brussels, though not before instructing Hüe to remove the diamonds from the royal crown, pack them into artillery cases and get them out of the country.

In command from the Tuileries Palace, Napoleon faced but one obstacle to complete success in France: Bordeaux, where a small army headed by the Duchesse d'Angoulême was entrenched. Despite instructions from the King that, for her own safety, she must join him in exile, Marie-Thérèse refused to leave. She wrote how she began and ended each day with her soldiers. Early morning Mass would be followed by inspection at their barracks where she would praise their loyalty, urge them on and confer with their leaders. Each day she would examine the list of volunteers at the town hall and each day the numbers would dwindle. It was getting harder to mobilize men now the King himself had fled France.

Napoleon understood that Marie-Thérèse would require careful handling and that he could not be seen to harm the 'Orphan of the Temple'. So he dispatched General Bertrand Clauzel to persuade the headstrong Princess to leave the country under the Emperor's protection. The ensuing standoff between Napoleon's aide-de-camp and the granddaughter of Empress Maria Theresa was detailed by Marie-Thérèse in her letter to Fanny and by General Clauzel in his reports.

Clauzel had stationed his troops on the banks of the Garonne River. He delegated a small group of prisoners to cross the river and deliver a message to Marie-Thérèse that read: 'Bordeaux is in my hands. I could enter it tomorrow if I chose to.' Disgusted with the disloyalty of so many of the French generals whom her uncle had decorated and who had become turncoats, like Decaen, causing local dissent, Marie-Thérèse refused to meet with Clauzel's emissaries. Instead, she sent a local politician, Monsieur Jean-Baptiste, Vicomte de Martignac to give Clauzel a defiant message of her own: she would never surrender. Clauzel retorted that he would 'occupy Bordeaux without firing one shot – when I want, how I want. Tell Madame well that I would already be in Bordeaux if I did not want above all to allow her to leave for wherever she wants to go. But tomorrow, I will have the emperor's authority recognized as sovereign in Bordeaux.'

Responding that she would 'teach the generals how one serves the King', she rode to the barracks of nearby Saint-Raphael, her horse flanked by two generals. As she stood calling for inspection, the regiment of National Guard formed a square around her. When the Princess charged them with their duty to fight, only twelve men stepped forward to swear their allegiance. One of the captains stepped forward and said, 'Your Highness can count on us to assure her personal safety.' She responded, 'It is not about my personal safety, but about service to the King! Will you or will you not serve?' The soldiers shrank, admitting they had no taste for civil war.

She traveled next to another barracks and here she faced further dissent. Some drowned out her words with cries of 'Vive l'Empereur!' Humiliated but not deterred, she proceeded to the Château Trompette, the ancient fortress that served as the home of the Régiment d'Angoulême, her own. Outside the castle walls a sentry stopped her and told her she could only proceed if her guards remained outside. 'I will enter alone,' she responded and passed across the drawbridge, but was stopped inside by the commander. 'What motive do you have, refusing my guards access to this fortress?' she demanded. 'I take orders from the King, not his relatives,' barked the soldier. 'Understand that my men will not fight other Frenchmen,' he warned. 'Then will you remain neutral if the National Guard and the King's loyal volunteers attack?' she asked. 'If the National Guard attacks, we will fire at them.' She looked at his subordinates and asked, 'Do you share the opinion of your leader?' They nodded affirmatively. At this precise moment she realized her efforts were futile. With great sadness she told them: 'Then you will no longer be considered Frenchmen, for they remain faithful to honor.'

One lone soldier broke ranks and stepped forward, 'Madame,' he said, 'I will not add to the number of traitors. I will die for the King, for you, before I betray my oath and I will follow you everywhere I can render myself useful.' Marie-Thérèse replied: 'I am happy with you, Captain; you will not make such a sacrifice.' The other soldiers voiced their disapproval but the soldier stood his ground. Marie-Thérèse issued them with a challenge stating that she was prepared to do her duty and they ought to follow her example. One last time, Marie-Thérèse surveyed the men: 'And do you not recognize me? Is this not the Angoulême Regiment to whom I speak? Is that not the name you carry? . . . And do you not call me your princess?' There was no response. Silence was her exit cue and she turned and reflected: 'It is so cruel, after twenty years of exile and unhappiness, I will have to expatriate once again. I, nevertheless, will never cease to swear – I make this vow: For France! Because I am French! You are no longer Frenchmen. About-face! Withdraw!'

She found Martignac and directed him to cross the river and tell General Clauzel 'that in happier times I distinguished him and now he has displayed his devotion. I only demand of him one thing: that is to postpone his entrance into Bordeaux until tomorrow. Tell him that is my wish.'

Marie-Thérèse determined to inspect the remaining 1,700 National Guard of the local garrison that afternoon and the people of Bordeaux crowded along the banks of the Garonne to watch. The white flag of the Bourbons flew on one side of the river while Clauzel and his men stood on the other displaying the colors of the Revolution. Clauzel, believing he had been duped, ordered his men to aim their guns at the royalists. The tension was unbearable as Marie-Thérèse arrived in her calèche. The crowd waited for her to speak, and she stood in the open-topped carriage so they could see and hear her. She addressed the Bordelaise: 'People of Bordeaux! The garrison will no longer protect you. I have come to ask you for one more sacrifice. Will you swear to obey my command?' The crowd replied that it would. She surveyed the throngs of people and the enemy on the other bank and declared: 'You have demonstrated great honor. Preserve your loyalty for better times. I order you to cease fighting.' The crowd then protested that they were willing to die for her. 'The King's niece commands you. Obey. Now, I am leaving you. It is time for me to bid you farewell.' As she sat down, the crowd broke ranks to cheer her. Clauzel, expecting an attack, ordered his soldiers to prepare to fire; but there was no onslaught. Instead, Marie-Thérèse threw ribbons and feathers from her hat to the cheering crowds as her carriage moved slowly out of the city.

Marie-Thérèse left behind her a farewell address to the citizens of Bordeaux, which someone pinned to the city wall the following morning. *The Times* of London published it in its entirety:

Brave Bordelais, Your fidelity is well known to me; your devotion, unlimited, does not permit you to foresee any danger: but my attachment for you, for every Frenchman, directs me to foresee it. My stay in your city being prolonged might aggravate circumstances, and bring down upon you the weight of vengeance. I have not the courage to behold Frenchmen unhappy, and to be the cause of their misfortune. I leave you, brave Bordelais, deeply penetrated with the feelings you have expressed, and can assure you that they shall be faithfully transmitted to the King. Soon, with God's assistance, under happier auspices, you shall witness my gratitude, and that of the Prince whom you love.

Marie-Thérèse

As crowds congregated to read her message, Clauzel arrived to take control of the city. The General told the people of Bordeaux that it was the Princess who had saved their lives. 'I would not have hesitated for one minute to shower you with bullets,' he told them, 'but she has written the most beautiful page of her own history. It is the duty of every soldier to respect such great courage.'

When apprized of his niece's actions, King Louis XVIII, now in Ghent, compared her to Marguerite d'Anjou, the fifteenth-century Princess of Lorraine, who married King Henry VI of England and led the Lancastrian troops on her husband's behalf in the War of the Roses. At the Tuileries, an awestruck Napoleon said of the Duchesse d'Angoulême: 'She is the only man in the family!'

Marie-Thérèse journeyed to the coastal town of Pauillac and boarded the English ship the *Wanderer* for a life in exile once more. As she explained to Fanny in her letter, although she had left most of her personal effects in Paris, she kept part of her diamond collection with her throughout. The ship sailed along the northern coast of Spain in bad weather and docked at last on April 8. The new King of Spain, Charles IV's son, Ferdinand, agreed to offer her asylum, but little military assistance, and realizing that once again it would be in England where she would find more help, she ordered her English captain to sail to the English Channel. On April 19, a year to the day that she had bid farewell to Hartwell for France, Marie-Thérèse came ashore at Plymouth at ten in the morning. Here, as she told Fanny, she was greeted by 'the sincerest cries of "hurrah!"' . . . women waved their handkerchiefs in the air and all of the carriages had been decorated with white cockades. This lasted through the many miles as I traveled to London, where I arrived on the 21st at the home of the ambassador [the Comte de la Châtre] to the King my uncle.'

La Châtre had distressing news for her: her husband had been taken prisoner by Napoleon's General de Grouchy in Pont-Saint-Esprit, despite a previous agreement to permit the Bourbon Prince to travel to Spain. The execution of the Duc d'Enghien came immediately to everyone's minds – Napoleon's message to the Bourbons some ten years since. La Châtre wrote to Blacas, Louis XVIII's minister, that the Duchesse d'Angoulême 'displayed the greatest courage on the receipt of this dreadful intelligence, but tears filled her eyes when she was alone with me'.

Marie-Thérèse had confided to Fanny that she had received a stream of threatening letters from Napoleon's generals, that 'everything demanded combat' and that, while she had been forced to flee, she was not ready to concede defeat. In London, she sprang into action, first writing to her cousin, the Duc de Bourbon, father of the murdered Duc d'Enghien, urging him, 'I know that the King desires that you immediately go to the Vendée, and I think that your presence there is very necessary: you will revive their spirits . . . this province is very important and necessary to our cause. Do not lose any time, I beseech you, to get there as soon as possible.' She also wrote to Louis XVIII in Ghent of her experiences in Bordeaux, proclaiming the Bordelais 'excellent', and her feelings of loyalty to the town where she had 'raise[d] the sword'. She angrily referred to Napoleon as 'that man', to Clauzel with contempt, and to the turncoat soldiers as 'cowards'.

A few days later, she received the welcome news that d'Angoulême had been set free, had sailed to Barcelona and had made his way to Madrid. She confided her deepest anxieties about her husband's whereabouts as well as her relief upon hearing about his safety in her letter to Fanny: 'how happy I am! He has suffered greatly, but Heaven has taken pity on him, and has returned him to us.' On May 9, she wrote again to the Duc de Bourbon. 'You can judge all I have suffered, upon learning that [my husband] had been taken prisoner and my happiness last Saturday, to learn from himself that he had arrived in Spain in good health'.

For a while, Marie-Thérèse and her husband had been able to correspond. Marie-Thérèse was told that these intimate letters had since found a wider audience as Napoleon had intercepted and published some of them. One could now read, for instance, that the Duke addressed his wife as 'my beloved *Gioia*' – meaning 'joy' in Italian. Although Marie-Thérèse had, in the past, accepted the fact that some of her letters would be opened by police and spies, she was furious that Napoleon would make her private letters public.

From the ambassador's home in London, Marie-Thérèse continued to wage her campaign to oust Napoleon. She knew that she could count on her old friend, the Prince Regent, so she petitioned him for men and munitions. The moment Napoleon had reached the shores of southern France, another allied coalition, comprising over 700,000 troops from England, Prussia, Nassau, Brunswick, Hanover, and the Netherlands, formed to do battle with 'the Usurper'. On June 12, Napoleon left Paris with 125,000 soldiers heading east, presumably to cross the Rhine. With about 74,000 of the troops, instead of waiting for an allied attack, he marched into Belgium. About seven miles southeast of Brussels, at Waterloo, 150,000 of the allied forces commanded by the Duke of Wellington and the Prussian General von Blücher surrounded the French army, and on June 18, 1815, the coalition pounded Napoleon's army into the ground, putting an end to what has become known as Napoleon's 'Hundred Days'.

The Duke of Wellington immediately sent a courier with word of the allied victory to Louis XVIII in nearby Ghent, who then made preparations for a second return to France and requested that Marie-Thérèse join him immediately.

The King entered Paris on July 8, but Marie-Thérèse decided to delay her return to the capital until the 27th. When she arrived she refused all pomp and circumstance. She was disgusted by both her uncle's cowardice and the fact that the Bourbons were returning to an occupied country. The allied governments were enraged that the former Emperor of the French seemed to enjoy the complicity and collaboration of so many French citizens, and they were going to be less forgiving now. This time, Marie-Thérèse resolved, she was not going to watch from the sidelines; this time, she would have a say in the governing of France.

CHAPTER XX
RESTORATION

W HEN THE BOURBONS were restored for a second time it was the
triumphant Duke of Wellington who presided as generalissimo
over the chaotic scenes in Paris. Prussian and British soldiers stood guard
on the road from Saint-Cloud to Paris and on the roof of the Tuileries.
When off duty they gambled at the Palais-Royal. Wellington had been
acting as mediator between the partisan politicians of France and the
ministers and monarchs of Europe who were in disunity about the
country's future. A number of proposals had been considered: one,
supported by the Czar, who was angry with Louis for having rejected
his daughter, Grand Duchess Anne, as the wife of the Duc de Berry
because of her religion, was to put the Duc d'Orléans on the throne. There
were factions who believed the monarchy of Louis XVIII to be impotent,
like that of his brother before him. Louis argued that he had not fled out
of cowardice, but because he had had insufficient military support. He
also pointed a finger at the allies for permitting Napoleon to serve out his
captivity in such proximity to France, and thus make easy his return. This
time Napoleon would be confined on the barren, remote South Atlantic
island of St Helena.

France would be forced to pay huge war reparations to the allies. In
Paris, representatives of the Austrian, Italian and Dutch governments
concentrated on retrieving artworks from the Louvre and elsewhere
looted by Napoleon from their respective countries. The most conspic-
uous of these was the famous bronze horses which the Emperor had had
removed from St Mark's Square in Venice and had perched atop the arch
at the Place du Carrousel. Despite Talleyrand's attempts to stop the
removal of the sculpture, the horses were now going home. The Pope sent

his own emissary, the sculptor, Canova, who reclaimed works of art and manuscripts belonging to the Vatican.

Marie-Thérèse deduced that, as she had always been most warmly welcomed in Bordeaux, that region would best serve as her stage. On August 15 she traveled there, after a brief stay in Paris, to consolidate her support. She and her husband, who had been traveling from the south after his sojourn in Spain, met on the road to the city of Bordeaux. Their visit was a triumph. On the banks of the Garonne a pavilion had been constructed to welcome the couple, who rowed toward it on a gondola. Once ashore, the Duke mounted a horse to enter the city while Marie-Thérèse was placed inside a specially prepared carriage. Her horses were unfastened and she was lifted in her carriage through the streets to cheering crowds. A new flag was commissioned by the citizens of Bordeaux: the Bourbon white now edged in a green trim – the color of the d'Angoulême livery.

From Bordeaux, at the beginning of September, Marie-Thérèse traveled to Toulouse where once again, the horses were detached from her carriage, it was hoisted in the air and she was received with cheers. On September 11, she returned to the Tuileries to stand by her uncle and ensure she had a say in the appointments of his ministers and to his court. Five days after her return, Joseph Fouché, a former Jacobin who had voted for the execution of Louis XVI and whom Marie-Thérèse called the 'butcher of Lyon' for his revolutionary misdeeds, was dismissed from his post as Minister of Police and sent to Dresden as ambassador. Shortly after that Talleyrand – 'Prince Weathervane' – was forced to offer his resignation. Marie-Thérèse also understood that it was time for her uncle to humor their 'cousin', Czar Alexander. On September 22, Marie-Thérèse met with the Czar at the Tuileries, and they talked for hours. Not long thereafter, despite Marie-Thérèse's antipathy toward the moderates, the Duc de Richelieu, whom the Czar had appointed Governor of Odessa in 1804 and who was Alexander's personal favorite as a choice for Louis's new Foreign Minister, was given the job.

As at Hartwell, Marie-Thérèse took charge of protocol at the royal palaces, relying on her own etiquette expert, Monsieur Abraham, whose memory of Versailles was flawless. It was decided that the King's livery would be blue, silver and red; the Comte d'Artois's, green and pink; and both the d'Angoulêmes and the Duc de Berry would have green and gold.

As she had during her return to France one year earlier, Marie-Thérèse selected her staff for the royal household at the Tuileries from among those who had been close to her mother and from her own friends from childhood and years of exile. This time, she embarked with less emotion and more calculation; although the King had stayed the course of the Charter, Marie-Thérèse felt little need for pretense: there would be little forgiveness for Bonapartists and absolutely no nobles of the Empire among her retinue.

King Louis XVIII, the parliamentary Bourbon King, began his day quite differently from that of previous Kings of France. Instead of allowing the public into his bedroom, he prayed there alone. Members of the court now congregated in the Salle du Trône and the Grand Cabinet, public rooms, and in rooms like the Salon Bleu and the Salon de la Paix, again, not in the chamber of His Most Christian Majesty, which was now on view to anyone in the city who wanted to pay for a ticket to enter. Adopting the more simple daily routine of country life he had observed at Hartwell, the King would begin his day early and eat his meals earlier than was the form at Versailles. Louis also liked to take afternoon drives: that exercise was not only a pleasurable holdover from his Hartwell days, but it was also a way for him to ensure a presence in Paris, the nexus of power. Although for the moment, the English dominion over France may not have been popular with the people, visiting Englishmen would always be welcome at the court of Louis XVIII, and he would never forget their kindness to him and his family.

The year before, when Louis stayed at Compiègne, he had, despite being appalled by the decor, chosen to ignore Napoleon's intrusive redecoration of the Bourbon home and referred to the Emperor as a 'good concierge'. Upon the family's second return, Marie-Thérèse ordered the removal of each and every bee, eagle and 'N' from all the royal palaces that Napoleon had occupied on the Île de France. She was not prepared to endure the presence of the Bonapartists any longer – not at her table, nor in the King's cabinet. Her father had asked that she forgive the people of France, but she would not tolerate Napoleon's warriors. Neither would she suffer the presence of her cousin, the Duc d'Orléans, whose movements she had been monitoring. During the Hundred Days, before his escape to England, Orléans had overtly shown his contempt for the regime of Louis XVIII. While Marie-Thérèse had been leading the King's troops in Bordeaux, Orléans, before leaving France, had ordered the soldiers under his command in Lille to return to their barracks rather than fight. Once in exile, he had refused to join his sovereign in Ghent and, in a signal that he was most definitely his father's son, he not only circulated pamphlets criticizing the Bourbon King, he attempted to persuade Wellington to place him on the throne of France instead of his cousin. For now, Louis decided to listen to his niece and banish Orléans from French soil.

Legitimists in France also proved unforgiving. Two of Napoleon's twenty-six Marshals were murdered toward the end of the Hundred Days: General Ramel was killed in Toulouse, and Brune's body was tossed into the Rhône River in Avignon. This course of vengeance was the beginning of what some refer to as *La Terreur Blanche* (The White Terror), when the Bourbons and their sympathizers, underneath their white banner, demanded justice. It was then that Louis began serially to dismiss ministers and strip men of their peerages. In December, Napoleon's accomplices were put on trial. Two Marshals, Ney and Labédoyère, and the Duc de La Valette, were condemned to death, and over 250 Bonapartists were given prison sentences. Despite the tearful pleas of Mesdames de La Valette and Ney, Marie-Thérèse refused to intervene and obtain pardons for any of them, believing that traitors had to be punished. The public was stunned by such seemingly uncharacteristic behavior and the episode earned her the new epithet 'Madame Rancune' – Rancor. She had absolutely no doubts that her judgment had been correct until the early 1820s when a book on Napoleon's expedition to Russia by the Comte de Ségur was published recounting tales of Ney's unsurpassed courage. Marie-Thérèse is reported to have said: 'If only I had known,' and wept, regretting her own stubborn refusal to intercede on Ney's behalf.[1]

During *La Terreur Blanche*, Marie-Thérèse decided to take action on an issue that had plaguing her since she was sixteen: she wanted corroboration, documentation and proof, once and for all, that her brother was dead. To this end she broke her silence and divulged the story told to her by Dr Pelletan to Louis XVIII so that his ministers could conduct an enquiry into the matter. Pelletan, now nearly seventy years old, was interviewed by many of Louis's advisors, but they could come to no conclusion. An extremely frustrated Dr Pelletan wrote to Marie-Thérèse detailing his attempts to place the jar containing Louis Charles's heart in her possession, and explaining that his efforts had been thwarted by bureaucrats. Although the courtiers who surrounded Marie-Thérèse remained sensitive to the pain any mention of her brother caused, it was in fact the very personnel on Louis's staff who, working on behalf of their King, should have followed the matter through to its completion. The King wanted public proof, as did his niece, that Louis Charles had perished in the prison. There could be no funeral or public memorial allowing the public to grieve as there was no body; instead there seemed to be ever more speculation and fascination with the mystery of the death of the boy King. Marie-Thérèse continued to walk the painful emotional line of being both suspicious of any deception and of discovering the truth about her beloved little brother. Dr Pelletan's letter, which detailed his account of the journey of her brother's heart, along with the reliquary itself, never reached her.

In 1815, Louis XVII would have been thirty years old. That December a young man aged about thirty arrived in Saint-Malo declaring to be Charles de Navarre, King Louis XVII of France. Shortly thereafter he was arrested in Rouen for vagrancy, but by this time his story had spread throughout France. He wrote pitiable letters to the Duchesse d'Angoulême begging her to come and see him. His trial, in a small town in Brittany, caused a bout of national hysteria. Decazes, the Minister of Police, took matters into his own hands and sent the man to jail to await trial. The fact that a senior minister had involved himself immediately aroused suspicion. Madame Simon was taken out of her asylum to testify and she once again claimed that Louis Charles was alive and that he had been lifted from Temple Prison in a laundry basket. When she publicly offered to travel to Saint-Malo to identify the young man, Decazes and his men declared her insane.

Locked away in a provincial prison, the young vagrant received extravagant presents from citizens all over France. His story was like that of Hervagault's before him, and bore similarities to Regnault-Warin's popular tale *Le Cimetière de la Madeleine*. For the King, each new young pretender raised questions as to the legitimacy of his monarchy; for Marie-Thérèse the uncertainty was debilitating. She secretly sent two men to visit and question the young man in his cell. Rumors spread that even Madame de Tourzel had visited the man, and that she, too, believed him. Marie-Thérèse gave her first *valet de chambre*, the Chevalier de Turgy, a list of questions to ask him. The note was intercepted by the police and never reached him; it did, however, confirm that Marie-Thérèse took seriously claims that her brother might be alive. On February 18, 1818, the young man was sentenced to seven years in prison but four years into his sentence he died in Mont-Saint-Michel jail. It was later revealed that the man was probably one Mathurin Bruneau, a shoemaker.

The issue would not die. That same month, the King recalled that a young man arrived at the Tuileries in the early evening. Somehow, he was able to trail the servants into the dining hall, where he announced to the King, 'I am Charles de Navarre.' It did not take long for everyone to determine that the man was delusional and yet another in a parade of men determined to be acclaimed as the long-lost brother of Marie-Thérèse of France. The King determined to try to quash the controversy once and for all and locate the body of little Louis Charles. He instructed Decazes to write a letter to the Prefect of the Police to find Louis XVII's remains and a long and expensive search began at the cemetery Sainte-Marguerite; but it, again, turned up nothing.

Eliciting even more focus on the imprisoned children of the late King and Queen, within a year after Bruneau's arrest, Marie-Thérèse's prison memoir, corrected and edited by Louis XVIII, was published along with the accounts by Cléry and Hüe in a book titled *Mémoires particuliers sur la captivité de la famille royale à la tour du Temple*. The King hoped that the circulation of this publication would not only garner sympathy for his reign, but that it would also lay to rest the public's notion that Marie-Thérèse might have any doubt about her brother's death as the prison memoir, again, emphatically stated that she, Marie-Thérèse, was absolutely certain that her brother had died in the Temple Prison. Although the book was a great success in terms of popularity and sales, both in France and abroad, rumor and counter-rumor concerning Louis Charles's fate continued. On March 5, 1817, *The Times* of London reprinted an abridged, third-person summarized version of the memoir, with the introduction: 'A work has appeared purporting to be written by this Princess, on the subject of the cruel confinement of herself and her Royal relations in the Temple. We know not whether it be authentic: at least it is written with simplicity and without exaggeration.'

Six years later, the journal of Marie-Thérèse would be brought out once again in a collection called *Mémoires relatifs à la Révolution*. At that same time, an unauthorized edition appeared. Marie-Thérèse accused Madame de Chanterenne of having betrayed her: it was the only dispute the two would ever have. Madame de Chanterenne had been in possession of two copies of the letters and journals written by Marie-Thérèse. The first was a copy that she herself had made before returning the original papers to Cléry when Marie-Thérèse had asked for them back. The second collection was, in fact, the original documents, which the Duchesse d'Angoulême had returned to her dear friend Renête, after King Louis XVIII had read and edited the account. Happily for Madame de Chanterenne, however, Marie-Thérèse learned that Renète was not responsible for the surreptitious edition. Marie-Thérèse found out that it was none other than Madame de Soucy, whom she had always found irritating, and to whom she had also given a copy as a souvenir of their journey to Vienna.

On Tuesday, January 16, 1816, *Le Moniteur* announced that Saturday, January 20, would be a national day of mourning. On that day, the King, Marie-Thérèse and the Princes of the Blood held a solemn prayer vigil at the royal crypt at Saint-Denis to commemorate the anniversary of the deaths of King Louis XVI and Marie Antoinette. Significantly, the King's last will and testament, in which he begged for Frenchmen to forgive one another, was read in churches around the country. While Frenchmen grieved in each other's arms, Marie-Thérèse wept inside the enclosed, underground crypt in private. Just two weeks later, in early February, Queen Marie Antoinette's last letter to her sister-in-law, Madame Elisabeth, was found and read aloud in the Chamber of Deputies. It had been among Robespierre's papers, which had been confiscated on 9 Thermidor. The letter made such an impression on the politicians that they decreed that each year, on October 16, the anniversary of Marie Antoinette's death, the text of the letter would be read in every church in France. When the deputies came to the Tuileries to inform Marie-Thérèse of their decision, one of their members made an emotional speech praising Marie Antoinette's 'lofty virtues', and flattering the Duchess by comparing her to her mother. Marie-Thérèse only offered a brief and perfunctory comment. The group waited for further reaction, but there was none.

Louis XVIII's new militia included the return of the Swiss Guard, a carefully appointed royalist 'Garde Royale'. Louis made his brother, d'Artois, head of the less loyal National Guard and in another act of reconciliation, on February 5, the National Guard was fêted at a celebration at the Tuileries. To wild applause, Marie-Thérèse visited all of the twelve banquet tables, which had been adorned with escutcheons of the great Kings of France. She had proved as valiant a soldier as any and the military admired her. Five hundred women and a thousand men, recalling Marie-Thérèse's gallant efforts in Bordeaux the year before, stood and cheered her. Shortly afterwards the King commissioned the painter Baron Gros to depict the moment the Duchesse d'Angoulême bid farewell to the people of Bordeaux in April 1815, another fine piece of propaganda organized by Louis XVIII.

Others continued to pay tribute to Marie-Thérèse for her suffering, bravery and piety. Madame de Chateaubriand, wife of the celebrated writer and statesman, founded the Infirmerie Marie-Thérèse in Paris, a shelter for former émigrés and priests who had suffered during the Revolution. The structure would be completed in 1819. First to contribute to the hospice in her honor was the King of Prussia, widower of Marie-Thérèse's great friend, Queen Louise. That same year Louis XVIII turned the prison cell at the *Conciergerie* in which Marie Antoinette spent her final weeks into a public shrine. And in recognition of her piety, the Church had given Marie-Thérèse the honor of naming bishops and cardinals.

While the King was building his portfolio of tributes to the past in an attempt to shore up the Bourbon legend, the Duc d'Angoulême, looking to the example of the revered first Bourbon King, Henri IV, found a new and productive role for himself. He sought to unite quarreling factions around France, and in doing so earned respect and a growing reputation as a thoughtful man and skillful negotiator. He also established a power base in the south and then toward the west as he rode to the borders to evacuate the Spanish soldiers who had invaded during Napoleon's return.

Although it was widely acknowledged that the d'Angoulêmes were the powers behind the throne, their union had failed to produce any children. Marie-Thérèse was nearly forty. The Bourbon dynasty needed a son and heir in order to continue, or at the very least, legitimate royal children. For this the Bourbons turned to the King's younger brother, the thirty-eight-year-old Duc de Berry. Although the Duke already had a common-law wife and two daughters in London, his English family was not recognized by his uncle, the King, nor by the Church. The King selected an official bride with the blessing of Marie-Thérèse. This would be seventeen-year-old Princess Marie Caroline of Naples, granddaughter of Marie Antoinette's favorite sister, Maria Carolina of the Two Sicilies, and niece of the wife of the current Duc d'Orléans. She was a Bourbon as well as a niece of the Habsburg Emperor, Franz of Austria.

In preparation for Marie Caroline's arrival, Marie-Thérèse organized the bride's multi-national household staff and a lavish ancien-régime-style wedding feast was set for June. A reception was prepared for Marie Caroline in the southern seaport city of Marseille echoing the welcome given in October 1600 to Henri IV's second wife, the Italian Princess Marie de' Medici, so spectacular and significant that it was immortalized by the great painter, Peter Paul Rubens. Cannon roared, a flotilla appeared, and the town was bedecked in crimson for the very young – and very sexy – Marie Caroline. She remained 'in quarantine' for two weeks and then was paraded through the towns of France, where she was warmly welcomed as the hope for the future of the dynasty.

On June 15, Marie Caroline arrived in the forest at Fontainebleau, which served as a romantic backdrop to the couple's first meeting. Tapestries had been placed on the grass inside a great tent inside which the royal family would host a great feast. Louis XVIII, who was now so

fat he could no longer walk by himself and had to be carried in a chair by
servants, made the formal introductions, and upon presenting the teenage
bride to her new sister-in-law, referred to Marie-Thérèse as 'our angel'.

Although the Duc de Berry had been corresponding with his fiancée,
and the two had flirted in their letters, he really had no idea what to
expect. When at last he met his bride he was immediately smitten. Despite
the fact that Marie Caroline's French was very bad, the young Sicilian
was recognized by everyone as a breath of fresh air. Just as Louis XV had
been enchanted with the delicious young Marie Antoinette, Louis XVIII
was sure that his nephew would find his bride irresistible – and, hopefully,
fertile.

Others were less impressed. James Gallatin, son of the now US
ambassador to France, Albert Gallatin, considered the new Duchesse
de Berry to be spoilt and bad mannered. James Gallatin recorded many
such private opinions of the French royal family in his journal. He
thought that the Duc d'Angoulême appeared very stern but knew that
he was, in fact, a kind man. The Duc de Berry was extremely handsome
and was great fun. As for Marie-Thérèse, she enjoyed a special place of
honor in Gallatin's heart. He, like many people, regarded her as a saint,
and the two exchanged many conversations during which he remained
impressed by her kindness, sweetness and compassion.

Two days after the Fontainebleau festivities, the official wedding
took place at Notre Dame cathedral in Paris. The interior of the
church was illuminated by thousands of candles. Baskets of fruits and
flowers, symbolizing the fertility of the dynasty, were suspended mid-
air, banners proclaiming the glories of France swagged across columns, and the nave was festooned with blue velvet embroidered with
gold fleurs-de-lys. Parisians had been celebrating since early morning
and women scrambled for their most elaborate gowns for the occasion. The bride, dressed in white satin embroidered with silver lamé,
wore a glittering diamond diadem. Marie-Thérèse was attired in white
silk, her hair coiffed with her rarely worn diamonds and a white
ostrich feather. The obese King, in vivid royal blue trimmed with lace
and pearls, ornamented himself with both the Regent and Sancy
diamonds, the legendary and historic gems that had disappeared
during the Revolution, when they were allegedly stolen from the
treasury by marauders. They had reappeared just as mysteriously as
they had disappeared. The Comte d'Artois sported the uniform of the
Colonel General of the National Guard; the Duc d'Angoulême the
uniform of Grand Admiral; the Prince de Condé the white and gold

uniform of Colonel General of the French Infantry; and the groom the court robes of King Henri IV.

The formal celebrations took place later that afternoon at the Tuileries Palace, contrary to Marie-Thérèse's wishes: Louis knew she hated the place and would have preferred Versailles but the King insisted the wedding take place in the capital. Marie-Thérèse, as ever, performed her duty impeccably and chose to place her own stamp on the festivities. For the wedding celebrations she had planned an evening of nostalgia. Two-thirds of the invited guests were courtiers from the ancien régime who had served at Versailles before the Revolution. With a wand in his hand, the first maître d'hôtel escorted the King to his table for the fabled *grand couvert* repast; whenever His Majesty required a drink, he would proclaim the monarch's desire in a loud voice, as was the ancient custom. The officers of the crown, the aides-de-camp, the men of the chamber and others on duty stood in lines on either side of the royal table. No one was permitted a seat except for the nobility with the rank of no lower than a duke or duchess. At the King's table sat the royal Princes and Princesses – with the exception of the Orléans family, who, because the event had been organized by Marie-Thérèse, had been pointedly excluded. There was a magnificent display of fireworks featuring a Temple of Hymen, a symbol of the bride's virginity and the hope that she would become the mother of a future king. After the illuminations, the King and the d'Angoulêmes escorted the newlyweds to their new home, the Élysée Palace on the Faubourg Saint-Honoré for the ceremony leading to the consummation of the marriage. The *grand aumônier*, the Bishop of Hermopolis, blessed the marriage bed and the royal party bid goodnight to the Duc de Berry and his bride.

That summer, the de Berrys settled into their home near the Champs-Élysées. They could often be seen arm in arm with their heads together on promenades. They were both fun loving: the young bride was vivacious, and it was clear that this was truly a love match. The people of Paris soon learned that the Duchesse de Berry, upon hearing the sound of her husband's footsteps, would run down the stairs and leap into his arms. Her husband would then carry her back up the stairs. Some of her household staff delighted in the romance; while others maintained that the young bride needed to be taught better manners. Marie-Thérèse for one dismissed her young sister-in-law as silly, frivolous and ill educated and brought in her etiquette expert, Monsieur Abraham, to teach the Duchess to dance and learn the ways of the French court, while she, herself, wasted little more time thinking about the young bride.

There may have been harmony at the Élysée Palace, but all was not well at the Tuileries. Almost immediately after the wedding of the de Berrys, the d'Angoulêmes left Paris again for a tour of the royalist south and west of France. Although Marie-Thérèse would be hailed, her husband's position there had changed. While Marie-Thérèse and the Comte d'Artois were deeply politicized ultra-royalists, wanting a return to such ancien régime policies as less freedom for the press, more power for the Church, and complete sovereignty for the King, Louis XVIII was more pragmatic – the consummate politician. The King and his inner circle, Richelieu, Decazes and a handful of others, were moderates. They adhered to the changes that the Charter of France had implemented, guaranteeing a parliamentary government.

There were frequent arguments between the King and his brother, d'Artois, and between the King and Marie-Thérèse, and Marie-Thérèse had begun to fight with her own husband, who had grown to admire the parliamentary form of government when he had lived in England. From that time on, although he served his family, he remained a moderate. Husband and wife often toured the regions of France at cross-purposes: she, to remind the royalists that their sacrifices would not ever be forgotten; he, on behalf of Decazes and the government position of compromise. The English statesman, Lord Glenbervie, wrote in his journal on Monday, November 24, 1817: 'It is universally said that the Duc d'Angoulême is become a proselyte to the Ministers, and that to make this generally known has been the principal object of his late tour. It is a common report that on this account he was very ill received in the Vendée.'

The King, for his part, continued to show his affection for his New Antigone, always kissing her hand in front of others; however, during one of their arguments, he accused her of becoming akin to 'Goneril and Regan', King Lear's treacherous daughters. She, whom some described as taut and emotionless, would apparently lie down on the floor and cry hysterically, pleading with her uncle to change his politics. The King wanted peace in the country, among his ministers and his family, and even went so far as to instruct his favorite, Decazes, to visit Marie-Thérèse on her birthday with good wishes from the politicians she abhorred.

That December there was indeed good reason for the King to be in a magnanimous mood: the Duchesse de Berry was pregnant. Marie-Thérèse was so excited about the prospect of a Bourbon heir that she put to one side her misgivings about Marie Caroline and her own longings for a child and decided she would oversee the pregnancy personally. The ebullient King softened to the extent that he allowed the Duc d'Orléans

back into the country. Marie-Thérèse was furious. It was Gaston d'Orléans who had joined the Frondeurs against Louis XIV; Philippe
d'Orléans who, she believed, had caused her parents to be murdered;
and she remained convinced that his son, Louis-Philippe, was nothing
more than a menace. Others agreed. James Gallatin recorded in his
journal that the Duc d'Orléans, like his father before him, had political
ambitions of his own. The Comte de Villèle asserted that the Duc
d'Orléans had publicly announced that he would have no trouble don-
ning the tri-colored symbols of the Revolution. According to Villèle,
Louis-Philippe had also openly declared his vehement disappointment
that, although Wellington's emissaries had discussed the idea of giving
him the crown, it had gone to the senior branch of the Bourbons. Almost
immediately upon his return, Louis-Philippe, in an echo of his own father,
installed himself at the Palais-Royal (a property returned to him courtesy
of the head of the family, Louis XVIII) and set about establishing it as the
rallying point for anti-Bourbon dissent.

While Marie-Thérèse, the Comte d'Artois and the King continued to
battle over politics, the Duchesse de Berry was concerned with but one
argument: her husband's refusal to give up his mistresses. Like father, like
son. In the 1770s after having married his own Italian bride, the Duke's
father, d'Artois installed one of the most sensual boudoirs imaginable at
his Château de Bagatelle in the Bois de Boulogne in Paris. Replete with
mirrors, erotic paintings and a rose-colored bed, d'Artois's 'pleasure
palace' provided an escape from the bride he found repulsive. There
he seduced a long list of paramours. De Berry, despite finding his wife
adorable, nonetheless maintained an exhaustive schedule of extramarital
liaisons with the likes of Marie Sophie de la Roche, Joséphine Deux de la
Roserie, and a Mademoiselle de Saint-Ange, who were all members of the
Comédie-Française, another actress named Résica Lebreton, the ballerina
Eugénie Virginie Oreille, and others, including Louise Thiryfoq, who gave
birth to a daughter fathered by de Berry.

James Gallatin recorded in his diary in 1817 an episode in which both
he and the Duc de Berry had been involved. The farcical scene, which
could have been written by Molière, transpired as follows:

I had rather an unfortunate adventure some few nights since, but I hope
will never get to father's ears. After going to the opera, a charming little
danseuse, whose acquaintance I had only just made, asked me if I
would sup with her at her apartment. Much to my surprise I found the
greatest luxury – some person evidently in the background. A round

table with *couverts* for two. We had just commenced to sup when I
heard a noise in the antechamber. My charmer exclaimed, '*Mon Dieu,
je suis perdue, cachez-vous*' [My God! I am lost! Hide!] I rushed behind
a curtain. The door opened, and to my dismay I recognized the voice of
the Duc de Berry. He said, 'So mademoiselle has an *amant.*' Clare
tremblingly answered, '*Non, Monseigneur*, it was only mamma who I
was giving a little supper to as you did not arrive.' He asked, 'What has
become of her?' 'She has gone, Monseigneur, as she was not properly
dressed to receive your Highness.' By bad luck I had left my hat on a
chair. The Duke picked it up and said with a laugh, 'So, madame, *votre
mere* wears a man's hat, which she has forgotten.'

I felt it was time for me to discover myself, no matter what the
consequences might be. I stepped out from behind the curtain, saying,
'Monseigneur, it is my hat; I am mademoiselle's mother.' He broke into
fits of laughter, poor Clare into tears. He laughed so heartily that I
could not help joining him; he then became serious and in the kindest
manner said, 'Young man, you have acted in a most honorable manner
not to play eavesdropper. *Tout est pardonné.* Let us sup together.'
Clare rang and ordered another *couvert* to be laid, and we had a most
cheerful supper. When he rose to leave he begged me to accompany
him, which of course, I did. Going down the stairs he took me by the
arm and said most kindly, 'Here we have met as Mr Smith and Mr
Jones' . . . He always speaks English to me, even at Court . . . I met the
Duc yesterday. He burst out laughing and said, with a twinkle in his
eyes, 'Have you seen your friend, Mr. Jones, lately? Mr. Smith, I hear,
has gone back to England.'[2]

On July 13, the day after these events, a baby girl was born to the Duc
and Duchesse de Berry, but died the following day. The heartbroken
young Duchess tearfully apologized to her husband for their loss, as well
as for the disappointment of having given birth to a girl. The Duc de Berry
tried to assuage her grief by gently joking that if the baby had been a boy
there would have been those who would have declared him another man's
son. That night, the infant was buried at the foot of the coffin of Louis
XVI in the royal crypt at Saint-Denis. Madame de Gontaut-Biron, who
had been chosen as governess to the child, recalled in her memoir that she,
the Bishop of Amiens and the Dowager Duchesse de Lévis accompanied
the tiny casket to its grave. The next morning, Madame Biron recounted
every detail of the baby's funeral to Marie-Thérèse, and when she
informed Marie-Thérèse that she had stopped to pray beside the coffin

of the late King, Louis XVI, Marie-Thérèse broke down, took the woman's hand and placed it on her own heart.

Miles away in Eishausen, Germany, Philip Scharre, the faithful servant of the Dark Count and Countess, also died, taking all information he had about 'Vavel de Versay' and his mysterious companion to the grave. The count replaced Scharre with Johanna Schmidt's husband, who was also instructed to operate under the same secretive conditions. On May 14, 1818, Charlotte, the Duchess of Hildburghausen died. Before she passed away, she gathered her children – including Joseph, the Duke of Saxe-Altenburg; Charlotte, later Princess of Württemberg; Thérèse, who married King Ludwig I of Bavaria; Louise, who married Guillaume, Prince and Duke of Nassau; and Eduard, who married a Hohenzollern princess – and, as a matter or urgency, made them swear that they would assume the responsibility of maintaining the secret of the identity of the couple who lived in Castle Eishausen and that they would offer the mysterious pair all the protection and assistance they required during their lifetimes.

CHAPTER XXI
BIRTH, DEATH
AND A NEW DAUPHINE

TWICE A YEAR, on January 21 and October 16 – dates she dreaded – Marie-Thérèse endured the public anniversaries of her parents' murders. Whilst mourning past events and the violent deaths of so many close to her she also feared for the future: the possibility that enemies – and there were many – would strike again. There were constant threats on her life and the lives of her family members stemming from various political factions as well as from the unbalanced who wanted notoriety. To the people of France, she remained a powerful symbol of suffering, but because she remained childless, she was also pitied.

Marie-Thérèse now focused her hopes on a new heir to the throne. Her sister-in-law became pregnant once again just a few months after the death of her daughter. On September 13, 1818, Marie Caroline gave birth to the son they had all hoped for, but sadly the infant lived for only a few hours. By the end of 1818, Marie Caroline was pregnant once more, and on September 21, 1819, she gave birth to a second baby girl. Although the Duc de Berry already had a daughter named Louise with his English common-law wife, who was now living in Paris with their children, the royal baby was christened Louise. Though of course not heir because of Salic law, this new baby, Princess Louise, was at least healthy, and the family was jubilant.

By 1819, the relationship between the King and Marie-Thérèse had become so fraught that he refused to allow her to visit her beloved Bordeaux. He was jealous of her popularity there and also afraid that her political campaigning would backfire on his own administration. So she remained in Paris, under his thumb. She sometimes visited Madame de

Chanterenne and other friends and also spent a great deal of time with her brother and sister-in-law, often stopping by the Élysée Palace to play her favorite game, 'loto'.[1]

On December 19, to celebrate Marie-Thérèse's forty-first birthday, the de Berrys asked the Théâtre du Vaudeville to put on the plays *M. Champagne* and *La Somnambule*. On New Year's Day, 1820, the royal family held their customary *grand couvert* at the Tuileries, and, on January 21, as usual, there was a mournful service at the royal crypt at Saint-Denis in memory of the late King Louis XVI. Although the entire family knew it took days for Marie-Thérèse to recover from the anniversary of the 21st, the de Berrys rather insensitively organized two balls to ring in carnival season, the first just two days later on January 23, at the Élysée Palace.

Shrove Tuesday, the last opportunity to frolic before the subdued Lent season, was approaching when on Sunday night, February 13, the Duc and Duchesse de Berry attended a performance at the Opéra, then on the rue de Richelieu. Marie Caroline appeared radiant. The de Berrys adored attending cultural events, while the Duke also found it a convenient place to recruit mistresses. This evening promised to be particularly stunning. To celebrate the end of a madcap month of masked balls, the program was to include two ballets, *Le Carnaval de Venise* and Starzer's *Les Noces de Gamache*, and the opera *Le Rossignol*. The first presentation was wildly popular in Paris at the time and was received with thunderous applause. During the intermission, the de Berrys left their box to visit the Duc and Duchesse d'Orléans in theirs. The curtain was about to go up on *Les Noces de Gamache* starring one of the Duc de Berry's mistresses, Virginie Oreille, when Marie Caroline informed her husband that she was exhausted and needed to go home. He, along with Marie Caroline's first equerry, the Comte de Mesnard, and her lady-in-waiting, Madame de Béthisy, escorted the Duchess to her carriage. The Duc de Berry waved goodbye from the doorway. Suddenly, Marie Caroline saw her husband stagger: he had been stabbed. Marie Caroline, without thinking that she might be the assailant's next victim, fought with Madame de Béthisy to get out of the carriage. She rushed to her husband's side and held him in her arms. Mesnard ordered the carriage driver to summon the Comte d'Artois, the King and the Duc and Duchesse d'Angoulême to the theater. Madame de Gontaut had also been awakened and was instructed to bring the infant Princess Louise to her father's side. By the time they all arrived, the Duke had been moved to a private room upstairs at the opera house.

Outside, crowds gathered to wait for news. The eminent author and statesman François-René de Chateaubriand made his way inside the theater via a door on the left. He found himself in an ante-chamber among members of the audience who had refused to evacuate the house. Chateaubriand spied the Duc d'Orléans and later wrote that he had a 'badly disguised expression of jubilation behind the contrite face he imposed; he saw himself closer to the throne'.[2]

Marie Caroline sobbed and whispered constant words of love while her husband lay gravely wounded. Marie-Thérèse quietly prayed and tried to be of service. Two doctors arrived, but there was little they could do as the knife had punctured a lung. James Gallatin, who was among the small group of people in attendance, was stunned when he heard de Berry, barely audibly, telling his wife, 'Stay calm for the sake of the child that you carry.' He had revealed their secret. The Duchesse de Berry was pregnant once again, though they had not yet told the family. Marie Caroline sent for her husband's English common-law wife and two daughters, and embracing the girls in front of their father, she assured him that they would always be her children as well. Madame de Gontaut-Biron recalled that she was overwhelmed by Marie Caroline's poise, and was equally awestruck when the Duchesse d'Angoulême interjected and said: 'We will all adopt them.' The King would later ennoble the two English girls 'Comtesse de Vierzon' and 'Comtesse d'Issoudun' and provide them with incomes.

In the middle of the night, the Duc de Berry asked for a priest. By dawn he was dead. James Gallatin recalled the private moment of grief:

> Monsieur de Brissac . . . motioned me to kneel and, handing the brush from the holy-water bowl, motioned me to sprinkle the corpse, which I did. I would not believe the Duke was dead. He was still sitting up in a large gilt armchair, his head supported by a cushion . . . It was a sight I will never forget.[3]

Distraught, Marie Caroline told Madame de Gontaut-Biron that she was to raise Princess Louise herself as she wished to die alongside her husband. Marie-Thérèse and Madame de Gontaut-Biron escorted the pregnant young widow back to her home and into her bedroom. Still drenched in her husband's blood, she grabbed a pair of scissors and cut off her hair, screaming, 'Charles! Charles! No hand but thine will caress my head.' Handing the clump to Madame de Gontaut-Biron, she directed: 'Give this hair to my daughter and tell her I cut it off the day her father died.' Marie-Thérèse and Madame de Gontaut-Biron helped undress the nearly delirious Marie Caroline and tried to persuade her to get some sleep. The young widow refused to sleep in any chamber but her husband's. The family, worried about Marie Caroline's health and the safety of her unborn child and her daughter, insisted that she move from the Élysée Palace, a place where she had known only love and happiness, into the Tuileries.

The Duke's assassin was a saddler named Louis-Pierre Louvel. A fanatical Bonapartist, Louvel had openly sworn that he would murder the last of the Bourbon line able to produce an heir. Louvel was arrested and in June was sent to the guillotine. D'Artois and Marie-Thérèse blamed the King's minister, Decazes, and his liberal policies for the incident. Decazes, the handsome young Minister of Police, had, in that capacity, repressed royalist protests against the Charter. He had become so influential over Louis that he was able to persuade the King to dismiss the House, which led to a moderate majority in parliament.[4] As the man who had roused the ire of the ultra-royalists, ironically, his new, moderate assembly had voted for fewer powers for the police. When interviewed by the police, the usually apolitical Marie Caroline railed against Decazes. The entire family pressured Louis to dismiss his most trusted advisor, but the King would not yield. On February 18, Marie-Thérèse went down on her knees, and in a vitriolic explosion of passion, told the King that she would no longer dine with him and that she was considering leaving Paris. The King understood this to be a veiled threat that she and her husband would head for the southwest, which might lead to insurrection. At last, but with great reluctance, Louis relented and dismissed Decazes. Four days after the emotional scenes at the Tuileries, the Duc de Berry was entombed in the royal crypt at Saint-Denis; his entrails were buried in Lille and his heart at Rosny, his country home in Rosny-sur-Seine, outside Paris.

The Tuileries Palace was draped in black and the royal family went into deep mourning. After the King surrendered his favorite, the Chamber of Deputies responded by convening to discuss the future of the monarchy. It was initially proposed that Salic law be abolished in order to allow Marie-Thérèse to ascend the throne upon Louis XVIII's death. The dignitaries then abandoned that suggestion, opting instead to postpone their decision and wait for the birth of the Duchesse de Berry's baby, due at the end of September or early October.

In April there was further violence. Explosives were detonated at the Tuileries and Louvre palaces. The Duchesse de Berry tried desperately to convince the police that she was the intended target and produced threatening letters to substantiate her claims. It was soon discovered, however, that it was the Duchess herself, with the assistance of a servant, who had fabricated the entire drama. She was terrified that her husband's enemies were still at large in Paris and thought that her scheme would get her better protection. James Gallatin remarked in his diaries that the Duchesse de Berry had confessed to her priest that it was she herself who had arranged for the explosives. The King instructed the police to forget the incident, the royal family excusing her as 'Italian' and prone to melodrama.

Her claims, however, were not unfounded. Two men were actually found and charged with having conspired to detonate explosives near the Duchesse de Berry's apartment: they had hoped, it was claimed, to frighten the Duchess into having a miscarriage. To make matters worse for the grieving Duchesse de Berry, one of her late husband's mistresses, Marie Sophie de la Roche, gave birth to a baby boy, christened Charles Ferdinand, whom she claimed de Berry had fathered. That spring, as Marie Caroline walked along the Seine, evidently pregnant, the public pitied her and she prayed desperately for a son.

In June, there was widespread student rioting and dissent caused by concessions made to d'Artois and his conservatives. To the students one of the most offensive of these was a reactionary educational system, nostalgic for the ancien régime when the Catholic Church and the State were inseparable and epistemology was absolute. The students, schooled under the secular Napoleonic system, opposed the Catholic pedagogy. Two days before the trial and execution of the Duc de Berry's assassin, one of the student demonstrators was murdered by a royal guard. With blood spilled on the streets of Paris, and tensions escalating between republicans and royalists, Marie-Thérèse feared that France would once again be overwhelmed by civil war.

The poet, novelist and dramatist Victor Hugo wrote an emotional prayer begging God, through the poor widow, the Duchesse de Berry, to save France by giving her a healthy son. The Duchesse de Berry, meanwhile, dreamt one night that she was indeed going to be mother to a King of France. She described her dream in a letter to the Comte de Brissac, 'I beheld Saint Louis enter my room, just as he is painted, his crown on his head, his great royal mantle sewn with the fleur-de-lys, and his venerable face. I presented my little girl to him. He opened his mantle and presented me with the prettiest little boy.'

Letters and presents streamed into the Tuileries Palace in excited anticipation. The King announced to all that because of the steadfast loyalty of the citizens of Bordeaux, if the Duchesse de Berry's baby were born a boy he would be given the title 'Duc de Bordeaux', while the people of Bordeaux begged the Duchess to have her baby in their province. The King appointed the Ducs de Coigny and d'Albuféra to be official witnesses at the delivery of the baby at the Tuileries.

On September 28, late in the evening, well after Marie-Thérèse had gone to bed, her sister-in-law went into labor. Sometime around 2 a.m. on the morning of September 29, Marie-Thérèse was awakened by one of Marie Caroline's maids and told to hurry to the Duchesse de Berry's room. Both Marie-Thérèse and Madame de Gontaut-Biron arrived simultaneously to the stunning sight that, amidst a room draped in black in mourning for her husband, Marie Caroline's baby had already been born. Neither doctor nor witnesses had been present. As the baby and mother were still tied together by the umbilical cord, Marie-Thérèse instructed the governess to find two witnesses – any witnesses. Two guards arrived post haste and confirmed that the baby was indeed the child of the Duchesse de Berry. The rest of the royal household began to arrive. Ten minutes after the two witnesses signed their testaments, at about 2.30 a.m., cannon-fire roared across Paris. If the baby were a girl, there would be twenty-one guns; if a boy – one hundred and one. The people of Paris anxiously counted. When they heard the twenty-second round, they dressed and hurried to celebrate in the streets. The little Duc de Bordeaux, named for the first city to have welcomed the return of the Bourbons in 1814, was named Henri (after the great Henri IV) Charles (after his father) Ferdinand (after his maternal great-grandfather, Ferdinand I of the Two Sicilies), Marie, and, lastly, Dieudonné ('Godgiven') – a name that had been given to the baby, born to his parents after a twenty-three-year childless marriage, who became King Louis XIV. Marie-Thérèse carried Henri, Duc de Bordeaux, to the windows of his mother's room, where she held him to be seen by the already swelling crowds. When the King arrived, he took the baby from her arms and said, 'This is mine!' and, beaming at Marie Caroline, handed her a staggeringly large, brilliant suite of diamonds, ebulliently declaring, 'And . . . this is yours!'

As the late Duc de Berry had once joked, if he had fathered a son with his wife, people would immediately question the baby's paternity. While the morning newspaper hailed the birth of the Duc de Bordeaux, it simultaneously published an unsigned protest questioning the legitimacy of little Henri Dieudonné. Although he denied having been its author, it was widely believed that it was written by none other than the Duc d'Orléans, who had, like his father on the occasions of the births of all of

Marie Antoinette's children, openly questioned the baby's paternity. Madame de Gontaut-Biron, who had observed the little boy still attached to his mother by the umbilical cord, was angry with the Duke when she was summoned to respond to a formal challenge that he put forth. When the Duc de Coigny was called to testify, d'Orléans asked the Duke if he was absolutely certain that the baby was Marie Caroline's. De Coigny replied: 'As certain as I am that you are the father of the Duc de Chartres.' James Gallatin, who was at the Palais-Royal with the Duc d'Orléans when he received the news of the birth of the Duc de Bordeaux, recalled: 'It did not strike me that the Orléans family looked or seemed particularly pleased.'[5] Gallatin recounted to d'Orléans the Duc de Berry's dying words to his wife, confirming his knowledge of the pregnancy, and tried to reason with d'Orléans that, since no one but the Duchesse de Berry and her husband knew about her pregnancy that early on, there was his proof that de Berry was the father.

Monseigneur Macchi, the papal nuncio, hailed Henri the 'Child of Europe'. The royal family, so dispirited after the death of the Duc de Berry, revived with the birth of his son. 'He is all of ours,' declared the King, joyfully. Louis was in a very good mood for another reason as well. In 1817, he had met the Comtesse Zoë du Cayla when the Countess's own mother-in-law, taking her daughter-in-law's side against her own son, petitioned the King for assistance with the couple's separation. By 1820, Madame du Cayla, a thirty-five-year-old woman whom most described as attractive and agreeable, was solidly ensconced as the King's 'favorite'. Despite the King's lack of mobility, he and Madame du Cayla enjoyed private time together every Wednesday afternoon at which times, commanded Louis, they were not to be interrupted. Marie-Thérèse treated Madame du Cayla with disdain, much as her mother had Madame du Barry. The Princess made her displeasure known and even begrudged a growing friendship between Madame du Cayla and her own friend, Madame de Choisy. The Duchesse de Berry was less judgmental and thought it politic to be kind to the King's special friend.

This proved a smarter strategy. The Duchesse de Berry, who had already earned the King's admiration for giving the family an heir, now earned his adoration. For the moment, anything she asked was granted. In order to keep her husband's memory alive, the Duchesse de Berry requested that his staff serve the Duc de Bordeaux. The King agreed. When, the morning after Henri's birth, a delegation of over five hundred soldiers asked to see the little Prince, the Duchesse de Berry asked the King if they could all pay their respects, regardless of rank.

Once again, the King agreed. At six o'clock in the morning, Marie-Thérèse greeted the regiments. At noon, the entire family went to the Tuileries chapel together for a *Te Deum* to give thanks for the birth of the little boy, the future of the Bourbon dynasty.

Earlier in the year, Maréchal Berthier's widow had induced the King to sell the Château de Chambord in the Loire Valley while a nationwide fundraising effort began to purchase it. Upon the birth of the Duc de Bordeaux, the committee presented the fabulous Renaissance castle as a gift to the new baby. Six weeks after the infant's birth, the poet Lamartine, traveling in Naples, offered his own contribution. In 'Ode on the Birth of the Duc de Bordeaux', Lamartine called Henri the 'Miracle Child':

> *He is born, child of a miracle*
> *Who inherited the blood of a martyr*
> *He is born of a belated oracle*
> *He is born of a final breath*

After the birth of the 'miracle child', Pauline de Béarn recalled how she heard her childhood friend, the Duchesse d'Angoulême, sigh and, as de Béarn described it, 'unselfishly' unburden herself: 'At last I am resigned forever to remain childless.' Marie-Thérèse's joy in life was often tempered by the caution of personal experience. The day after all of the festivities and celebrations surrounding the birth of Henri, a servant found Marie-Thérèse in a pensive mood. 'Your Highness was very happy yesterday,' he said. 'Yes, very happy yesterday, but today I am reflecting on the destiny of this child,' she replied. James Gallatin, too, recalled that at a ball at court in October, when 'some near-sighted Hungarian officer, not seeing he was in front of the Duchesse d'Angoulême, caught his spur in the lace of her dress and tore yards of splendid lace . . . she was so gracious, so womanly . . . the "descendant of a hundred kings" certainly applies to her . . . [yet, he] had never seen so sad a face'.

Miracles seemed to be in the air and at the age of forty-two, Marie-Thérèse believed that she was pregnant. While royalists were certain of the connection between the Bourbon blood and the divinity, liberal sympathizers like the Duchesse de Broglie, the daughter of Madame de Staël, were skeptical. On November 25, 1820, she wrote to her friend the Comtesse de Castellane: 'One hears everywhere the noise about the pregnancy of Madame; but it is sheer stupidity.' Jean-Baptiste-Jacques Augustin, Painter in the Cabinet of the King, sought to please his patron with a portrait of the Duchesse d'Angoulême pregnant. Keenly aware of Louis's devotion to Henri IV, Augustin chose to base the image on a scandalous late-sixteenth-century portrait of one of Henri IV's mistresses, Gabrielle d'Estrées. Allegedly to signify that d'Estrées was pregnant with César, the King's bastard son, d'Estrées is seated in a wash-tub with her sister, who is pinching her nipple. In his painting, Augustin depicted the Duchesse d'Angoulême with her right hand on her left breast – a clear message that she was, like Gabrielle d'Estrées, expecting a child. On February 15, 1821, in another note to the Comtesse de Castellane, just two months after her complete dismissal of the possibility that the Duchesse d'Angoulême was with child, de Broglie reluctantly conceded: 'They say positively the Duchesse d'Angoulême is pregnant; Madame the Duchesse de Berry is only half-smiling.'

James Gallatin recorded in his diary that on February 16, there was

> a magnificent ball at the Tuileries . . . the Duchesse d'Angoulême was superbly regal; her train of white velvet thickly embroidered with gold fleurs-de-lys with a broad gold border, lined and faced with ermine; her dress entirely of superb lace, which they told me had belonged to her mother; the highest diadem of emeralds and diamonds that I have ever seen, it was quite four inches. A veil of superb lace hung down below her shoulders; a belt and stomacher of diamonds and one enormous emerald in the center; from the shoulders hung great strings of diamonds.[6]

Marie-Thérèse was radiant, and then subsequently devastated when it became clear that she was not pregnant at all. She had mistaken the symptoms of the onset of menopause for pregnancy. Her childbearing days were now behind her and instead she would have to be content in the role of aunt. Ironically, the public had often considered her the 'Mother of France', and, in newspapers, it was often she, and not Marie Caroline, who appeared in illustrations holding the miracle child.

On the first day in May, the Duc de Bordeaux was baptized at the cathedral of Notre Dame with full pomp and splendor, though not without threat of incident. The young Prince and his governess, Madame de Gontaut-Biron, traveled in the first coach of a cortège of twenty-seven carriages. On their way out of the Tuileries, a stranger approached the governess and handed her a note warning: 'Urgent. Be on your guard at the Pont Neuf where the carriage will stop, and then take care of the Prince.' She called out to the commander of the soldiers escorting their carriage, 'This concerns you,' and handed him the note. The soldier read it and swore that nothing would happen to the baby. Indeed, they all arrived safely at the cathedral and after the holy water, prayers and acclamations, the King signed the baptismal certificate and the royal family returned to the Tuileries Palace without incident.

That evening, fireworks filled the skies in many towns around France. Ten thousand packages of sugared almonds were distributed on the streets of Paris and the Opéra and theaters staged spectacles commemorating the event. The Duchesse de Berry had stated that if she were to give birth to a son, she would make a pilgrimage to the shrine of Notre-Dame de Liesse in Picardie, and she left for the shrine on May 20.

By the end of the summer, the Duchesse de Berry was back in Paris and ready to resume her social life. Her hair had grown back, and, naturally vivacious, she began to entertain and attend parties once again. Nearly eleven hundred people attended the first reception she hosted since her husband's death. The social calendars reveal balls, dinners and theatrical presentations hosted by the Duchesse de Berry on a regular basis. Things looked very good for the Bourbons: they had an heir, and, earlier that summer, Napoleon Bonaparte, 'the Usurper', had died.

While the Duchesse de Berry planned her day around her evenings, Marie-Thérèse ached to play the role of mother. When Madame de Gontaut-Biron contracted scarlet fever, the children were invited to sleep in their aunt's bedroom. Marie-Thérèse, recalling her own early, idyllic childhood at her mother's Hameau and the Petit Trianon, decided she needed a country estate. She wanted a place where the children could breathe clean air and where they could frolic without concern for the formalities of the Tuileries. Besides, she disliked the capital for its dirt, its chaos and its memories. On December 29, 1821, ten days after her forty-third birthday, Marie-Thérèse purchased the estate of Villeneuve-l'Étang to the west of Paris in Marnes. Its previous owner had planted an Orangerie on the estate out of admiration for the great gardens at Versailles. Marie-Thérèse hired the architect Maximilien Villiers to completely renovate the house.

Villeneuve-l'Étang would be a place where, reminiscent of her mother, she could be herself and where she would invite only those people whose company she enjoyed. Most importantly she hoped to create a second home for her niece and nephew and to organize parties for them. There was a billiard room for the adults' enjoyment, and a library which she stocked with travel books and histories of the Revolution. She instructed her agent to find furniture for the home, and she approved the purchase of several pieces commissioned by her mother. She assembled a menagerie for the children's delight – and for their health. Her very own herd of cows provided the Duc de Bordeaux and the Princess Louise with fresh milk and cream. Marie-Thérèse was so proud of her farm that she often brought samples of the excellent cream back with her to Paris, and regarded it as a special treat for her favorite guests. A well-known story illustrating Marie-Thérèse's less-than-saintly side concerns a dinner party at the Tuileries at which the Duc de Richelieu, whose politics she openly disliked, was a guest: she offered her homemade cream to the person to the Duke's right and to his left, but refused to share it with Richelieu himself.

Villeneuve-l'Étang also gave Marie-Thérèse the perfect excuse to avoid going to Versailles. James Gallatin recalled attending a party at Versailles on April 20, 1821, hosted by the Comte d'Artois. Gallatin reflected in his diary that at one point during the party he found himself peering out a window toward the Cour d'Honneur and thinking about Marie-Thérèse: 'Most people are leaving Paris now . . . The Court is at St Cloud. The Duchesse d'Angoulême loves it [at Saint-Cloud], but nothing will induce her to go to Versailles. I am not surprised – the memories would be terrible for her.'[7]

Gallatin admitted in his diary that he knew for sure that Marie-Thérèse believed her brother was still alive, a belief only made more painful for her by the steady trickle of pretenders coming forward with fantastical tales. In early 1823, as the Gallatins were preparing to return to the United States, they were approached by a woman from the American West who told Albert Gallatin that she had met Louis XVII, 'the little boy Dauphin', and that he had arrived in America dressed in the finest clothing. The boy had been raised by Native Americans, had converted to Christianity and was known to many as 'Indian Williams'. Now a grown man, he claimed that he could only remember a prison, a mob and a very beautiful mother and insisted that he was the brother of the Duchesse d'Angoulême. When it was discovered that he received a regular stipend from a French nobleman, his story was given credibility for many. In truth, his real name was Eleazar Williams and he was the son of a Native American woman and a Caucasian father. Unlike Louis Charles, whose eyes had been blue, Williams's eyes were hazel-colored. The difference in eye color did nothing to deter Williams from his claims, and he magnanimously offered to allow King Louis XVIII to retain his right to the throne in exchange for a large cash settlement. Another story that circulated at the same time was the tale of Pierre Louis Poiret, who claimed that he had been smuggled out of the Temple Prison and sent to the Seychelles. There, he presided over his own tropical court for believers.

The Gallatins had been very close to the Bourbons for years, and on the eve of their return to America, the Duchesse d'Angoulême surreptitiously handed Albert Gallatin a sealed packet, 'begging him to take great care of it'. Albert Gallatin arrived back at his Paris home at 21 rue de l'Université and opened the package.

> It contains several copies of letters addressed to her from America from people who imagine they are the Dauphin (Louis XVII) and from others who state that the poor child was given into their care. A note from her begging father to investigate the matter if he possibly can, as it is the great wish of her life if her brother is alive to be able to find him. Of course father will do all he can, but he is very skeptical on the matter and fears that wicked people are trying to prey on her feelings with a view of making money.[8]

Gallatin went back to America with the lasting impression that Marie-Thérèse was the consummate performer. Always gracious and serene in public, she was evidently in constant turmoil. At the beginning of 1823, she had yet another trial to endure. King Ferdinand VII of Spain, descended from the Bourbon Henri IV and the Habsburgs, had been deposed by rebel soldiers. Louis XVIII appointed the Duc d'Angoulême head of the French army that was sent to invade Spain and return Ferdinand to the throne. Marie-Thérèse feared for her husband's safety and set off at the end of April for the Spanish border in order to be closer in case of news with a retinue that included Pauline de Béarn.

On May 11, 1823, the Comte de Villèle wrote to the Duc d'Angoulême that the people of the southwest were 'in heaven to have Madame; she has had the kindness in passing through Toulouse to receive my mother who is very happy'. It was noted again that the Duchesse d'Angoulême became far happier when she was far from Paris. 'I went with her on several voyages,' wrote Pauline,

> to Bordeaux, to the waters, to the provinces, to the Vendée . . . she was always, for me, good, always tender . . . In 1823, during the war in Spain, when M. le Duc d'Angoulême was the head of the elite French army, Madame la Duchesse d'Angoulême established herself at Bordeaux, to be closer to the news . . . what charming affability she displayed every day at the tables and in the salons of the various

business leaders of Bordeaux. It was so touching to see the goodness with which the princess entered conversation with each of these men, these details of business, which could not have had any interest for her; nonetheless Madame always found something to question them about and listened to them, leaving all of those so happy who had had the honor to meet her.[9]

With 100,000 men, d'Angoulême marched without resistance through Madrid, and, on August 31, after seizing the fortress of Trocadero, restored Ferdinand VII to the throne. D'Angoulême was hailed as the man who accomplished what Napoleon could not. It was essential for Marie-Thérèse to now return to Paris for her husband's official welcome. The Bourbons regarded his victory as a victory for the monarchy – and for the idea of monarchy. A triumphal return to the French capital was planned for December 2, the anniversary of Napoleon's victory at Austerlitz. The royal family waited on the balcony of the Tuileries Palace as the Duc d'Angoulême and his regiment marched through the gates of Paris. Marie-Thérèse beamed with pride. She was so euphoric that she had decorated an entire room at Villeneuve-l'Étang with paintings to commemorate his military triumphs.

Marie-Thérèse and 'The Hero of Trocadero' later attended a performance of the play Le Cid by Corneille, put on in her husband's honor. Although she savored the moment, Marie-Thérèse soon left the capital once more to embark on another tour of the provinces, visiting Bordeaux, Provence and the always-loyal Vendée, where she laid the first stone of a new chapel. She was always cognizant of the mistakes that her parents had made in neglecting the provinces and remaining insular at Versailles and had long ago decided that she would have a power base outside Paris and its vicinity.

In 1824, France was in a strong position. The treasury was sound and, since its suppression of the revolt in Spain, France had recovered its international power and prestige. Many other European territories, however, were experiencing turbulence. The newspapers were filled with reports of the Greek revolution and the daring exploits of Lord Byron. In Jena, the formation of the Burschenschaft in 1815, which espoused the ideals of the French Revolution, led to a rise of secret societies and student riots which persisted well into the mid-1820s. Curiously, at the same time, oblique references to 'the Dark Countess' appeared in German and French newspapers, one claiming, for example: 'one has discovered in a small corner in Thuringia, the trail of a long-lost French princess . . . but there may have been reasons why the trail was no longer pursued'.[10]

On March 12, 1824, anticipating the spread of social unrest, the Duke of Hildburghausen signed a *Schutzbrief* (protection letter) stating that all authorities in Hildburghausen are to know that 'Vavel de Versay and his companion' are under his special protection and are to continue to receive all consideration as they had 'from the very moment' they had arrived. Not only was it clear that, in case of upheaval, this couple demanded special attention, but it obviated the fact that the Duke of Hildburghausen had 'from the very moment' – for some twenty years – known the couple's identity and special requirements. This document, the statement that he had personally taken responsibility for their safety, would form part of his legacy. In 1826, the Duchy of Hildburghausen was subsumed into Meiningen. The new government required registration of Vavel de Versay, which he refused. Princess (Paul) Charlotte of Württemberg offered the couple asylum; however, when the *Schutzbrief* from Duke Frederick of Hildburghausen, now Duke of Saxe-Altenburg, was produced, the Duke of Meiningen intervened, and the identities of Vavel de Versay and his mysterious female companion, now in her late forties, remained undisclosed to the community.

In an unexpected turn of events, in May of the following year, Vavel de Versay was proclaimed an honorary citizen of the town in appreciation for his many years of local philanthropy. Needless to say, he had not in any way sought any kind of public acclamation.

A fiscally and militarily sound France was to be the legacy of Louis XVIII, and by the spring of 1824, it was clear that he was dying. His obesity had caused a variety of complications from gout to gangrene, and he was having difficulty breathing. That summer, at Saint-Cloud, he insisted on returning to Paris for the annual August 25th Fête Saint Louis. The King had always hated leaving Paris. He had been told a prediction that he would not die at the Tuileries and so he avoided going outside the capital or anywhere else whenever possible. Dressed in full uniform with golden epaulettes, he was a pitiable sight and it was apparent to all that he was clinging to life. Over the next few weeks, Louis withered away at the Tuileries. Marie-Thérèse was often by his side, crying and praying, but it was his mistress, Madame du Cayla, who had wrested a fortune out of her lover, who insisted on calling for a priest so that Louis could make his last confession, which he did before the Abbé Rocher on Monday, September 13 at 7.30 a.m. Marie-Thérèse and the Duc d'Angoulême were at his bedside when the King said: '*Adieu, mes enfants, je vous bénis; que Dieu soit avec vous.*' (Good-bye, my children, I bless you; may God be with you.') At 3 p.m., the infant Duc de Bordeaux and his sister were brought to his bedside so that Louis could say goodbye. He could no longer see them, but heard their voices, smiled at them and blessed them. He had always been very tender with the children and their governess noted that, despite their age, they understood that he was dying and they were very sad on their drive back to Saint-Cloud.

On the evening of Tuesday, September 14, a crowd assembled in the Tuileries courtyard to keep vigil. Visitors and doctors recalled that during the King's final days Marie-Thérèse stayed by his side in a constant state of grief. Each time he had difficulty breathing, he would see her tear-soaked eyes, hold her hand and say: 'It is not yet the time. Do not worry.' On Wednesday, September 15, the Abbé returned to speak with Louis. When, at 8 p.m., the King's fever spiked and continued to rise, the priest placed a cross at his lips for him to kiss. The King's Directeur-Général des Postes, the Duc de Doudeauville, gave the order to assemble the Ministers.

Among those present in the King's room at 3 a.m. on Thursday, September 16, 1824, were his doctor, Alibert, the royal family – including the Duc and Duchesse d'Orléans – Talleyrand, Charles de Damas, the Ducs de Duras and Blacas, the Marquis d'Avaray and Baron Hüe. An hour later the King died. Louis XVIII's surgeon took a candle and held it near the King's mouth. When the flame was not extinguished, he pronounced, 'The King is dead'. Turning to Louis's brother and heir, the Comte d'Artois, the doctor added, 'Long live the King!'

D'Artois, now Charles X, wept and turned to leave his brother's chamber. The rest of the family followed. Marie-Thérèse, as the daughter of a king, would have followed immediately behind her uncle had it not been for the fact that her husband was now second in line to the throne. Obeying a thousand years of etiquette, she turned to d'Angoulême and said, 'Proceed, Monsieur le Dauphin.' Marie-Thérèse was now Dauphine of France.

CHAPTER XXII
MENDING FENCES

ARIE-THÉRÈSE WAS an expert equestrienne. She had grown up riding with her mother, had resumed her passion in England, and the sport became a form of escapism for her from life at the Tuileries. She spent many a day on horseback in the Bois de Boulogne. When she asked her father-in-law, the new King, for her own stable at the Louvre, he ignored her. Instead he offered stables there to the Duc d'Orléans on the grounds that there were none at the Palais-Royal. Irritated, but aware that Charles X was determined to extend an olive branch to the junior branch of the Bourbon family, she bought her own stables in the Faubourg St Germain, directly across the Seine from the Tuileries, just to make a point. Days later, by royal ordinance, the Duc d'Orléans was granted the right to be called 'Royal Highness'.

More was to come. When, on September 23, Louis XVIII's body was brought to Saint-Denis, Marie-Thérèse was forced to share a carriage in the funeral cortège with the Duc d'Orléans in a show of family solidarity. At the chapel, they watched as the chief herald threw the late King's sword, helmet and buckler one by one down the stairs – as had been enacted for hundreds of years – repeating three times with each throw, 'The King is Dead!' After the ritual, the Master of Ceremony, who apparently felt that he could have done a better job, apologized to the new King and innocently blundered: 'There were so many mistakes. Next time we will do better.' Charles replied with a smile, 'I am not in a hurry.' In fact, Louis XVIII would be the last King of France to be buried in the royal crypt at Saint-Denis.

Charles X formally entered Paris on September 27, 1824. Seated on a stallion, the King, as handsome and debonair as his brother was bloated and unattractive, entered the city followed by a dazzling parade of carriages. Once more the Duc d'Orléans traveled in line with the rest of the family. There was a 101-gun salute, the Prefect of the Seine gave Charles X the keys to the city, and the King paraded through the streets of Paris. On the rue du Faubourg-Saint-Honoré he was distracted by excited shouts of 'Bon-papa! Bon-papa!' and, looking up, saw his grandchildren, Princess Louise and four-year-old Duc de Bordeaux, waving from an upper-floor balcony. Princess Louise had been initially upset that her grandfather was to be King of France. She had only known the other King to sit in a wheelchair and she thought that a wheelchair was a requirement for the job, but once she saw her grandfather slender and handsome riding his Arabian horse, she could hardly contain herself. Breaking with the solemnity and etiquette of the pageant, and to the delight of the crowds, Charles broke away from the procession, rode toward the building that housed his little ones, lifted his hat, and shouted up words of adoration to the children. As he had once charmed the late Queen Marie Antoinette with the twinkle in his eye, the nearly white-haired, affable man, who would turn sixty-seven in two weeks, but who looked much younger, sent the crowds into a dither.

Paris was clearly smitten with its new King. To the surprise of many, the ultra-conservative Charles decided to immediately loosen the restrictions on press censorship. He also maintained the status quo among his late brother's ministers. Villèle would remain Chief Counsel and Minister of Finance and Damas, Minister of Foreign Affairs. The Duchesse de Berry had heard that others were receiving honors and asked the King if she could be known as 'Madame', a title typically reserved for the daughter of the King, the sister of the King or the wife of the brother of the King. Charles refused her request stating that she had no right to it. 'Madame, la Dauphine' Marie-Thérèse was outraged that the Duchess had tried to obtain a title not rightfully hers. She was also becoming increasingly annoyed with her sister-in-law for what she saw as her neglect of her children – Madame Gontaut-Biron wrote that their mother rarely saw them – and for failing to perform her role as mother to a future King of France.

Like Marie-Thérèse, Marie Caroline detested the Tuileries, for its formality rather than its memories. The young Princess was determined to have fun. She traveled, attended balls and hunting parties, and, in general, avoided the ceremonial solemnity that always surrounded the royal family of France. Marie-Thérèse wrote to her sister-in-law reminding her of her duties: 'Who could possibly have suffered more than me to find myself once again in these places where I was with my parents and where I saw them so unhappy? And yet, my duty is to be there and my heart calls me there because that is where I find my family.'[1] Her entreaty fell on deaf ears, however, and Marie Caroline's behavior became even more outrageous. The King, who as the Comte d'Artois had famously sown his own wild oats, understood to some extent, but he advised his daughter-in-law that she must channel her energies into her children, host parties for them and be sure to invite all the Orléans children.

On December 22, Charles presided over the opening of the Chamber of Deputies and invited his entire family along to the ceremony to show a united front. The majority of those who served in the parliament at that time were ultra-royalists. They represented a country of approximately 32 million people, most of whom had no memory of the ancien régime. A huge crowd waited to see what the King would say. Charles X reaffirmed his loyalty to the Constitutional Charter that had been forced on his brother, but he also attempted to further restore property to those families whose lands had been confiscated in the 1790s and reinstate a religious presence in a now largely secular country. The latter included the re-introduction to France of the Jesuits, who had been banned for over fifty years, which proved a deeply unpopular decision. In response to dissent on the matter, Marie-Thérèse privately remarked: 'I am sure that those who shout "A bas les Jésuites!" do not even know what the Jesuits are.'[2]

Although Marie-Thérèse could never forgive the d'Orléans clan, she still believed in the primacy of etiquette of rank. Madame de Gontaut-Biron recalled that after the King's speech, there was a little step, which His Majesty did not see. He stumbled and his hat, which was under his arm, fell to the ground. The Duc d'Orléans retrieved it. The Duchesse d'Orléans, Marie-Thérèse's first cousin, Marie Amélie, turned to Gon-taut-Biron and said: 'The King would have fallen, but my husband saved him.' Gontaut-Biron disagreed: 'No, Madame, Monseigneur only picked up His Majesty's hat.' The children's governess recalled that Marie-Thérèse gave her a very frosty look and would not speak with her for years because she had contradicted a royal Princess, and even then Madame Gontaut-Biron believed that the Dauphine never truly forgave her. Similarly, despite the Dauphine's personal animosity toward the son of Philippe Égalité, Marie-Thérèse performed her duty impeccably and obeyed her King, who had set the tone for reconciliation. Marie-Thérèse began a monthly pattern of either inviting the Duke and his Duchess to the Tuileries, as she did on February 24, 1825, or accepting an invitation to dine at the Palais-Royal, where she was a month later.

Marie-Thérèse had become comfortable with the notion that she could perform her public duty while she maintained a balance with her own personal preferences. On the one hand, she would celebrate Easter at Saint-Germain-l'Auxerrois, the church in which she had been confirmed in 1790, and go to Vichy in the summertime for the waters. On the other, while the parties at the Tuileries contained none of the magic of Versailles, she would appear at the dinners that were important to the crown. While King Charles X prepared for his coronation at Reims, scheduled for Sunday, May 29, Marie-Thérèse served as his hostess in April at the Tuileries for the Prince of Saxe-Coburg and Chancellor Metternich, in May for Prince Esterhazy, and, after the coronation in Reims, she remained in Paris for a time in June to entertain the Queen of Württemberg and the Prince of Salerno.

The famous salon hostess, Madame Récamier, recalled with amusement in her own diary that she had been absent from France after having been in Italy for three years, only to find that when she returned to Paris at the end of May, 1825, the city was deserted, everyone having gone to Reims. Alone in the capital, she received a letter from her friend, the writer-statesman, Chateaubriand, who described a personal moment during the coronation when: 'At the ceremony of the *chevaliers des ordres*, I fell on my knees before the King . . . The King, having gone to the trouble of removing his gloves to take my hands in his, said to me, smiling: "A gloved cat cannot capture a mouse".'[3]

After the King's formal coronation, there was a splendid dinner in the two-tiered *grande salle* of the fifteenth-century Palais de Tau, the home of the Archbishop of Reims. Marie-Thérèse stayed in Reims for a few days, on June 1 visiting two hospitals for sick soldiers and a third for the public. The next day, in Châlons, she toured the cathedral, a hospice, the royal school of the arts, and a convent, after which she remained to dine with local dignitaries who hailed her as 'the heroine of Bordeaux'. She returned to Paris to participate in the King's own celebratory grand fête to which 8,000 people had been invited. On June 8, she attended the King's own official gala and as the next in line as Queen of France was seated to his right. A few days later, the entire royal family attended the Théâtre-Français for a performance of *Clytemnestra*, and on June 19, once again, the whole family, in a grand show of solidarity, attended the Théâtre Italien for the premiere performance of *Il Viaggio a Reims* by Rossini. The opera, a delightful account of a group of people desperately trying to get to the coronation of Charles X on time, had been composed in the new King's honor.

Twice a year for two weeks, in March and October, the royal family would retire to the royal palace at Compiègne, where Marie Antoinette had first met her husband. The Comte Alexandre de Puymaigre, Prefect of l'Oise during the reign of Charles X, and a frequent guest, recalled that Charles X preferred to do very little work when he was at Compiègne. He would hunt every day until around five in the evening. At 7 p.m. the royal family and their guests would congregate in a grand salon. Dinner would be served and would last about an hour. Puymaigre noticed that the King 'did not serve first-rate wines'. After dinner, Marie-Thérèse would socialize with the women and give the children sweets. The King liked to play billiards. Sometimes Marie-Thérèse would put down her needlework and join the King at the billiard table. They would play whist, often enjoy a late-night serving of punch, and sometimes stay awake until two in the morning playing various card games. Puymaigre noted that, when it came to gambling, the Dauphine placed a limit on the stakes of 5 francs, but he recalled that sometimes, after Marie-Thérèse went to bed, the tone of the party would change, the rules would loosen, and behavior would degenerate, which suited the Duchesse de Berry who preferred a riskier game and racier conversation.

Puymaigre, however, did not regard Marie-Thérèse as a prude or a sourpuss and commented, as many did, that she had a wonderful sense of humor. One day, Marie-Thérèse informed him that she wanted to visit the gardens of Plessis-Villette, owned by the Marquis de Villette. Puymaigre said he would send word ahead to warn that the Princess was coming but Marie-Thérèse insisted that she wanted no fuss made. Puymaigre protested and looked uncomfortable. At last, he explained that the Marquis de Villette often invited inappropriate women – 'actresses' – to his house. Marie-Thérèse burst out laughing, laughed heartily for a while and then told her nervous escort to go ahead and do whatever he liked. She enjoyed Puymaigre's company and requested that he accompany her on many of her trips around France as a *chevalier d'honneur*. Once, a gust of wind blew the Dauphine's skirt up indecently high. He offered her a scarf to tie around her skirt and protect her modesty, and, when she teased him that he had not rescued her in time, he responded: 'If Madame had been on fire, I would have been there to put it out, but I cannot do anything against the wind.'

Marie-Thérèse's greatest private pleasure as she approached middle age was her maternal role with the Children of France. Despite their rift, Madame de Gontaut-Biron had nothing but praise for the Dauphine's devotion to Princess Louise and the little Duc de Bordeaux, in the absence of their own mother. The children often went to Bagatelle, the d'Artois family home in the Bois de Boulogne, when they were in Paris, so that they could play in the park. Their aunt, often on horseback, would meet the children and join them on nature walks. As the royal family spent the summer at Saint-Cloud, their governess suggested that the children also needed a park there in which they could play. Marie-Thérèse and the King thought it was a wonderful idea. In an old flower garden they set about constructing a playground for the children which they named the 'Trocadéro' in honor of the Dauphin's victory in Spain, complete with an iron bridge leading directly from the playground to the children's apartments. They put on parties in the park and invited the children from the key aristocratic families such as the de Maillé, de Meffray, de Nadaillac and the Orléans. At one party, they lit a bonfire after supper. When the Bourbon flag almost went up in smoke, little Henri rescued it, waved it above his head and shouted: 'I have saved the flag!'[4]

According to Gontaut-Biron, the Dauphine also concerned herself with the children's education, and she was quite exceptional in her requirements. Marie-Thérèse regarded the Duc de Bordeaux as her responsibility and she was going to do everything she could to ensure his place in history. She tutored him on his bloodline and the divine right of kings. In an unusual and forward-thinking move, instead of engaging her own friends as was the custom in previous French courts, Marie-Thérèse insisted on appointing tutors of great principle and learning so that Henri could be properly prepared to rule. In addition, she hired language tutors to teach Princess Louise and Henri Italian, German and English. These children were going to be truly European.

While on New Year's Day, Marie-Thérèse made a point of giving presents to the Orléans children, she gave none to the de Berry children, upon whom she usually lavished much love and attention. Princess Louise and the little Duc de Bordeaux, however, had been well versed in the story told by their aunt of how her mother, the late Queen, Marie Antoinette, would offer her own children a splendid array of toys and then send them away. Marie-Thérèse repeatedly explained to the little Louise and Henri that this was a lesson about 'blessings and want'. When the de Berry children exhibited no complaints, their governess and the King were proud of them, and, just as she had been given an allowance, and had been instructed to give a portion of it to charity, Marie-Thérèse saw that the children received their money and then shared it with those less fortunate.

Although the Dauphine's rank and bearing intimidated many adults, children universally adored her. Even the young members of the Orléans branch of the family remembered her with the utmost love and affection. The Prince de Joinville, a grandson of Philippe Égalité, recalled in his memoirs that on January 6, 1824, when the whole family, including the Orléans children, were together to celebrate Twelfth Night, he broke open his cake and found the traditionally lucky bean within. His mother explained to the six-year-old that if he were to receive the bean he would be 'King' of the festivities.

> I got up from the table, and carried the bean on a salver to the Duchesse d'Angoulême. I loved her dearly even then, that good kind Duchess! For she had always been so good to us, ever since we were babies, and never failed to give us the most beautiful New Year's gifts. My respectful affection deepened as I grew old enough to realize her sorrows and the nobility of her nature . . . She broke the ice by being the first to raise her glass to her lips, when I had made her my queen.

The boy did not understand the silence at the table at that time, but upon reflection and later events, he did. While others at the table were uncomfortably awaiting her reaction, Marie-Thérèse, aware of the symbolism of the moment, when an Orléans was being made 'King', displayed only graciousness to the child. The Prince de Joinville later acknowledged that even 'after we were separated by the events of 1830', when his father would betray the King and steal the Bourbon crown, she was still 'the queen of his heart', and he tried 'to take every opportunity of letting her know how unalterable my feelings for her were'.

Despite the 'nobility of her nature', the sorrows of the past still found their way into Marie-Thérèse's life, including even her daily routines. Instead of allowing her ladies of honor to dress and prepare her toilette, Marie-Thérèse did it all herself, as she had in prison. For hours on end, even with guests present, Marie-Thérèse would sit at her needlework, performing her craft at a staccato pace, as she had in jail where, with the skill her mother and aunt taught her, she sewed and embroidered diligently for both her sanity and her self-preservation. Her rooms in the Pavillon de Flore, once her mother's, and the Pavillon de l'Horloge, contained reliquaries of her loved ones. Fastened to her bedroom wall was a tapestry of white velvet embroidered with lilac daisies, which had been sewn by her mother and Aunt Elisabeth. There was also a stool seat that her brother used to say his prayers on in prison. The stool contained a drawer in which she had placed her most cherished possessions: the white bloodstained shirt that had been worn by her father to the guillotine, a lace bonnet her mother had worked on in the Conciergerie, confiscated by Robespierre, and a fichu that Madame Elisabeth wore to the scaffold that had blown into the hands of someone in the crowd, who had sent it to Marie-Thérèse. And of course she still carried with her a pronounced vocal defect from the time in the Temple Prison when she had stubbornly refused to speak with her captors – her trophy of defiance.

Thirty years after the Terror, Marie-Thérèse was still a target. On July 24, 1825, at a meeting of the King's cabinet, Charles X showed a letter to his ministers containing an anonymous death threat to the Dauphine. The same year, yet another man claiming to be Louis Charles stepped forward to cause the Dauphine further torment. The man, who traveled from Modena, Italy, called himself the Baron de Richemont and he proved to be more insidious than any of the previous pretenders. Richemont, whose tales included little known details about life at Versailles and in the Temple Prison, went so far as to publish his memoirs and he harassed Marie-Thérèse with a barrage of letters from his apartment on the rue de Fleurus. When she refused to meet with him, he started a public campaign to 'regain his throne'.

In December 1825, when Marie-Thérèse learned that her long-time paladin, Czar Alexander, had passed away, his death affected her deeply. Charles X would soon be seventy, and Marie-Thérèse worried what the future would bring upon his death. Louis-Antoine was next in line to the throne, but privately she and her husband held different political views. The Dauphin maintained the liberality he had learned in England where the King shared his power with parliament; Marie-Thérèse was steadfast in her conviction in the God-given right for the Bourbons to rule France. They, nonetheless, depended on each other, both for now comfortable in their separate roles for their common cause. He was the military hero; she the ambassador of goodwill. In 1826, the Dauphin went off to tour military barracks around France, and his wife left on her own public relations trips.

The problems arose when Louis-Antoine meddled in politics. Somewhat eager to involve himself in the affairs of State, anticipating the day not too long off when he surely would be King, the Dauphin irritated his father's ministers by choosing to attend their meetings. Charles X would convene with his advisors four times a week. They would begin at four o'clock in the afternoon, break for supper for an hour, and continue until eleven at night. Openly acknowledged as less intelligent than his wife, although a fine soldier, the Dauphin would arrive at the meetings and spend the time making his own notes in a portfolio without listening to what was going on around him. When he would every now and then tune in to the discussion, he would interrupt typically saying, 'This might be stupid, but . . .' forcing the group to recount what he had missed and making the meetings even more drawn out. Even his wife believed that he was better off paying attention to the army than taking an interest in political affairs.

The young Comtesse d'Agoult, who in 1827 was presented at court, believed that the marriage of the d'Angoulêmes was not a happy one. She found the Dauphine perennially grumpy and attributed it to her having married not for love but for duty. Formerly Marie Catherine Sophie de Flavigny, the Countess had just married the nephew of the Vicomtesse d'Agoult, the Dauphine's great friend and lady-in-waiting. To be presented at court, young ladies needed two important sponsors, usually godmothers, who submitted their names and credentials to be considered. In Marie's case, it was her new aunt the Vicomtesse d'Agoult who submitted her name.

The court of Charles X was beginning to reflect the changes of post-imperial France. Official rank gave one status, allowing admission to Jews and Protestants. Young girls from ancient noble families, from *nouveau* noble families as well as the merely *nouveau riche*, vied to be presented. Families of the young girls who longed to make their debuts at court hired Monsieur Abraham for instructions, and he made a tidy business. The brand new Comtesse d'Agoult recalled that it was Monsieur Abraham, in his lace-trimmed shirts, who taught her how to maneuver the long court dress with walks and counter-walks because one never turned one's back on royalty. He instructed the young woman on the art of lowering one's eyes to the ground, inclining one's head and at what point to perform each movement. He educated the girls in the subtle signals of the King's procession and what to wear that would please Marie-Thérèse, who, in the end, controlled the invitation list. If you wanted to be invited back to the Tuileries, you were instructed to wear her favorite hairstyle for your debut and to wear a gown that the Dauphine would find appropriate. D'Agoult was presented in a white gown festooned with silver lamé tulle embroidered with silver flowers. Her hair was piled suitably high and pinned with stiff combs, shells and ostrich feathers. The front was divided in half into cascades of tiny curls and then ornamented with a small diadem of jewels and flowers. She also wore an exquisite suite of gorgeous emeralds.

Marie d'Agoult recalled being extremely nervous before her appearance because, thinking that she was doing her niece a special favor, the Vicomtesse invited the young woman to meet privately with Marie-Thérèse for her approval before the official soirée began. The Vicomtesse escorted her to the Dauphine's private rooms. Marie-Thérèse looked her over from head to toe and, echoing Louis XVIII's own criticism of herself when she first appeared in Paris upon the return of the Bourbons, snapped, 'She is not wearing enough rouge.' Without saying another word, Marie-Thérèse turned on her heels and left the room. 'How did I not see that?' the elder d'Agoult nervously fretted, but there was nothing that the two women could do at that point.

The Comtesse d'Agoult, despite her pallor, was indeed invited back on many occasions. She, like most women, was completely enamored of the King and enjoyed his company hugely. On the other hand, she never changed her mind about her first impression of Marie-Thérèse, often wondering what her aunt found so appealing about the woman. Marie d'Agoult wrote that the Dauphine had a glacial temperament and that she thought it was ridiculous for a forty-six-year-old woman to be called 'Dauphine', a word that evoked a fresh young bride. (In fact, the titles of Dauphin and Dauphine, which dated back to 1349, were absolutely correct for the d'Angoulêmes.) D'Agoult wrote that the Duc d'Angoulême was puny, ugly and had a nervous tic. Offered admittance to the Dauphine's informal gatherings owing to her aunt's close friendship with Marie-Thérèse, the young Countess claimed that on many occasions she observed Marie-Thérèse sitting at her needlework, while the guests, lined in two rows according to their rank, sat completely bored.

The Comtesse d'Agoult enjoyed the company of the Duchesse de Berry, whom she regarded as fun and, while the Dauphine would not budge from her position that the Duc d'Orléans wanted to steal the crown, the Duchesse de Berry harbored no ill will and was quite friendly with the members of the junior branch of the Bourbons. The Countess also stated that people had begun to gossip that Princess Louise would be married to the Duc de Chartres, the eldest son of the Duc d'Orléans, but that everyone knew that the Dauphine was adamantly against that union, which meant that it would never happen.[5]

While the Comtesse d'Agoult may never have understood the Dauphine's charm, there were countless lifelong admirers of Marie-Thérèse. Among them was Maurice Esterhazy, who also met the Dauphine in 1827. For years, Marie-Thérèse had begged her old friend, the Comtesse Esterhazy, to return to her native France. In June of 1827, 'Fanny' arrived in Paris with her twenty-year-old son, Maurice, whose father had asked the young man to keep a journal of his time with the French royal family. Maurice did, indeed, keep daily notes of his visit, which include many warm, insightful anecdotes about Marie-Thérèse and her family.

His own mother, whose friendship with Marie-Thérèse began on January 10, 1796, when she 'first laid eyes' on the Bourbon Princess, had accompanied Marie-Thérèse to Prague and to Belvedere and had enjoyed many years of intimate correspondence with the Dauphine. Their very cordial relationship allowed Maurice a perspective of Marie-Thérèse that very few people were privy to. He had heard that she was formal and dry, but he recalled that when they arrived she greeted his mother effusively, as if the two were still young, giggly girls. He remembered her as an exceedingly warm, pleasant and hospitable host who possessed a wonderful sense of humor. One day, she had a bit of fun grilling them about the Bonapartes – Napoleon's mother, his famously promiscuous sister, Pauline, and various nieces and nephews – who were now living in Rome, 'in general and on each in particular, their mannerisms, their social relations, the way they were with others, and if the Pope had seen them. She finished by asking us if we had been invited to their parties. After a sudden and involuntary expression escaped us as a result of her last question, she was really amused.'

While the Esterhazys were guests of the Dauphine they were treated like members of the family. They dined with the Bourbons, went to church with the Bourbons and visited Saint-Cloud, Compiègne, the Tuileries, Rosny, and the Dauphine's estate at Villeneuve-l'Étang, where Maurice saw his mother's portrait on a table placed alongside some of the Dauphine's most personal treasures. They saw the rooms commemorating both her stay in Vienna and her husband's victory in Spain. Maurice wrote that the Dauphine spent a great deal of time with her niece and nephew, which allowed him to get to know the children and he found them well-mannered and quite adorable. He recounted an episode at the dining table when the six-year-old Henri could not cut his bread. His grandfather, Charles X, managed the bread for the boy who responded simply 'very much obliged, Sire'.

Six weeks after their arrival, Marie-Thérèse shocked everyone by taking the Esterhazys to Versailles. Maurice was concerned that this particular tour was going to be very difficult for his mother's friend, and he was amazed that she had offered to take them there. 'It is interesting,' he wrote, 'to find oneself with the daughter of Louis XVI in the apartment which he occupied, to be at the place where the bed stood of Marie Antoinette, the little secret exit through which she was forced to save herself, the place where the unfortunate *garde du corps* defended the entrance to the chamber of the Queen, the balcony where she showed Louis XVII to his people.' Marie-Thérèse took them to the theater in the town of Versailles and three days later showed them around the Petit Trianon. Maurice was in complete awe of Marie-Thérèse as they walked about the gardens, saw the rustic Hameau, entered the theater where her mother had performed in comedies and visited the family chapel. He wrote that she 'showed us with great tenderness a small room, where she would take her lessons, when the rain kept her from playing outside in the gardens'. All of the furniture that was still in place at the Trianon, he wrote, had belonged to the Bonapartes. The Bourbons had not bothered to change any of it. Certainly, Marie-Thérèse had avoided the house since her return, making this tour of Versailles, he believed, afforded him by the only surviving child of Louis XVI and Marie Antoinette, a singular experience. Marie-Thérèse had summoned her strength, mastered her pain and thought only about his and his mother's enjoyment and for this she was a heroine in his eyes.

On November 17, 1827, a slate of liberals was elected to the Chamber of Deputies in parliament. The Duc d'Angoulême saw this as the perfect opportunity for his father to get rid of the ultra-royalist Villèle. According to Villèle in his memoir, although the King acted as though the turn of events was not dramatic, Marie-Thérèse was alarmed. Villèle recalled that she warned the King on December 11 of that year: 'You abandon M. de Villèle: that is the first step that your throne descends.' In early 1828, Villèle resigned, and the King replaced him with the equally ultra-royalist Vicomte de Martignac. Martignac was the very same man who had assisted Marie-Thérèse in her confrontation with General Clauzel in 1815. His ambitions had taken him from local politics in Bordeaux to the center of power in Paris.

Others also sensed unrest in the air and one in particular felt he had an important mission to accomplish. In May of 1828, an eighty-one-year-old Dr Pelletan, after many failed attempts to give the heart he claimed was that of Louis Charles to the royal family, approached the Archbishop of Paris, Monsieur de Quélen, and begged him to keep the relic safe. De Quélen acknowledged receipt of the heart on May 23. When, sixteen months later, the doctor died, the heart, preserved in alcohol and stored in a crystal jar, stayed hidden behind some books on a bookshelf in the Archbishop's library.

Throughout 1827 and 1828 Marie-Thérèse continued her steady round of public appearances and served her King as his ubiquitous emissary of charity and kindness. The Parisian newspaper *Le Moniteur* chronicled that among her appearances during this period the Dauphine presided over a ceremony for the Children of Providence, traveled to Oise, visited a candle factory in Versailles, an artist's atelier in Montmartre, placed the first stone at a church in the village of Grenelle, journeyed to Normandy, to Caen, opened a theater at Saint-Cloud for a charity benefit, and visited a hospice in Melun; she made trips to Troyes, Chaumont, Plombières, Nancy, Strasbourg, Metz, Bar-le-Duc, Besançon and visited the ruins of the ancient chateau of the Princesse de Clèves. She also continued to pay out a staggering amount – hundreds of thousands of francs per year – to charities, living the concept of noblesse oblige and refusing to accept receipts for her charitable donations, saying that it was the duty of the donor to forget his gift. *Le Moniteur* would frequently report on the lavish gifts given by other members of the royal family; it would report on the Dauphine's frequent visits to military hospices, convents and hospitals, but it would never include the considerable amounts of money she left at the end of each visit.

In truth, the Dauphine, famous for her forbearance, was growing quite impatient with her family, remarking that they were 'like goats tethered at pasture'. For one, she wished that her husband would adopt a more robust political stance. Further, she had come to the conclusion that the Duchesse de Berry was utterly inane. Her sister-in-law's vacuity and complete insensitivity in her eyes reached new heights when, on Monday March 2, 1829, Marie Caroline hosted an extravagant costume ball – in imitation of those hosted by Marie Antoinette at Versailles – and made a grand entrance dressed as Mary Queen of Scots, the Stuart Queen who had, like Marie-Thérèse's mother, been decapitated.

People read about the Duchesse de Berry's succession of parties and balls, but, as the economy in France was still in a strong position, few complained about the cost to the public purse. Neither was the court of Charles X criticized, even though it was far more extravagant than that of the guillotined King Louis XVI. Charles X, like Louis XVI, loved to hunt, and he organized lavish post-hunt parties, and liked to play cards. It would often be Marie-Thérèse who read the newspapers and kept him abreast of political developments in Europe. Charles X supported a total of 2,219 court officials and servants. By the end of the 1820s, the little Duc de Bordeaux had more than one hundred servants, compared to the Dauphin of France in 1789 who had forty-five. As in the days of the ancien régime, throughout the reign of Charles X, the other courts of Europe looked to France for its style. The King of Bavaria sent his pages to the French court to study their equivalents; the King of Sardinia received reports detailing receptions at the Tuileries, and copied their plan; the Czar Nicholas I, younger brother of the childless Czar, Alexander I, of Russia emulated the *menus-plaisirs*; Emperor Pedro I of Brazil sent an envoy to the court of Charles X to study its organization and etiquette; and the United States commissioned *tabourets,* a kind of straight-legged stool, from a Parisian furniture manufacturer for installation at the White House. Despite the widely held notion that the Dauphine seemed to be unconcerned with style, preferring understated simplicity, her formal gowns and jewels were fabulous and courtiers and fashionable women around the world followed her lead, as they had that of her mother.

The 1820s had seen the rise and expansion of industrialization in parts of Europe and in America. The first phases of railroad systems as well as new technologies had created new fortunes. Bankers were now heroes, and a prosperous class of capitalists was beginning to dictate social values. Although she had always anticipated an arranged marriage for herself, Marie-Thérèse could not quite grasp the notion of alliances among merchant families where young girls were bartered into marriage for the sake of business. Money became the new virtue, and people were rewarded for simply having a lot of it. Marie-Thérèse had been raised in a world where bloodline and Christian ideals gave one dignity, and she was quite uncomfortable with this burgeoning, modern and very secular civilization. People pointed to material success with pride, but it would not be for extravagance that the Bourbons would be faulted.

As the great novelist Stendhal remarked, at the very moment when the average citizen, the 'everyman', had begun to believe in his own self-importance and had begun to take an aggressive role in his own self-determination, success and personal liberty, the Bourbons had been returned to the throne. They had created a government profoundly ill at ease with itself. The Charter under which King Louis XVIII had been forced to rule had presented an incongruous mixture of ancien-régime and revolutionary concepts, two orders so paradoxical their union was almost destined to fail. Although Louis liked pomp and ceremony, his more conservative brother demanded it. At the court of Charles X, there were six classes of '*entrées*' – permissions and entitlements to enter a room in the presence of the King. There were those who could enter the King's bedroom while he slept, the first of the Cabinet, or the *grand*; those who could enter at anytime as long as they were announced and the *entrées* of the Cabinet; those who could enter a room a little before the hour when the King would hear Mass (which included the military household of the King, royal guards, the cardinals, Chancellor of France and the President of the Chamber of Deputies); those of the Hall of the Throne, who could appear when the King sat for his formal audience; those with admittance to the first salon preceding the Hall of the Throne; and those who could enter the second salon (subsets of equerries and those who participated tangentially in ceremonial positions). The Dauphine too had her own staff of clergy, ladies of honor, ladies of the bedchamber, companions, ladies-in-waiting, military aides, equerries and the like. A return to such formal protocol was regarded as an echo of the past and had little in keeping with democratic reform.

In the summer of 1829, Charles X himself began to make reactionary decisions that even Marie-Thérèse thought unwise and too extreme. The first of these was to place Prince Jules Auguste de Polignac in his ministry. Polignac, forty-nine years old, was thought to look very much like the King – and, therefore, like the late Louis XVI. He was the son born on May 14, 1780 to GabrielleYolande de Polignac, whose special friendship with the late Louis XVI had caused great pain to her best friend, Marie Antoinette.

The name of Polignac was infamous in France. It was hated by those who had believed in the Revolution as well as those members of the ancient nobility who recalled that the mother of Prince Jules had arrived at the court of Versailles with an insufficient pedigree. It was Louis XVI who had ennobled her with the title of 'duchess' when this boy was born. Those French men and women born years after the Terror had heard stories of the excessive favor given to the Polignacs at court, which had contributed to the eruption of great violence. And when, in 1815, Jules de Polignac had refused to swear allegiance to the Charter; he antagonized a great many people. Immediately after Charles X appointed Polignac, a new political faction headed by Lafayette and Talleyrand, and funded by the Duc d'Orléans for whose benefit this party was created, banded together to reaffirm the Charter and oppose the policies of Charles X. Marie-Thérèse shrewdly cautioned the King that his association with Polignac could be politically disastrous; he ignored her, but she sensed a familiar ill wind in the air.

That autumn, the King and Marie-Thérèse went on a goodwill tour of eastern France. While on the road the Dauphine became extremely agitated and asked an escort where she was. On being told she was in Varennes, she screamed at the officers to get her out of there as quickly as possible. The news of her erratic behavior spread and when she appeared on a balcony with the King in Nancy she was greeted with jeers. That winter, General Clauzel, the man who had forced her out of Bordeaux nearly fifteen years earlier, was elected to serve in parliament. Marie-Thérèse took the public affirmation of this man as a personal insult.

In May, the Dauphin left for the southern coast to see off a contingent of French troops bound for France's expansionist war against Algeria. On June 14, 1830, when 34,000 French soldiers landed near Algiers, the royal family was in Paris hosting a series of feasts in honor of the King and Queen of Naples. On July 5, the Algerians surrendered. The French celebrated their victory and Marie-Thérèse, who made her father-in-law promise that he would not do anything rash while she was away, set off on her annual pilgrimage to take the waters in Vichy. In her absence the King yielded to Prince Polignac's plans. On the morning of July 26, *Le Moniteur* reported that on the previous day, Sunday, the King had taken the extraordinary measure of signing an ordinance from his home at Saint-Cloud that revoked the fifteen-year-old Charter – an instrument that at least acknowledged libertarian concepts – and repealed freedoms that had been granted to the press.

Marie-Thérèse only learned of the King's betrayal on reaching Mâcon on her way back to Paris. She immediately realized that the end was near, telling her traveling companion, the Comte de Puymaigre: 'It is the worst pity that I was not in Paris.' On July 27, she appeared at the theater in Dijon and was met with hostility. As she traveled toward the Île de France, she discovered that Paris was once more under siege. For three days – 'Les Trois Glorieuses' – angry men and women refused to work. Carts were overturned to form barricades and gunfire was heard once again in the capital's streets. Royal ensigns that hung over shop windows were torn down and symbolically burnt. The police fired into the crowds, killing several people. A powder magazine was ransacked, with citizens turning the Place Louis XV, the Place Vendôme and the Carrousel into artillery batteries. It was an excruciatingly hot July, and over the next two days cannon fire ripped through Paris, church bells pealed continuously and a black flag was hoisted over the Madeleine church. Marauders invaded and ransacked the palace of the Archbishop of Paris. The crystal jar that was claimed to contain the heart of Louis XVII fell to the floor and splintered into pieces. A man who found Dr Pelletan's papers took them to the home of Pelletan's son, Philippe-Gabriel Pelletan. Two days later, the younger Pelletan went back to the Archbishop's home, where he found what remained of the heart smelling of ethyl alcohol – as his father had described – and covered in sand and glass. Nonetheless, Philippe-Gabriel was able to collect it, remove the shards of glass and place it in a new jar, thus preserving his father's secret.

Madame de Boigne recalled the violence perpetrated during those three days in Paris and the hatred once again directed toward the monarchy: 'I can positively affirm that throughout this and the following days I heard no cries except "Long live the Charter!"' A deputation of the Chamber appeared at Saint-Cloud and begged the King to rescind his decree. The Marquis de Sémonville urged him, for the sake of the safety of the Dauphine who was en route to Paris, to placate the people. The King replied that Madame, the Dauphine, was as prepared to die for France as he was. The Dauphin, Louis-Antoine, had joined the infantry to fight the rebels and soon returned to be with his father when troops began to march on Saint-Cloud. The King, however, remained blasé, explaining to the Comte de Broglie: 'Jules [Polignac] has seen the Holy Virgin again last night. She ordered him to persevere, and promised that all would end well.'[6]

Marie-Thérèse, however, was not as cavalier. She arrived at Tonnerre on July 30 at five in the morning in her grand royal carriage. She was met by her secretary, Baron Charlet, who had traveled to meet her to apprize her of the violence that had raged in Paris for the previous three days. With Charlet's help, she abandoned her carriage and luggage, changed into the costume of a maid and transferred to a rather basic coach in order to avoid detection by the National Guard, once again under the command of Lafayette. As she journeyed toward Saint-Cloud, Charlet went on ahead with orders to take care of her affairs, including to sell her beloved Villeneuve-l'Etang. The house was purchased by the Vicomte Decazes, brother of the minister Marie-Thérèse had blamed for the Duc de Berry's death.

The King and the Duchesse de Berry had been able to watch some of the insurrection through a spy-glass that had been placed on the top floor at Saint-Cloud. On the morning of July 30, they watched with horror as the tri-colored flag was raised over the Tuileries. The Dauphin made a brave effort to rally French forces, but was hindered by conflicting and incomplete information and directives. Even his own soldiers were beginning to grumble that his wife had been a better general in 1815. Most of the military defected and fighting spread throughout the entire Île de France.

On July 31, Charles X, determined to appear strong and uncompromising, but fearing for his life and for his family, packed up his grandchildren and the Duchesse de Berry and left Saint-Cloud accompanied by about 4,000 *garde royale* and *gardes du corps*, and headed for Versailles. The Duc d'Angoulême rode on horseback among the soldiers. Along the way they faced obstructive and hostile crowds and by the time they reached the Grand Trianon, Charles decided that it was time to make haste to his hunting lodge at Rambouillet, an even greater distance from Paris. The Duchesse de Berry, who adored the novels of Sir Walter Scott, seized the opportunity to dress as a man and arm herself with pistols, her father-in-law remarking that she looked just like one of Scott's heroines. The party reached Rambouillet at about nine in the evening.

While the King and his family had been making good their escape from the capital, in Paris, outside the Hôtel de Ville, General Lafayette embraced the Duc d'Orléans in front of a delighted crowd of thousands.

As Marie-Thérèse journeyed from the provinces she saw that everywhere the white flags of the Bourbon dynasty had been replaced with the banner of the Revolution. That evening, July 31, she reached Fontainebleau and found the palace virtually deserted. She learned of her family's whereabouts, and left for Rambouillet the next morning. When she arrived, the King's first words to her were: 'My daughter, will you forgive me?' She replied simply: 'Let us forget the past.'

As Marie-Thérèse had predicted, Charles X was forced to abdicate. On August 2, the King and the Dauphin signed a document relinquishing their hereditary rights to the throne in favor of Henri, the Duc de Bordeaux. Many historians have claimed that for the twenty minutes between the time the King signed the document, the ink dried, and the Dauphin read and put his own name to the paper, Marie-Thérèse was the last Queen of France from the senior Bourbon line. In truth, to legitimists, she would only become Queen upon the death of her father-in-law. The three – the King, the Dauphin, and Marie-Thérèse – all believed that this gesture of devolution to the young boy would ensure his place on the throne.

When the Duc de Bordeaux was informed that he was King of France, the boy and his sister were in another room arranging chairs into a carriage. Seated high on the group of chairs playing coachman with an imaginary whip in his hands, the nearly ten-year-old boy was told that his grandfather, despite all of his best efforts, had not succeeded in making the people of France happy. Little Henri replied that he could not believe that his wonderful *bon-papa* could make anyone unhappy and continued lashing his invisible horses.

Four months before the revolution of 1830, on March 29, King Ferdinand of Spain abolished Salic law in favor of his daughter, Isabella, to the prejudice of his younger brother, Charles. When the French Bourbons were told of the news, Marie-Thérèse grumbled that France should have done the same thing long ago.

CHAPTER XXIII
SUSPICIONS CONFIRMED

O N AUGUST 3, approximately 14,000 armed Parisians and members of the National Guard marched toward the royal family's hide-out at Rambouillet. As soon as the King received word of the threat of impending violence he knew it was time to go. Marie-Thérèse, the aging King and Louis-Antoine prepared to leave France once more. They packed their personal effects, silver and other finery into splendid carriages; the King arranged for the crown jewels to be returned to the treasury in Paris, and Marie-Thérèse packed every one of the treasured souvenirs that remained to her of her parents and siblings. The Duchesse de Berry, with the vainglorious notion that she would, like other great matriarchal figures of history, Marguerite de Navarre, Margaret of Austria and Louise de Savoie, influence a King, planned to remain in France as Regent of her son.

Marie-Thérèse bid a tearful farewell to Pauline de Béarn. It would be the last time the childhood friends would ever see each other. Pauline recalled that the Dauphine, who said she had nothing more precious to give her cherished friend, relinquished the seal that had belonged to her mother which the Queen had worn suspended from her watch. Marie Antoinette had given her daughter this memento the day she was removed from the Temple Prison.

The Duchesse de Berry, her children and members of the royal households accompanied Marie-Thérèse and the reluctant party on their journey to France's northern coastline. Charles X rode his own horse behind his grandson's carriage for reasons of protocol as well as safety. Much like a funeral procession, the majestic but grim convoy proceeded toward the Château de Maintenon at a slow pace, giving the Chamber of

Deputies time, if it were needed, to recall the King. At the chateau, its proprietor, the Duc de Noailles, offered them hospitality and his condolences. Along the route Marie-Thérèse had noted the tricolors being waved – horribly familiar portents – and knew that the King would not be asked to return.

Rumors had spread that Charles was riding toward the coast to rendezvous with British naval vessels leading to an invasion of France on his behalf. In the small town of Dreux, armed peasants surrounded the Bourbon procession and shouted abuse. En route to L'Aigle, an open packet of arsenic was found in the kitchen being used to prepare meals for the King and his family. On to Saint-Lô, and Valognes, where, early in the morning, Marie-Thérèse was able to attend Mass and, later that day, Charles bid an emotional farewell to his bodyguards. As his most loyal soldiers bowed to kiss the hand of the Dauphine, many of the men observed a look on her face of sad resignation.

Traveling slowly from town to town, Charles still hoped that once the legislators learned of his abdication in favor of the young Duc de Bordeaux, they would appoint a regent and recall the family. Charles had asked his cousin, the Duc d'Orléans, to read the declaration before the Chamber of Deputies. Unbeknown to him, when Louis-Philippe read the document he deliberately omitted the portion that named the King's grandson successor to the throne. The King had naively placed his trust, and his family's future, in the hands of Louis-Philippe: the man who Marie-Thérèse always believed had learned treachery at his own father's knee. In an eerie echo of the tactics of 'Philippe Egalité' and of his ancestor, Gaston d'Orléans, who had tied his ambitions to the dissenting Frondeurs against his nephew, King Louis XIV, Louis-Philippe had already struck his own deal with the politicians. Many also accused him of engineering the violence of 'Les Trois Glorieuses' by bribing soldiers and mobs to come out onto the streets.

It was only when the party arrived in the town of Carentan and the King read Le Moniteur that they learned that young Henri would not be the next King. Instead the Chamber of Deputies had elected the Duc d'Orléans to the throne, as France's new 'Citizen King'. Charles was stunned. It was he who had insisted on reconciliation between the two branches of the family. It was he who had asked his cousin to serve as his emissary to the parliament, while Marie-Thérèse, her instincts as ever quite correct, had remained distrustful. It was she who had withstood and sacrificed so much, and whose trust in the King he had dishonored.

At first named Lieutenant-General, Louis-Philippe d'Orléans focused all his diplomatic efforts on appeasing Europe's foreign ministers and making his grab for power seem less a revolution than an easy transition from one political party to another. Once installed as King, Louis-Philippe reinstated the Charter and substituted the tri-colored flag of the Revolution for the white flag of the Bourbons. He distanced himself from his own lineage, refusing to be crowned at Reims, insisting instead on a ceremony at the Palais-Bourbon, across the Seine from the Tuileries. He would live at neither the Tuileries nor Versailles but remained in the center of Paris at his home, and that of his late father, the Palais-Royal. For all of his seemingly good intentions, he was, however, like his father: a social chameleon and a hypocrite. Heinrich Heine, the German poet, arrived in Paris shortly after Louis-Philippe ascended the throne. While there, Heine associated with a group of utopian socialists, and was less than impressed with the new monarch's claims of '*égalité*'. Heine noted that the King was known to wear dirty pairs of gloves to shake hands with the common people and clean, fresh, kid gloves when among noblemen. His reign would soon be characterized by the entreaty '*Enrichissez-vous!*' – 'Get rich!'

One person who, surprisingly, did not endorse the 'Citizen King' was Louis-Philippe's own wife, the new Queen. Marie Amélie was horrified that her husband was prepared to sacrifice the senior branch of the Bourbon family. After all, she herself was a granddaughter of Empress Maria Theresa, a daughter of the sister of Marie Antoinette, and first cousin to the Dauphine. She was embarrassed that the rest of her family, which included her brother, the King of Two Sicilies, as well as the Austrian clan, would now regard her husband as the new 'Usurper'.

When the senior, legitimate, branch of the Bourbons arrived at last at Cherbourg on August 16, to embark for whereabouts unknown – they found that their cousin, the new King, had thought of everything. He had arranged for two American packet boats, the *Charles Carroll* and the *Great Britain*, to be placed under the command of a French rear admiral, Dumont d'Urville, and be readied to remove the party from France. Charles and his family had little choice but to board the ships, though they had no idea where they would be taken. Marie-Thérèse hurriedly dispatched a letter to her secretary Baron Charlet instructing that he write to her under her new pseudonym 'Comtesse de Marnes' (after Villeneuve-l'Étang in Marnes) in London and in Hamburg – believing these to be the two most likely final destinations.

The newly styled 'Comtesse de Marnes' said farewell to her cherished friends. Many of them begged her to allow them to join her wherever in the world she was heading, but she sadly refused their pleas. Each member of the royal family was escorted on board by a trusted friend – the small task being regarded as a great honor; the tiny walk of great symbolic importance to history. Yet again, Marie-Thérèse of France steeled herself for an uncertain future. If anyone in the family could have been prepared for the unknown, it was this now fifty-one-year-old woman, who had so courageously faced uncharted waters throughout her life.

On board the *Great Britain*, Marie-Thérèse asked a sailor if he knew what the captain's orders were. He told her, 'to fire on and kill anyone who tries to regain the coast of France'. As the ships set sail, the Duchesse de Berry cried openly, but Marie-Thérèse, dressed in black, kept her grief hidden. She remained on deck as the *Great Britain* left harbor and watched until the French coastline was a faint blur. Suddenly two French ships of war, the *Seine* and the *Rôdeur*, approached with their guns aimed toward the ships containing the royal fugitives. Madame de Gontaut-Biron began to speak in English with one of their ship's sailors. The French captain on board the *Great Britain*, afraid of a conspiracy that would take the ships to the royalist Vendée, ordered the governess to speak only in French so that he could understand all communication on board. Marie-Thérèse laughed, told Gontaut-Biron to ignore the captain and find out as much information as she could about their destination. Gontaut wondered aloud, again, in English, about where they were heading. One of the sailors overheard her and curtly replied: '*Saint Helena*'. In an absolute panic, she ran with the news to Marie-Thérèse. The confusion was sorted out after some discussion when it was revealed that they were destined for St Helens on the Isle of Wight in the English Channel and not the remote island in the South Atlantic where Napoleon had died in exile nine years earlier.

After days of terrible storms, they finally reached the waters of Spithead. At St Helens three of the former King's most trusted men were dispatched to London to ask the Duke of Wellington, now Prime Minister, for asylum for the royal family. The ship was loaded with more commodities and Marie-Thérèse and her sister-in-law discovered that trunks containing their clothes had been stolen, probably at Cherbourg. At Cowes they registered at a small inn under assumed names and were provided with some garments by the waiting Lady Anglesey and Lady Grantham. When Charles X had lived in England as the Comte d'Artois he had been a well-liked figure. Now, owing to his revocation of the Charter, many Englishmen had revised their opinion of him. Charles's emissaries returned with a message from the Prime Minister that he was trying to find a place where the Bourbons could live quietly. As the royal party crossed the Solent and approached the southern coast of England, Madame de Gontaut-Biron watched for activities on the English mainland through a telescope. When they arrived at a pier in Portsmouth, a small boat pulled near the gangway and an officer, attired in the uniform of an English aide-de-camp, announced: 'A letter for the Duchesse de Gontaut!' The children's governess, completely surprised, was handed a letter, which she passed to Charles X. The former King returned the note to the Duchess, stating: 'It *is* for you.' Gontaut-Biron then handed it to Marie-Thérèse, who also said: 'It's for you.' Madame de Gontaut-Biron then opened the note and the two women read it together.

It was a missive from the Duke of Wellington, who, on behalf of His Majesty, King William IV of England, explained that he had been authorized to offer them refuge provided that they arrive as private citizens. Marie-Thérèse had already adopted the name the Comtesse de Marnes; the Duchesse de Berry followed suit and, taking the name of her country estate, became the Comtesse de Rosny; the former King became the Comte de Ponthieu, after one of his royal domains in Normandy, and little Henri, the Comte de Chambord after the palace bought for him by the people of France after his birth.

It was obvious to the Bourbons when they saw the flags of the Revolution being waved mockingly at them on the streets of Portsmouth that Wellington had had to walk a political tightrope to secure their stay. They were on their way to Lulworth Castle in Dorset, which the Catholic Sir Thomas Weld had agreed to rent out to the Bourbons. Lulworth had been built as a hunting lodge in 1610. Four English Kings, James I, Charles I, James II and George III had been regular visitors there. While the exiled Bourbons installed themselves in the West Country, they realized that, as Lulworth was exceedingly cold and drafty, it would be uninhabitable in winter and that they needed to make more permanent plans. Also, unhappily for Charles X, many of his former creditors – from his high-spending days in London – began to resurface. Fortunately, Marie-Thérèse – due to some planning on her part and on the part of her trusted secretary, Baron Charlet – arranged to receive a very large sum of money from the London banker, Werth, to take care of the family.

One month after their arrival in England, they received an unpleasant surprise. The Citizen King had dispatched his own hand-picked ambassador to England. It was none other than the consummate survivor, the man who had shed his skin and transformed himself and his allegiances infinite times – Charles Maurice de Talleyrand. When Talleyrand arrived on September 25 at Dover, he was greeted by an impressive salvo of artillery. Thirty-six-years earlier, penniless and held in contempt, the émigré Talleyrand had fled England for America in disgrace. It had been the era of Pitt and Fox when men wore powdered wigs and silk knee-breeches. It was now a different society with Gladstone and Disraeli on the rise. The wardrobe of the bourgeoisie was in style, as was, apparently, Talleyrand, who was now fêted and celebrated, and, very much to his own personal pleasure, invited to join London's most exclusive private men's clubs.

The local populace in the countryside near Lulworth Castle was very curious about their royal visitors. Mary Frampton recorded in her journal that her brother, James, called on the 'Comte de Ponthieu' and his family and was thunderstruck when the former King extended his hand, offering to shake Mr Frampton's instead of placing it for Mr Frampton to kiss. James Frampton was thoroughly delighted when, a few days later, he received a return visit. James's daughter, Harriot, thought that the woman dressed shabbily in a light brown dress, yellow-ish shawl, cotton stockings, very short petticoats and a coarse, weather-beaten bonnet was a maid. When she asked this servant woman whether Marie-Thérèse-Charlotte of France was still at Lulworth Castle, the woman replied: 'Yes, I am' – Harriot was appalled at her own mistake. The women discussed the fact that Harriot was engaged and about to be married. Harriot reported to her Aunt Mary that the Dauphine was quite surprised to learn that Harriot and her fiancé were well acquainted. Mary also had an opportunity to see the Dauphine, whom she had last spied in London in the spring of 1814 during the euphoric festivities upon the defeat of Napoleon. She had heard that the Dauphine often looked somber. Mary believed that as no one had suffered her 'unpar-alleled misfortunes' no one had more of a right to appear sad; but Mary was not of the opinion that Marie-Thérèse, whose red-rimmed eyes she noted as had so many others, seemed the least bit grumpy. In fact, when the royal family appeared unannounced at the Framptons' home, as ordinary neighbors paying a call, Mary expressed to one of their attendants how astonished she was to have just had the honor to meet the Princess, who was quite fun. He replied: 'It was just what the Duchesse liked, to surprise people.'

The meeting prompted Mary to record in her journal an event re-counted by a friend, a Mr Okeden, which confirmed her own assessment of the Dauphine:

In the year 1818, Mr Okeden happened to be at Paris, and he related to me a strong instance of these qualities, displayed at a moment when she had no time to prepare her mind for their exhibition.

At the annual fair held at Vincennes, the crowd was extreme, and the pressure very great and dangerous to the people, on the arrival of her carriage with herself and attendants in it, preceded and followed by a detachment of guards on horseback. The mob murmured, and cries were heard; the 'La Dauphine', then only Duchesse d'Angoulême, dared not to venture to the fair unaccompanied by guards. Upon which she stood up in her carriage, ordered the coachmen to stop, and then, in the most cool and dignified manner, commanded the troops to retreat, and leave her. The order was immediately obeyed, and the Duchesse then drove several times backward and forward through the fair, accompanied by the applause instead of the hisses of the crowd.[1]

Mary and Harriot enjoyed their social engagements with Marie-Thérèse; they found her easy to talk to and completely at ease among the country folk. They were very impressed that the de Berry children spoke perfect English. Harriot was also flattered by the Dauphine's interest in her nuptials. Apparently, although the French had a custom of a *gâteau de noce*, Marie-Thérèse was intrigued by the English wedding ritual of sending around among friends and neighbors pieces of the wedding cake. Harriot's fiancé, Mr Mundy, concurred, remarking that the French royals, who were 'great walkers', 'having shown themselves everywhere' and who had entertained the locals with 'historical gossip', would be very much missed when they left the area, which happened sooner than anyone had expected.

The 'Trois Glorieuses' in France had begun to rumble throughout Europe. The Tories were nervous and by early October the Bourbons were shuttled to Holyrood Palace in Edinburgh, away from Charles's creditors; but even more importantly, removed from the political spotlight. In November, Wellington was ousted, making way for the more liberal Lord Grey and his Whig party. In 1831, uprisings in Italy, Portugal and Poland would parallel France's 'July Revolution'. In France, Louis-Philippe issued decrees reversing those of his Bourbon predecessors. It was now illegal to observe with reverence the anniversary of the death of Louis XVI; he also shut down the memorial to Marie Antoinette at the Conciergerie. Although members of the Chamber of Deputies pleaded in public for Marie-Thérèse to be allowed to return to the country for which she had sacrificed so much, Louis-Philippe greeted these entreaties with silence. The Orléans family had, at last, attained the throne they had sought for nearly two hundred years.

Although Charles was familiar with life in Edinburgh, and with Holyrood, having lived at the palace during the 1790s, Marie-Thérèse hated the place and immediately rented a small house close by in Canongate at 31 Regent Terrace for herself, her husband and eleven-year-old Princess Louise. The 'Comte de Ponthieu' and his ten-year-old grandson shared the palace, which was open to the public for tours at various times and on various days, with a small staff. Marie-Thérèse and her father-in-law often went out riding together.

While Marie-Thérèse spent hours each day at Holyrood with her family, reading of world affairs in the newspapers and performing her needlework, the Duchesse de Berry would take off on jaunts around England. She soon installed herself in the resort town of Bath, enjoying the spa and the gaming. Reporting back to the French government on the royal group's activities, Talleyrand recounted how he had seen the 'Comtesse de Rosny' at a party in London at the Neapolitan Embassy. According to the French ambassador, a minister from Naples joked that although she was the niece of his King, the new French Queen was the King's sister. Both men, according to Talleyrand, noted that apparently the 'Comtesse de Rosny' had no concept of the meaning of discretion. She refused to keep a low profile, or simply did not know how to.

The exiled King Charles X philosophically remarked on many occasions that it was fitting that he be allowed to spend his waning years with his grandchildren. Louis-Antoine was not as resigned. He openly expressed his frustration at not having done more and would often comment bitterly that he wished he had fought to the last. Captain Dumont d'Urville wrote in his journal that he had heard the Dauphin expressly admit: 'I have only one regret . . . that I was not killed in Paris.' Some thought that Louis-Antoine wanted to recapture the crown for himself; but Marie-Thérèse continued to meet with sympathizers who insisted that such a route was impossible. They told her that the people of France would never accept him, and even if there were ever a change of heart, it would most likely be the young Comte de Chambord whose ascension would be agreed upon. After this point of view was explained repeatedly to Marie-Thérèse, she realized that any plan for her own husband would be fruitless. She had always determined to educate and prepare her nephew for monarchy; now she resolved to chart his return. While keeping abreast of political movements in France and holding audiences with royalist spies, she would spend the majority of the day with the Comte de Chambord, impressing upon him his Bourbon heritage as well as the lessons of the past.

At the age of six, the Comte de Chambord's education, supervised by Marie-Thérèse, had been turned over to the Duc de Rivière. As Marie Antoinette had prepared an informative account of her young son's character for Madame de Tourzel, the Duc de Bourdeaux's governess, Madame de Gontaut-Biron had done likewise for his new tutor. She described the boy as honest, straightforward, serious, and a champion of the underdog. Gontaut-Biron admitted that, although Henri was prone to having a quick temper, he was stoic and could display remarkable self-control for one so young. She also affirmed that he genuinely adored his sister, Princess Louise.

The relationship between her niece and nephew often reminded Marie-Thérèse of the most tender and precious bond that she and her little brother Louis Charles had shared. She fostered their closeness, and made every effort to teach the children about love and charity. Marie-Thérèse had learned long ago to make her home wherever she was, and it was, despite her distaste for the Protestant country, in Edinburgh that she oversaw Princess Louise's first communion. She was intent on teaching the children to bring their customs, values and traditions with them even when they were outside France; for, in France, many of their family celebrations were public events. In exile, their rituals were performed for their own benefit. Marie-Thérèse's influence had a lasting impact on the children as evidenced by the letter from Madame de Gontaut-Biron to the Duc de Rivière, which stated that the young Henri was exceedingly charitable, often giving much of his own allowance to others in need. Many years later, as an adult, Henri would claim that it was his aunt, Marie-Thérèse, who was his most significant mentor, that she taught by example and that she remained, for him, the embodiment of piety and charity.

Marie-Thérèse's long periods in exile had taught her to appreciate the necessity of always having contingency plans, and although she departed France without much preparation, she and her secretary, Charlet, had arranged for monies from the sale of Villeneuve-l'Étang to be placed abroad. She also carried, tied into her skirt, a small bag of significant diamonds. The Bourbon family was entitled to yet another source of income that would provide for them all. The always fiscally prudent Louis XVIII had put away a fortune in a London bank during his reign – 'just in case'. So, when King William IV began to encounter serious political problems with Parliament in 1831, and it became clear that it was best for a foreign monarchy to situate itself elsewhere, the Bourbons prepared to relocate, but, this time, it would not be for an impoverished lifestyle. While William IV battled with his two political parties over the parliamentary reforms of 1831–32, the Bourbons, cast down by the Scottish weather anyway, contacted Marie-Thérèse's aging cousin, Franz of Austria.

Franz, whose power had been diminished during the Napoleonic era, was once again a ruler of supremacy, owing to Napoleon's demise and the 1814–15 Congress of Vienna, which not only returned Austrian and Italian lands to his Empire, but expanded his control, naming him President of a newly drawn German Confederation. The Emperor could afford to be magnanimous to his cousins and offered the Bourbon family hospitality in Prague at the fabulous and historic Hradschin Palace, Franz's residence when he visited his domains in Bohemia. Marie-Thérèse was quite looking forward to returning to the Catholic country that was part of her mother's homeland. When in France, Marie-Thérèse had responded to those who believed that Franz and his Viennese court had imprisoned and mistreated her that she had, in fact, been very happy amongst her Habsburg cousins. On July 7, 1832, she wrote to the Emperor: 'I would like His permission to pass through Vienna to verbally express to Him my very deep acknowledgment of his past and present benevolence.'

The Duchesse de Berry, however, would not be going to Austria. In early 1831, Charles X issued a half-hearted statement in order to mollify Marie Caroline. She had previously harangued him to appoint her the Comte de Chambord's official Regent, but he had refused. In late January, the exiled King signed a document that stated that the Duchesse de Berry would be Regent of France during her son's minority 'when they return to France'. Shortly after this proclamation was issued, the peripatetic Duchess disappeared. Using various disguises and pseudonyms from Italian operas and the tales of Sir Walter Scott, she had returned to the continent on a mission to put her son on the throne of France. She journeyed through Holland, Germany, Switzerland, and Italy, going from one escapade to another. Her Bourbon relatives read of her adventures in the daily newspapers with increasing horror.

The Duchesse de Berry arrived in Genoa and went on to Sestri, Massa, and Florence. Local princes hurriedly dispatched missives to France's King Louis-Philippe reassuring him that the Duchesse de Berry was unwelcome in their principalities. When she arrived in Rome, the Pope, equally alarmed, also contacted the Citizen King swearing that he had no intention of harboring the royal fugitive. From Rome, she contacted her own family in Naples, and even they were unimpressed to see her. Her half-brother, King Ferdinand III of the Two Sicilies, was annoyed with the Duchess's lack of circumspection. The Duchess later admitted that, while in Italy, she had engaged in a romance, not reported on by the press, but one that would result in serious repercussions regarding her future. In addition to this alleged liaison, she embarked on another wild exploit, one that would turn out to be extremely dangerous.

In April 1832, the Duchess sailed to Marseille. Her plan was to reach the royalist Vendée where she would lead an insurrection. When Marie-Thérèse and Charles X learned of Marie Caroline's ambitions, they were dismayed. The Duchesse de Berry's attempt failed; she was arrested and imprisoned at Blaye fortress. It was then discovered that she was pregnant. Most thought that the father of the baby was her co-conspirator, the equerry Mesnard, or Guibourg, a handsome local attorney who was often at her side. Mesnard, a married man in his sixties, could certainly not marry his pregnant lover and Guibourg was not of the appropriate station. Charles X was outraged, and he demanded the Duchesse de Berry provide a marriage license immediately. Eventually the Duchess did so claiming that when she was in Naples she had resumed a teenage love affair with Comte Ettore Lucchesi-Palli and had secretly married him. Most chose not to believe her: there were too many holes in her story, not least the fact that it had been over a year since she had even been in Naples and therefore Lucchesi-Palli could not be the baby's father. Those who believe her story insist that proof was revealed in secret records at the Vatican in 1899 when papal secretary Petrus Chicchi asserted that the couple had married on December 14, 1831, and that the ceremony had been performed by a Jesuit priest, Father Rozaven, with the knowledge of Pope Gregory XVI. Skeptics insist that no such marriage license ever existed, that the powerful King of the Two Sicilies, in an effort to save his family's honor, had something planted in the archives.

At last, Marie Caroline became the heroine of her own invented story, the solipsistic theme of which was that she had been underestimated. In her tale, which she would tell to the poet-statesman Chateaubriand, she claimed that on her way to the Vendée she had started a letter-writing campaign, begging Europe's monarchs to assist her in an invasion of France. They all turned her down except one. Through exceptional negotiations on her part and on the part of the Comte Ettore Lucchesi-Palli, King William I of the Netherlands agreed to cede Belgium to

France if Henri V acceded to the throne. Marie Caroline insisted that during the summer of 1832, she and Ettore Lucchesi-Palli were working together hammering out an agreement. Ettore Lucchesi-Palli claimed that he had visited his bride on more than one occasion in Nantes; and she, once again, acting the role of playing a favorite figure from a Sir Walter Scott saga, made a dangerous and covert trip from west to east through France, to the Hague and back to Nantes, her theater of operation. Their meetings, in fact, do coincide with the correct timing for the conception of her baby, due the following May; however, once again, there is ample testimony that those meetings could not have taken place. Many tried and failed to find proof of these claims on the Duchess's behalf, and there is still disagreement about their veracity today.

Once she landed on French soil, Marie Caroline issued her own proclamations as 'Regent of France'. Appalled by the commotion caused by the Duchess's behavior, Charles X issued a new statement making it clear that the Duchesse de Berry was not Regent of France. Meanwhile, he and Marie-Thérèse went ahead with their own plans. Charles, Louis-Antoine and Henri would sail from Leith for Hamburg at the end of September 1832, while Marie-Thérèse would take Princess Louise on a trip to London and then meet the men in Prague.

In London, William IV's Queen, Adelaide of Saxe-Meiningen, called on Marie-Thérèse and Princess Louise to pay her respects. General de la Rochejaquelein, namesake and nephew of the General and great hero of the Vendée uprising of the 1790s, then accompanied Marie-Thérèse, Princess Louise and Madame de Gontaut-Biron to their ship and on to Rotterdam. During the crossing, the General decided to speak with Marie-Thérèse about a matter that was weighing heavy on his mind. Understanding that it was a very delicate subject, he approached Marie-Thérèse and took a portrait out of his pocket. He showed the picture to her and stated that he thought it was a picture of her brother, and that he believed he was still very much alive. Madame de Gontaut-Biron recalled that Marie-Thérèse grew visibly agitated and then screamed at him: 'How could you believe that if there had been the slightest possible doubt, I could have hesitated to proclaim it? Is it probable that I should prefer my uncle to my brother?' Princess Louise wanted to know what her aunt had meant, so Marie-Thérèse, who explained that she simply could not bring herself to speak about it, asked Madame de Gontaut-Biron to tell the young girl about her aunt's sad past. Madame de Gontaut-Biron complied and told Princess Louise: 'You shall know all; and then you will understand, my child, a sadness which you have sometimes mistaken for brusqueness.'

One day, during a carriage ride in the Dutch countryside, Marie-Thérèse unburdened her heart to her niece, and told Louise about her years in prison. In her cell, she told her, she had learned *The Day of the Christian* by heart because it comforted her. She recalled that she would twist wool that her aunt had left behind, and that she hated not knowing at which hours the guards would enter her cell. She told Louise that it was her own dear Aunt Elisabeth who, before she was taken to her death, had asked the guards to promise that they would allow her beloved young niece to dress before they entered. She recounted for Louise how she would wash her own laundry and then smooth it by putting it under her mattress. She explained that she would spend the days and nights listening: listening for the sound of approaching guards; listening to all she could hear within the prison walls. Wrenchingly, she then confided to Louise that she knew for certain that her mother had heard Louis Charles being tortured. At that point the memory proved so overwhelming that Marie-Thérèse stopped the carriage and alighted for some air. She walked alone for a while and then returned to the coach, calmer. When she resumed her place, she very sweetly asked Louise not to mention the subject ever again.

Marie-Thérèse was nearing fifty-four years of age; yet, the painful memories of the Reign of Terror remained in clear focus. Other memories from her past proved a little more pleasant, and when, on October 8, 1832, Marie-Thérèse and her entourage arrived at the Hofburg, she claimed to be very happy to return to the home of her maternal family. She was, once again, a guest of the Habsburgs, whom she described as 'amiable' and 'attentive'. She slept in the rooms she had occupied over thirty years ago, and aside from the sad anniversary of her mother's death, which she commemorated with her mother's relatives, she displayed obvious enjoyment showing Princess Louise around Vienna. At the end of the month, on October 28, she returned, after thirty-five years, to Prague, where she had been sequestered, for her safety, in a convent in 1797 when Napoleon had marched on Vienna. Although in 1797 she had not been overjoyed to remain at the side of her sickly aunt, Maria Anna, Marie-Thérèse had always found convent life soothing.

Now in Prague people lovingly called her 'Majesté'. The ground floor at Hradschin Palace was kept vacant for the Emperor, and the Bourbons and their small coterie of courtiers occupied the second floor. From their windows they could see the church domes and bridges and peer over the rooftops at one of the most beautiful cities in Europe. It was a lavish and truly splendid home. Louis-Antoine and her father-in-law would meet with sympathizers and she would care for her niece and nephew. Her own staff included her almoner, the Bishop of Hermopolis, her equerry, a Mr O'Haggerty, who became like a son to her, another priest named Trébuquet, and her longtime friend, the Vicomtesse d'Agoult. Marie-Thérèse was delighted when the Duc de Blacas, who had so ably served King Louis XVIII, and knew every rule of etiquette, joined them and assumed the role of head of household. Charles paid for guards out of his own funds and the Bourbons in exile lived comfortably and with many familiar rituals.

While Charles X maintained that the family's dream was to see his grandson on the throne of France, Louis-Antoine continued to minister to his father and proclaim publicly that his King's wish was his command. Privately he felt some resentment. He was a man used to leading troops into battle and he was now visibly bored. Marie-Thérèse felt great sympathy for her husband's pain; however, she would not cause a schism with her father-in-law, the rightful King of France.

In the spring of 1833, Marie-Thérèse decided to visit the popular spa at Carlsbad, where she leased a riverside house on the edge of town. She went for walks, had treatments, and spent what she would later recall as delightful moments with friends. She was enjoying a pleasant, relaxing time when trouble abruptly interrupted her quietude, and came knocking at her door.

CHAPTER XXIV
BLACKMAIL

ON MAY 10, 1833, the Duchesse de Berry, now Contessa Lucchesi-Palli, gave birth in Blaye prison to a daughter whom she named Anna Maria Rosalia. One month later, in a seemingly magnanimous gesture, Louis-Philippe released the infant and her mother from the tower fortress. In truth, the Citizen King was well aware that Marie Caroline posed little threat to his monarchy: she had proved herself daring but fatuous, was regarded as something of a joke and, given her liberty, would doubtless continue to be an embarrassment and a liability to the senior Bourbon line. Although Charles X was extremely fond of his effervescent daughter-in-law he maintained her banishment for the sake of family honor. Instead of reuniting with her family in Prague, Marie Caroline headed for Italy, where she and her new husband placed their daughter in the care of a foster couple. Sadly, Anna Maria Rosalia would die at only three months of age.

Marie Caroline now possessed only a very minor title and began to realize that as the Contessa Lucchesi-Palli she had little standing among the noble houses of Europe. She desperately wanted to make amends with her late husband's family and asked her friend François-René de Chateaubriand to serve as her emissary to the Bourbons. Chateaubriand left for Prague in May 1833. His mission was to meet with the former King and to deliver a packet of letters – one to Henri and Louise, one to Charles X, and some others to the Dauphine. Henri, Comte de Chambord would turn thirteen that autumn, the historic age of majority for Kings of France. In her letter to Charles, Henri's mother asked her father-in-law to make a public proclamation announcing the great day; to her children she wrote declaring her love.

At the Hradschin Palace, Chateaubriand asked the King's permission
to deliver the note to the children, but the King refused. Chateaubriand
then relayed Marie Caroline's request to see her children, and once again
he was told this was not possible as the children had not yet been told of
their mother's remarriage. Chateaubriand spent some time with Henri
and Louise, whom he found cheerful and charming, reporting that the
brother and sister amused each other, teased each other, and were very
respectful of their guest. However, Chateaubriand was distressed about
the manner in which the children were being educated. He had been under
the assumption that the tutors were preparing the de Berry children to
face the new, modern and industrialized social order of Europe; instead,
he found that the Jesuits were in charge of the children's education,
inculcating them, he felt, with antiquated dogma.

In France, although moderates were happy with the constitutional
monarchy as a compromise, republicans wanted elections. Within the
royalist legitimist movement there were divergent factions: a few sided
with Marie Caroline, some dismissed her, some believed that Charles
X should return to the throne, some urged the Dauphin to gather an
army, and others thought it best to wait for Henri to come of age.
Chateaubriand, a staunch royalist, believed that if France were going
to keep pace with the other nations of Europe its King needed to be
in step with his people. Agrarian economies that were socially
paternalistic were changing with the advent of the industrial revolution. Every bourgeois merchant now fancied himself as king in his
own right and wanted prestige and prosperity for his family. Would
any of the Bourbon men in Prague be fit for the future? The aging
Charles X was unlikely. The Dauphin now seemed listless and
pitiable, and having witnessed for himself the schooling and shaping
of the future Henri V, Chateaubriand determined that even Henri
would be unsuitable as King unless he was better guided. Chateaubriand thought it was his patriotic duty to ask to have himself
appointed the boy's tutor.

The first step was to reconcile the family. Learning that Marie-Thérèse
was in Carlsbad, Chateaubriand took his leave of the King and proceeded
to the spa. He arrived there at the end of May and made his way to the
little house at the edge of town that Marie-Thérèse had rented for the
season. He memorialized every detail of his visit with the Dauphine and
wrote that before being presented to her he was 'so filled with emotion
that I did not know if I could face the princess'. At the Dauphine's house,
a servant opened the door, and he saw

Madame la Dauphine seated in the corner of the salon on a sofa, between two windows embroidering a piece of tapestry . . . She raised her head from her work, and as if hiding her own emotion, addressed me: 'I am happy to see you, M. Chateaubriand; the king told me you were coming. You have traveled the night? You must be tired.' I respectfully presented her with the letters from the Duchesse de Berry; she took them, placed them near her on the sofa and said: 'Sit. Sit.' She then returned to her embroidery with a rapid machine-like convulsive movement.[1]

He noted that aside from her eyes being 'red-rimmed', they had an extraordinary intensity lending her a beauty 'that made her resemble the Virgin at Spasimo' by Raphael. Still stitching, Marie-Thérèse first enquired if Chateaubriand had seen the Comte de Chambord and asked the poet to confirm that Henri was indeed a marvel. Chateaubriand responded that Henri was certainly strong and fine, but, after having witnessed a little temper tantrum, during which the boy's sister called him 'a beast', he smiled and suggested that the Dauphine may have indulged the boy a little. Marie-Thérèse laughingly dismissed that notion. It was clear to Chateaubriand that Marie-Thérèse had a deep mother's love for her nephew.

Their conversation turned more solemn when he voiced his concerns over the direction of the boy's education. Marie-Thérèse swept his criticisms aside and then asked wistfully after her 'sister', the Duchesse de Berry, saying: 'She is very unhappy, very unhappy. I feel very much for her. I feel very much for her.' When Chateaubriand addressed Marie-Thérèse as 'Majesty' he observed that she made an involuntary response of pleasure, suddenly appearing to him as if she were wearing a diadem, before quickly recovering, 'Oh no! I am not Queen.' 'By the laws of our realm you are and you will be the mother of Henri V,' Chateaubriand responded. He then went on to explain his mission. He had come on behalf of the Contessa Lucchesi-Palli and he was to give Marie-Thérèse her sister-in-law's formal permission to continue the job that the Dauphine had already long assumed. He handed the Dauphine a packet of letters written by Marie Caroline while she had been in prison. The notes were written in lemon juice. Marie-Thérèse had long ago – when she had written and received secret communiqués in Vienna in the late 1790s – learned how to decipher this kind of missive. She placed the notes near a flame, and she and their messenger read them together. In essence, Marie Caroline relinquished her children to their aunt and she begged her sister-in-law to care for them. Marie-Thérèse turned to Chateaubriand and said simply: 'She is right to count on me.'

Marie-Thérèse understood that her sister-in-law's gesture was merely that, a gesture, made by a woman powerless to do otherwise. Appreciating Chateaubriand's difficult errand, Marie-Thérèse treated him graciously. She spent two hours with the writer, after which she explained that, unfortunately, she had to leave because it was time for her *régime des eaux*. She invited him to come back at 3 p.m. at which time he could join her for lunch.

When he returned that afternoon, many of the Dauphine's retinue were present also. Chateaubriand met Mr O'Haggerty, the Comte de Trogoff, the Comtesse Esterhazy and her daughter. They all ate together in the drawing room as the house did not have a formal dining room. Chateaubriand was appalled at the poor quality of the food and even more surprised when, after dinner, the Dauphine gossiped with her friends. Apparently, she was not quite the saint he had believed her to be, and he was stunned when she made underhand comments about, among others, the Duchesse de Guiche, whose husband was maliciously rumored to be the Dauphine's lover. Chateaubriand concluded philosophically that at that moment the princess of thrones and the scaffold 'descended from the heights of her life to the level of other women', and proved she was, after all, human.

Chateaubriand and Marie-Thérèse continued to chat while she sewed. At five she went out for a drive in her calèche again asking him to join her later on, at 7 p.m. He returned that evening and it was much of the same – the same people, the same needlepoint, the same chatter. She paid close attention to all her guests, including Chateaubriand, and as he watched her from a side view, he felt an eerie sensation. As he watched Marie-Thérèse bend over her handiwork, he saw an image of the late King on his way to the scaffold. He suddenly realized that she had come to resemble her father, especially in profile.

A few days later, Chateaubriand met again with Marie-Thérèse at the Mühlenbad baths. She was dressed in a shabby, gray silk dress, shawl and old hat. As the Dauphine and the poet took their promenade around the gardens, passers-by stopped to drink from the fountains and took no notice of them. Chateaubriand reflected sadly that every clock in town and every chapel bell measured time because of this woman's grandmother, and now, she, Marie-Thérèse, the Empress's namesake, seemed inconsequential. They met again later that day. Marie-Thérèse had written a response to the Contessa Lucchesi-Palli, which she handed to Chateaubriand. The note was dated the very first day of Chateau-briand's arrival in Carlsbad, yet Marie-Thérèse had not given it to the statesman until the day of his departure. She told him that she had intentionally omitted his name from the note for his own protection, and he recalled that she handed it to him with great caution. It read:

I experienced a great deal of satisfaction, my dear sister to at last receive news directly from you. I feel for you with all my heart. Count on me always when it comes to the constant interest in you and, above all, your dear children, who are most precious to me as ever. My existence, however long it will be in duration, will be consecrated to them. I have not yet been able to deliver your commissions to our family, my health having demanded that I come here to take the waters. But I will discharge them as soon as I return, and believe that we will never, they and I, have but the same sentiments concerning everything. Good-bye my dear sister. I feel pity for you from the bottom of my heart, and I tenderly kiss you.

M.T.

Despite the fact that Marie Caroline had thoroughly embarrassed her entire family, Marie-Thérèse conveyed nothing but love and loyalty toward the children and kindness toward their mother, yet Chateau-briand judged the letter to be cold. His assessment is mystifying, as minutes before he read the note he had acknowledged the extreme care with which she had placed the letter in his hands and the fact that she had taken great pains to reassure her sister-in-law that she and, especially, her children, would be loved. Tensions were growing for the Bourbons as Henri's thirteenth birthday drew near. Chateaubriand was aware of that, nonetheless he mistook the Dauphine's political prudence for an act of neglect, which it was not. He then asked the Dauphine if she had any further instructions for him. She replied: 'Tell your friends how much I love France; that they know well that I am French.' He reminded her that France had made her suffer, but she countered: 'No, Monsieur Chateau-briand, do not forget. Tell everyone well that I am French, that I am French.' As he left Carlsbad, Chateaubriand steeled himself to deliver the unpleasant news to Marie Caroline that her husband's family would not receive her.

Chateaubriand made his way westward through the Germanic fairytale towns of Weissenstadt, Berneck, Bayreuth, Hohlfeld, Bamberg, Dettel-bach and Würtzburg, comparing his journey to the great romantic epics of literary mythology. On through Wiesenbach, Heidelberg, across the Rhine to Manheim, Dunkheim and Frankenstein, Chateaubriand contemplated the scenery as 'the region of dreams'. That summer thousands would make this same journey in reverse on a pilgrimage to Prague to hail the young man who, turning thirteen in September, should, to those faithful to the ancient laws of France and dreaming of its past glories, rightfully one day be King of France.

When Chateaubriand passed through Bamberg, he was within just a few miles of Hildburghausen where the Dark Count and his now fifty-four-year-old companion still resided at Castle Eishausen. The Count had decided that the couple should remove themselves for the summer to the bucolic retreat called 'Schulersberg' just outside the town, which he had recently purchased. There, they could enjoy the tranquil charms of summer away from the prying and still curious eyes of their neighbors – and the many who would pass through on their way to hail Henri in Prague.

In France, thousands of people had applied for their passports to make the pilgrimage to Prague but were refused the proper papers. Louis-Philippe made all kinds of threats, even going so far as to station officials at the eastern borders of France in towns such as Strasbourg. As many made their way through the German principalities without documentation, in essence, as refugees, Franz of Austria prepared himself for turmoil and strained relations with the Citizen King. Charles X was unwilling to exacerbate the situation with Louis-Philippe and as soon as Marie-Thérèse returned from her spa treatment he whisked the entire family to the remote town of Buschtierad, in the countryside outside Prague. Some also believed that Charles was jealous of Henri and could not face the throngs of people who came to worship at his grandson's feet rather than his own.

Once he learned that the royal family had departed Prague for the little town of Buschtierad, the Vicomte de la Rochefoucauld made his way there toward the end of July 1833. De la Rochefoucauld, whose father, the Duc de Doudeauville, had been a trusted advisor to Louis XVIII and Charles X, had been given an assignment by the editor of the journal *Paris, ou le livre des Cent-et-un*, to cover the royal family at the time of Henri's coming-of-age. The editor knew that de la Rochefoucauld would be afforded a rare kind of access to the Bourbons.

De la Rochefoucauld described his journey as a vista of immense plains, scenery that made one sad. He rode past the rows of apple trees to the secluded house, which he deemed ugly, and walked beneath the cloister-like arches to pay his respects to his father's dear friend. He informed the royal family that he was there to write a story and, because of his father's longstanding and very close friendship with Charles X, they all agreed to cooperate. De la Rochefoucauld was disappointed to learn that the house was filled to the brim and he would have to stay elsewhere. However, the King invited him to dine with the family the next day, and 'on leaving, I went to offer my homage to Madame the Dauphine, to whom I asked for a particular audience'.

De la Rochefoucauld spent a week with the royal family at Buschtierad, observing them separately and together at dinners, at Mass and in their daily activities. He was aware that it was a sensitive time for them because of the strain caused by Marie Caroline. He noted that the family observed a simple daily routine: at ten in the morning, they would convene for breakfast; dinner with their entourage would be at six in the evening. After breakfast, the royal family would separate for their own tasks. At two in the afternoon, Marie-Thérèse and Louis-Antoine would go for a carriage ride together. He observed Henri at his lessons and agreed with Chateaubriand that the choice of Jesuit tutors was a mistake.

When de la Rochefoucauld interviewed Marie-Thérèse, he probed her to ascertain her views on the splinter group that wanted her husband to return immediately to France with troops to claim the throne for himself. She insisted that neither she nor her husband had any designs on the throne, that it belonged to Henri, and advised those people who wished them to take up arms to 'arm themselves with patience' – meant also as criticism of her sister-in-law. She told him: 'We so love France . . . we so love the French people. They have banished us, but all of our prayers are for them and France; speak from time to time of us, so that they do not forget us in our exile. How long to endure this punishable exile!' When de la Rochefoucauld voiced his opinion that Henri ought not to be super-vised by Jesuits, Marie-Thérèse countered that he was learning valuable lessons about discipline from the priests. While many people might think wearing the crown enviable, she explained, it was in fact, 'a heavy burden, and a prince renders it dignified through his virtue and reason'. She told de la Rochefoucauld that it was very important to her that Henri possessed those values above all, and reiterated:

Who would, today, envy the crown? A crown is a terrible weight to bear. One has called me ambitious: all of my ambition is for the happiness and glory of France . . . a journal dared to say that I was not French . . . what a cruel injustice! That is the only injury that could wound me. Oh! Believe and repeat that I am French, uniquely French, French before everything. All of my sentiments are French, all of my thoughts, all of my prayers are for France. We are raising the Duc de Bordeaux for France, but it is France alone that could and ought to reclaim him.

De la Rochefoucauld spoke with Marie-Thérèse for many hours. He believed that she was very open and frank with him and that no subjects were out of bounds. There was one request she made to de la Rochefoucauld that was not allowed on the record, involving a favor. The rest of their conversation was reported for posterity.

Although the King had appointed Marie-Thérèse Regent of France she had, as she explained to her secretary Baron Charlet, accepted the position not out of ambition but out of duty. However, Marie Caroline was not going to surrender her position as mother to a future King of France that easily. When she realized that Chateaubriand had failed in his mission to reconcile her with her children and family, she recruited the help of the elderly, retired Comte de La Ferronays. In August 1833, de La Ferronays arrived in Buschtierad to re-open negotiations on her behalf. The Count, a loyal ally of the Bourbons, reported that during these discussions, while Charles remained stubbornly opposed to forgiving his errant daughter-in-law, it was Marie-Thérèse who worked at softening the King's heart. She was the 'pacifier', and it was she who convinced the King to at least consider dialogue with young Henri's mother.

Marie Caroline, meanwhile, approached Chateaubriand once more, in Paris, and implored him to meet her in Italy. He was not at all optimistic that he could be of any further service but at the beginning of September he set out to join the Countess in Venice. When he arrived, he discovered that Marie Caroline had set off for Ferrara instead. It seemed that Charles X's aide-de-camp, Blacas, had worked in concert with the Austrian statesman Metternich and the royal governor of Lombardy to deny the Princess visas that would bring her closer to her children. In Ferrara, a crowd and armed guards awaited Contessa Lucchesi-Palli's arrival. As she descended from her carriage she loudly announced to the waiting Chateaubriand: 'My son is your king! Help me pass.' Inside the Hotel des Trois-Couronnes, Marie Caroline pleaded her case to Chateaubriand. They then proceeded to Padua where the Countess was told that she could not go any further. Since she could not set foot on Austrian soil, she begged Chateaubriand to go to Prague once again on her behalf. She wanted the Bourbons to formally proclaim her son their King on his thirteenth birthday, and she needed to see her children. After much cajoling, Chateaubriand acquiesced and set out for Prague.

In Udine, Chateaubriand had a chance encounter with the Comte de La Ferronays who informed him that he had just left the Bourbons, who were in Buschtierad, not Prague. At Buschtierad, Marie-Thérèse received the writer warmly and, on the evening of September 27, two days before Henri's thirteenth birthday, Charles X, mildly ill, greeted Chateaubriand from his bed. The King accepted the note from Marie Caroline, read it, and exploded. 'What right does this woman have to dictate what I do?' he railed. 'She is nothing . . . she is merely Madame Lucchesi-Palli, a woman unknown to my family. She no longer has any domain over her children; the French code does not recognize secret marriages; the code dispossesses her of guardianship upon this second marriage.' Charles then informed Chateaubriand that he had no intention of ever setting eyes on Marie Caroline again.

When the time came, on September 29, for Charles X to acknowledge his grandson's majority he did so with a small, simple announcement. Those who had arrived in Prague expecting a grand celebration and formal declaration were disappointed and angry. Fervent legitimists, determined to be with Henri on this day, had made the arduous journey to Prague and then found their way to Buschtierad. When she learned that there were French citizens who had made this pilgrimage, Marie-Thérèse opened the doors of their home, greeted as many of them as she could, and welcomed them all to celebrate with Henri.

On that same day, thanks once again to Marie-Thérèse, Chateaubriand was able to write to the Contessa Lucchesi-Palli from Prague that, despite the King's initial fury, there was good news. Marie-Thérèse had convinced the King to see his daughter-in-law. Charles, who either feigned ignorance that Marie Caroline was not allowed on Austrian soil or, less likely, had not been told by his ministers of this fact, advised Chateaubriand that the entire royal family were going to travel to a town in the central Austrian region of Styria called Leoben, and, if Marie Caroline were to travel there – and the King would arrange for her to do so – they might meet. The King's minister, Blacas, invited Chateaubriand to accompany the royal family; ironically, however, the author of *Atala,* an epic tale of adventure, rescue and suicide, decided that he wanted no further part of this particular family drama, and returned to Paris.

Chateaubriand imagined that fireworks would erupt among the Bourbon family, and he was right. Their reunion took place at the Hotel Emperor in Leoben on October 13. En route to Leoben, the King informed his grandchildren that not only had their mother remarried, but she had had a baby. Henri and Louise were so shocked that they refused to see their mother. According to Comte Montbel, the boy at first remained immobile and silent and then he shouted that he was now an orphan:

> No! No! Now what remains is my grandfather, my uncle and my aunt to guide me with their good advice and their good examples . . . for the present, I will only be silent toward my mother. What am I to do with this M. de Lucchesi? I hope that no one expects me to see a man like that! My mother has a baby, but this infant cannot be my sister, and if there are more babies, what would you expect me to do with these urchins?

At Leoben, the King and Marie Caroline met face to face. Marie-Thérèse and the Comte Lucchesi-Palli remained in the hotel's salon. Marie Caroline made the initial and crucial mistake of making demands. She wanted to be reunited with her children, to have a proper proclamation of majority for her son, and to replace his tutors with educators, like Chateaubriand, who could prepare him for the future and not the past. Charles, amazed at what he considered to be stunning high-handedness, refused each and every one of Marie Caroline's demands. When she realized that her method had backfired, Marie Caroline began to sob, plead, thrash, and scream to get her way. In the hotel's drawing room, Marie-Thérèse hurriedly ran from window to window, slamming them shut, and finally, to the front door, which she also closed, anxiously telling those present: 'They can hear her in the street!' although a crowd had already formed outside. The three-day encampment, with Marie Caroline and her entourage in the Hotel Maure and the King and his staff in the Hotel Emperor, and negotiations going back and forth between them, ended badly for Marie Caroline. She would be returning home without her children.

The Bourbon royal family returned to the Hradschin Palace in Prague and resumed their quotidian life in exile. Mass, breakfast, walks, lessons for the children, letter-writing, making gifts for the poor, and dinners with friends. Marie Caroline, meanwhile, persisted. She obtained permission to travel to Vienna to visit Emperor Franz. In an effort to compromise with all of the warring factions in his and his wife's families, he agreed to allow Marie Caroline to visit the Chateau Brandeis in Bohemia at a safe, but honorable, distance from her children. The following summer, when she arrived at the Chateau Brandeis for her visit, she was not surprised to learn that Marie-Thérèse had seized the moment to take a trip to Carlsbad. Friends of Contessa Lucchesi-Palli insisted that the de Berry children wept with delight and kissed their mother with joy when they saw her; those at Hradschin Palace insisted differently.

Marie Caroline moved from her temporary home at the Chateau Brandeis and relocated to Schloss Brunnsee near Graz. She would also live part of each year at the Palazzo Vendramin in Venice and over the next few years would have four children with the Comte Lucchesi-Palli, all of whom would survive into adulthood.

As soon as the issue of Marie Caroline had been settled, Marie-Thérèse encountered two other matters that weighed heavy on her heart. On October 5, 1832, the now elderly and ailing Madame de Soucy, learning that Marie-Thérèse was en route to Vienna, seized what she thought was an opportune moment to remind Marie-Thérèse that after their last trip together to the Austrian capital in early 1796, Marie-Thérèse had promised undying loyalty to her traveling companion. De Soucy produced a copy of a letter that Marie-Thérèse had originally written to her in which the then teenage Princess thanked her for her kindness and acknowledged all of de Soucy's 'sacrifices that you have made leaving your country and your children to follow me'.

Marie-Thérèse was also greatly relieved when de Soucy was asked to leave Vienna. Marie-Thérèse thought she had heard the last of the woman, but de Soucy, who had been handsomely remunerated by the Emperor (and, for that matter, the Directory, when she was allowed an entire wardrobe at their expense), was always on the lookout for money. In 1823, it was she who had published Marie-Thérèse's unedited account of life in the Temple Prison, no doubt at a profit; and when, in October 1832, de Soucy received no immediate reply from Marie-Thérèse, the former *sous* governess wrote a second letter. On October 17, de Soucy informed Marie-Thérèse, 'cherished princess of my heart', that she needed money to pay for her care needs because her children had refused to assist her.

On December 5, having still no response from the Dauphine, Madame de Soucy wrote to advise Marie-Thérèse that she had written a book about her life with the Princess which contained information that Marie-Thérèse would not want made public. Madame de Soucy explained that she had turned over the manuscript to her doctor, Magneux Lavergne, who was instructed to exchange the book with the Princess for a large sum of money; or, if the Princess would not be forthcoming with cash, Lavergne was to publish the manuscript, which would contain unflattering accounts of Marie-Thérèse.

Madame de Soucy wrote again on January 14, 1833, offering the Princess a peek at the manuscript's conclusion, which read: 'I received my princess at her entrée to life . . . but, alas, my princess has refused me everything.' She wrote again on January 20 and February 16. A week later, Dr Lavergne, with Madame de Soucy's supervision, wrote an account of what they thought they could sell the manuscript for and the profits they might reap, but stated that if Marie-Thérèse could meet those sums, they would destroy the manuscript. In conclusion Lavergne warned that Madame de Soucy had 'stored in her bosom a secret that only the heart of a mother was worthy of containing' and that 'only your Royal Highness has the means to destroy the manuscript in question'.

Although Marie-Thérèse's charity was legendary, Madame de Soucy had made a tactical mistake. She was trying to intimidate the woman who had led the troops at Bordeaux. Instead of gaining the sympathy of Marie-Thérèse, whose sense of obligation, duty and Christian compassion made her greatly admired, de Soucy's behavior, as it had in the past, only served to reinforce the Dauphine's dislike and mistrust of her. In a letter dated March 15, 1833, Marie-Thérèse admitted to her secretary Charlet that whatever she may have confided to Madame de Soucy, and she was not sure that she had ever confided anything of a very personal nature, would have been at a time when she 'was very young, very innocent, when I traveled with this woman . . . I could have said some things that she misunderstood . . . but I never confided secrets of that nature'. In this same note, Marie-Thérèse wrote: 'Tell, then, this man to never write me again . . . that he is master to do whatever he likes with the book, that one more calumny added to those that have already been said about me is no great thing. Tell him that I would have given help to this woman as long as I had the means, knowing that she was ill and unhappy, but from the moment that she menaced me, it was all over.'

Charlet contacted Lavergne and demanded the manuscript. The doctor refused to hand it over, claiming that the information contained within ought only to be seen by Marie-Thérèse. De Soucy continued to bombard Marie-Thérèse with threatening letters, imploring the Princess to send her money. This time, it was Marie-Thérèse who erred. On July 2, 1833, she decided that since the former governess claimed destitution, she would instruct Charlet to send her the sum of 500 francs, 'on the condition that I never hear any more from her or her book – or from that doctor'. In 1837, nearly five years after Madame de Soucy had instigated the blackmail affair, Charlet and Lavergne came to an agreement. He demanded 30,000 francs; Baron Charlet offered 24,000 in two installments. Charlet paid Lavergne 10,000 francs and informed Marie-Thérèse that he had received the manuscript. She wrote to Charlet: 'I would like you to remit the 14,000 F left to pay. I will authorize my banker to give the money to you, but after this, I will not give any thing more to this man, nor will I listen to him speak. As for the writing, you can burn it if you like, although I hope you will live a long enough time so that I can see you again.'

Madame de Soucy died in 1840, but Dr Lavergne kept a copy of the manuscript. He wanted to be named 'personal physician to the Dauphine', which would elevate his career if she and her family returned to the throne. Although she refused this request, Marie-Thérèse did make more payments to the doctor, including 10,000 francs in August 1845 and another 1,000 in July 1847. Each time Marie-Thérèse insisted that the payment would be the last, but each time she sent more. Lavergne, never satisfied, wrote to Charlet: 'I could have sold them to the government, then I would have had *real* money.'

In a letter dated 'Paris, March 29, 1838', in Madame de Soucy's handwriting, the Marquise admitted that she received money in exchange for a journal she kept 'relative to my voyage to Austria to accompany Her Royal Highness, Madame, child of the deceased Louis XVI'. Some historians have seen this as confirmation that Marie-Thérèse's putative half-sister Ernestine de Lambriquet changed places with the real Madame Royale somewhere between the gates of the Temple Prison and Vienna. It was, after all, Madame de Soucy, and very few others, who knew where Ernestine de Lambriquet was sequestered while Marie-Thérèse languished in jail. It was also Madame de Soucy who accompanied the young, blonde woman to Vienna in 1795–96; and it was Madame de Soucy who was permitted to bring along 'a son' and 'a maid' on the journey. Others were convinced that de Soucy's information pertained to some admission on the Princess's part during their journey about Louis Charles. Did Marie-Thérèse confess that she suspected that the little King's real father was Comte Fersen? Or, did Marie-Thérèse divulge her own personal anguish that, since she had never seen her brother's dead body, she was not certain that Louis Charles had died in prison?

Marie-Thérèse decided to stop paying the doctor and Dr Lavergne never did publish the manuscript. If, in fact, there had been secrets of such import, and not merely youthful indiscretions or mistakes of an embarrassing nature, surely Madame de Soucy could have made available her own book, and not just the memoir of a teenage girl, to the highest bidder long before the Bourbon exile of 1830 when, if the matter were that explosive, for example, a state secret or matters concerning a conspiracy, she could have received far more money.[2]

The Bourbon fortune, of course, was always attractive to adventurers. Among those who came forward to claim their 'entitlement' was a woman named Pauline Verber. Verber insisted that she was the daughter of Marie-Thérèse of France, born in the Temple Prison as a result of the Dauphine having been raped by one of her jailers. There were at least a dozen other women in France, the Holy Roman Empire and the United States, each of whom claimed to be the daughter of Marie-Thérèse of France, born of rape or adultery.

One story concerned the daughter of a Dr Thiollier. Thiollier had served as physician to Louis XVIII's wife, Marie-Joséphine, while they lived in Mitau around 1799–1800. While he was in Mitau, Dr Thiollier, a bachelor at that time, suddenly came in the possession of a baby girl. The doctor raised the girl, and after the Bourbon Restoration in 1815 they moved back to his home town, Lyon. That same year, the girl, named Joséphine Thiollier, married. On the marriage documents her mother is listed as an English woman the doctor claimed he had married in Switzerland in a town whose civil offices had burned down at the turn of the century, destroying all records. Dr Thiollier was named 'Baron Villeneuve' by Louis XVIII, apparently on the suggestion of Marie-Thérèse, who visited Lyon, where she happily received the Baron and his daughter, the new bride. Joséphine Thiollier eventually divorced her husband and assumed the name Madame Plasaret de Villeneuve. After her death in 1880, one of her daughters claimed that, although her mother would never divulge the secret of her origins, the family believed that she was, in reality, the daughter of Marie-Thérèse and a lover.

There were also at least forty men who, over the years, dragged Marie-Thérèse and her family through various court systems claiming to be her long-lost brother, Louis Charles. In France, the self-styled Baron de Richemont continued his campaign to be acknowledged as King of France. In the early 1831 he published his 'memoir', which caused a sensation. In it, he challenged Louis-Philippe and disparaged Marie-Thérèse, his 'sister'. In response, in 1831, the historian A. Antoinette de Saint-Gervais wrote a powerful book called *Preuves authentiques de la mort du jeune Louis XVII*. Saint-Gervais's book refuted Richemont's allegations. Saint-Gervais was not the only one to take action against the

Baron de Richemont. In 1833, King Louis-Philippe, irritated by the pretender's fantasies, had him thrown in jail.

That same year, another man claiming to be the rightful heir to the throne of France also began to create disturbance. His story was first published on August 16, 1831, in the German newspaper *Leipziger Zeitung*. According to this report, a man named Carl Wilhelm Naundorff insisted that he, too, was the real King Louis XVII of France. Naundorff arrived in Paris in the spring of 1833, just as Marie-Thérèse had begun her treatments in Carlsbad. During the summer of 1833, Naundorff was able to meet with Madame de Rambaud, who had served as Louis Charles's maid. Madame de Rambaud was overcome with emotion when she met with Naundorff. They reminisced about Versailles and he told her about his daring escape from the Temple Prison. According to Naundorff, a mute child named Tardif had been substituted for the Dauphin in November 1794. Later the child was replaced with one dying of tuberculosis. Naundorff asserted that after he was removed from the Temple Prison, among his various and astonishing adventures, he had been kidnapped, captured by a French ship on the open seas and eventually, in 1810, he arrived in Germany where he became a clockmaker.

In August 1833, after her meeting with the German clockmaker, and examining his vaccination marks, moles and a scar on his lip, which she remembered Louis Charles had received from a rabbit bite, Madame de Rambaud was almost convinced that the man before her was Louis Charles. She set one more trap: she held up a little blue suit she had kept that had belonged to the Dauphin and asked Naundorff: 'Do you remember when you wore this in Paris?' Naundorff replied: 'No. I only wore it once at Versailles.' Rambaud nearly fainted and immediately wrote to Marie-Thérèse in Prague with the thrilling news that King Louis XVII of France was, indeed, still alive. Others who also believed Naundorff included Marco de Saint-Hilaire, Chamberlain to Louis XVI, and Monsieur de Joly, a former minister of the murdered King.

Marie-Thérèse tried to remain calm and insisted that she would wait for more evidence. During a private meeting with the Vicomte de la Rochefoucauld she asked him to investigate thoroughly this Mr Naundorff. On returning to Paris, de la Rochefoucauld set out to follow him. On November 16, de la Rochefoucauld reported back to Marie-Thérèse that, in fact, not only did Naundorff bear a striking resemblance to Louis Charles but his mannerisms and demeanor were so convincing that de la Rochefoucauld felt a bit light-headed with anxiety about the whole affair.

Marie-Thérèse proceeded with caution; despite Naundorff's pleas to meet with 'his sister', she refused. Some of his supporters thought her callous and claimed that the Dauphine was reluctant to meet with Naundorff because she, herself, was a fraud and her charade would be uncovered. After the New Year, in January 1834, Marie-Thérèse agreed to meet with Naundorff's lawyer, Morel de Saint-Didier, so that he could present his client's case and offer her evidence. The elderly Madame de Rambaud, so earnest in her support for Naundorff, traveled to Prague with Saint-Didier. Marie-Thérèse, concerned that de Rambaud herself was an impostor, refused to meet with the woman and would only accept documents from Saint-Didier. Former courtiers who had taken up Naundorff's cause pleaded with Marie-Thérèse, but she refused to meet with him.

At the end of January, Marie-Thérèse received a note from de la Rochefoucauld who told her that two men had tried to assassinate Naundorff in the Place du Carrousel. Naundorff seized the moment to write 'his sister' that he had been longing to see her for many years, that he had written to her over the years, and that he suspected it had been King Louis XVIII, to whom he had also written, who had kept brother and sister apart.

In October 1834, Baron de Richemont was put on trial. In the middle of the trial, Morel de Saint-Didier rose and, with great melodrama, exclaimed that *he* represented the real Louis XVII of France. Baron de Richemont was found guilty of defrauding the people of France. Mr Naundorff continued his claims for years to come, even going so far as to file a lawsuit against Marie-Thérèse in the hope that she would appear in court in person. He, too, was eventually arrested and details of a nefarious past as a con artist and arsonist surfaced. So intent was he on his story, that he and his family had assumed the name of 'Bourbon'. When Naundorff died on August 10, 1845, his survivors – wife and children – insisted that his death certificate read, 'Louis XVII'. After his death, his widow tried to sue Marie-Thérèse for her 'husband's inheritance', asked the court to invalidate the 1795 death certificate of Louis Charles, and restore rights to her children.[3]

The summer of 1833 had brought the picaresque adventures of Marie Caroline, the appearance of Carl Wilhelm Naundorff and the blackmail attempts by the venal Madame de Soucy and Dr Lavergne, causing Marie-Thérèse much vexation and threatening her well-being. Gossip had surrounded her for years, like the scandalmongering that the Duc de Guiche was her lover and this had allowed him to advance quickly in his career, or the stories about illegitimate children, or the rumor that the real

Marie-Thérèse was living quietly in a small town in Germany and that she, the Dauphine of France, was, in fact, a substitute. During each of these trials, she, as always, found solace in prayer. In France, in England, in Prague, wherever she lived, Marie-Thérèse maintained an altar in her bedroom. It was an armoire where she kept candles and the relics that had belonged to her mother, brother and father.

Here she would kneel many times a day. She would sometimes show visitors, especially children, her collections. She would tell them the stories about her parents, their deaths, and her own personal recollections of prison, her escape, and her life as the daughter of the King of France. Marie-Thérèse's mother had delighted in her birth, telling her newborn daughter, 'You shall be mine', and although Henri and his sister Louise would eventually be reconciled with their mother, for now these children were hers, and she would show them, and tell them, and teach them.

CHAPTER XXV
QUEEN OF FRANCE

IN MARCH 1835, Marie-Thérèse's cousin, friend and adversary, Emperor Franz of Austria, died. The new Emperor, Ferdinand I, an epileptic who was also considered mentally impaired, wished to use the Hradschin Palace for his coronation. Marie-Thérèse, having many times experienced a change in the wind with a change in régime, understood that their time in Prague was coming to an end. In May, she suggested that the family travel to the spa at Teplitz and when it seemed evident that the new Emperor would be installing himself in a more permanent manner at the Hradschin, the family instructed the Duc de Blacas to purchase the chateau at Kirchberg. At first the Bourbons hoped to make this their new home, but the region was soon engulfed by a cholera epidemic. Henri developed a serious fever, causing everyone great anxiety. As soon as he was recovered, Charles X, who would soon be seventy-nine, decided that he would establish his family elsewhere and in a milder climate.

In early October, the royal family set off toward Trieste and the Adriatic. They stopped in Linz at the Hotel Canon and proceeded to Slovenia. They crossed the Ponte del Torrione, which spanned the Isonzo River, and arrived in Gorizia, famous for its fine air. It was here, for a time, that Marie-Thérèse's elderly great-aunts had lived during the Revolution. The Count Coronini-Cronberg, head of an ancient noble family in the region, had placed a castle at the disposal of the exiled Bourbon King and it would be here that Charles would reside with his grandson. Marie-Thérèse, Louis-Antoine and Princess Louise rented the medieval Castello di Strassoldo in the center of town.

While cholera ravaged much of the Austrian territories, the exiled Bourbons, thinking they had escaped the plague, began to enjoy the simple daily pleasures of Gorizia. Not two weeks after their arrival, however, on the morning of November 3, Charles began to feel unwell. For two days, he suffered extreme fever and bouts of vomiting. Charles's doctor, Bougon, pronounced that the exiled King had indeed contracted cholera. While Marie-Thérèse remained at Charles's bedside, there were many decisions to be made in the event of the death of the exiled King of France.

Communications were immediately dispatched to the Austrian Emperor since Charles's final resting place was still a matter of political importance. France was out of the question. Emperor Ferdinand offered a Cappucine crypt where many of Marie Antoinette's family members had been buried; however, Metternich did not want to cause friction with King Louis-Philippe. Other proposed sites included Graz, where the Comtesse d'Artois had been buried, and Naples, where a collateral branch of the Bourbons were interred. Another solution was considered. From the moment of his arrival in Gorizia, Charles had enjoyed taking walks to a distant hill where a Franciscan convent stood nestled on the mountain-top. The cloister, called Castagnavizza, had harbored a number of French citizens seeking refuge during the Revolution. Castagnavizza was under the protection of the Thurn und Taxis family. When approached they immediately granted their permission for the exiled Bourbon King to be buried at the convent.

Charles X died at 1.30 a.m. on November 6, 1836. To honor him, many of the townspeople draped the windows of their homes in black. He was buried days later in a white marble sarcophagus bearing the inscription: 'Here rests the Very High, Very Powerful, Very Excellent Prince, Charles X by Name, By the Grace of God, King of France and of Navarre, dead in Gorizia the sixth of November, 1836, age seventy-nine and twenty-eight days.' He left his considerable fortune of 6 million francs to his son and to his grandchildren. Although many in France mourned the late King, Louis-Philippe flaunted custom and chose not to wear mourning clothes in honor of his late cousin.

In early January 1837, Marie-Thérèse, Louis-Antoine (now King Louis XIX to legitimists), Prince Henri and Princess Louise traveled to Vienna for the wedding of a Habsburg cousin. Another Marie-Thérèse, the daughter of Archduke Karl, was about to become Queen of the Two Sicilies and sister-in-law to Marie Caroline, the former Duchesse de Berry. The wedding took place at the same church in which the bride's father had acted as stand-in for Napoleon, when the Emperor of the French had married his Austrian Princess in 1810.

It was nearly forty years since Marie-Thérèse had seen her onetime intended husband Archduke Karl. He had married Princess Henrietta of Nassau-Weilburg, a great beauty, some thirty years younger than himself and twenty years younger than Marie-Thérèse of France. She was a great-great-granddaughter of King George II of England, and proved quite fertile. The couple had seven children together. Their eldest son, who would also become a famous military leader, would marry the daughter of Ludwig I of Bavaria and his Queen, Thérèse of Saxe-Hildburghausen, one of the daughters of Charlotte, the Duchess of Saxe-Hildburghausen, who had sworn to keep the secret and protect the identity of the 'Dark Countess'.

Karl had continued his career as field marshal even after Napoleon's defeat, and after his wife's premature death in 1829, he spent his time writing books on military strategy. He still presented an impressive figure when Marie-Thérèse saw him at the wedding that January: the patriarch of a large and happy brood, he was strong, upright and dashing, in stark contrast to the Duc d'Angoulême whom Chateaubriand described as nearly stick-thin, old beyond his years and attired in shabby clothes. For Marie-Thérèse her visit to Vienna was bittersweet: it was both a pleasant time among family and a reminder of the sacrifice she had made for her own dynasty, a sacrifice which, ironically, had resulted in neither realm nor issue.

After the wedding, the exiled, legitimate King and Queen of France returned to their very simple life at the Castello di Strassoldo in Gorizia. Many Frenchmen traveled to see them in Gorizia to offer their condolences, often arriving at the Castello di Strassoldo with news and books from France as they knew that 'Queen Marie-Thérèse' loved to read. An old friend, Alexandrine du Montet, asked if she had read Victor Hugo's *Notre-Dame de Paris*, which had been a wild success throughout Europe, and was surprised for a moment but then understood when Marie-Thérèse admitted that she simply could not bear to.

They were now a family of four, living in one house: King Louis XIX of France and his wife, Queen Marie-Thérèse, Henri and his sister Louise, the remnants of the thousand-year-old Capetian dynasty all living together in Slovenia with a skeleton staff and their most loyal friends, the people who refused to abandon them. The members of the French contingent continued to include, among others, the Duchesse de Blacas and the Vicomtesse d'Agoult, Marie-Thérèse's friend of nearly forty years. Marie-Thérèse also enjoyed making new friends, and she grew especially fond of the members of the Coronini family.

Their days followed a routine that rarely changed. Marie-Thérèse and Louis-Antoine rose early and attended Mass. Marie-Thérèse, who left her home about six in the morning to go to church, was usually seen wearing black. While she was at church, the teenage brother and sister would begin their own morning of lessons. At ten the family would reunite for breakfast. A menu would be placed on the table. Their maître d'hôtel would ceremoniously announce that breakfast was served and everyone would eat off plates decorated with fleurs-de-lys. Each member of the family would then go about their business for the day. The children would continue with their lessons; Marie-Thérèse would perform her needlework and visit the poor. Every afternoon, she and her husband would take a walk together, sometimes around town, sometimes to the convent of Castagnavizza.

Twice weekly, in the early evenings, the doors of the Castello di Strassoldo opened to the local aristocracy. The guests wore evening clothes and gloves – black or gray, depending on the season – and all would rise whenever 'King Louis XIX and his Queen' entered or left a room. Marie-Thérèse would do likewise in deference to her husband. They would play loto and whist; sometimes there were concerts; sometimes, if someone spontaneously burst into song, an amateur musician would play an accompaniment on the piano. Princess Louise depicted one of these merry soirées in a *gouache* painting; it hangs today in the Musée des Arts Décoratifs in Bordeaux. At other times they visited friends in Hungary and Germany, actively taking part in *la belle saison*.

The Dark Count and Countess, like a couple in a fairy tale, continued to live in seclusion, locked away with their secret in Castle Eishausen. In November 1837, on one of her solitary promenades along the forest paths, the Countess caught a chill, was confined to bed and died days later, on November 25. Before sunrise on the 28th, the old servant Schmidt, a tailor named Marr, two brothers named Schmidt, six pallbearers and a *Totenfrau* ('death's woman') assembled in the entrance hall of Castle Eishausen around the open casket. Inside, a corpse of a woman lay dressed in white. The casket was lifted into the hearse and it was accompanied by another carriage to the graveside. On a small hillside, nearly hidden under brush, a prayer was said as the casket was lowered to its final resting place. All of this was completed in darkness and without the presence of the Dark Count who was too distraught to participate. In a note to Pastor Kühner's widow, Vavel de Versay admitted that his loss was almost impossible to bear. In the most revealing comments that he ever made about the 'Countess', he referred to 'Sophie Botta' as a 'poor orphan'.

Days after the funeral, some local women acquired a number of chemises embroidered with fleurs-de-lys that had been given away. Years later, a Dr Lommler, who performed the autopsy on the body, admitted that he was stunned by the corpse's resemblance to Marie Antoinette. Vavel de Versay continued to live in the vicinity of Castle Eishausen until his death on April 8, 1845. Items that had belonged to 'Sophie' were among his effects and in September of that year Charlotte, Princess Paul of Württemberg instructed her attorney to buy some of 'Sophie's' belongings including a gold embroidered bag that she herself had given the woman whose identity had for so long been a mystery.

There were very few around in the late 1830s who could still have remembered Marie-Thérèse from her youth at Versailles, and their numbers were growing fewer by the month. Madame de Tourzel had long since died. In 1838, Renée de Chanterenne passed away at the age of seventy-six. The Comte de la Rochefoucauld (the Duc de Doudeauville) had also died. In 1839, the Vicomte de la Rochefoucauld, who had assumed his father's title, appeared once again at the door of the exiled French royal family to write another story. Although Charles X had approved of the story of the journalist's trip to Buschtierad, when de la Rochefoucauld arrived in Gorizia on March 22 he was given a very chilly reception by Louis-Antoine's staff. He wrote in the *Pèlerinage à Goritz* that he found the locals ugly and dirty. The Castello de Strassoldo was small, sad, inadequate and bourgeois. 'Although there is a porter, no one stops you as you enter the courtyard and head under a vaulted ceiling to a staircase. Straight opposite the stairs you open a double door that opens onto a large room which serves as both drawing room and dining room, and "Voilà", the habitation which contains the Bourbon dynasty.'

The rooms, he noted, were basic. To the right of the main salon was the suite belonging to Henri, comprising a bedroom and a study. Here he kept two pretty vases from Paris, locks of his mother's hair, a portrait of his father, and paintings that he and his sister had executed. In Princess Louise's room was an iron bed sent from Paris, two paintings – one of her brother and one of her mother. There was a work-table, some simple furniture, a small library, a few statuettes, and some Bohemian glass in different colors.

Unlike her husband, Marie-Thérèse was delighted to see her old friend. De la Rochefoucauld interviewed people in the town of Gorizia who claimed to admire the Bourbons living among them. He wrote that he was in awe of Marie-Thérèse, this 'long-suffering woman', and that she was, for him, and for so many others, the example of Christian compassion. He reported that Marie-Thérèse took him to a Mass at the local cathedral in honor of the recent death of Marie, a Princess of Württemberg. She was also a daughter of Louis-Philippe, the Citizen King. De la Rochefoucauld noted that although Marie-Thérèse was quite complimentary about Louis-Philippe's wife, Marie Amélie, saying that her Italian cousin was 'very charitable', she refused to refer to her as Queen.

Louis-Antoine told de la Rochefoucauld that he and his wife repeated a prayer daily that Madame Elisabeth had taught her: 'Seigneur, whatever may arise, or whatever may arrive, we are convinced that You have wished the greatest good for us.' Marie-Thérèse reminisced with de la Rochefoucauld about other women who had meant so much to her during her childhood and who were now gone, like Madame de Tourzel. She seemed grateful that she could open her heart to him, commenting that 'women so rarely find the occasion to express their feelings'. He noted that she was extremely hospitable to the townspeople as well as to visitors. On Easter Sunday, March 31, de la Rochefoucauld joined a group of French legitimists, determined to hail the man they saw as their rightful King, gratefully gathered at the Castello de Strassoldo to dine with the royal couple.

However, what de la Rochefoucauld really wanted to know related to a far more substantial matter. Now that Charles X was dead would Louis XIX be prepared to return to the throne in the event of another revolution, or would he honor his abdication in favor of his nephew? Although Louis-Antoine was not happy to speak about the matter, Marie-Thérèse had no qualms about telling the writer that she and her husband had but one common desire: to see their nephew on the throne of France. She told de la Rochefoucauld that his visit to Gorizia and, indeed, his story should be about how she and her husband were preparing Henri, 'our child', to rule. The journalist may have found little majesty in their lifestyle, but he readily admitted that he found majesty in her sentiments.

De la Rochefoucauld was then allowed to meet with Henri and his tutors. He described him as a young, vigorous, healthy and handsome young man who, like his father, loved the arts. Although he studied, rode well and fenced brilliantly, Henri admitted that his greatest teacher was his aunt. De la Rochefoucauld had his story. Upon his departure, Henri and Louise each presented him with a gift. Henri had painted a castle, and Louise, angels. The eighteen-year-old young man gave a message to the people of France of his own. 'We love all who love our cherished country and who serve her loyally,' he declared, his aunt looking on with an approving smile. Days later de la Rochefoucauld saw Marie-Thérèse on a personal matter. He requested some memento of the late King Charles X. Handing him the cup from which the late King had drunk his hot chocolate, Marie-Thérèse apologized: 'This is the only thing I can offer you. The jewels of my father were shared among his friends and his *garde robe* was given by us to Monsieur Gros, the son-in-law of Basset, his faithful *valet de chambre*.'

De la Rochefoucauld traveled homeward with his notes. Henri had informed the writer of the code his aunt had taught him to live by: 'Princes are no more than the last of men before God . . . when one humbles oneself before the Supreme Majesty one does not humiliate the rest.' It was Marie-Thérèse who also taught him that court was a place of chimera, where a king could be led astray by those of ambition, and she advised him to live among the people. Marie-Thérèse, who had lived in so many European countries, insisted that part of Henri's continuing education should be to see as much of the world as he could. The days of the King of France living in isolated splendor were no more. If Henri were someday to rule France – and both Louis-Antoine and Marie-Thérèse were convinced that their nephew would, indeed, be recalled by the people – then it was imperative for Henri to understand the world around him.

Henri traveled throughout Switzerland, Italy, Germany and Austria, where he had meetings on politics with Metternich, 'the coachman of Europe'. He also made a point of traveling to the towns of Banat de Temesvar, Charleville, Saint-Hubert and Seultour, Romanian villages that were established by the citizens of Alsace and Lorraine who, upon the call of the Empress Maria Theresa, had settled there in the 1770s to provide Austria with a cultural buffer from the Muslim world. Henri spent time in each of these places, talking to people, soaking up local customs, and learning about industry. When he went to Rome to meet with the Pope, Louis-Philippe's envoy there issued a strong protest. On September 30, 1843, Henri wrote to Chateaubriand from Magdeburg, Germany that his intentions were to travel to England. On November 22, Chateaubriand wrote to Madame Récamier that he was setting out to meet 'my king'. In London, over two thousand legitimists organized a demonstration demanding that Henri ascend the throne of France.

In early December 1843, Louis-Antoine became ill with cancer, and his health declined rapidly. He saw local doctors, experts from Padua and specialists sent from Vienna by Metternich. He suffered terribly for six months, went blind, and died on June 3, 1844. At his bedside, his sobbing wife repeated the same words that the Abbé Edgeworth had uttered at the scaffold at her father's death: 'Son of Saint Louis, ascend to heaven!' Louis-Antoine had written a last request which read: 'I wish to be buried as simply as possible in the very place where I died.' His funeral took place on June 8 and the entire town turned out to line the streets as the cortège proceeded to the cathedral. The exiled 'King Louis XIX' was then interred at the convent of Castagnavizza near his father.

Now that both her father-in-law and husband were dead, Marie-Thérèse, like many widows, decided that she needed to make some changes in her life. She felt that Marie Caroline had been banished long enough and it was time for the family to reconcile. It was also time for a change of scenery. Marie-Thérèse set about purchasing a new home. In the 1830s, the Duc de Blacas had bought a home about fifty kilometers south of Vienna named 'Frohsdorf', named for the little village in which it stood. He offered it to Marie-Thérèse and she accepted it. Frohsdorf, or 'village of frogs', was formerly known as 'Krottendorf', 'village of toads'. Krottendorf, of course, was also the name of the General who became the butt of a private joke between Marie Antoinette and her mother, the Empress, and was used to refer to Marie Antoinette's maddeningly regular menstrual periods. When 'General Krottendorf' at last did not arrive, it had signaled the conception of Marie-Thérèse-Charlotte; and Krottendorf – now Frohsdorf – would be the place where she would die.

CHAPTER XXVI
THE MATRIARCH

S CHLOSS FROHSDORF WAS described by some as a simple white country house, unfit for a queen. It was, in fact, a lovely place. It was two stories high, with nine large windows on each level and a balcony flanked by pillars. It also had a tower and a moat and faced a large plain, which ended at the foot of the mountain range that united the Styrian Alps with the Carpathian range, separating Styria from the Archduchy of Austria. The snow-topped mountains provided an idyllic distant vista. It was from this house, in the presence of such luminaries as Marie-Anne of Savoy, now the Empress of Austria, and the Dowager Queen Caroline of Bavaria, that in 1845 Princess Louise married Ferdinand-Charles de Bourbon, Prince of Lucca, who would become Charles III, Duke of Parma upon his father's death in 1849.

After her father-in-law's death, Marie-Thérèse had been referred to as 'Queen'; however, with Louis-Antoine dead the now Dowager Queen, Marie-Thérèse, insisted on following ancient protocol and curtsying to her nephew whenever he entered or left the room and rising in his presence. While Marie-Thérèse settled in at Frohsdorf, she dispatched her niece and nephew to Venice to meet with their mother. From Venice, Henri wrote to Marie-Thérèse and, on June 9, 1845, she replied: 'I thank you so much, Dear Child, for your letter of June 3. It is so full of sense . . . so touching, so well expressed.' She then went on to tell him that they were suffering a terrible heat, asked him to send 'a thousand loves to your mother', and reminded him that they were all to work together for the wedding of his sister, Louise, to take place that autumn.

For all of the foolish things that Marie Caroline had done, she had also kept her word to her late husband. She had honored his memory and taken care of the children that the Duc de Berry had had with Amy Brown and then grandchildren born of those daughters. De Berry's English-born daughter, entitled the Comtesse d'Issoudun upon his death, had married the Prince de Faucigny-Lucinge. Their son, born only four years after Henri, was as much a member of the Lucchesi-Palli brood as the Countess's own children. The young Prince de Faucigny-Lucinge recalled arriving with Marie Caroline at Frohsdorf in September 1845, for the wedding of Princess Louise of France. He had not seen Marie-Thérèse since staying with her at Holyrood in 1831, he recalled, and when he saw her now, 'at about sixty-seven years', he noted that her carriage was straight as it had been years before. He also commented that for all of the time she spent at her needlework, she stood quite erect, displaying none of the round-shoulderedness he had expected. She moved with great dignity, in fact, majesty; her hair, still abundant, had turned gray, and she immediately tried to put him at his ease. 'The august and sainted daughter of the martyred king', although kind, seemed to always have a sad expression on her face, and he thought that she was most serious.

Faucigny-Lucinge was surprised at how quickly Marie-Thérèse ate her meals. Scarcely had one finished, or even if one had not, if she had finished the plates were immediately cleared. He quickly learned that this was a habit from the days when, having to eat at the King's table in public view, she learned 'to get it over with' as rapidly as possible. Later, when she was a guest in other's houses, he recalled, her sense of urgency disappeared, and she relaxed and laughed among her friends and family.

Faucigny-Lucinge, as had many others, wrote about the salon evenings where the men would play cards, and the women would work on embroidery. The Dowager Queen bid her company goodnight at nine o'clock, and, after the ladies left, he would join the men in the *fumoir* where he questioned her staff as to the etiquette at Frohsdorf. They advised him to be on time for everything. He made a point, then, of rushing to his room to gargle, in order to rid himself of the smell of smoke, and comb his hair ten minutes before each outing with Marie-Thérèse. One day, she invited him to accompany her on a carriage ride. It was a small carriage, built for two passengers. He was surprised when she had invited a friend along and instructed him to sit in the front seat with the driver. At first he felt insulted and agitated. He then smiled to himself, remembering that his uncle, Gaspard, had sat similarly when he smuggled the Princess from Vichy to Rambouillet in 1830. They drove for a while until Marie-Thérèse asked the driver to stop. Alighting from the carriage, she took the young Prince by his arm and, as if she had read his mind, recounted to him the very same story he had been thinking about. As she told him of her adventure and of her affection for his uncle, Faucigny-Lucinge fully relaxed, understanding that she had seated him with that intention, and recalled that he, in her presence, felt part of that history.

On November 10, 1845, the whole family celebrated the marriage of Louise, who would remain very close to her aunt. She and her husband purchased a house near Frohsdorf and when their first child, a daughter, was born in 1847, they named her Marie-Thérèse. Little Marie-Thérèse, known as 'Marguerite', would go on to marry her cousin, the Duke of Madrid, and during the First World War lived under house arrest at Frohsdorf. 'Marguerite' was followed by Robert, who would marry twice and have twenty-four children, countless grandchildren, great-grandchildren and great-great-grandchildren, many of whom are still living today. Two more children followed: Alice, who would marry Ferdinand IV of Habsburg-Tuscany, and Henri, who became the husband of the daughter of Ferdinand of Modena. There are hundreds of Bourbons, directly descended from the late King Charles X, many of whom are male, alive today.

In the summer of 1846, Marie Caroline returned Marie-Thérèse's kindness and invited her sister-in-law to her home in Brunnsee. Henri accompanied his beloved aunt on the journey. Faucigny-Lucinge recalled that there was much merriment when they arrived at Brunnsee. Marie Caroline was the same vivacious, fun-loving woman she had always been. One of her charms was that she had never quite mastered French, despite the fact that it was the language of the aristocracy. One time in Venice she felt unwell and arrived late for an appointment with an important German aristocrat. Transforming the Italian word *constipato*, meaning 'suffering from a cold or bronchitis', she apologized, telling him in French: '*Je suis si constipé*' – 'I am constipated'. The German was stunned. Another time in Venice, she remarked that she loved the city, and she loved to be among its people, its crowds. Instead of saying, '*dans le tas*', she said, '*dans la tasse*' – 'in the cups', or 'drunk'. Faucigny-Lucinge recognized that one of the secrets to Marie Caroline's success with people was that she was a wonderful hostess, and before her sister-in-law's arrival they spent days planning activities and entertainment for Marie-Thérèse's comfort and amusement. They put on plays in which they all took parts, went on merry jaunts around the countryside, and had very pleasant evenings during which the two women would conspire on how to marry off Henri. It would not be an easy task because, although he was called Henri V by legitimists, he had no throne and therefore his prospects were limited.

There had been discussions with Naples for Henri to marry an aunt, and with Russia, for Henri to marry an archduchess. Neither materialized. Finally, in 1846, Henri married the elder, less attractive, daughter of the Duke of Modena, the head of the house of Austria-Este, the younger branch of the house of Austria. She, too, was called Marie-Thérèse. Although it was not a love match, Marie-Thérèse of Modena made a very good impression on the woman who mattered most to her husband – Marie-Thérèse-Charlotte of France who, with great relief at a good match, declared her nephew's fiancée 'an angel'.

Despite Metternich's admonishment that their attendance might displease King Louis-Philippe, two Austrian empresses – the fourth wife of Franz II and the wife of Ferdinand I – and a number of princes and princesses made the trip to Frohsdorf for the wedding. Faucigny-Lucinge recalled that when Marie-Thérèse appeared at the wedding dinner she was absolutely radiant – resplendent in a soft gray gown, a diamond diadem, and wearing a fabulous suite of jewelry that had belonged to Marie Antoinette. She appeared luminous, majestic and young. According to Faucigny-Lucinge, the illusion was so strong he thought his eyes were deceiving him.

Marie-Thérèse happily agreed for Frohsdorf to be the main residence of Henri and his very rich bride – that is, when they were not traveling. The pair became quite international, visiting many popular and very social places around Europe, and Henri, the King without a throne, was welcomed at many fashionable resorts, balls and shooting parties. They bought the Palazzo Cavalli on the Grand Canal in Venice, where they would entertain many aristocrats and, with his aunt's encouragement, Henri would frequently call on his mother, Contessa Lucchesi-Palli, and her rather large family.

It was in Venice, in February 1848, that Henri heard news of the first rumblings of strife that would lead to a series of revolutions across the West. The year 1848 was to be one of seismic events around the world. Europe and North America had seen a groundswell of demonstrations for women's rights, workers' rights, and equal rights for all. While republicans, socialists and abolitionists drafted manifestos, Marie-Thérèse remained quietly at Frohsdorf, where she would turn seventy at the end of the year. She had lived through revolutions, assassinations, coups, political uncertainty and exile; at seventy, she was undaunted and prepared for any outcome.

Early in the year, the King of Sardinia, Charles-Albert, had been forced to sign a new constitution. On February 22, violence erupted in Paris and

France was once again in turmoil. On February 24, King Louis-Philippe abdicated. The following day the Citizen King fled Paris and on March 2 sailed to England under the alias 'Mr Smith'. The Venetian police, unsure whether Henri's life was in danger, or if he was himself a threat – a spy – immediately surrounded the Palazzo Cavalli. Growing nationalist movements became a serious problem for the Austrian Empire. There were uprisings among the Czech population, a Croatian army invaded Hungary and rioting in Vienna and Hungary forced the Emperor and Metternich to make sweeping democratic reforms. By the end of the year, they were both deposed, the Emperor in favor of his nephew, Franz Joseph. In Germany as well, where there was an immediate demand for the unification of several states, turbulence threatened. Through all of this, Marie-Thérèse waited and hoped for the people of France to call upon her nephew; but no such communiqué came.

Instead, the French turned to Charles Louis Napoleon Bonaparte (known as Louis Napoleon), son of Hortense de Beauharnais, the daughter of Napoleon Bonaparte's first wife, Joséphine de Beauharnais, and her first husband. Although Hortense was married to her stepfather's brother, Louis Bonaparte, her series of adulterous affairs left her son's paternity in question. For the most part, however, in order to avoid embarrassment, people accepted his claim that he was his father's son, and, therefore, the nephew of Napoleon Bonaparte, the Emperor of the French. A combination of nostalgia for the legend of Napoleon and the power of the name secured Louis Charles Napoleon Bonaparte's election as President of the Republic of France.

Two years after the Revolution of 1848, Louis-Philippe died in exile. A visitor to Frohsdorf, impressed that Marie-Thérèse showed no pleasure in the sufferings of the Orléans family, commented nonetheless that God had punished the man for his role in the downfall of his own cousins. 'It is impossible not to see God's finger in the fall of Louis-Philippe,' said the guest. 'It is in everything,' Marie-Thérèse replied, steadfast in her teleology, before organizing a memorial service for her treacherous cousin.

Her compassion, her kindness and even her wit kept her at the center of a loyal circle of loved ones. Those who were still alive and had adored her when she was seventeen adored her when she was seventy; young people who had the opportunity to meet her were awed by her spirit. She remained active in her charity work, busy with guests, and was always hospitable to anyone who showed respect to the cause of the legitimists. Madame de La Ferronnays described Marie-Thérèse as having a heart that 'was a treasure of indulgence'. Indeed, Marie-Thérèse's own journal of her time in the Temple Prison had displayed no bitterness despite all that she had suffered. She could be fun and enjoyed lighthearted moments with family and friends, where she displayed the side of her personality that, as a child, her mother had named 'Mousseline'.

Henri, her nephew, continued to depend on his aunt as his most reliable source of affection. She was his most significant source of strength. When he and his supporters were negotiating to return to Paris after the abdication of Louis-Philippe, she was his mainstay. She knew him better than anyone. He would write to her regularly from his travels, concerned for both her safety and her health. In the early summer of 1849, he wrote to her from one of his fact-finding journeys that he had taken without his wife. She received his letter and answered from Frohsdorf, on July 8, 1849: 'My Dear Child . . . With what pleasure did I receive at last your letter of your arrival . . . I share your pain that you are separated from your wife . . . and I thank you for sharing the details of your route.' She offered him news of her visitors and her activities – 'two German comedies' – and told him that she had plans to go to Leibnitz, but she would not go to Spitz because cholera had broken out there, along the Danube. His sister and her family were all fine; she, herself, was 'quite tranquil', and she signed off, 'Adieu, my most beloved Child.'

Robert de Bourbon-Parme, Princess Louise's eldest son, remembered an early childhood memory of his great-aunt, Marie-Thérèse. In a story he repeated to his own children about her many years later, he recalled that he was just a tiny boy when he went with his sister, their mother and great-aunt – 'the Queen' – for a ride in a carriage. He remembered Marie-Thérèse's scratchy voice and understood enough to know that she intimidated many people. He, however, mostly remembered her gentleness. As the children, jammed into the coach, were being wildly tossed about, Robert began to cry. Marie-Thérèse placed him on her lap, cuddled with him and told him the following story: She was just a little girl when her mother, Queen Marie Antoinette, brought her to ride in a carriage that was part of a tailgating hunting party. Their carriage lost track of the hunt. When it arrived at a crossroads, they stopped to listen for the sounds of the bugles to determine their route. All of a sudden, and the very young Madame Royale could see this all from her window, a stag appeared. The men aimed their muskets to shoot, but the Queen commanded them to spare the animal. The trembling beast escaped, crossing a pool of water. One could thereafter only see his head and antlers. On the other side, he rose from the water, turned, as if to say 'thank you', and disappeared into the copse. Soon thereafter, the hunting party arrived, but the deer was gone. The King, Louis XVI, approached his wife's carriage door and asked: 'Have you passed the deer?' She told him exactly what had happened and added: 'He is my stag. I do not want him touched.' The King laughed, declared the hunt over, and said to his Queen: 'You have made the best catch of the year.'

Marie-Thérèse, nearing seventy-three years old, continued to promenade daily. It was during one of her customary walks, on October 12, 1851, that she caught a chill. The next day, after Mass, her condition had grown visibly worse. Dr Thévenot was called. On the 14th, she seemed a bit improved and received a visit from Archduchess Sophie, mother of the young Emperor. On the 15th, when her most devoted family members and friends arrived to celebrate her 'Saint's Day', she was so ill that only Henri was permitted to enter her room. She lay in bed under the portrait of her father, Louis XVI, ascending to heaven with the Angel of Consolation. She also permitted Madame de Sainte-Preuve to assist her. On the 16th, she insisted on commemorating the fifty-eighth anniversary of her mother's death. When the people around her protested that she was too frail to go to church, she contended: 'Nothing could stop me from going to the chapel to render to the memory of my mother; I have never failed those duties.' That morning she made every effort to get to the chapel and partake of communion but she was so ill she simply could not get there. Instead the Abbé Trébuquet came to her room and dispensed it to her there.

Alarmed, her Habsburg cousins dispatched the Emperor's personal physician, Dr Seeburger, who diagnosed pneumonia and pleurisy. Owing to the quantity of people wishing to pay their respects, she was transferred from her bed to a divan. On the morning of the 17th, with the help of her secretary Charlet, she organized her papers and asked her trusted assistant to burn many of them. She instructed that after her death her parents' rings, her father's bloodstained shirt and her brother's prayer stool should all remain at Frohsdorf with Henri. She also made a list of people dear to her heart to whom she would leave other personal possessions. She made Charlet promise to give generously to the poor on her behalf.

Her closest friends and family were called to her side. On the evening of the 18th, her fever was very high, and by the middle of the night as morning approached on October 19, she was nearly comatose. At 11.15 a.m., she uttered her final words to her beloved nephew, Henri: '*Je suis anéantie*' – annihilated. The Abbé Trébuquet softly said, 'Daughter of Saint Louis and of Louis XVI, ascend to heaven!'

On Saturday October 25, a funeral service was held at the Frohsdorf chapel, and according to her wishes, the casket of Marie-Thérèse remained closed. Her nephew, Henri, read her last will and testament, which included her thanks to the Emperor and the people of Gorizia and the prayer:

I die in the Roman Catholic and Apostolic religion . . .
After the example of my parents, I pardon, with my entire soul, and without exception, all those who have injured or offended me . . .
I pray to God to shower down His blessings upon France –
France, that I have never ceased to love even under my bitterest afflictions.

She made her nephew her executor and heir and stated, 'I have always considered my nephew Henri and my niece Louise as my children, I give them my maternal benediction . . . worthy descendants of Saint Louis.'

The next day the casket began its journey to Gorizia. The funeral cortège that traveled from Vienna included Marie Caroline Lucchesi-Palli. On October 28, Marie-Thérèse-Charlotte of France was buried in the Franciscan convent of Castagnavizza alongside her husband and father-in-law. On October 29, Henri left for Venice and his biological mother for Brunnsee. The woman he called 'more than a mother . . . the visible sign of divine protection', lay at rest in what for many is 'the Saint-Denis crypt in exile' for two Kings and a Queen of France, her tombstone bearing the inscription: 'All you who pass this way, behold and see if there be any sorrow like unto my sorrow.'

The people of France did not forget her. They, too, mourned her death. In Paris, Louis Napoleon, one year from becoming Emperor Napoleon III, held a private service for the daughter of the late King of France at the Chapelle de l'Élysée; and, on November 6, with the full diplomatic corps from a multitude of foreign countries present, a solemn and dignified Mass was held at the Madeleine church. The writer Sainte-Beuve eulogized her on November 3, 1851. In his essay, Sainte-Beuve chronicled the life of this Child of France and wrote: 'She was not eleven years old when, with the terrible days of October 1789, her public role beside her mother began.' In truth, she had been the object of worldwide fascination from the very moment that her parents announced her impending birth.

In the later half of the nineteenth century, after the demise of the Second Empire, Henri, Comte de Chambord, was offered the crown. In 1871, from the Château de Chambord, Henri issued a manifesto. In homage to his aunt, he insisted on the abolishment of the tri-colored flag of the Revolution. When informed that the people of France would not accept the white banner of the ancien régime, Henri returned to exile, paving the way for the Third Republic of France, the unwitting legacy of Marie-Thérèse to her people.

AFTERWORD

Although there have been a handful of novels published over the past hundred and fifty years that have advanced the possibility that the 'Sophie' who died at Castle Eishausen was the real Marie-Thérèse, nobody has been able to verify this claim. In 1853, when the book *The Dark Count* by German author Ludwig Bechstein, Librarian to the Grand Duke of Saxe-Meiningen, made this assertion, the author merely articulated what had already been widely speculated. In 1872, *The Mystery of Hildburghausen* by Brachvogel offered another account. Hungarian author Jókai Mór contributed *Névtelen vár* to the legend in 1877. This compelling tale, translated into English as *The Nameless Castle*, was published in England in 1889 and in the United States in 1898. Rumors started to fly that the coffin buried in Hildburghausen did not, in fact, contain a body, but a wax figure. On July 8, 1891, the coffin was opened and a female corpse was found within, laying one part of the fable to rest. In 1926, the first investigations by O. V. Maeckel were published in Germany, and the book by Saxe-Altenburg in 1954. In 1980, Mór's book was made into a six-part German television series entitled *Die Namenlose Burg*.

There has been a recent revival and groundswell of attention focused on the theory of a switch. For the past decade, each September, a large group of eminent European scientists, doctors and historians have convened in Ingelfingen, Germany to discuss the controversy and they have demanded that the two bodies, one buried in the Castagnavizza convent in Slovenia, the other in Hildburghausen, north of Nuremberg, be exhumed. In 2005, a 'union of interest' was formed with the hope of discovering the truth. A contemporary play, *Marriage at Heidegg*, about a filmmaker meeting the ghost of Marie-Thérèse as the Dark Countess, was performed at Heidegg Castle, which overlooks Lake Baldegg in Switzerland. In 2006, *Die Frau mit den Seidenaugen* by Guido Dieckmann, another fictionalized account of the switch theory, was published. And public interest in this controversy, it seems, is far from on the wane. Attendance at the Ingelfingen symposium has increased dramatically and the convention itself is now broadcast on European radio. In 2007, a nine-month jubilee to commemorate the two-hundredth anniversary of the arrival of 'the Dark Count and Countess' was celebrated in the town of Hildburghausen.

There is also a third theory that needs to be considered. According to official French records, Ernestine de Lambriquet married a widower named Jean-Charles-Germain Prempain in Paris on December 7, 1810, and died in Passy, a Parisian suburb, on December 30, 1813, leaving no children of her own. Three months after her alleged demise, the Bourbons were restored to the throne and returned to Paris. The cemetery in Passy was destroyed in 1819.

In 1979, French historian Robert Ambelain published his *Crimes et Secrets d'État 1785–1830*, in which he provided documentary evidence that Ernestine de Lambriquet had, in fact, married and died in a suburb of Paris. On December 7, 1810, in the presence of two imperial notaries, Marie-Philippine de Lambriquet – 'Ernestine' – married Prempain. The official death certificate number '41561 n. 2745', states, according to Ambelain: 'the Mayor of Passy, arrondissement of Saint Denis, department of the Seine declared that on December 31, 1813, at nine o'clock in the morning, in Passy, dead at age thirty-five years, daughter of Jacques Lambriquet and Marie-Philippine Noirot, his wife, both deceased, married to Jean-Charles-Germain Prempain, proprietor . . . signed: Amavet.'

Ambelain wrote that he had seen the handwriting on the marriage certificate and it did not in any way match that of Marie-Thérèse-Charlotte. If, in fact, Ernestine de Lambriquet was the illegitimate child of King Louis XVI, and therefore of no political consequence, she could have quite easily remained in France without threat throughout the reign of Napoleon I.

Had there been a conspiracy, a charade? If there had been, who were the players? After having pieced together the protagonists at the border of France at the time that Madame Royale was exchanged for prisoners, it was clear that, other than Marie-Thérèse's traveling companions, only Bacher, the representative of the Directory, had close enough access to Marie-Thérèse to have affected a switch. The Austrians did not even see Marie-Thérèse until Switzerland; the Comte de Provence and his minions were miles away without permission to approach. There would have been nothing for the Directory to gain in organizing such a scheme and, if it had, at the time of the Bourbon restoration it would certainly have been to Napoleon's advantage to reveal such a fraud.

I wanted scientific proof, the kind of proof provided by Dr Jean-Jacques Cassiman concerning the heart of the Dauphin. I contacted an old friend, Prince Charles-Henri de Lobkowicz, the great-great-great-great-grandson of King Charles X and great-great-grandson of Princess Louise, sister of Henri, Comte de Chambord. Prince Charles-Henri offered me unprecedented access to private family letters and a parcel containing a lock of hair. The handwriting on the parcel was confirmed to be that of the Comte de Chambord. His notation states that the lock of hair within had been taken from the head of the 'Duchesse d'Angoulême' and the date '1830' recorded. The packet had been preserved by the Comte de Chambord and, subsequently, his heirs. We turned over a portion of the lock of this hair to the team headed by Dr Jean-Jacques Cassiman, but unfortunately their results were inconclusive because the DNA in the sample had disintegrated.

I still hoped for a scientific resolution to our mystery. Dr Cassiman suggested that I obtain a tooth or a bone. As a Professor of Comparative Literature and author, I had never dreamed that my work would lead me to a place where I would even entertain the thought of opening graves to help perform experiments. I began with the Bourbon grave in Gorizia and casually asked Prince Charles-Henri if we could open it and maybe borrow a tooth. When I learned more about the 'Saint-Denis in exile' royal crypt at the bucolic convent Castagnavizza in Slovenia, I discovered that it had been the scene of incredibly bloody battles of the First World War, so horrific that the area actually became known as the 'Isonzo Front'. In order to safeguard the graves of the last of the Bourbons, Empress Zita of Austria, herself a Bourbon-Parme, had arranged for the caskets to be moved. After a nearly twenty-year exile, they were subsequently returned to Gorizia in 1932.

The removal of the caskets led to another controversy. Those who believe in an ongoing conspiracy believe that the bodies of the Dark Countess of Hildburghausen and the false Duchesse d'Angoulême were switched at some point in time when the caskets from Gorizia were being transported to Vienna. Although those espousing this theory can offer no substantiation of time or day, their strength of conviction that there has been some cover-up made me suspect that even if I could offer proof from the Gorizia grave, it would not be acceptable to many.

In his delightful travel book *Dunkelgräfin, Kahlbutz & Co.*, published in 2006, Reiner Hammeran journeys throughout Germany to follow the legend of the 'Dark Count'. He proposes that the lore of the 'Dunkel-gräfin' is so pervasive a phenomenon and so ingrained in the German mythology that one could visit almost every town in Germany – and Hammeran made it to twenty-seven of those villages – where the tale of a

mysterious count ensconced in a castle persists to this day. The Hildburghausen legacy, which coincides with the birth of German Romanticism in
that very area, relates specifically to the story of the switch of Marie-
Thérèse-Charlotte of France. There could be no story more emblematic of
the *zeitgeist* of the *Frühromantik*, the early German Romantic movement
that took root right in the vicinity of Hildburghausen, than the Dark
Count holding captive in his mysterious castle the daughter of the
murdered Most Christian King. The strong motif of the doppelgänger,
a hallmark of the Romantic epoch, also distinguishes this story.

The Hildburghausen Museum still houses 'Dark Countess' artifacts, and
has its own website that states 'the secrets surrounding the mysterious Dark
Countess attract many guests from Germany and abroad'. I contacted the
Mayor of Hildburghausen to find out about the grave marked by a head-
stone that reads 'Sophie Botta'. As it turned out, the grave in Hildburghausen is on town property and scientific examination could, in fact,
proceed with approval of the Mayor and town council. After having
corresponded and spoken with the Mayor, it was clear that I was not going
to receive permission for Dr Cassiman and his team to perform DNA testing.
The reason, though not expressly stated, was apparent. Hildburghausen, a
tiny village that was for years behind the Iron Curtain, receives much of its
income from tourism owing to this mystery; the people are in no hurry to put
to bed this controversy. It is simply good for business.

It was clear that we needed to pursue other methods in order to solve the
two-hundred-year-old mystery about the fate of Marie-Thérèse-Charlotte
of France. I felt that what I had learned about her character offered me
sufficient proof; she was the same strong, young woman in Vienna when
she confronted the Holy Roman Emperor as she was in the Temple Prison
when she refused to speak with her jailers. Yet, she could also be sweet and
most virtuous. All of these qualities, which defined the young Marie-
Thérèse, the 'Mousseline Sérieuse', as her mother called her, delineated
a unique blend of traits that indicated, to me, a singular character.

The next obvious choice was to search for girls named 'Sophie Botta'
born in Europe who would have been the same age as Madame Royale.
There was one such girl born in Landau, a town in Alsace, on November
25, 1779. Not only would that have made her both French and German
speaking, it would also have placed the day of the Hildburghausen death
on exactly the girl's fifty-eighth birthday, the age marked on the tomb.
This 'Sophie Botta', however, perished at only four years of age. To date,
it has not been possible to locate any other girls born in Europe of the
appropriate or approximate age who were named 'Sophie Botta' at birth.

I needed to locate letters that could be authenticated as having been written by Marie-Thérèse. One would have to be a letter written before she left the Temple Prison and before there was any possibility of a switch; the others would have to exhibit the same penmanship. I raked the archives and private collections from Russia to Sicily in search of the evidence. Here, I offer two handwriting samples: the first, a fragment of a poem written by Marie-Thérèse in the Temple Prison during the winter of 1794, which I have quoted from in Chapter XI.

Handwriting Sample 1. Poem written in the Temple Prison (given by the family of Madame de Chanterenne to the Comte de Chambord).

The second is the letter that Marie-Thérèse wrote to Madame de Chanterenne from the Hôtel du Corbeau detailing her escape from the Temple Prison on the arm of Monsieur Bénézech and her journey toward the frontier. Discussed in Chapter XII, this letter was penned on Christmas Day, 1795, and is incontestably from the same hand as the one that wrote the poem in the Temple Prison.

Handwriting Sample 2. Excerpt of letter from Marie-Thérèse to Madame de Chanterenne, December 25, 1795 (given by the family of Madame de Chanterenne to the Comte de Chambord).

Once Marie-Thérèse arrived in Vienna, many of the letters that she wrote her family members and friends were intercepted and copied by the Austrian Imperial police and therefore none of the letters held in the Österreichisches Staatsarchiv are in her own handwriting. One private note, however, that Marie-Thérèse personally handed to her guardian, Madame de Chanclos, dated September 13, 1796, was not intercepted by the Emperor's agents, and is offered here as the third example of Madame Royale's own handwriting. This sample demonstrates that the person living in Vienna was the same as the person writing from Huningue, France. The letter to Madame de Chanclos, which was on the back of a drawing, has been in the possession of the family of the Count Coronini-Cronberg in Gorizia since the 1840s. It was in Gorizia that Marie-Thérèse resided for nine years along with her dwindling entourage, which included the Vicomtesse d'Agoult, Madame de Chanclos's niece.

Handwriting Sample 3. Letter from Marie-Thérèse to Madame de Chanclos, September 13, 1796 (Fondazione Palazzo Coronini Cronbergonlus, Gorizia, Italy).

The fourth piece of evidence is the April 9, 1804 letter that Marie-Thérèse wrote to her cousin, the Prince de Condé, which I have quoted from in Chapter XVII. The handwriting in this letter of condolence from the Archives Nationales de France in Paris matches that of the other three.

We know that both in the tower and on her journey from the Temple Prison, Madame Royale was permitted neither secretary nor servant, and that she wrote the poem and her letter to her 'dear Renète' in her own

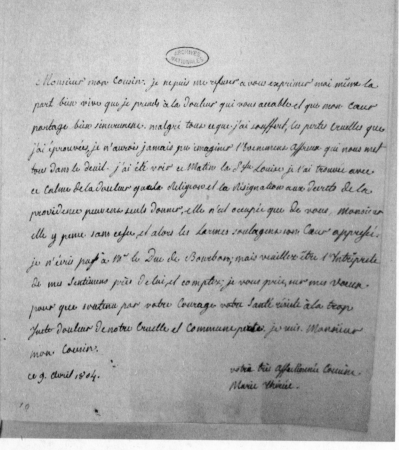

Letter from Marie-Thérèse to the Prince de Condé, April 9, 1804 (Centre historique des Archives nationals, Paris, 34AP7#10. Cliché Atelier photographique du Centre historique des Archives nationales, Paris).

hand. The other two letters shown here are also in her own hand and not of the calligraphic quality attributed to professional amanuenses. In addition, taking into consideration the alteration of vision and dexterity that comes with age, their brushstrokes are the same that appear in letters penned by Marie-Thérèse from the early Bourbon Restoration, many years later, as well as those she wrote into the late 1840s, provided to me by Prince Charles-Henri de Lobkowicz.

In contrast, an excerpt from a note written on September 22, 1808, by the 'Dark Countess' to her protector, wishing him a 'Happy Birthday' and signed 'Sophie', bears absolutely no resemblance to any of the missives signed 'Marie-Thérèse'.

As Ernestine de Lambriquet lived in Paris throughout the Napoleonic era, and all of the letters written by Marie-Thérèse provide substantiation that Madame Royale did, indeed, marry her cousin, the Duc d'Angoulême and went on to become Dauphine and Queen of France, who, then, was the woman, believed to be the daughter of the King, so mysteriously veiled in Hildburghausen? The fact that she possessed items engraved or embroidered with the recognizable fleur-de-lys or pieces of jewelry that may have belonged to Marie Antoinette is insufficient as we know the murdered Queen's belongings made their way via auctions and antique dealers all around the world. After I had asked Dr Jean-Jacques Cassiman to perform the DNA testing on the hair labeled 'Duchesse d'Angoulême' that was in the possession of Prince Charles-Henri, the Prince went even further in the name of friendship, pulling out some of his own hair so that we could study as well his mitochondrial Bourbon DNA. Those results, successfully documented by Dr Cassiman, might assist in other studies. In other words, if someone were to step forward claiming to be a Bourbon, we now have the proper sequencing with which to compare DNA. If the 'Dark Countess of Hildburghausen' was indeed a member of the Bourbon family, the DNA is now available to verify this assertion, and, although she may well have been a Bourbon, she was not, however, Marie-Thérèse-Charlotte, daughter of Queen Marie Antoinette and King Louis XVI of France.

NOTES

PART I: SINNER
Chapter I: *Sex and Politics*

1. The members of the Austrian royal family corresponded with each other in French, the preferred language of the aristocracy.
2. According to Madame Campan, Marie Antoinette's First Lady-in-Waiting, and eyewitness to the Emperor's visit, Joseph II loved to gossip, especially about his brothers and sisters. Despite his counsel to Marie Antoinette to follow a sober path, he was, apparently, quite indiscreet. Madame Campan reported that the 'Emperor was fond of describing the Italian Courts that he had visited. The jealous quarrels between the King and Queen of Naples amused him highly; he described the life, manner and speech of that sovereign, and the simplicity with which he used to go and solicit the First Chamberlain to obtain permission to return to the nuptial bed, when the angry Queen had banished him from it.' (*Memoirs of the Court of Marie Antoinette, Queen of France*, p. 228).
3. In the 1780s, 24 *livres* was the equivalent of about one English pound sterling. After 1814, the *livre* was replaced by the franc, and in 1814, there were approximately 24 francs to one English pound sterling.

Chapter II: *Child of France*

1. In addition to the Princesse de Guémenée, others who had already been appointed included *sous* governess Comtesse de Mackau, religious instructors, a first doctor, a surgeon, medical specialists, a foot surgeon, and chambermaids including Mesdames Buot de Leschevin de Billy, Pollart Le Moine, and de Fréminville.
2. This was the same Cardinal de Rohan later implicated in the 'diamond necklace scandal'.

Chapter IV: *Once Upon a Time*

1. The Cordon Bleu and the Orders of Saint-Esprit, Saint-Louis, Saint-Michel and the Golden Fleece were the most prestigious.
2. When Chateaubriand, citing *Guirlande de Julie*, wrote 'I have on the display of my birth', he erred in his literary reference. *Guirlande de Julie* was actually a collection of poems written by a number of poets at the request of the Duc de Montausier in 1641 in honor of his fiancée. What Chateaubriand meant to draw on was the play called *La Fleur d'Oranger*.
3. Records concerning the expenditures made on behalf of Ernestine are in the Archives Nationales de France in Paris (Series O).

Chapter V: *Storm Clouds Over the Palace*

1. C. Hippeau, 'Le Premier Dauphin, fils de Louis XVI', *Revue des Provinces*, vol. 11, Paris: June 15, 1866, p. 494; Monsieur Lefèvre's account.
2. Lord Glenbervie, *The Diaries of Sylvester Douglas (Lord Glenbervie)*, ed. Francis Bickley, London: Constable, 1928, vol. I, p. 25, December 21, 1793.
3. Letter from Marie Antoinette, la Duchesse de Tourzel, *Mémoires*, Paris: E. Plon et Cie, 1883, July 25, 1789.

Chapter VII: *A New Home*

1. Cited in Baron Hüe, *Souvenirs*, Paris: Calmann-Lévy, 1903, pp. 21–23, and Comtesse Pauline de Béarn, *Souvenirs de Quarante Ans 1789–1830*, Paris: Jacques Lecoffre et Cie, 1861, pp. 56–58.
2. Cited in de Tourzel, op. cit., chapter III.
3. Cited in de Béarn, op. cit., p. 58.
4. Today, the Eiffel Tower faces the Champ de Mars.

Chapter X: *Two Orphans*

1. A series of bulletins in French went from English spies in Paris, to Francis Drake in Genoa, to Foreign Secretary Grenville in London as England had no ambassador to France in 1793. The collection, known as the Dropmore Papers (see bibliography entry for J. B. Fortescue), includes the reports on the treatment of Louis Charles in the Temple Prison. See Number 12, February 12, 1794. Lord Glenbervie, op. cit. (ed. Bickley, vol. I, p. 25), December 21, 1793.
2. Juror priests professed loyalty to the government rather than to the Church.
3. Cited in Joseph Turquan, *La Dernière Dauphine, Madame duchesse d'Angoulême (1778–1851)*, Paris: Émile-Paul, 1909, pp. 58–59.

Chapter XI: *Sole Survivor*

1. Cited in Lord Glenbervie, op. cit. (ed. Bickley, vol. I, p. 73).
2. Archives Nationales de France, AF, II 300, 88.
3. Marie-Thérèse to Maria Carolina, letter dated January 10, 1796, Österreichisches Staatsarchiv, Vienna.

PART II: SAINT
Chapter XII: *Every Inch a Princess*

1. The Public Library of Basel has a complete list of the trousseau that Marie-Thérèse left behind. The two trunks included: four dozen blouses, two dozen toile handkerchiefs, two dozen batiste handkerchiefs, three muslin toile and embroidered peignoirs, three muslin and batiste embroidered peignoirs, two dozen napkins de toilette, six dozen wardrobe napkins, six cotton twill skirts, six English dimity muslin embroidered underskirts, twelve pairs of embroidered pockets, eighteen balls of wool for washing, twelve lace evening caps, twelve hair bands, twelve linen bonnets embroidered with lace, six linen handkerchiefs embroidered in lace, twelve double linen fichus, one linen needlepoint-embroidered lap cover, one English-style lap cover, two decorated lap covers made of linen, four dozen lace neckerchiefs, four dozen *frottoirs* muslin and cotton twill, two *ajustements,* one organdy dress with embroidery, one linen dress embroidered in white, four pieces of embroidered muslin, two pieces of linen batiste, two pieces of cotton percale for four morning dresses, one piece of English dimity for two dresses, one pink velour dress, one white satin dress with taffeta, one dress of satin moiré, two white taffeta skirts, one pink taffeta skirt, one piece of muslin for undergarments (camisoles), one piece of embroidered muslin to decorate the camisoles, English dimity for six corsets, twelve pairs of white silk stockings, two dozen pairs of lisle stockings, two dozen pairs of tricot slippers, twelve lengths of ribbon, one taffeta quilted redingote, one muff, and a hat. This inventory list was signed by Gomin, Lasne, who saw it in Paris, and Baron Hüe and the cook Meunier who saw it in Basel.
2. Archives Nationales, F42315.

Chapter XIV: *The Émigrés*

1. Cited in Duchesse d'Abrantès, *At the Court of Napoleon: Memoirs of the Duchesse d'Abrantès*, New York: Doubleday, 1989, p. 167.
2. Cited in A. C. Morris (ed.), *The Diary and Letters of Gouverneur Morris*, New York: Charles Scribner's Sons, 1888, vol. II, p. 212.
3. Ibid., pp. 238–39.
4. Ibid., pp. 226–27.

Chapter XVI: *A Bride*

1. Alfred H. Bill, *Highroads of Peril*, Boston: Little, Brown & Co., 1926, p. 169.

Chapter XVII: *The New Antigone*

1. British Library: Add. Mss 33793.

Chapter XVIII: *Country Life*

1. *Gentleman's Magazine*, January–June 1797, vol. LXXXI, p. 587.
2. Lord Colchester, *Diary and Correspondence*, London: John Murray, 1861, pp. 336–38.
3. Cited in Baron André de Maricourt, *Les Bourbons (1518–1830)*, Paris: Émile-Paul Frères, 1937, pp. 241–42.
4. Archives Nationales, 34AP180.

Chapter XIX: *The Only Man in the Family*

1. Archives Nationales, 1309 f. 302sq.
2. In 1809, when Napoleon had asked the Magyars to find a new king to replace the Habsburgs, overtures were made to Esterhazy, whose family had presided over the area for hundreds of years, before and during the Habsburg era. Nicolas refused the honor, earning the esteem of many.

Chapter XX: *Restoration*

1. Although witnesses have stated that Ney, famous for his bravery, actually gave the signal to his own firing squad, controversy emerged regarding his death. In 1818 a man named Peter Stuart Ney arrived in South Carolina and on his deathbed claimed to be the famous soldier. Some handwriting experts have asserted that the handwriting of Peter Stuart Ney matches that of Napoleon's General.
2. James Gallatin, *The Diary of James Gallatin*, London: William Heinemann, 1914, p. 107.

Chapter XXI: *Birth, Death and a New Dauphine*

1. James Gallatin recorded that the game 'Boston', which had been popular during the ancien régime, was still popular. He noted that he believed the game had been invented by French sailors while on duty in Boston Harbor during the American Revolutionary War.
2. François-René de Chateaubriand, *Mémoires d'outre-tombe*, Paris: Classiques Garnier, 1998, Livre XV, pp. 50–51.
3. Gallatin, op. cit., p. 158.
4. Some believe that Decazes was the model for Balzac's ruthlessly ambitious character, Rastignac, in the *Comédie humaine* series of novels.

5. Gallatin, op. cit., p. 166.
6. Gallatin, ibid., p. 177.
7. Gallatin, ibid., pp. 210–11.
8. Gallatin, ibid., pp. 241–42.
9. Béarn, op. cit., pp. 299–300.
10. Cited in Armin Human, *Der Dunkelgraf von Eishausen*, Hildburghausen: Keffenbringsche Hofbuchhandlung, 1883, 1886, pp. 72–73.

Chapter XXII: *Mending Fences*

1. Cited in André Castelot, *La Duchesse de Berry*, Paris: Perrin, 1996, p. 194.
2. Cited in Philip Mansel, *Paris Between Empires: Monarchy and Revolution 1814–1852*, New York: St Martin's Press, 2001, p. 218.
3. Chateaubriand, op. cit., Livre VI, pp. 179–80.
4. Ironically, it would later be that flag, the white banner of the ancien régime, which he would insist upon when offered the crown and which would turn out to be the 'deal breaker'.
5. Cited in Comtesse de Boigne, *Memoirs*, New York: Helen Marx Books, 2003, p. 174. The Comtesse d'Agoult's own marriage would prove to be miserable: she divorced her husband after eight years and lived with the composer Franz Liszt, with whom she would have two illegitimate daughters, one of whom, Cosima, would marry another musical giant, Richard Wagner. D'Agoult also went on to become a famous writer under her own name and under the pen name 'Daniel Stern'.
5. Cited in Turquan, op. cit., p. 383.

Chapter XXIII: *Suspicions Confirmed*

1. Cited in Mary Frampton, *The Journal of Mary Frampton from the Year 1779, Until the Year 1846*, London: Sampson Low, Marston, Searle & Rivington, 1886, p. 356.

Chapter XXIV: *Blackmail*

1. Chateaubriand, op. cit., Livre XXXVIII, pp. 316–17.
2. There are nearly eighty letters that relate to the de Soucy/Dr Lavergne affair. See the Mackau files at the Archives Nationales: AN 156 AP I 11 dossier 1.
3. Dr Jean-Jacques Cassiman, whose DNA testing in 2000 resulted in indisputable proof that the boy who died in the Temple Prison was Louis Charles, also conducted DNA testing on a piece of a bone from Naundorff's corpse. Although the DNA pattern from the bone from the Naundorff skeleton did not match that of Marie Antoinette, Naundorff's descendants, who still go by the name 'Bourbon', insist that they are the rightful heirs to the Capetian dynasty.

BIBLIOGRAPHY

Unpublished Sources

Archives du Ministère des Affaires Étrangères, Paris
Archives Nationales de France (Series AB, AF, AP, C, F, H, O), Paris
Département des Manuscrits de la Bibliothèque Nationale de France, Paris
Fonds Bourbon, Paris
Österreichisches Staatsarchiv (Haus-, Hof-, and Staatsarchiv), Vienna
Private collection of HSH Charles-Henri de Lobkowicz (letters and diaries)

Published Sources

d'Abrantès, Duchesse, *At the Court of Napoleon: Memoirs of the Duchesse d'Abrantès*, New York: Doubleday, 1989.

d'Agoult, Comtesse, *Mes Souvenirs, 1806–1833*, Paris: Ancienne Maison Michel Lévy Frères, 3ème édition, 1880.

d'Allonville, Comte Armand-François, *Mémoires Secrets de 1770 à 1830*, Paris: Werdet, 1838.

d'Amarzit, Pierre, *Barnave: Le Conseiller Secret de Marie-Antoinette*, Paris: Le Sémaphore, 2000.

Ambelain, Robert, *Crimes et Secrets d'État 1785–1830*, Paris: Robert Laffont, 1979.

Les Amis du Comte de Chambord, vols 1–11, Angers, France: Dominique Lambert de la Douasnerie, October, 1992–March, 1998.

d'Angoulême, Duchesse, 'Souvenirs de 1815', *Le Correspondant*, August 25, 1913, pp. 650–83.

d'Arblay, Madame (Fanny Burney), *Diary and Letters*, 6 vols, London: Macmillan and Co. Ltd, 1905.

Aspinall, A., (ed.), *Correspondence of George Prince of Wales 1770–1812*, vol. VII, London: Cassell & Company Ltd, 1970.

———*The Later Correspondence of George III*, Cambridge: Cambridge University Press, 1963.

———*Letters of the Princess Charlotte, 1811–1817*, London: Home and Van Thal, 1949.

Autié, Léonard Alexis, *Recollections of Léonard*, New York: Sturgis & Walton Company, 1909.

Babeau, Albert, *Paris en 1789*, Paris: Albin Michel, 1989.

Bader, Luigi, *Album Le Comte de Chambord et les siens en exil*, Paris: Diffusion Université-Culture, 1983.

Barbey, Frédéric, *Madame Atkyns et La Prison du Temple*, Paris: Perrin et Cie, 1905.

Barras, Paul, *Mémoires*, Paris: Éditions Paleo, 2004.

Barthélemy, François, *Papiers de Barthélemy, ambassadeur de France en Suisse, 1792–1797*, VI, ed. Alexandre Tausserat-Radel; published under the auspices of the Commission of Diplomatic Archives, Ministry of Foreign Affairs, France.

Beales, Derek, *Joseph II*, Cambridge: Cambridge University Press, 1987.

Béarn, Comtesse Pauline de, *Souvenirs de Quarante Ans 1789–1830*, Paris: Jacques Lecoffre et Cie, 1861.

Beauchesne, Alcide Hyacinthe du Bois de, *Louis XVII: Sa Vie, Son Agonie, Sa Mort*, Paris: Henri Plon, 1867.

Beiser, Frederick C., *The Romantic Imperative (The Concept of Early German Romanticism)*, Cambridge: Harvard, 2003.

Belcroix, Cyr, *Autour de Louis XVII: La Comtesse des Ténèbres*, La Chapelle: Éditions Le Relais, 1999.

Bernier, Olivier, *Imperial Mother, Royal Daughter*, London: Sidgwick & Jackson, 1986.

Berry, Mary, *A Comparative View of the Social Life of England and France (From the Restoration of Charles II to the French Revolution)*, London: Longman, Rees, Orme, Brown, and Green, 1828.

————*Social Life in England and France from the French Revolution in 1789 to that of July 1830*, London: Longman, Rees, Orme, Brown, and Green, 1831.

Bertière, Simone, *Les Reines de France au Temps des Bourbons: Marie-Antoinette l'insoumise*, Paris: Éditions de Fallois, 2002.

Besenval, Baron de, *Mémoires du Baron de Besenval Sur La Cour de France*, Paris: Mercure de France, 1987.

Bill, Alfred H., *Highroads of Peril* (The memoirs of Franklin Darlington's adventures among the spies of Louis XVIII), Boston: Little, Brown & Co., 1926.

Bled, Jean-Paul, *Les Lys en exil (ou la seconde mort de l'Ancien Régime)*, Paris: Fayard, 1992.

Blum, Carol, *Rousseau and the Republic of Virtue: The Language of Politics in the French Revolution*, Ithaca, New York: Cornell University Press, 1986.

Boigne, Comtesse de, *Memoirs*, New York: Helen Marx Books, 2003.

Bordonove, Georges, *Les Bourbons de Louis XVI à Louis-Philippe (1774–1848)*, Paris: Pygmalion, 2004.

Bourbon-Conti, Stéphanie-Louise de, *Mémoires historiques*, Paris: Pierre Horay, 1986.

Brett-James, Anthony, *The Hundred Days (Napoleon's Last Campaign from Eye-Witness Accounts)*, New York: St Martin's Press, 1964.

Breunlich-Pawlik, Maria, *Kriegsminister Beurnonville und vier Mitglieder des Nationalkonvents als Staategefangene in Österreich 1793–1795*,

Wien: Mitteilungen des Österreichischen Staatsarchiv, 24 (pp. 371–99), 1971.

Broglie, Duchesse de, *Lettres*, Paris: Calmann-Lévy, 1896.

Brunyer, Madame, *Dans l'Ombre de Marie-Antoinette, le journal de Mme Brunyer*, Paris: Direction des Archives de France, 2003.

Burke, Edmund, *Reflections on the Revolution in France*, Buffalo, NY: Prometheus Books, 1987.

Cadbury, Deborah, *The Lost King of France*, New York: St Martin's Griffin, 2002.

Campan, Madame, *Mémoires*, Paris: Mercure de France, 1988 (first published Paris: Baudouin Frères, 1822).

———*Memoirs of the Court of Marie Antoinette, Queen of France, vols I & II*, Boston: L. C. Page and Company, 1900.

Carlyle, Thomas, *The French Revolution*, Oxford: Oxford University Press, 1989.

Cartron, Michel Bernard, *Louis XIX Roi Sans Couronne*, Paris: Communication & Tradition, 1996.

———*Marie-Thérèse, duchesse d'Angoulême (La vertu et le malheur)*, Paris: Communication & Tradition, 1999.

Castelot, André, *Le Secret de Madame Royale*, Paris: Sfelt, 1949.

———*La Duchesse de Berry*, Paris: Perrin, 1996.

Challice, Mrs, *Illustrious Women of France*, London: Bradbury, Agnew & Co., 1873.

Chalon, Jean, *Chère Marie-Antoinette*, Paris: Perrin, 1988.

Chastenay, Madame de, *Mémoires*, Paris: Librairie Plon, 1896.

Chateaubriand, François-René de, *Mémoires d'outre-tombe, Livres I-XLII*, Paris: Classiques Garnier, 1998.

———*Mémoires sur le duc de Berry (Éditions 1820 et 1825)*, Paris: Communication & Tradition, 1998.

Chazet, Alissan, *Louis XVIII à son lit de mort, ou, Récit exact et authentique de ce qui s'est passé au Chateau des Tuileries les 13, 14, 15 et 16 septembre 1824*, Paris: Ponthieu, 1824.

Chiappe, Jean-François, *Le comte de Chambord*, Paris: Perrin, 1999.

Cléry, Jean-Baptiste, *Journal*, Paris: Pays & Terroirs, 1861.

Colchester, Lord (Charles Abbot), *Diary and Correspondence*, vol. II, London: John Murray, 1861.

Condé, Prince Louis Joseph de Bourbon, *Journal d'Émigration (1789–1795)*, Paris: Le Comte de Ribes, 1924.

Conti, Conte Egon Caesar, *Ich, Eine Tochter Maria Theresias*, Munich: Verlag F. Bruckmann, 1950.

Cooper, James Fenimore, *Autobiography of a Pocket-Handkerchief*, Evanston, Illinois: Golden Book Press, 1897.

Courtot, Baroness Cécile de, *Memoirs*, New York: Henry Holt and Company, 1900.

Daehne, Paul, *Das Geheimnis der Dunkelgräfin*, Leipzig: Max Beck Verlage GMBH, 1933.

Daudet, Ernest, *Histoire de l'Émigration (Pendant La Révolution Française)*, Paris: Librairie Poussielgue, 1904.

———'Louis XVIII et Bonaparte', parts I-VI, *Le Correspondant*, February 25, 1905, pp. 666–94; March 10, 1905, pp. 849–81.

———*Madame Royale (Fille de Louis XVI et de Marie-Antoinette)*, Paris: Hachette & Cie, 1912.

David, Saul, *Prince of Pleasure: The Prince of Wales and the Making of the Regency*, New York: Atlantic Monthly Press, 1998.

Deffand, Marquise du, *Correspondance Complète*, Paris: H. Plon, 1865.

Delorme, Philippe, *L'Affaire Louis XVII*, Paris: Tallandier, 1995.

———*Louis XVII, La Vérité: sa mort confirmée par la science*, Paris: Pygmalion Gérard Watelet, 2000.

———*Marie Antoinette, Épouse de Louis XVI, mère de Louis XVII*, Paris: Pygmalion Gérard Watelet, 2000.

Desmond, Alice Curtis, *Marie Antoinette's Daughter*, New York: Dodd, Mean & Company, 1967.

Destremau, Noëlle, *Madame Royale et Son Mystère*, Paris: Nouvelles Editions Latines, 1991.

Ditchfield, the Reverend P. H., *Memorials of Old Buckinghamshire*, London: Derby, Bemrose and Sons Ltd, 1901.

Dolan, Brian, *Ladies of the Grand Tour*, New York: HarperCollins, 2001.

Dunlop, Ian, *Marie-Antoinette*, London: Phoenix, 1998.

Earl, John L, III, 'Talleyrand in Philadelphia 1794–1796', *Pennsylvania Magazine of History and Biography*, vol. 91, pp. 282–98, Philadelphia: Historical Society of Pennsylvania, 1967.

Egret, Jean, *The French Pre-revolution 1787–1788*, Chicago: University of Chicago Press, 1977.

Esterházy, Comte Maurice, *Le Journal: Un Témoin Hongrois de l'Époque de Charles X*, Budapest: Société de la Nouvelle Revue de Hongrie, 1940, pp. 1–47.

Evans, Joan, *Madame Royale*, London: Museum Press Ltd, 1959.

Faucigny-Lucinge, Prince de, *Souvenirs Inédits du Petit-Fils du duc de Berry*, Paris: Librairie Académique Perrin, 1971.

Fejtö, François, *Un Habsbourg Révolutionnaire, Joseph II, Portrait d'un despote éclairé*, Paris: Librairie Plon, 1953.

Félix, Joël, *Louis XVI & Marie-Antoinette (Un couple en politique)*, Paris: Éditions Payot & Rivages, 2006.

Ferronnays, Madame de la, *Mémoires*, Paris: Librairie Paul Ollendorff, 1899.

Fersen, Count Hans Axel, *Diary and Correspondence*, Boston: Hardy, Pratt & Co., 1902.

Feydeau, Elisabeth de, *Jean-Louis Fargeon, parfumeur de Marie-Antoinette*, Versailles: Perrin, 2004.

Foreman, Amanda, *Georgiana: Duchess of Devonshire*, New York: Random House, 1998.

Fortescue, J. B., *Manuscripts Preserved at Dropmore* (Historical Manuscripts Commission), vol. II, London: Eyre and Spottiswoode, 1894.

Frampton, Mary, *The Journal of Mary Frampton from the Year 1779, Until the Year 1846*, London: Sampson Low, Marston, Searle & Rivington, 1886.

Fraser, Antonia, *Marie Antoinette: The Journey*, New York: Nan A. Talese/Doubleday, 2001.

———*The French Revolution and the Creation of Modern Political Culture*, Oxford: Pergamon Press, vol. I, ed. Keith Michael Baker, 1987; vol. II, ed.

Colin Lucas, 1988; vol. III, ed. François Furet and Mona Ozouf, 1989; vol. IV, ed. Keith Michael Baker, 1994.

Furet, François, *La Révolution de Turgot à Jules Ferry 1770–1880*, Paris: Hachette, 1988.

Gallatin, James, *The Diary of James Gallatin*, London: William Heinemann, 1914.

La Gazette Nationale, nos. 73, 91, 108, 113, 134, 139, 173, Paris: December, 1795–March, 1796.

Genlis, Comtesse de, *Mémoires* (vols I-X), Paris: Chez Ladvocat Librairie, 1825.

Girault de Coursac, Paul et Pierrette, *Louis XVI a la Parole (Lettres, Discours, Écrits Politiques)*, Paris: François-Xavier de Guibert, 1997.

——————*Provence et Artois: Les deux frères de Louis XVI*, Paris: François-Xavier de Guibert, 1999.

——————*Sur la route de Varennes*, Paris: François-Xavier de Guibert, 2000.

Girouard, Mark, *Life in the French Country House*, London: Cassell & Co., 2000.

Glenbervie, Lord, *The Glenbervie Journals*, ed. Walter Sichel, London: Constable & Co. Ltd, 1910.

——————*The Diaries of Sylvester Douglas (Lord Glenbervie)*, ed. Francis Bickley, London: Constable & Co. Ltd, 1928.

Goncourt, Edmond and Jules de, *Histoire de Marie Antoinette*, Paris: Librairie de Firmin Didot Frères et Cie, 1863.

Gontaut-Biron, Duchesse de, *Memoirs*, New York: Dodd, Mead & Company, 1894.

Guichen, Vicomte de, *Le duc d'Angoulême (1775–1844)*, Paris: Émile-Paul, 1909.

Guizot, François, *De la démocratie en France*, Paris: V. Masson, 1849.

Hall, Major John R., *The Bourbon Restoration*, Boston: Houghton Mifflin Company, 1909.

Hammeran, Reiner, *Dunkelgräfin, Kahlbutz & Co.*, Germany: Wagner Verlag, 2006.

Hardman, John, *The French Revolution: The Fall of the Ancien Régime to the Thermidorian Reaction 1785–1795*, New York: St Martin's Press, 1982.

Hazlitt, William, *Notes of a Journey Through France and Italy*, London: Hunt and Clarke, 1826.

Henri, Comte de Chambord, *Textes Politiques*, Paris: Communication & Tradition, 1995.

Herold, J. Christopher, *Mistress to an Age: A Life of Madame de Staël*, New York: The Bobbs-Merrill Company, 1958.

d'Hézecques, Félix, Comte de France, *Souvenirs d'un Page de la Cour de Louis XVI*, Paris: Gérard Monfort, Éditeur, 1998.

Hippeau, C., 'Le Premier Dauphin, fils de Louis XVI', *Revue des Provinces*, vol. 11, pp. 492–96, Paris: June 15, 1866.

Hoehling, A. A., *Women Who Spied*, Lanham, Maryland: Madison Books, 1993.

Horne, Alistair, *La Belle France (A Short History)*, New York: Alfred A. Knopf, 2005.

Hüe, Baron, *Souvenirs*, Paris: Calmann-Lévy, 1903.

Huertas, Monique de, *Madame Royale* (*L'énigmatique destinée de la fille de Louis XVI*), Paris: Pygmalion/Gérard Watelet, 1999.

Human, Armin, *Der Dunkelgraf von Eishausen*, Hildburghausen: Keffenbringsche Hofbuchhandlung, Part I: 1883; Part II: 1886.

Hunt, Lynn, *The Family Romance of the French Revolution*, Berkeley, California: University of California Press, 1992.

———*L'Idée de Nation Et l'Idée de Citoyenneté En France et Dans Les Pays de Langue Allemande Sous la Révolution*, Belfort: Institut de Recherches et d'Éducation Permanente du Territoire de Belfort, Actes du Colloque International de Belfort, October, 1988.

Imbert de Saint-Amand, Arthur Léon, *The Duchess of Angoulême and the Two Restorations*, New York: Charles Scribner's Sons, 1892.

———*The Duchess of Berry and the Court of Charles X*, New York: Charles Scribner's Sons, 1892.

———*La Jeunesse de la Duchesse d'Angoulême*, Paris: Librairie de la Société des Gens de Lettres, 1892.

———*Marie Antoinette and the Downfall of Royalty*, New York: Charles Scribner's Sons, 1891.

Ingrao, Charles, *The Habsburg Monarchy 1618–1815*, Cambridge: Cambridge University Press, 1994.

Jehaes, E. and H. Pfeiffer, K. Toprak, R. Decorte, B. Brinkmann, J. J. Cassiman, 'Mitochondrial DNA analysis of the putative heart of Louis XVII, son of Louis XVI and Marie Antoinette', *European Journal of Human Genetics* 9 (2001), pp. 185–90.

Jehaes, E. and R. Decorte, A. Peneau, H. J. Petrie, P. Boiry, A. Gilissen, J. P. Moisan, H. Van den Berghe, O. Pascal, J. J. Cassiman, 'Mitochondrial DNA analysis on remains of a putative son of Louis XVI and Marie Antoinette', *European Journal of Human Genetics* 6 (1998), pp. 383–95.

Jérome (Le Roi) et Catherine (La Reine), *Mémoires et Correspondance* (vols I – VII), Paris: E. Dentu, 1861.

Joinville, François-Ferdinand-Philippe-Louis-Marie-d'Orléans, Prince de, *Memoirs*, New York: Macmillan and Co., 1895.

Jókai, Maurus, *The Nameless Castle*, New York: Doubleday, Page & Co., 1898.

Kelly, Linda, *The Young Romantics*, New York: Random House, 1976.

Kent, HRH Princess Michael of, *The Serpent and the Moon*, New York: Touchstone Books, 2004.

Kremers, Hildegard, *Marie Caroline Duchesse de Berry*, Graz: Verlag Styria, 1998.

Maisonfort, Marquis de la, *Mémoires d'un agent royaliste* (*sous la Révolution, l'Empire et la Restauration 1763–1827*), Paris: Mercure de France, 1998.

Lamartine, Alphonse de, *Histoire de la Restauration*, Paris: V. Lecous, Furne et Cie, 1851.

Lamballe, Princess de, *Secret Memoirs* (2 vols), London: H. S. Nichols & Co., 1895 (original edition published in 1826).

Lambert de la Douasnerie, Dominique, *Le drapeau blanc en exil*: *lieux de mémoire* (*1833–1883*), Paris: Librairie Édition Guénégaud, 1998.

Langeron, Roger, *Madame Royale* (*La Fille de Marie-Antoinette*), Paris: Librairie Hachette, 1958.

La Rochefoucauld, Duchesse de, *Lettres*, Paris: Mercure de France, 2001.

La Rochefoucauld, Vicomte de, *Mémoires*, vol. V, Paris: Allardin Librairie, 1837.

———*Pèlerinage à Goritz*, Paris: E. Houdaille, 1839.

———'Voyage à Buschtierad', *Paris, ou le livre des Cent-et-un, Tome XIII*, Bruxelles: Louis Hauman et Cie, 1833.

La Tour du Pin, Madame de, *Memoirs*, London: Harvill, 1969.

Lenotre, G., *La Fille de Louis XVI*, Paris: Perrin et Cie, 1928.

Lescure, M. F. A., de, *La Vraie Marie Antoinette*, Paris: Librairie Parisienne, 1863.

———*Marie Antoinette et sa Famille*, Paris: P. Ducrocq, 1879.

Lever, Evelyne, *Louis XVIII*, Paris: Fayard, 1988.

———*Marie Antoinette: The Last Queen of France*, New York: Farrar, Straus and Giroux, 2000.

Levinger, Matthew, *Enlightened Nationalism* (*The Transformation of Prussian Political Culture 1806–1848*), Oxford: Oxford University Press, 2000.

Lévis, Gaston de, *Souvenirs et Portraits 1780-1789*, Paris: François Buisson, 1813.

Louis XVIII, *Lettres d'Artwell, Correspondance Politique et Privée*, Paris: Jules Lefebvre et Cite, 1830.

———*Mémoires* (vols I-XII), Paris: Mame-Delaunay, 1832.

Maeckel, O. V., *The Dunkelgraf Mystery*, London: Hutchinson & Co., 1930.

Mansel, Philip, *The Court of France 1789–1830*, Cambridge: Cambridge University Press, 1988.

———*Louis XVIII*, London: Blond & Briggs, 1981.

———*Paris Between Empires: Monarchy and Revolution 1814–1852*, New York: St Martin's Press, 2001.

Maricourt, Baron André de, *Les Bourbons* (*1518–1830*), Paris: Émile-Paul Frères, 1937.

———'Le Cygne d'Or de M. le Dauphin', *L'Écho de Paris*, October 1, 1910.

Marie Antoinette, *Correspondance*, Tome I, 1767–1787, Paris: Éditions Paleo, 2004.

———*Correspondance*, Tome II, 1788–1793, Paris: Éditions Paleo, 2004.

———*Correspondance Secrète entre Marie-Thérèse et le Comte de Mercy-Argenteau*, 3 vols, d'Arneth, Alfred & Geffroy, M. A., eds, Paris: Librairie de Firmin-Didot Frères, Fils et Cie, 1875.

———*Correspondance Secrète Inédite de Marie Antoinette, Louis XVI et Madame Elisabeth*, 6 vols, Paris: Plon, 1864.

Marie-Thérèse-Charlotte de France, *Mémoire écrit par Marie-Thérèse Charlotte de France, sur la captivité des princes et princesses, ses parens, depuis le 10 août 1792, jusqu'à la mort de son frère, arrivée le 9 juin 1795*, Paris: Librairie Poulet-Malassis, 1862.

Maurois, André, *Chateaubriand* (*Poet Statesman Lover*), New York: Harper & Brothers, 1938.

McMahon, Darrin M., *Enemies of the Enlightenment: The French Counter-Enlightenment and the Making of Modernity*, Oxford: Oxford University Press, 2001.

McPhee, Peter, *A Social History of France 1789–1914* (2nd edition), London: Palgrave Macmillan, 2004.

Mellor, Anne K., *Romanticism and Gender*, New York: Routledge, 1993.

Mignet, (François) Auguste, *Histoire de la revolution française, depuis 1789 jusq'en 1814*, Paris: F. Didot Frères, 1837.

Monroe, James, *James Monroe Papers*, 1772–1836.

Montet, Baronne du, *Souvenirs de la Baronne du Montet (1785–1866)*, Paris: Librairie Plon, 1914.

Montjoye, F. L. C., *Histoire de Marie-Antoinette-Josèphe-Jeanne de Lorraine, Archduchesse d'Autriche, Reine de France*, Paris: Madame Ve, Lepetit, 1814 (second edition with notes by the author and new dedication to the duchesse d'Angoulême; first edition published in 1797).

Morinerie, Baron de la, 'Papiers du Temple', *Nouvelle Revue*, XXVII, p. 587, Paris: 1884.

Morris, Anne Cary, (ed.), *The Diary and Letters of Gouverneur Morris*, vols. I & II, New York: Charles Scribner's Sons, 1888.

Nolhac, Pierre de, *Marie-Antoinette*, Paris: Librairie Arthème Fayard, 1951.

———*The Trianon of Marie-Antoinette*, London: T. Fisher Unwin Ltd, 1925.

d'Oberkirch, Baronne, *Mémoires (sur la Cour de Louis XVI et la Société Française Avant 1789)*, Paris: Mercure de France, 1989.

Ozouf, Mona, *Festivals and the French Revolution*, Cambridge: Harvard University Press, 1988.

Paroy, Comte de, *Mémoires*, Paris: Librairie Plon, 1895.

Petitfils, Jean-Christian, *Louis XVI*, Paris: Perrin, 2005.

Pimodan, Comte de, *Les Fiançailles de Madame Royale (fille de Louis XVI) et La Première Année de son Séjour à Vienne*, Paris: Librairie Plon, 1912.

Polignac, Diane, Comtesse de, *Mémoires Sur la Vie et le Caractère de Mme, la Duchesse de Polignac*, London: Debrett, 1796.

Puymaigre, Comte Alexandre de, *Souvenirs sur l'Émigration, l'Empire et La Restauration*, Paris: Librairie Plon, 1884.

Rasky, Marie Magdeleine de, *La Révolution française: une affaire de famille (Tome I: Louis XVII & Tome II: Madame Royale)*, Paris: Éditions Scriptoplan, 1977.

Récamier, Madame, *Souvenirs*, Paris: Michel Lévy Frères, 1859.

Regnault-Warin, J. J., *Le Cimetière de la Madeleine*, Paris: Lepetit, 1800.

———*L'homme au masque de fer*, Paris: Frechet et Cie, 1804.

Reiset, Vicomte de, *Autour des Bourbons*, Paris: Éditions Émile-Paul Frères, 1927.

Roederer, Pierre-Louis, *Chronique de 50 jours, du 20 juin au 10 août 1792, rédigée sur pièces authentiques*, Paris: L'Imprimerie de Lachevardière, 1832.

Romer, Isabella Frances, *Filia Dolorosa, Memoirs of Marie-Thérèse-Charlotte, Duchess of Angoulême, the last of the Dauphines*, London: Richard Bentley, 1852.

Rothenberg, Gunther E., *Napoleon's Great Adversaries The Archduke Charles and the Austrian Army, 1792–1814*, London: B. T. Batsford Ltd, 1982.

Sainte-Beuve, Charles-Augustin, *Galerie de Femmes Célèbres*, Paris: Garnier Frères, 1862.

Samuels, Maurice, *The Spectacular Past: Popular History and the Novel in Nineteenth-Century France*, Ithaca, NY: Cornell University Press, 2004.

Saxe-Altenburg, Frédéric de, *L'Énigme de Madame Royale*, Paris: Flammarion, 1954.

Schama, Simon, *Citizens*, New York: Alfred A. Knopf, 1989.

Schiff, Stacy, *A Great Improvisation: Franklin, France, and the Birth of America*, New York: Henry Holt, 2005.

Scott, John, *A Visit to Paris in 1814*, Philadelphia: Edward Parker, 1815.

——*Paris Revisited in 1815*, London: Longman, Hurst, Rees, Orme & Brown, 1816.

Seillan, Fabienne, 'Le château de Villeneuve-l'Étang', *L'Objet de l'Art*, no. 414, Paris: Juin, 2006.

Seth, Catriona, *Marie Antoinette, Anthologie et dictionnaire*, Paris: Robert Laffont, 2006.

Singh, Simon, *The Code Book*, New York: Anchor Books, 2000.

Sion, Madeleine Louise de, *Le vrai visage de Madame Royale Duchesse d'Angoulême*, Paris: Beauchesne et Ses Fils, 1959.

Spitzer, Alan B., *The French Generation of 1820*, Princeton: Princeton University Press, 1987.

Staël, Madame de, *Considerations on the Principal Events of The French Revolution*, London: Baldwin, Cradock & Joy, 1821.

——*Réflexions Sur le Process de la Reine par Une Femme*, August, 1793.

Stenger, Gilbert, *The Return of Louis XVIII*, New York: Charles Scribner's Sons, 1909.

Stewart, John Hall, *A Documentary Survey of the French Revolution*, New York: The Macmillan Company, 1951.

Tackett, Timothy, *Becoming A Revolutionary (The Deputies of the French National Assembly and the Emergence of a Revolutionary Culture 1789–1790)*, Princeton: Princeton University Press, 1996.

Tarente, La Princesse de (Louise Emmanuelle de Châtillon), *Souvenirs*, Nantes: Émile Grimaud et Fils, 1897.

Thierry, Augustin, *De la réorganization de la société européene, our De la nécessité et des moyens de rassembler les peoples de l'Europe en un seul corps politique: en conservant à chacun son independence nationale*, Paris: A. Egron, 1814.

Thompson, Stith, *Motif-Index of Folk Literature* (6 vols), Bloomington: Indiana University Press, 1989.

Tourzel, la Duchesse de, *Mémoires*, Paris: E. Plon et Cie, 1883.

Tulard, Jean, *Les Vingt Jours: Louis XVIII our Napoléon? 1er-20 mars 1815*, Paris: Fayard, 2001.

Turquan, Joseph, *La Dernière Dauphine, Madame duchesse d'Angoulême (1778–1851)*, Paris: Émile-Paul, 1909.

Tussaud, Madame, *Memoirs and Reminiscences of France*, London: Saunders and Otlay, 1838.

Vigée-Lebrun, Madame, *Memoirs of Madame Vigée Lebrun*, New York: George Braziller Publishers, 1989.

Villèle, Comte de, *Mémoires et Correspondance* (5 vols), Paris: Perrin et Cie, 1888.

Vovelle, Michel, *La Chute de la monarchie, 1787–1792*, Paris: Éditions du Seuil, 1999.

Walzer, Michael, (ed.), *Regicide and Revolution: Speeches at the trial of Louis XVI*, Cambridge: Cambridge University Press, 1974.

Waquet, Françoise, *Les Fêtes Royales Sous La Restauration*, Geneva: Droz, 1981.

Weber, Caroline, *Queen of Fashion: What Marie Antoinette Wore to the Revolution*, New York: Henry Holt and Company, 2006.

Weber, Joseph, *Mémoires concernant Marie Antoinette Archduchesse d'Autriche, Reine de France*, 3 vols, London: Daponte & Vogel, 1804.

Weiner, Margery, *The French Exiles, 1789–1815*, London: John Murray, 1960.

Williams, H. Noel, *A Princess of Adventure: Marie Caroline, Duchesse de Berry*, New York: Charles Scribner's Sons, 1911.

Williams, Helen Maria, *Narrative of the Events which have taken place in France, from the landing of Napoleon Bonaparte, on the first of March, 1815 till the Restoration of Louis XVIII*, Philadelphia: Moses Thomas, 1816.

Wilson, R. McNair, *Women of the French Revolution*, Port Washington, New York: Kennikat Press, 1936.

Winock, Michel, *1789, l'année sans pareille*, Paris: Perrin, 2004.

Wormeley, Katharine Prescott, (trans.), *The Ruin of a Princess*, New York: The Lamb Publishing Co., 1912.

Yalom, Marilyn, *Blood Sisters: The French Revolution in Women's Memory*, New York: Basic Books/Harper Collins, 1993.

Young, Arthur, *Travels in France During the Years 1787, 1788 & 1789*, London: Cambridge University Press, 1929.

Zurich, Comte Pierre de, *Madame de la Briche (1755–1844)*, Paris: Éditions de Boccard, 1934.

Zweig, Stefan, *Marie Antoinette: The Portrait of an Average Woman*, New York: The Viking Press, 1933.

INDEX

to safekeeping 100–1, 126, 189;
plan and preparations for escape
from France 100–2, 102–5; effects
of traumatic attempt to escape 112;
desperate letters written while under
house arrest 117–18; disposal of
sensitive papers after Brunswick
Declaration 122; grief at fate of
Princesse de Lamballe 131; grief-
stricken reaction to Louis XVI's
death sentence 135; reaction to
death of Louis XVI 135–6; moved
to Conciergerie prison 138, 138–9,
139–40; ill-fated attempts to rescue
139; final letter to Mme Elisabeth
140–1, 147, 276; trial and charges
against 140; execution of 141, 143;
initials on ring given to M-T as
wedding present 210; grave in
Madeleine cemetery 230, 258;
retrieval and burial of remains of
230; altar situated at place of
execution 248–9; re-burial of body
in royal crypt 261, 262; anniversary
of her death 276, 284, 363;
resemblance of 'Dark Countess' to
353; in story told by M-T to great-
nephew 362–3; 'Dark Countess'
and jewelry possibly belonging to
376
Marie Caroline of Naples *see* Berry,
Marie Caroline, Duchesse de
Marie Christine (sister of Marie
Antoinette) 40–1, 189
Marie Joséphine (wife of Louis XVIII)
194, 208, 211, 229, 235, 236, 238;
death and funeral of 241–2
Marie-Anne, Empress of Austria 357
Marie-Thérèse, Queen of the Two
Sicilies 350
Marie-Thérèse of Modena (daughter
of Henri, Duc de Bordeaux) 360
Marie-Thérèse (of Sardinia), Comtesse
d'Artois 207
Marie-Thérèse-Charlotte of France:
birth, baptism and ensuing
celebrations 22–6, 43; parents'
love for 24–5, 37; consideration of
marriage prospects for 27–8, 39–

40; education and upbringing 29–
30, 38; teething problems 31–2;
presented to powerful figures
visiting Versailles 33; love for her
father 37, 48; protective and close
relationship with Louis Charles 42,
50, 326; early life and demands of
ritual and pageantry 43–4, 45;
dubbed 'Mousseline Sérieuse' by
mother 45, 362, 370; character
and qualities shown as young girl
46–7, 48, 185; lessons in humility
given to her by mother 47;
experience of divisions among
family members 48, 113, 117;
letters to Mme de Polignac 67, 89;
recollections of days of terror 70,
72, 73, 76, 78, 79, 80, 82, 125,
128, 129, 130, 131, 137;
unhappiness at Tuileries 86, 88;
lessons learnt and observations
during revolutionary times 87–8,
94, 95; first communion 91–3;
sensitivity to parents' suffering 95,
112, 119; courage and composure
during worst ordeals 99, 121, 145,
152, 157, 166, 170, 172, 177;
recollections of attempt to escape
from France 105, 106, 110;
subject to crowd violence after
failed escape attempt 109; as
deprived of childhood and youth
119; suffering with pains and
illness in Temple Prison 134, 136,
143; hysteria at news of father's
death sentence 135; official
concerns regarding prison
treatment of 147–8, 149, 151; on
sixteenth birthday 149–50; poetry
written in private diary 150–1,
158, 371, 373–4; relationship with
Mme de Chanterenne (Renète) in
prison 154, 156, 157, 158, 160;
grief on finally being told of death
of family 156; loyalty to her
beloved France 157, 166–7, 250–
1, 336; memoir of time in Temple
Prison 158, 160, 220, 275, 361–2;
release from Temple Prison 160; at